FRIEDRICH SCHILLER

An Anthology for Our Time

In new English translations
and the original German

With an account
of his life and work by
FREDERICK UNGAR

FREDERICK UNGAR PUBLISHING CO.
New York

SECOND PRINTING, 1960

Copyright 1959© by
FREDERICK UNGAR PUBLISHING CO.

Printed in the United States of America

Library of Congress Catalog Card No. 59-15923

MOTTOES

Into your hands the dignity of man is given.
Now keep it well!
It sinks with you! With you, again, it rises.

> *Der Menschheit Würde ist in eure Hand gegeben,*
> *Bewahret sie!*
> *Sie sinkt mit euch! Mit euch wird sie sich heben.*

Only the morning gate of beauty
Leads you into the land of truth.

> *Nur durch das Morgentor des Schönen*
> *Dringst du in der Erkenntnis Land.*

Genuine art, on the other hand, does not have
as its object a mere transitory game. Its serious
purpose is not merely to translate the human
being into a momentary dream of freedom, but
actually to *make* him free.

> *Die wahre Kunst aber hat es nicht bloß auf ein*
> *vorübergehendes Spiel abgesehen; es ist ihr ernst*
> *damit, den Menschen nicht bloß in einen augen-*
> *blicklichen Traum von Freiheit zu versetzen, son-*
> *dern ihn wirklich und in der Tat frei zu machen.*

A poetic truth, because it is true in the absolute, can never be congruent with reality.

> *Eine poetische Wahrheit kann, eben weil sie*
> *absolut wahr ist, mit der Wirklichkeit niemals*
> *zusammenfallen.*

What has never, what has nowhere happened,
Only that can not turn stale.

> *Was sich nie und nirgends hat begeben,*
> *Das allein veraltet nie.*

Virtue is nothing else but inclination to duty.

> *Tugend ist nichts anders als eine Neigung zu der*
> *Pflicht.*

The mind grows narrow in a narrow sphere,
And man grows great with greater purposes.

> *Im engen Kreis verengert sich der Sinn,*
> *Es wächst der Mensch mit seinen höhern Zwecken.*

Every individual human being . . . carries within himself, as his potential and destination, the pure ideal image of man. To be in accord with its immutable oneness through all changes is the great task of his life.

> *Jeder individuelle Mensch . . . trägt der Anlage*
> *und Bestimmung nach einen reinen idealischen*
> *Menschen in sich, mit dessen unveränderlicher*
> *Einheit in allen seinen Abwechslungen überein-*
> *zustimmen die große Aufgabe seines Daseins ist.*

                    The century is
Not ripe for my ideal. And I live
A citizen of ages yet to come.

> *Das Jahrhundert*
> *Ist meinem Ideal nicht reif. Ich lebe*
> *Ein Bürger derer, welche kommen werden.*

A WORD TO THE READER

A SCHILLER anthology for today's readers has long been a cherished personal project. The bicentennial anniversary of Schiller's birth presented a unique occasion for such a volume. Beyond the satisfaction of celebrating a significant anniversary, however, is the conviction that our cultural life has been the poorer because one of the world's greatest writers has remained almost unknown to a wider public in English-speaking countries. The language barrier is a formidable one for any poet; for Schiller, the classical poet of freedom and brotherhood, it has proved almost insurmountable. But it is we who have suffered the major loss.

Schiller has much to say to us today, much that is vitally important for the continuity of our cultural tradition—intellectually, politically, ethically. If the birth of the American nation was spurred by the spirit of "rational idealism," if this same spirit has remained the chief characteristic of American thought and practical endeavor, it finds its counterpart in the works of the principal old-world exponent of that very "rational idealism"—Friedrich Schiller himself.

The anthology consists of two parts. Part One comprises a descriptive and analytical account of Schiller's life and thought, interwoven with selections and quotations from his work, most of them newly translated. Longer selections that would have disrupted the continuity of the opening section are included in Part Two.

If Schiller has not reached a wider audience in Eng-

lish it is mainly because of the difficulties of translating him adequately. Although his German is limpid and in a sense quite simple, it is borne along by something outside the realm of grammar and lexicography, and this "something," so essential to a full understanding of Schiller, easily gets lost in an English rendering. For this volume new translations were made of all selections with the exception of three poems. In most instances the new translations are the first to be done since the nineteenth century. How far they succeed where their predecessors failed must be left to the reader to decide.

Because of the special problems of translation, the inclusion of the German text seemed essential. To make room for this text, some aspects of Schiller's work were omitted, and others were treated less fully than might have been desirable.

It is customary for an editor to acknowledge his obligation to those who have lent him assistance. It may truly be said, first, that this work would not have been possible without the continuing inspiration found in Schiller himself. The writer is also greatly indebted to his friend, the noted linguist, Alexander Gode-von Aesch, for his numerous valuable suggestions and for his translations.

This anthology was conceived and prepared with the hope of kindling new interest in Friedrich Schiller, the writer, and Friedrich Schiller, the man. If the volume offers the reader at least the pleasure of meeting or renewing acquaintance with a truly great man, it will fulfill its purpose.

F. U.

CONTENTS

PART ONE

For complete listing of selections in the text,
see following page

PART TWO

Longer selections

GUIDE TO SELECTIONS

Translations were prepared especially for this volume by Jane Bannard Greene (JBG); Charles E. Passage (CEP); Alexander Gode-von Aesch (GVA)

PART ONE

The account of Schiller's life and work, JBG, *except for certain passages added by Frederick Ungar*

PART TWO

Selections in prose, JBG; selections from the dramas, CEP; "The Cranes of Ibycus," *Harold Lenz*, after E. P. Arnold-Forster; "The Song of the Bell," *Henry Wadsworth Longfellow*

FRIEDRICH
SCHILLER

An Anthology for Our Time

PART ONE

THROUGHOUT the English-speaking world, the name of Schiller evokes today at best a hazy image. In his native land, too, his fame has steadily declined, although during his lifetime and for a half century thereafter he was the most beloved and most widely read of German poets, excepting none, not even Goethe. The causes of this remarkable change must not be sought in Schiller but in ourselves, not in the poet's works as such but rather in what has happened to our modes of thought throughout the past one hundred years.

There are many who call the works of Schiller outmoded, either because they do not know those works or because they are not prepared to grasp the author's unique greatness. The voice of Schiller—if we but try to listen—rings out boldly to us today and beyond us to future generations. Few poets or thinkers have a greater message for mankind than Schiller, or one with a more direct bearing on men's daily lives. This is indeed no small claim, and he who makes it must be prepared to back it up with tangible proof.

Schiller has left us a twofold legacy: the grandeur of his literary and philosophical work and the heroic example of his personal life. His own age saw in him the embodiment of all that is most noble in man, enabling him, as an individual, to rise to greatness in a time of mediocrity and to preserve his integrity in hardship and suffering. If we today approach Schiller in this spirit, we shall find that the anxious questions of our age find answers and interpretations in him—in

his ideas or in his attitudes—which may be ignored only to the detriment of a better, a more humane future.

The significance of Schiller's work for us today lies in its simultaneously political and moral nature. It is not only his poetic work that reveals this quality, but also his historical and philosophical writings, which too may be considered poetic because of their brilliance of language and lofty flight of imagination.

In an era when a fragmented Germany was powerless against foreign enemies, and the individual's lack of freedom seemed hopeless, Schiller's voice—particularly as it resounded from the rostrum of the stage—was bound to exert a tremendous influence. He gave stirring expression to the timeless, supranational ideas with which his age was struggling.

Schiller was indeed the poet for times that try men's souls, times that move towards great goals and decisions. In the era of satiated quietude, however, that marked the middle of the nineteenth century, his influence could not but decline. Materialism increased steadily. Belief in progress was unquestioned, and there was no bridge to connect it with a concept of life that gives the tragic its rightful place. Such an atmosphere was not receptive to a spirit which regards "the ennoblement of feeling and the moral purification of the will" as the indispensable prerequisites for the higher development of political and social conditions and which is profoundly aware of the extent to which man is at the mercy of fate.

Thus Schiller's high integrity, his heart that beat for all mankind, became a source of embarrassment to those who wanted to use the weight of his name for their own dubious purposes. Such misuse could only result in Schiller's being the most misunderstood of German poets, the one whose aims have been most misrepresented. Those groups which, in absolute con-

tradiction to his unequivocal word, cited him as a champion of nationalistic aims were guilty of complete falsification.

It is necessary to recognize this falsification as such before the image of Schiller's human greatness can be seen in its purity. He can, of course, be called a patriotic poet—and his influence in this role was by no means small—but he was never an advocate of patriotism in a political sense. To him family and state are institutions provided by nature itself. They constitute man's earthly home and the roots of his existence. On them depends his spiritual health. The state must assure the human being of the possibility of fully developing all the talents latent within him and it must so organize social conditions that he is guaranteed the freedom requisite for this.

In the essay entitled "The Legislation of Lycurgus and Solon," which is included here, Schiller sketches the terrifying picture of a totalitarian state built according to the specifications of the mythical Spartan lawgiver, Lycurgus. With this he contrasts the humane legislation of Solon, the Athenian. In praise of the latter, Schiller says that "he had a respect for human nature and never sacrificed the human being for the state, nor the end for the means, but saw to it that the state served man. His laws were loose reins within which the minds of the citizens could move freely and easily in all directions without feeling that they were being guided." Under Lycurgus' legislation, the human being is completely sacrificed to the military might and durability of the state. Of this Schiller says: "If a constitution hinders the development of all the powers in man . . . it is harmful and worthless. . . . The state is never an end in itself. It is important only as a means to the realization of an end . . ." What explosive power is contained in this essay even today

17

is evident from the fact that it was used as a pamphlet against the Nazi dictatorship by the student youth of Munich under the leadership of Hans and Sophie Scholl, the brother and sister who were later executed.

Schiller believed that no man could attain to a higher humanity unless he were independent and self-reliant in his thinking and in his search for the truth. It was Schiller's humanity that led him to politics, but not to the pursuit of political aims such as the establishment of a specific social order or the interests of a certain social class. Rather he made politics as such the subject of his thought and writings.

At the center of his thinking throughout his life were these questions: how can the opposing demands for control and for freedom be reconciled, how can the world be changed so that a life more worthy of man becomes possible? And the question which took precedence over all others: how can man develop the totality of his being, how can he bring to fruition all of his talents? Only when he has succeeded in reaching a higher level of human development will he be able to apply himself successfully to the solution of political problems. This will be possible only when agreement has been reached as to what is meant by the term "humanity." And it is not enough for a single nation to agree upon this meaning; it must be accepted by all peoples.

Schiller's political aims are concerned with what is universally human. In his opinion these aims are to be realized only through a complete abandonment of the sort of politics that exists in the traditional state, and they require a deeper and more comprehensive knowledge of human nature and existence. Politics, which aims at shaping the present and the future, is worthy of consideration only in so far as it attempts to bring

reality closer to the ideal or has already done so. As regards the past, this means that only peoples and communities are worth studying which in certain periods of their history have succeeded in accomplishing something that is, or should be, of concern to all humanity. However, in Schiller's conception it is not peoples or communities as collective bodies that perform those actions and thereby advance the humanization of humanity. They are represented in this endeavor by individual men. Only individual men exert an influence that will be felt down through the ages.

"I do believe," Schiller wrote to his sister-in-law, Caroline von Beulwitz, "that every individual human soul that develops its powers is more than the greatest society taken as a whole. The greatest state is a work of man; man is the work of incomparable great Nature. The state is a product of chance, but man is a necessary being, and by what is the state great and venerable except the power of its individuals? The state is only a product of human endeavor, it is a creation of thought, but man is himself the source of the endeavor and the creator of the thought."

"[Ich] glaube . . . , daß jede einzelne ihre Kraft entwickelnde Menschenseele mehr ist als die größte Menschengesellschaft, wenn ich diese als ein Ganzes betrachte. Der größte Staat ist ein Menschenwerk, der Mensch ist ein Werk der unerreichbaren großen Natur. Der Staat ist ein Geschöpf des Zufalls, aber der Mensch ist ein notwendiges Wesen, und durch was sonst ist der Mensch groß und ehrwürdig als durch die Kräfte seiner Individuen? Der Staat ist nur eine Wirkung der Menschenkraft, nur ein Gedankenwerk, aber der Mensch ist die Quelle der Kraft selbst und der Schöpfer des Gedankens."

This "humanism" remained a permanent trait of Schiller's thinking. At a different period of his life he expressed it still more strikingly in a letter to the Christian philosopher Friedrich Heinrich Jacobi:

"Let us remain citizens of our age *in the flesh,* for there is no other way. But *in the spirit* it is the privilege and the duty of philosopher and poet to belong to no nation and no age but to be in the full sense of the term a contemporary of all ages."

"Wir wollen dem Leibe nach *Bürger unserer Zeit sein und bleiben, weil es nicht anders sein kann; sonst aber und* dem Geiste nach *ist es das Vorrecht und die Pflicht des Philosophen wie des Dichters, zu keinem Volk und zu keiner Zeit zu gehören, sondern im eigentlichen Sinne des Wortes der Zeitgenosse aller Zeiten zu sein."*

All this should leave no doubt that Schiller was quite averse to every form of emotional or intellectual nationalism. As he put it in a letter to his friend, Christian Gottfried Körner:

"We of the modern world are endowed with a realm of interest unknown to Greek and Roman alike. With it the patriotic interest simply cannot compete. This latter is really significant only for immature peoples, the youth of the world. It is something quite different to be concerned with representing in a humanly significant way whatever noteworthy occurrence involved human beings. It is a poor and paltry ideal to write for *one* nation. A philosophical mind will find such a restriction quite unbearable. It simply cannot stop with so changeable, accidental, and arbitrary a form of humanity, with such a fragment, for indeed, what else is even the greatest of nations? The philosophical mind can take an interest in one nation or one national occurrence only in so far

as it appears significant to him as a condition for the betterment of the whole race. When an historical event—of whatever nation or time it be—can be dealt with in this manner and can thus be linked to the whole race, then it fulfills all the prerequisites to become interesting in the hands of the philosopher, and this interest can dispense with all further adornment."

"*Wir Neueren haben ein Interesse in unserer Gewalt, das kein Grieche und kein Römer gekannt hat und dem das vaterländische Interesse bei weitem nicht beikommt. Das letzte ist überhaupt nur für unreife Nationen wichtig, für die Jugend der Welt. Ein ganz andres Interesse ist es, jede merkwürdige Begebenheit, die mit Menschen vorging, dem Menschen wichtig darzustellen. Es ist ein armseliges, kleinliches Ideal, für eine Nation zu schreiben; einem philosophischen Geiste ist diese Grenze durchaus unerträglich. Dieser kann bei einer so wandelbaren, zufälligen und willkürlichen Form der Menschheit, bei einem Fragmente (und was ist die wichtigste Nation anders?) nicht stille stehen. Er kann sich nicht weiter dafür erwärmen, als soweit ihm diese Nation oder Nationalbegebenheit als Bedingung für den Fortschritt der Gattung wichtig ist. Ist eine Geschichte (von welcher Nation und Zeit sie auch sei) dieser Anwendung fähig, kann sie an die Gattung angeschlossen werden, so hat sie alle Requisite, unter der Hand des Philosophen interessant zu werden, und dieses Interesse kann jeder Verzierung entbehren.*"

This may serve to explain Schiller's enthusiasm for the early struggle for freedom on the part of the Netherlands, France, and Switzerland—reflected in *The History of the Revolt of the Netherlands, Don Carlos, The Maid of Orleans,* and *William Tell*—and it also explains why he presented no great national

drama to his own people, addressing the Germans instead in these challenging words:

> "Vainly you Germans attempt to set yourself up
> as a nation.
> Strive to grow freer instead, freer as men—
> and succeed."

> *"Zur Nation euch zu bilden, ihr hoffet es, Deutsche, vergebens.*
> *Bildet, ihr könnt es, dafür freier zu Menschen euch aus!"*

But let us return to the history of Schiller's influence on posterity. The age of unqualified belief in progress and in the everlasting increase in material power came to a close with the catastrophes of the two World Wars and the aftermath of political collapse and personal hardship. Once more people became deeply conscious of the tragic aspects of life, and in their new awareness the figure of Schiller stood forth in its forthright militancy, face furrowed with suffering but an arm stretched high in a gesture of victory. No one has stressed the moral necessity of maintaining spiritual independence in the face of destiny so strongly as Schiller; no one has experienced so deeply the fact that the tragic in human existence lends nobility and dignity to the human being, and has expressed it so movingly in the sublime beauty of tragic poetry. It is abundantly clear why responsible German thinkers are bringing Schiller's figure into true focus and are opening up a new approach to him with remarkable success.

What is it that endeared Schiller to so many? It is probably that no other poet has been so strong an advocate of man and his rights, that he believes in the high destiny of man and that he can kindle the divine

spark once again in an oppressed or spiritually lazy humanity. In his battle for recognition and for liberation from the limitations that restrict men physically and spiritually he was nothing less than heroic, particularly in the light of the hardship of his own life and his depressing physical suffering. It is "the great subjects of humanity" that are the basis of his works, and the living breath of freedom blows through all of them. To Schiller all human value is based primarily on freedom. His concept of "freedom," however, is so far removed from the catchword used in the political arena that to understand his thought it is necessary to inquire more closely into the range of meaning he included in this term.

Freedom, as Schiller conceives it, never has a merely material meaning, but involves all aspects of human life. He sees in it man's ultimate destiny and at the same time an absolute prerequisite of man's existence. Any moral value his action may possess is of necessity derived from the fact of his freedom. And indeed, what made Schiller a disciple of Kant was above all else "the great idea of self-determination" based on freedom.

"Certainly," he wrote in a letter to Körner, "no greater words were ever spoken by mortal man than these of Kant which represent at once the essence of his entire philosophy: *Determine yourself from within.*"

"*Es ist gewiß von einem sterblichen Menschen kein größeres Wort noch gesprochen als dieses Kantsche, was zugleich der Inhalt seiner ganzen Philosophie ist: Bestimme dich aus dir selbst.*"

The same idea is developed in greater detail in the opening paragraphs of the essay "On the Sublime" where the famous words from Lessing's *Nathan* are quoted, "There is no must that men must bow to"

(*"Kein Mensch muß müssen"*). This leads up to the following passage:

> "All other things must; man is the being that wills. It is precisely for this reason that nothing is so unworthy of man as the toleration of force; for force negates him. Whoever inflicts force upon us denies us nothing less than our humanity. Whoever submits to it out of cowardice casts away his humanity."

> *"Alle anderen Dinge müssen; der Mensch ist das Wesen, welches will. Eben deswegen ist des Menschen nichts so unwürdig, als Gewalt zu erleiden, denn Gewalt hebt ihn auf. Wer sie uns antut, macht uns nichts Geringeres als die Menschheit streitig; wer sie feigerweise erleidet, wirft seine Menschheit hinweg."*

When man obeys foreign laws without being able to consent to them inwardly, he renounces his essential humanity. This deprives his action of any moral value and makes it a mere means to an end.

On the other hand, it is man's obligation to conduct himself morally that justifies his claim to freedom. This must not extend merely to things physical and political, preventing violence and disfranchisement. It must also apply to the spiritual realm where its purpose is to preserve independence of thought, to protect man from modes of thinking imposed upon him from without, so that he will not become the slave of ideological systems. Finally, it must enable the human being to preserve his independence in the face of those tendencies in him that are opposed to the idealistic goals towards which he strives. Thus this spiritual freedom absorbs the tension prevailing between the sensual and moral natures of man, enabling him to live in harmony with himself. But it also en-

ables him to remain uncommitted to things which are but ephemeral ornaments of life and to vanquish the sensual portion of his being when it involves him in a tragic conflict, acting in accord with the closing words of the chorus in *The Bride of Messina:*

> "One thing I clearly feel and here aver:
> Of all possessions life is not the highest,
> The worst of evils is, however, guilt."

> *"Dies eine fühl' ich und erkenn' es klar:*
> *Das Leben ist der Güter höchstes nicht,*
> *Der Übel größtes aber ist die Schuld."*

Schiller lived in a period of political upheaval. The French Revolution separated feudal and clerical Europe, the Europe of the decadent social orders from the future Europe of class realignments and revolutions. To be sure, the French people were still under the yoke of absolutism, but it was regarded as obsolete, and the grumbling which was becoming increasingly audible more than presaged the disruption of the old order. And in distant America the British colonies led the cause of enlightened freedom to victory and established their independence from the English crown.

The German lands were still wholly dominated by the oppressive power of the absolute principalities that prevented the Germans from achieving national unity and rendered impossible the free development of civic life. The feeling of impotence and intellectual slavery was coupled with another feeling quite opposed to either which set its stamp on this period. This was the belief in the unlimited power of reason.

It was reason that restored to man the feeling of being free at least in his thinking and of therefore being able to subject the powers of oppression to his criticism and condemnation. If reason had been able

to probe into the laws of nature, which were created by God, and even to shake the authority of Biblical revelations, it might also be expected to discover the basic laws of government and society. Reason had only to find the power to thrust aside all the unnatural obstacles that opposed it and to construct a new human society based on the demands of philosophy.

The happy anticipation of an approaching victory of such magnitude intoxicated men's hearts and minds. Men saw themselves and the earth on the threshold of a new creation. But the French Revolution mercilessly destroyed the mirage that had captivated their minds. How clearly the Revolution, soon drowned in blood, showed that the utopian dream world still lacked the people to build and inhabit it! The gulf that was opened between ideal and reality forced many to reorient their thinking entirely.

Realization that neither social revolution nor changes of governmental forms can produce a society worthy of humanity as long as the individual citizen has not been educated to be a human being, caused many people, including some of the most important minds, to retreat into resignation and indifference. But not Schiller, for whom these problems had been of central importance long before the French Revolution.

For him the Revolution was an attempt to instate abstract reason as the "sole and absolute lawgiver" and to decide public affairs according to hard and fast principles. Can a socially ideal situation be produced in this fashion? Does not this method fail to take into account the limitation of human powers so that in the end it results in destruction? Schiller repeatedly states that the realization of ideal social conditions by violent means can never result in the sovereignty of reason, but only in that of despotism, and that "man may trust

the inspiration of his heart or his individual sense of right and wrong far more safely than the dangerous guidance of universal, rational ideas that he has artificially created for himself." Salvation lies only in the training and education of free men. Art owes its high significance to the fact that it plays an indispensable role in accomplishing this purpose and thus proves its value by contributing to the formation of historical reality.

Schiller's basic reflections on this subject, which he developed in the "Aesthetic Letters," are as follows: In man as a being who explores and dominates nature lie the possibilities of achieving the highest freedom and self-determination, but also of falling into deepest slavery and self-estrangement. The farther man progresses in his ability to dominate nature and to shape his world, the more dependent he becomes on his creation, the more he forfeits of his freedom.

Man as a moral being requires a higher form of society in which he can develop freely and realize all the possibilities residing in his nature. To be sure, neither this higher form of society nor this ideal human nature is to be found anywhere in the actual world, but they are both given to man as ideals and ultimate goals. Both are demanded by reason on the basis of natural necessity. Though knowledge of this higher goal is the origin of all great political and social movements in behalf of the freedom of mankind, Schiller nevertheless makes extremely clear the contradiction inherent in all revolutionary movements that pursue their ideological goals blindly, and the inevitable disaster to which they are thus doomed.

He has no desire to sacrifice the given reality, the existing order for the invented, ideal state, to allow the idea of freedom in its absolute form to become a source of slavery which will result in a totalitarian

27

state. But he is also not ready to sanction the existing order even in theory, for this would hinder the development of a higher humanity. Both possibilities, the ideal demand for a higher form of society and the physical existence of the actual society, must be preserved, but at the same time the dangers of both must be combatted.

The solution of this paradoxical situation, the inevitable consequence of man's nature which is both moral and sensual and so contains within it two conflicting tendencies, is the center of Schiller's political work and often the central problem of his tragedies. And what is typical of his position is his unyielding protest against any fixed, abstract position that can only lead to intolerance and to blindness to the true nature and needs of one's fellow man, to a blindness also to the actual situations of life, which is forever changing. But the uninhibited striving for material gain must also be resisted as it is bound to result in erosion of the moral values and the coherence of the social structure.

How then can human society be changed on the basis of an idea without threatening its permanent existence and transforming freedom into slavery? Only by keeping alive the feeling for the goal of a higher, more human form of society, but without losing sight of human relations, so that respect for the otherness of one's fellow man is preserved. But with the realism of a responsible thinker Schiller sees this as "a task for more than a single century."

Whoever reads Schiller's philosophical writings with real sympathy cannot escape the impression that his words are the product not only of his thinking but also of his experience. We sense that when he describes the fate of modern man he is in reality revealing his own fate. He himself was caught in the spiritual con-

flicts of his time. He himself, in the years of his spiritual growth, was subject to the tyranny of an absolute prince, saw his plans for a career wrecked by it and became for a long time a homeless fugitive.

Johann Christoph Friedrich Schiller was born on November 10, 1759, in the little town of Marbach on the Neckar in the Grand Duchy of Württemberg, the second child and only son of Johann Kaspar Schiller and Elisabeth Dorothea, née Kodweiss.

The Schiller family had been small landholders in Swabia, where bearers of that name can be traced back to the fourteenth century. With Johann Kaspar it attained the social, intellectual, and economic status of the petty bourgeoisie. Driven by an unsatiable desire to improve himself and to see the world, Johann Kaspar Schiller had become a soldier. The Bavarian regiment of hussars in which he served was hired out— as was the custom in those days—to foreign powers in need of military assistance, and so Johann Kaspar came to take part on the side of the Dutch in the war which Holland, in alliance with Austria and England, was waging against France. When he returned home in 1749, he brought back with him not only his own horse and considerable savings but also a rich store of practical knowledge and experience which he had gathered during his stay in Holland, Belgium, France, and England. He married the daughter of an innkeeper at Marbach, but after four years he returned to military service and saw much of the Seven Years' War as a member of one of the corps which the Duke of Württemberg had put at the disposal of the French in their fight against Prussia. After the end of the war he was given the rank of lieutenant and stationed as a recruiting officer at Gmünd. From 1764 on he lived

with his family in the village of Lorch near Gmünd, where he devoted much time to the study and practice of agriculture, especially the cultivation of trees. Eventually he became the director of the ducal gardens and school for foresters, providing (as it has been put) the whole country with trees.

At Lorch, young Friedrich Schiller attracted the interest of the village pastor, Philipp Ulrich Moser, who exerted on him an influence hardly less important than his father's. Moser taught him Latin and the rudiments of Greek and inspired him with a strong desire to go into the church. At the age of seven Schiller entered the Latin School for an eight-year course, after which he was to continue his studies in a more advanced institution, the Klosterschule. But this plan had to be abandoned when the all-powerful Duke made it known that he wished young Schiller—who was now twelve years old—to be sent to the Karlsschule, which he had recently founded.

This "military nursery" was designed to train loyal officers, officials and artists for Duke Karl Eugen. The Duke's method of recruiting pupils for the school was simply to order his officials to send their sons to it. Because of its exclusively secular curriculum, Schiller was unable to pursue his theological studies there. His father tried, without stirring up trouble, to put off the moment of complying with the Duke's request. But the order was repeated more sharply and he had no choice but to obey. And so at the beginning of 1773, when he was not yet fourteen, Schiller had to leave home and for the first time in his life found himself dependent upon a power against which his parents could not protect him.

Schiller was to remain at the Karlsschule for eight long years. During all that time he never had a day's furlough and never saw his parents except for brief

visits which were always strictly monitored. The school took the place of the family, and every detail of the daily routine was arranged in accordance with the Duke's decrees, for the Duke left nothing to his subordinates, not even the pettiest punishment for the pettiest infraction of one of the innumerable rules.

Not being allowed to pursue his chosen study of theology Schiller had to take up law. When a medical course was added to the offerings of the Karlsschule, Schiller was allowed to give up his legal studies and take up medicine, but neither field could ever arouse his enthusiasm.

The spirit of absolutism (and not the strict discipline as such), the complete isolation from the realities of life, and above all the prevailing stupid contempt for poetry—these were characteristics of the Karlsschule atmosphere that were bound to result in the most adverse reactions in young Schiller's mind. What harm the Karlsschule did him he stated repeatedly in later years, most poignantly perhaps in the account he gave of himself in announcing to the public his plan to edit a theater periodical under the title of "The Rhenish Thalia." It may be well to note that that passage was written at a time when Schiller had little to his credit in the eyes of the public beyond the initial success of his drama *The Robbers,* which he himself already recognized with greater or lesser clarity as an uncouth product of his genius trying to rid itself of the ugly memories of the Karlsschule years.

"I write," he said, "as a citizen of the world who serves no prince. At an early time I lost my fatherland to exchange it for the wide world, which I knew only through a telescope. A strange misjudgment of nature condemned me to being a poet in my native land. Love of poetry was at odds with the laws of the institution in which I was

reared and did not accord with the plans of its founder. For eight years my enthusiasm wrestled with the military statute, but passion for the poet's art is as fiery and strong as first love. What was to be stamped out grew only the stronger. To escape from conditions that were torture to me, my heart took refuge in a world of ideals, but: without knowledge of the real world from which I was separated by iron bars; without knowledge of human beings, for the four hundred that were around me were but one single creature, the faithful copy of one model, of just that one model which plastic nature solemnly disclaimed; without knowledge of the hopes and the desires of free unfettered beings—for here but one desire could mature, one desire that I shall not name: all remaining strength of will grew weak while only one attained convulsive tenseness, and every whim and every fancy of multiply playful nature perished in the monotonous measure of the prevailing order; without knowledge of the fair sex—the gates of that institution admit women only before they begin to be interesting and after they have ceased to be so; without knowledge of men and the lot of man, I could not prevent my brush from missing the midline between angel and devil,— it was bound to paint a monster which fortunately exists nowhere in the world, and if I wish it immortality, I do so only to perpetuate the example of a birth which resulted from the unnatural mating of subordination and genius. I mean *The Robbers."*

"Ich schreibe als Weltbürger, der keinem Fürsten dient. Frühe verlor ich mein Vaterland, um es gegen die große Welt auszutauschen, die ich nur eben durch die Fernröhre kannte. Ein seltsamer Mißverstand der Natur hat mich in meinem Geburtsort zum Dichter verurteilt. Neigung für Po-

esie beleidigte die Gesetze des Instituts, worin
ich erzogen ward, und widersprach dem Plan
seines Stifters. Acht Jahre lang rang mein Enthu-
siasmus mit der militärischen Regel; aber Leiden-
schaft für die Dichtkunst ist feurig und stark wie
die erste Liebe. Was sie ersticken sollte, fachte sie
an. Verhältnissen zu entfliehen, die mir zur Folter
waren, schweifte mein Herz in eine Ideenwelt
aus—aber unbekannt mit der wirklichen, von wel-
cher mich eiserne Stäbe schieden, unbekannt mit
den Menschen (denn die vierhundert, die mich
umgaben, waren ein einziges Geschöpf, der ge-
treue Abguß eines and eben dieses Modells, von
welchem die plastische Natur sich feierlich los-
sagte), unbekannt mit den Neigungen freier, sich
selbst überlassener Wesen; denn hier kam nur
eine zur Reife, eine, die ich jetzo nicht nen-
nen will; jede übrige Kraft des Willens er-
schlaffte, indem eine einzige sich konvulsivisch
spannte; jede Eigenheit, jede Ausgelassenheit
der tausendfach spielenden Natur ging in dem
regelmäßigen Tempo der herrschenden Ord-
nung verloren—unbekannt mit dem schönen Ge-
schlechte (die Tore dieses Instituts öffnen sich, wie
man wissen wird, Frauenzimmern nur, ehe sie an-
fangen interessant zu werden, und wenn sie auf-
gehört haben, es zu sein)—unbekannt mit Men-
schen und Menschenschicksal, mußte mein Pinsel
notwendig die mittlere Linie zwischen Engel und
Teufel verfehlen, mußte er ein Ungeheuer hervor-
bringen, das zum Glück in der Welt nicht vorhan-
den war, dem ich nur darum Unsterblichkeit
wünschen möchte, um das Beispiel einer Geburt
zu verewigen, die der naturwidrige Beischlaf der
Subordination und des Genius in die Welt setzte.
Ich meine Die Räuber."

At last, at the age of twenty-one, Schiller was allowed to leave the Karlsschule. He was given a post as regimental physician with an extremely small salary. Instead of the freedom he had dreamed of there lay ahead of him another spell of the drudgery and the thralldom of garrison confinement.

During this period of military service at Stuttgart, Schiller prepared for publication *The Robbers,* which was a direct expression of his pent-up resentment. Since he was unable to find a publisher, he had it printed at his own expense, incurring a debt which was to be a burden to him for a long time. The book made a tremendous impression and its author became famous overnight.

Although Schiller considered *The Robbers* merely a "dramatized novel" and thought it was not suitable for the stage, it turned out to be an extremely effective drama. The bookseller, Schwan, persuaded the Baron von Dalberg, intendant of the National Theater in Mannheim, to produce it. No other German play up to that time had ever enjoyed so great a success, and Schiller received tremendous acclaim.

A contemporary report runs as follows: "The theater was like a madhouse, rolling eyes, clenched fists, hoarse outcries from the audience. Strangers fell sobbing into one another's arms. Women staggered to the door nearly fainting. There was general confusion like a chaos out of whose mists a new creation is about to break forth." And the earliest review that has been preserved says: "If ever we can expect a German Shakespeare, this is he." This success was also to have a decisive effect on Schiller's future life, for it brought him to the realization of his talents as a dramatic poet.

Karl Moor, the hero of the play, thinks that "the order of nature" has been abolished because, as he mistakenly believes, he cannot obtain the forgiveness

of his father for an unfortunate duel. "His private bitterness toward his hard-hearted father surges up into a universal hatred of the whole human race," as the poet explains in his own critique of *The Robbers*. It is his rebelliousness that plunges Karl into guilt and makes him presume to set himself up as a moral judge. The rebel against society commits one act of violence after another until he realizes with horror that he has been blind. At last he recognizes the reasons for his decision to assume the leadership of the robber band and sees the consequences. However, he is still responsible to the band. Finally he makes up his mind to expiate his guilt by a free moral act through which he restores in principle the order he had destroyed.

"I remember on my way over I was talking to a poor devil who has eleven live children and makes a living doing odd jobs.—A thousand louis d'or has been offered for bringing in the great robber alive—that man can be helped. (Exit)"

"Ich erinnere mich, einen armen Schelm gesprochen zu haben, als ich herüberkam, der im Taglohn arbeitet and elf lebendige Kinder hat.—Man hat tausend Louisdore geboten, wer den großen Räuber lebendig liefert—dem Mann kann geholfen werden. (Er geht ab.)"

Thus the drama ends, not with the victory of the revolutionary idea, but with that of conscience. But the poet's indignation is directed not only against the hero's guilt, but also against the evil and corruption of the absolutist state, and even today the motto of the play, "In Tyrannos!," is a battle cry against the forces of oppression.

For all the success and fame that *The Robbers* brought him, Schiller was by no means unaware of

the many defects of his play, in particular of the mixture of styles. This is evident from a review which he himself wrote and which appeared under a pseudonym in a literary quarterly. His criticism is detached and humorous.

"One wishes the language and the dialogue were more even and on the whole less poetic. In one place the expression is lyrical and epic, in another it is, by God, metaphysical, in a third place it is Biblical and in a fourth place it is trite. Franz should be speaking altogether differently. A flowery style can be excused only if it flows from a heated imagination, and Franz simply has to be cold. The girl has been reading too much Klopstock to suit me. If it is not the beauties of his work that make us suspect that the author is head over heels in love with his Shakespeare, we certainly can tell by his excesses. . . . Where the poet's feelings were the truest, where the impression he made was the deepest, there he spoke like any one of us."

"Die Sprache und der Dialog dürften sich gleicher bleiben und im ganzen weniger poetisch sein. Hier ist der Ausdruck lyrisch und episch, dort gar metaphysisch, an einem dritten Ort biblisch, an einem vierten platt. Franz sollte durchaus anders sprechen. Die blumigte Sprache verzeihen wir nur der erhitzten Phantasie, und Franz sollte schlechterdings kalt sein. Das Mädchen hat mir zu viel im Klopstock gelesen. Wenn man es dem Verfasser nicht an den Schönheiten anmerkt, daß er sich in seinen Shakespeare vergafft hat, so merkt man es desto gewisser an den Ausschweifungen. . . . Wo der Dichter am wahrsten fühlte und am durchdringendsten bewegte, sprach er wie unsereiner."

For years—till the appearance of *Don Carlos* and in

a sense much longer—*The Robbers* was Schiller's work that identified him in the eyes of his countrymen. The "ghost" of *The Robbers* haunted him long after he had freed himself from and had outgrown the angry spirit of this as well as the other dramas of his early years. It was the outcry of abused youth.

Schiller managed to make his first trip to Mannheim for the opening performance of *The Robbers* without being discovered. But a second secret journey was reported to the Duke who punished him by two weeks' arrest and peremptorily forbade him to indulge in any further literary activities on pain of imprisonment. The great success of *The Robbers* had opened the door to an attractive career, and the contrast between the artistic atmosphere of Mannheim and the barracks life and philistinism of Württemberg had made a deep impression on Schiller. It is no wonder, therefore, that he felt he had no choice but to take flight. He reached Mannheim after a series of dramatic adventures. His hope of receiving an appointment there as a playwright, however, was doomed to frustration.

He had placed his hopes primarily on a second drama, *Fiesco's Conspiracy at Genoa*. He had practically completed the manuscript and was convinced that it represented indeed a great advance over *The Robbers*. But Dalberg refused to accept it or to advance any money on the play until it was finished, and finally rejected it as unsuitable. Schiller's friends, who believed that his position was precarious, urged him to remain in hiding outside of Mannheim.

Schiller was now without resources or hope of receiving any income in the immediate future. He was also burdened with the debts he had been forced to leave behind him in Stuttgart. Apart from his belief in his vocation as a dramatist, he had nothing but the

respectful devotion of his friends who had as much admiration for his human qualities as for his genius and who stood by him selflessly in his desperate situation.

It was the young musician Andreas Streicher who gave him the greatest assistance in escaping from Stuttgart. He had left Stuttgart with Schiller to go to Hamburg where he wished to complete his musical training. When the two men received word from Dalberg in Frankfurt that *Fiesco* would have to be finished before he could make a decision, Streicher changed his plans and went with Schiller to live in Oggersheim, a little village near Mannheim. The money he contributed from his own scanty funds made it possible for Schiller to finish *Fiesco*.

After Dalberg's rejection of *Fiesco,* the mother of one of his Karlsschule schoolmates, Henriette von Wolzogen, offered him a refuge at her country estate in Bauerbach, a little village near Meiningen. In the middle of winter, with only scant protection from the bitter cold, he made the long journey by coach to the remote village where he spent six months. Here he completed his third drama, *Luise Millerin* or, as it was later called, *Intrigue and Love*. Here too he wrote the first draft of his last early drama, *Don Carlos*.

In the spring of 1783, Dalberg got in touch with him again and offered him the post of dramatist. Schiller, for whom a close connection with a stage was of the utmost importance, accepted without lengthy negotiations. The National Theater at Mannheim was one of the best in Germany at that time and was to enable Schiller to lay the foundation of his technical mastery of the stage. He promised to rewrite *Fiesco* and *Intrigue and Love* and to have ready for performance still another play, all within a season. Now began the years of the most difficult struggles and hardships. To add

to his heavy burden of work, he was subject to attacks of malaria caused by the unwholesome climate. Drastic remedies—emetics and strong doses of quinine—which were supposed to preserve his working capacity, undermined his health still further. It is quite likely that we have here the ultimate causes of his later illness and his untimely death. He himself felt that "this winter gave him a shock for the rest of his life." When *Fiesco* was finally performed in January 1784, it was a failure. Not altogether undeservedly so.

There is much in the drama that is true to life and very effective. Here, far more than in *The Robbers,* he tries to portray the world of reality. However, *Fiesco* shares the faults of all the plays of Schiller's youth: high-flown rhetoric and an extravagant style.

Here too the idea of freedom in its absolute form turns against the hero. Fiesco's attempt to free Genoa from tyrants threatens to set up a new rule of violence. What he considers necessary to do to win freedom is just what threatens to destroy it. This thought appears again in *Don Carlos,* expanded and deepened, and was to recur throughout Schiller's later work.

Intrigue and Love is a middle-class tragedy in the manner of Lessing's *Emilia Galotti.* The German middle-class tragedy of the eighteenth century takes its characters from the period. It is realistic, if not prosaic, but it provides an opportunity for social and political commentary. Schiller himself had had all too bitter an experience of the tyranny of an absolute prince. At this very time he was still living in fear of the long arm of the Duke and felt that he was in constant danger of extradition. So the tyrannical power of German princes was no matter of history or theory to him, but a practical reality that was oppressively close.

The theme of *Intrigue and Love* is the unbridgeable

gulf between nobility and bourgeoisie, and it is a passionate indictment of the conditions that prevailed in many German courts. Although the production of the play was a brilliant success, Dalberg did not renew the contract. In the meantime he had discovered in Iffland, a leading actor in the Mannheim theater, a playwright whose plays exactly suited the public taste and who could be relied upon to produce them whenever they were needed. Anonymous denunciations to the effect that the theater funds were being squandered on a revolutionary and a deserter also entered into Dalberg's decision.

On the other hand, it was during his stay at Mannheim that Schiller was given the honor of full membership in the "German Society," an association of men of learning not unlike a regular academy. At a public meeting of the society Schiller read his paper, "What Can a Well-Established Theater Really Contribute?" It is known today as "The Stage Considered as a Moral Institution" and appears as such in this volume. In it the stage is celebrated as an instrument of popular education in the most comprehensive sense. The idea that the stage has the immediate function of teaching moral lessons is vigorously rejected by Schiller. He holds instead that the art of the drama and hence of the stage is concerned with uncovering the secret workings of the human soul. In this sense it may be said that the stage teaches knowledge of men and thus preaches purer ideas and sounder principles.

When Schiller's contract at Mannheim was not renewed, he found himself without an income. This was the signal for his Stuttgart creditors to start pressing him even harder than before. His situation was desperate. He considered leaving Germany altogether and going into military service somewhere out in the

world, but, as so often in his life, kind friends came to his rescue when his need was greatest.

This time it was Christian Gottfried Körner who was chiefly responsible for getting him out of the intolerable situation in Mannheim. Three years older than Schiller, the son of a prominent and well-to-do theologian, Körner was an unsalaried lecturer on law at the University of Leipzig and was about to assume a post in the Dresden government. A man of broad and deep culture, he was, with Goethe and Wilhelm von Humboldt, Schiller's most intelligent reader and most constructive critic. He remained on terms of intimate friendship with Schiller throughout his life. The poet Theodor Körner, who was killed in the Wars of Liberation, was his son.

The first contact between Körner and Schiller dates back to the early summer of 1784. At that time Schiller received from four unknown and unnamed admirers in Leipzig a delicately embroidered silk portfolio with four unassuming portrait sketches and a letter which read in part: "At a time when art degrades itself more and more to the status of a meretricious slave of rich and mighty libertines, it is consoling to see a man appear ready and able to show what the human soul has in its powers even now." The senders, later identified, were two sisters, Dora and Minna Stock, the latter's fiancé Gottfried Körner, and a friend of theirs, the young writer Ludwig Ferdinand Huber.

When Körner learned of Schiller's desperate situation at Mannheim, he liberally and tactfully provided the means that enabled Schiller to move to Saxony and join the circle of his new friends. In April, 1785, he arrived in Leipzig, and in September he followed Körner and his young bride to Dresden. He stayed there for two years—two whole years of freedom from

41

worry and of a heretofore unknown association with people who really meant something to him. There grew up in his will to live an element of the joy of life which found expression in the great "Ode to Joy." In it, what had had its inception as a feeling of friendship and love for individuals assumed the dimensions of a rapturous love "embracing all mankind." It was this universal love of man that aroused in Beethoven a lifelong admiration for Schiller and inspired him to compose for the "Ode to Joy" in his Ninth Symphony the now universally known, heroically transfigured melody. In Beethoven's first plan the hymn itself was to have been preceded by the recitative: "Let us intone the hymn of the great Schiller."

ODE TO JOY

Joy, of flame celestial fashioned,
    Daughter of Elysium,
By that holy fire impassioned
    To thy sanctuary we come.
Thine the spells that reunited
    Those estranged by Custom dread,
Every man a brother plighted
    Where thy gentle wings are spread.
      Millions in our arms we gather,
        To the world our kiss be sent!
        Past the starry firmament,
      Brothers, dwells a loving Father.

Who that height of bliss has provèd
    Once a friend of friends to be,
Who has won a maid belovèd
    Join us in our jubilee.
Whoso holds a heart in keeping,
    One—in all the world—his own—

Who has failed, let him with weeping
From our fellowship begone!
All the mighty globe containeth
Homage to Compassion pay!
To the stars she leads the way
Where, unknown, the Godhead reigneth.

All drink joy from Mother Nature,
All she suckled at her breast,
Good or evil, every creature,
Follows where her foot has pressed.
Love she gave us, passing measure,
One Who true in death abode,
E'en the worm was granted pleasure,
Angels see the face of God.
Fall ye millions, fall before Him,
Is thy Maker, World, unknown?
Far above the stars His throne
Yonder seek Him and adore Him.

Joy, the spring of all contriving,
In eternal Nature's plan,
Joy set wheels on wheels a-driving
Since earth's horologe began;
From the bud the blossom winning
Suns from out the sky she drew,
Spheres through boundless ether spinning
Worlds no gazer's science knew.
Gladsome as her suns and glorious
Through the spacious heavens career,
Brothers, so your courses steer
Heroes joyful and victorious.

She from Truth's own mirror shining
Casts on sages glances gay,
Guides the sufferer unrepining
Far up Virtue's steepest way;
On the hills of Faith all-glorious
Mark her sunlit banners fly,

She, in death's despite, victorious,
  Stands with angels in the sky.
    Millions, bravely sorrows bearing,
      Suffer for a better time!
      See, above the starry clime
    God a great reward preparing.

Men may never match Immortals;
  Fair it is like Gods to be
Welcome to our joyous portals
  Sons of Want and Poverty.
Rancor and resentment leaving,
  Be our mortal foe forgiven,
Not a sorrow for his grieving,
  Not a tear to mar his heaven!
    Pardon every debt ungrudging,
      Let all nations be atoned!
      God above the stars enthroned
    Judges us, as we are judging.

Savages drink gentler notions
  While the meek learn to be bold
Through the joy of sparkling potions
  In the goblet's liquid gold.
Brothers, rise! In kindred feeling
  Let the goblet make the rounds.
While the foam spurts to the ceiling,
  Drink to Him whose love abounds.
    Him whose praise through stellar spaces
      Like a seraphs' chorus sounds,
      Drink to Him whose love abounds,
    Praise Him by your joyous faces.

Hearts in direst need unquailing,
  Aid to Innocence in woe,
Troth eternally unfailing,
  Loyalty to friend and foe!
Fronting kings, a manly spirit,
  Though it cost our wealth and blood!

Crowns to nought save noblest merit,
Death to all the Liars' brood!
Close the holy circle. Ever
Swear it by the wine of gold,
Swear these sacred vows to hold,
Swear it by the stars' Lawgiver.

AN DIE FREUDE

Freude, schöner Götterfunken,
Tochter aus Elysium,
Wir betreten feuertrunken,
Himmlische, dein Heiligtum.
Deine Zauber binden wieder,
Was die Mode streng geteilt,
Alle Menschen werden Brüder,
Wo dein sanfter Flügel weilt.
Seid umschlungen, Millionen!
Diesen Kuß der ganzen Welt!
Brüder—überm Sternenzelt
Muß ein lieber Vater wohnen.

Wem der große Wurf gelungen
Eines Freundes Freund zu sein,
Wer ein holdes Weib errungen,
Mische seinen Jubel ein!
Ja—wer auch nur eine Seele
Sein nennt auf dem Erdenrund:
Und wer's nie gekonnt, der stehle
Weinend sich aus diesem Bund.
Was den großen Ring bewohnet,
Huldige der Sympathie!
Zu den Sternen leitet sie,
Wo der Unbekannte thronet.

Freude trinken alle Wesen
An den Brüsten der Natur,
Alle Guten, alle Bösen
Folgen ihrer Rosenspur.

Küsse gab sie uns und Reben,
Einen Freund, geprüft im Tod,
Wollust ward dem Wurm gegeben,
Und der Cherub steht vor Gott.
   Ihr stürzt nieder, Millionen?
   Ahnest du den Schöpfer, Welt?
   Such ihn überm Sternenzelt!
   Über Sternen muß er wohnen.

Freude heißt die starke Feder
In der ewigen Natur.
Freude, Freude treibt die Räder
In der großen Weltenuhr.
Blumen lockt sie aus den Keimen,
Sonnen aus dem Firmament,
Sphären rollt sie in den Räumen,
Die des Sehers Rohr nicht kennt.
   Froh, wie seine Sonnen fliegen
   Durch des Himmels prächtgen Plan,
   Wandelt, Brüder, eure Bahn,
   Freudig wie ein Held zum Siegen.

Aus der Wahrheit Feuerspiegel
Lächelt sie den Forscher an.
Zu der Tugend steilem Hügel
Leitet sie des Dulders Bahn.
Auf des Glaubens Sonnenberge
Sieht man ihre Fahnen wehn,
Durch den Riß gesprengter Särge
Sie im Chor der Engel stehn.
   Duldet mutig, Millionen!
   Duldet für die beßre Welt!
   Droben überm Sternenzelt
   Wird ein großer Gott belohnen.

Göttern kann man nicht vergelten,
Schön ist's, ihnen gleich zu sein.
Gram und Armut soll sich melden,
Mit den Frohen sich erfreun.

Groll und Rache sei vergessen,
Unserm Todfeind sei verziehn,
Keine Träne soll ihn pressen,
Keine Reue nage ihn.
  Unser Schuldbuch sei vernichtet!
  Ausgesöhnt die ganze Welt!
  Brüder—überm Sternenzelt
  Richtet Gott, wie wir gerichtet.

Freude sprudelt in Pokalen,
In der Traube goldnem Blut
Trinken Sanftmut Kannibalen,
Die Verzweiflung Heldenmut.
Brüder, fliegt von euren Sitzen,
Wenn der volle Römer kreist,
Laßt den Schaum zum Himmel spritzen:
Dieses Glas dem guten Geist!
  Den der Sterne Wirbel loben,
  Den des Seraphs Hymne preist,
  Dieses Glas dem guten Geist
  Überm Sternenzelt dort oben!

Festen Mut in schweren Leiden,
Hilfe, wo die Unschuld weint,
Ewigkeit geschwornen Eiden,
Wahrheit gegen Freund und Feind,
Männerstolz vor Königsthronen—
Brüder, gält es Gut und Blut:
Dem Verdienste seine Kronen,
Untergang der Lügenbrut!
  Schließt den heilgen Zirkel dichter,
  Schwört bei diesem goldnen Wein,
  Dem Gelübde treu zu sein,
  Schwört es bei dem Sternenrichter!

Schiller himself judged the poem later on rather harshly. Indeed, the accumulation of disconnected images in it and the sweep of its rhythm are at times somewhat forced. And yet—with or without Beetho-

ven's music—there is something irresistible in this majestic flow of words.

Schiller's removal to Saxony meant the close of a chapter in his life. But it meant much more. It marked a turning point in his intellectual and artistic development. The middle-class tragedy with its down-to-earth realism had never really been an adequate mold for his artistic endeavors. This he now recognized and turned his attention to more universal concepts with a consciously greater stress on what concerns humanity in general.

The principal literary product of Schiller's two years in Saxony was *Don Carlos*. The first outline of this play goes back to his sojourn at Bauerbach. He worked on it off and on for five years and carried it through no fewer than four different versions. This work reflects more clearly than any other the transition from youthful ferment to mature assurance in Schiller's human and spiritual development. Originally conceived as a sort of "middle-class tragedy" in an aristocratic setting, the play in its final form transcends the confines of a drama of passion and is now a drama of human freedom and political necessity.

The argument of the play revolves around Don Carlos' love for his stepmother, who had been his betrothed before his father, King Philip, married her for reasons of state. In an early version, the character of the king as a jealous father and husband emerges sharply, while the Marquis of Posa is only a minor personage. All this, as well as Schiller's own statements in his letters, leaves no doubt as to his original intention. If he had finished *Don Carlos* without having to stop to work on *Fiesco* and *Intrigue and Love*, it would have been a love tragedy with Don Carlos and the Queen as the chief characters. However, the intervening years drastically altered his thinking and his plans.

It is no longer the love of Don Carlos and the Queen that is the central focus of the tragedy; now it is the Marquis of Posa who overshadows Don Carlos and who, as the exponent of a new age of enlightenment, tolerance and intellectual freedom, wishes to bring this new order about through Don Carlos. This is not to say, however, that *Don Carlos* has become a play with a political purpose. No play of Schiller's is that. His concern is always with human problems, and he clearly demonstrates the dubiousness of action directed toward an absolute goal that fails to take into account the limitations inherent in the human situation.

Don Carlos occupies a central place in Schiller's intellectual development and leads to his historical and philosophical writings. As in the other early dramas, man appears as a victim of the state and of various power interests. The play illustrates the contrast between the absoluteness of the idea and the profound equivocalness and unpredictability of human behavior.

It would be erroneous to regard the great Marquis of Posa scene from Act III, included here, as no more than a demand for the limitation of the power of the absolute state and a plea for the good as against the bad state or for the enlightened ideas of the period of the French Revolution. Rather it shows the conflict between personal and political life, between the unity and totality demanded of the individual human being and the "sad mutilation" caused by the state's demand for totality. It is Posa's claim that the human being "should be allowed to continue to be a human being," "that restored to himself, he should awaken to the feeling of his own value." And the "freedom of thought" he demands includes the inalienable human right not to allow his thinking to be determined by others and to be permitted to give spontaneous expression to his thoughts and feelings. Thus *Don Carlos*

leads us into the heart of the conflict between the demand for humanity and politics, a subject which to Schiller, as the spokesman for all that concerns humanity, is of decisive importance and which we shall meet again in many forms in his work.

Don Carlos is also a milestone in the sense that Schiller now recognizes clearly that the verse drama is the form best suited to him in that it automatically excludes the triviality of everyday life and frees the essence of things, their ideal form, from the accidental and insignificant. At the same time his verse, despite its lofty tone, has a greater naturalness than his dramatic prose. Since he felt that the prose dialogue of his early dramas was too close to ordinary speech to be great art, he not infrequently, in his effort to avoid realism, fell into exaggeration and a certain unnaturalness of dialogue.

Schiller had taken the blank verse from Lessing's *Nathan the Wise*, but from the very first he endowed it with the lofty thought and brilliant language which are typical of him and which constitute what is known as Schiller pathos. Goethe's *Iphigenie* appeared the same year as *Don Carlos*, and when shortly thereafter August Wilhelm Schlegel began his classic Shakespeare translation, a permanent German verse drama was finally established.

Don Carlos was first performed at Berlin in 1788. Schiller had reason to be satisfied with the initial success of his play. Yet, although he fully realized that he had produced a work immeasurably superior to his first three plays, he could not free himself from gnawing doubts about his qualifications as a dramatist or as a poet and creative writer in general. His habitual self-criticism did not allow him to overlook the fact that there were serious gaps in his education, both in knowledge and understanding. The awareness of such

shortcomings implied to him that he was not ready to satisfy the exacting requirements he expected every creative writer and poet to fulfill. Thus he reached the decision to dedicate the ensuing years to a rigorous discipline of self-training, accepting freely the implication that for a long time he would have to renounce all manner and form of poetic work. In fact, for fully a decade he wrote nothing for the stage and for several years not a single poem. If we consider the difficulties of his material situation at the time, we cannot but feel that we witness here an act of intellectual and spiritual responsibility which has few if any parallels in the history of German letters or elsewhere.

The perseverance with which Schiller applied himself throughout the ensuing years to his studies, first of history, then of the literature of the ancients, and finally of philosophy, reflects the extraordinary will power of which he was possessed. It also indicates the seriousness and severity of his self-criticism. This could not spring from a passing mood, and indeed, the motive of dissatisfaction with his intellectual accomplishments and his intellectual equipment appears repeatedly in his correspondence from the time of his flight from Stuttgart on. A particularly impressive passage of this kind is found in a letter which Schiller addressed to Körner a few days after the two had met for the first time.

"It was with gentle shame—a feeling which does not depress but arouses a manly decision—that I looked back to a past I had abused in the most unfortunate dissipation. I sensed the bold inherent disposition of my talents, the failure of Nature's perhaps great intentions for me. *One* half was destroyed by the insane method of my education and the ugly mood of my fate, the *other* and *greater* one by myself. All that, dear friend, I

felt most deeply, and in the general ferment and ardor of my feelings, my heart and my head were at one in the herculean vow—to make up for the past and start out anew in the noble race for the highest goal."

"Mit weicher Beschämung, die nicht nieder-drückt, sondern männlich emporrafft, sah ich rückwärts in die Vergangenheit, die ich durch die unglücklichste Verschwendung mißbrauchte. Ich fühlte die kühne Anlage meiner Kräfte, das miß-lungene (vielleicht große) Vorhaben der Natur mit mir. Eine Hälfte wurde durch die wahnsinnige Methode meiner Erziehung und die Mißlaune meines Schicksals, die zweite und größere aber durch mich selbst zernichtet. Tief, bester Freund, habe ich das empfunden, und in der allgemeinen feurigen Gärung meiner Gefühle haben sich Kopf und Herz zu einem herkulischen Gelübde ver-einigt,—die Vergangenheit nachzuholen und den edlen Wettlauf zum höchsten Ziele von vorn an-zufangen."

Considering the rigid training imposed upon Schiller at the Karlsschule and his life of hardship as a fugitive in the years that followed, it is eloquent proof of the fineness of his character that he took upon him-self so much of the blame for his faulty education.

As we read Schiller's severe criticism of the poems of Gottfried August Bürger (who was an older con-temporary of his), we are doubtless right in sensing that all these warnings and exhortations were ad-dressed as much to himself as to their purported ob-ject. Referring to poetry he wrote:

"It should be a mirror in which the customs, the character, and the full wisdom of its age are gathered in a purified and ennobled form. Out of the age and by means of the art of idealization it

should create a model for the age . . . A man of culture cannot possibly be expected to seek pleasure for head and heart in the offerings of an immature youth or be content with finding again in poetic products the very prejudices, vulgar demeanor, and spiritual vacuousness that repel him in real life. He has a right to expect the poet, who . . . is to be his cherished companion through life, to stand on the same intellectual and moral plane with him, for even in hours of leisure he does not care to sink below himself. Hence it is not enough to depict emotions in exalted colors: one must feel them exaltedly. Enthusiasm as such is not enough; what is wanted is the enthusiasm of a cultivated mind. All the poet can give us is his individuality. This, therefore, must be worthy of being exhibited to the world of today and tomorrow. To ennoble his individuality as far as possible, to raise and refine it to the purest, the most wonderful humanity is the poet's first and foremost concern . . . Only such a mind may express itself for us in works of art. We shall recognize it in its least utterance, and vainly will a mind not thus qualified attempt to cover up its essential shortcomings by artificial skill."

"*Die Sitten, den Charakter, die ganze Weisheit ihrer Zeit müßte . . . [die Dichtkunst], geläutert und veredelt, in ihrem Spiegel sammeln und mit idealisierender Kunst aus dem Jahrhundert selbst ein Muster für das Jahrhundert erschaffen . . . Unmöglich kann der gebildete Mann Erquickung für Geist und Herz bei einem unreifen Jüngling suchen, unmöglich in Gedichten die Vorurteile, die gemeinen Sitten, die Geistesleerheit wiederfinden wollen, die ihn im wirklichen Leben verscheuchen. Mit Recht verlangt er von dem Dichter, der ihm . . . ein teurer Begleiter durch das Leben sein soll, daß er im Intellektuellen und Sittlichen*

auf einer *Stufe mit ihm stehe, weil er auch in Stunden des Genusses nicht unter sich sinken will. Es ist also nicht genug, Empfindung mit erhöhten Farben zu schildern, man muß auch erhöht empfinden. Begeisterung allein ist nicht genug; man fodert die Begeisterung eines gebildeten Geistes. Alles, was der Dichter uns geben kann, ist seine Individualität. Diese muß es also wert sein, vor Welt und Nachwelt ausgestellt zu werden. Diese seine Individualität so sehr als möglich zu veredeln, zur reinsten, herrlichsten Menschheit hinaufzuläutern, ist sein erstes und wichtigstes Geschäft . . . Nur ein solcher Geist soll sich uns in Kunstwerken ausprägen; er wird uns in seiner kleinsten Äußerung kenntlich sein, und umsonst wird, der es nicht ist, diesen wesentlichen Mangel durch Kunst zu verdecken suchen."*

It is perhaps no accident that Schiller's decision to make a sustained effort to acquire belatedly the educational background for which his years at the Karlsschule had made no provision coincided in time with his realization that he could not indefinitely continue to play the part of an "adopted son" to his friend Körner. There was little hope that he might be able to make himself financially independent in Dresden by literary work or by securing for himself a position at the royal court. Körner, to be sure, was ready to go on providing for him—liberally and freely, as though it were the most natural thing in the world—but Schiller had made up his mind to face the uncertainties of his situation and to build for himself, by his own resources, a life of economic independence. In July 1787 he left for Weimar, from where he intended to go on to Hamburg to meet the famous actor and stage director Schröder. This plan was never carried out.

From Weimar Schiller went to pay a short visit to his old benefactress, Henriette von Wolzogen. At her

54

home he met Charlotte von Lengefeld, a distant relative of hers, as well as Charlotte's mother and her older sister Caroline. The two young ladies were great admirers of Schiller's work and took a lively interest in his plans, which he enjoyed discussing with them. Schiller spent the following summer at Rudolstadt as the guest of the Lengefeld family, and he and Charlotte became engaged—secretly at first, because the assent of Charlotte's mother seemed by no means assured. The reason for this was not so much the difference in social class—the Lengefelds belonged to the nobility—but once again the simple fact that Schiller could not provide a solid material basis on which to establish a family. However, Frau von Wolzogen had always thought highly of Schiller. She shared Schiller's own trust in his future, and with her unqualified blessing Schiller and Charlotte were married in February 1790.

The years of unsettled living had come to an end for Schiller. For a long time there had been in his correspondence, especially in his letters to Körner and other close friends, a sporadic undertone of the homeless wanderer's longing for a life of settled and harmonious security. In his happy companionship with Charlotte this longing was now fulfilled. The following passage from a letter to Körner describes touchingly what marriage meant to Schiller.

> "What a beautiful life I am leading now," Schiller wrote. "I look around me in a spirit of joy, and out there my heart finds everlasting gentle satisfaction and my spirit the most beautiful sustenance and comfort. My existence has been arranged in harmonious evenness. It is not in passionate tenseness but in quietude and light that these days have gone by for me."

*"Was für ein schönes Leben führe ich jetzt.
Ich sehe mit fröhlichem Geiste um mich her,
und mein Herz findet eine immerwährende sanfte
Befriedigung außer sich, mein Geist eine so schöne Nahrung und Erholung. Mein Dasein ist in
eine harmonische Gleichheit gerückt; nicht leiden-
schaftlich gespannt, aber ruhig und hell gingen
mir diese Tage dahin."*

A smaller man might have succumbed to the temptation to postulate such happiness as life's ultimate
objective, bending every effort toward providing for
it the material security it required. To Schiller, this
felicitous turn of events in his life could only signify
that he must take the more seriously what he had once
recognized as his duty to the unique gifts he knew
were potentially his. Briefly, then, the task before him
was to perfect his education and to raise money, and
to do the one not only while but by doing the other.

Schiller reached the conclusion that his best chance
of achieving his dual objective lay in the field of historical writing, where he was confident of being able
to make a significant contribution. The plan seemed
particularly appealing because of the special challenge
inherent in the fact that German historiography had
so far produced nothing in any way comparable to
the brilliant histories written in France and England
by men like Voltaire and Gibbon. And indeed, while
German historical writing had hitherto consisted of
little more than pedantic accumulations of facts, Schiller did succeed in raising it to a high literary level
and in thus making it attractive to a wide circle of
readers.

History, for Schiller, is the story of man's struggle
for freedom. "From this point of view," he wrote in
his essay "On the Sublime," "and *only* from it is the
history of the world to me a sublime object."

In his historical writings Schiller is primarily a philosopher of history. His aim is the philosophical elucidation of history, and few if any of his works in this field lack a philosophical discussion of man as the moving force in history.

All of Schiller's work and thought bears witness to his antidespotic attitude which demands freedom for the individual for the sake of the nation, and for the nation for the sake of humanity. This attitude is impressively reflected in his *History of the Rebellion of the Netherlands,* which glorifies the decade-long victorious struggle of a small nation against overwhelming odds.

The introduction to *The History of the Revolt of the Netherlands* (which is included in this volume) was first published separately in Wieland's periodical, "Der teutsche Merkur." The whole work, whose aim it is to celebrate the victory of the principle of freedom of thought over religious intolerance, is written in a clear and noble prose and gives a most effective presentation of historical events. Immediately upon the publication of its first volume in 1788 it made such an impression that quite a few people thought that Schiller had only now found his true profession. He was offered an unsalaried professorship at the University of Jena. Although the position was to bring him only the extremely meager fees paid by his students, he accepted the offer and moved to Jena in March 1789. However, since the teaching took up a considerable amount of time, time that had to be taken from his now more lucrative literary work, the position became more and more of a financial liability.

Next came *The History of the Thirty Years' War* in three volumes published 1789-1791. This book had the greatest sales success ever enjoyed up to that time

by a work of non-fiction in the German language. But Schiller was particularly concerned with his plan for a "universal history," an idea he had developed in his famous inaugural lecture in Jena, "What is Universal History and for What Purpose is it Studied?" What he had in mind was really a philosophy of history, i.e. the outline of a coherent system evolved from the totality of his philosophical insights and his historical knowledge and applied to a meaningful interpretation of the history of humanity.

At the age of thirty-one Schiller at last had what he had struggled to achieve through the long, hard years. He was married to Lotte and had his own little home. His historical writings and his editorial work for the first time had brought him an adequate income and he could look forward to a happy future. Now, after the hard years that he had devoted to pursuing his education he felt that he had earned the right as a mature man to embark on a new literary work. He could feel that he had left his early works behind him and would be capable of producing poetry of a higher order. It is Wallenstein, the figure he had portrayed in his *History of the Thirty Years' War*, that was to occupy him for many years and to engross his attention more and more.

His historical work and the other writing he was doing at this time was produced, however, by dint of fourteen-hour workdays and with a complete disregard for his health. A consequence of this continuous exertion was physical collapse. In the early days of 1791, during a short vacation trip to nearby Erfurt, Schiller developed a high fever and violent pains in his chest and came down with pneumonia. The doctor diagnosed the symptoms of tuberculosis and gastric disturbances, but the medical science of the day could offer nothing but palliatives. On the basis of recent

research, which is borne out by Schiller's own precise statements, it is probable that suppuration from a pleurisy infection spread through the peritoneum and brought on a progressive paralysis of the abdominal organs.

In the course of the ensuing months, Schiller suffered a series of severe attacks, always accompanied by painful spells of dyspnea. He knew now that his years were numbered, but this knowledge seemed merely to increase the power with which his will forced his weakened body to go on working. The premonition of an early death could not unnerve him.

"All in all," he wrote to Körner, "this terrible illness did me great good, deep within. I looked death in the eye more than once, and my courage has grown the stronger. Tuesday especially I did not think I would last the day; every moment I thought I would succumb to the terrible strain of breathing; my voice was gone, and with a trembling hand I was barely able to write what I still wanted to say. This included also a few words for you which I shall keep now as a memento of that sad occasion. But my spirit was serene, and the only pain I felt was that caused by the sight and the thought of my wonderful Lotte who would not have survived the blow."

"Überhaupt hat dieser schreckhafte Anfall mir innerlich sehr gut getan. Ich habe dabei mehr als einmal dem Tod ins Gesicht gesehen, und mein Mut ist dadurch gestärkt worden. Den Dienstag besonders glaubte ich nicht zu überleben; jeden Augenblick fürchtete ich der schrecklichen Mühe des Atemholens zu unterliegen; die Stimme hatte mich schon verlassen, und zitternd konnte ich bloß schreiben, was ich gern noch sagen wollte. Darunter waren auch einige Worte an Dich, die ich jetzt als ein Denkmal dieses traurigen Augenblicks

aufbewahre. Mein Geist war heiter, und alles Lei-
den, was ich in diesem Momente fühlte, verur-
sachte der Anblick, der Gedanke an meine gute
Lotte, die den Schlag nicht würde überstanden
haben."

The pride and strength of a great soul rising triumphantly above toil and torment even while succumbing to it, the heroic greatness of mind and soul which he so often demanded as a thinker and depicted as a poet, he himself now was called upon to practice. He rose to the occasion. He lived his ideals. The words *heiter* and *Heiterkeit*—which we may try to render by "serene" and "serenity"—occur from now on ever more frequently in his correspondence, in his writing and conversation. They stand as an expression of his triumph over fate and death, of the freedom he had achieved in the struggles of life. It is a basic tenet of his philosophy that the true stature of a man is measured by the degree of his inner freedom and that such inner freedom is manifest in the ability to face death. For beyond the realm of matter there is a higher life which can be won only by the triumph of the spirit over the misery of the body and every form of physical bondage.

Schiller's recuperation progressed very slowly. The abdominal spasms and the pressure in his chest persisted with rare intervals of relief. To the end of his days he was completely free from them for only the briefest periods of time. But the worst was that he could but rarely sleep at night and was often forced to make up for lost sleep in the morning and during the hours of the forenoon.

It was not until the fall of that year that Schiller was able to resume his work, but he was painfully aware that his strength was depleted and that this would result in financial difficulties. And so at the

end of his first year of marriage he found himself faced with the choice of taking the necessary rest and starving or of resuming work and inviting a relapse of his illness. He had indeed every reason to look upon the future with anxiety.

During Schiller's illness a rumor of his death had spread to Denmark, which at the time was still an important center of German cultural life. Through the initiative of the young Danish poet, Baggesen—who had paid Schiller a visit the year before and had become an ardent admirer of his works—a small circle of like-minded friends had arranged an obituary celebration in honor of the great poet. When it was learned that Schiller was still alive but that his life was in grave danger because his financial situation did not permit him to take the rest needed for recovery, Baggesen persuaded two Danish noblemen, Prince Friedrich Christian von Augustenburg and the Danish Minister of Finance, Count Ernst Schimmelmann, to offer him without obligation a stipend sufficient to support him for three years. Here is the text of their letter to Schiller:

"Two friends, whose bond is the interests they share as citizens of the world, are writing this letter to you, noble man! Both of them are unknown to you, but both honor and love you. Both admire the lofty flight of your genius which has been able to impress upon several of your more recent works the stamp of the highest human endeavor. . . . May the lively interest which you inspired in us, noble and honored man, protect us from the appearance of presumptuous importunity! May it make impossible any misunderstanding of the intention of this letter; we have composed it with a respectful diffidence inspired in us by the delicacy of your feelings. . . .

Your health, which has been ruined by too much strain and work, we are told, requires complete rest for a time if you are to recover and the danger to your life is to be averted. Only the state of your affairs prevents you from taking this rest. Will you give us the pleasure of making its enjoyment easier for you? We are offering you for this purpose an annual gift of 1000 talers for three years. Accept this offer, noble man! Do not let the sight of our titles cause you to refuse it; we know no pride except that of being men, citizens of the great republic whose boundaries include more than the life of individual generations, more than the boundaries of a globe."

More illuminating than Schiller's letter of thanks to the two noblemen is the following to Baggesen in which he sums up his past life and work.

"From the cradle of my conscious life till now when I write this, I had to fight fate, and since the time when I learned to value the freedom of the spirit, I have been condemned to be without it. A rash decision ten years ago deprived me forever of the possibility to exist by means other than my work as a writer. I had chosen this occupation without taking stock of its requirements and before I had learned to survey its difficulties. The need to practice it came upon me before I was equal to it in knowledge and maturity of mind. That I was able to sense this, that I did not reduce my ideal of the writer's obligations to the narrow confines within which I found myself enclosed I deem a God-given favor which does keep open for me the possibility of rising higher and progressing further, but in the situation in which I lived it only added to my misfortune. I saw now the immaturity of everything I produced and was aware of the distance by which it lagged behind the ideal alive within me. Vaguely aware of the

perfection that could have been achieved, I had
to display my unripe fruit before the eyes of the
public; so much in need of guidance myself, I had
to produce myself against my will as a guide and
teacher of men. Every product that came out half-
way successful despite these unfavorable conditions made me sense the more painfully what
potentialities fate kept repressed within me. I was
saddened by the masterpieces of other writers, for
I abandoned the hope of sharing their happy
leisure which alone permits the works of the genius to ripen. What would I not have given for
two or three quiet years which, free from all work
as a writer, I might have devoted exclusively to
studying, to evolving my thoughts, to maturing
my ideals! To satisfy the stern demands of art
and to provide, simultaneously, the bare essentials
of support for one's poetic industry, cannot be
achieved—as I have finally come to realize—in the
present world of German letters. For ten years I
strove to combine the two; but if I succeeded half-
way at best, I did so at the expense of my health.
Devotion to my work and the few beautiful flowers of life which fate did cast upon my path prevented me from noticing this loss until, early this
year, I was—you know how—aroused from my
dream. At a time when life began to show me its
full worth, when I came close to uniting within
me reason and imagination by an eternal bond of
love, when I girded myself for a new venture in
the realm of art, death came near me."

*"Von der Wiege meines Geistes an bis jetzt, da
ich dieses schreibe, habe ich mit dem Schicksal
gekämpft, und seitdem ich die Freiheit des Geistes
zu schätzen weiß, war ich dazu verurteilt, sie zu
entbehren. Ein rascher Schritt vor zehn Jahren
[die Flucht aus der Heimat] schnitt mir auf immer
die Mittel ab, durch etwas anders als schriftstel-*

lerische Wirksamkeit zu existieren. Ich hatte mir
diesen Beruf gegeben, eh ich seine Forderungen
geprüft, seine Schwierigkeiten übersehen hatte.
Die Notwendigkeit, ihn zu treiben, überfiel mich,
ehe ich ihm durch Kenntnisse und Reife des
Geistes gewachsen war. Daß ich dieses fühlte,
daß ich meinem Ideale von schriftstellerischen
Pflichten nicht diejenigen engen Grenzen setzte,
in welche ich selbst eingeschlossen war, erkenne
ich für eine Gunst des Himmels, der mir dadurch
die Möglichkeit des höheren Fortschritts offen
hält, aber in meinen Umständen vermehrte sie
nur mein Unglück. Unreif und tief unter dem
Ideale, das in mir lebendig war, sah ich jetzt
alles, was ich zur Welt brachte; bei aller geahn-
deten möglichen Vollkommenheit mußte ich mit
der unzeitigen Frucht vor die Augen des Publikums eilen, der Lehre selbst so bedürftig, mich
wider meinen Willen zum Lehrer der Menschen
aufwerfen. Jedes unter so ungünstigen Umständen nur leidlich gelungene Produkt ließ mich
nur desto empfindlicher fühlen, wie viele Keime
das Schicksal in mir unterdrückte. Traurig machten mich die Meisterstücke anderer Schriftsteller,
weil ich die Hoffnung aufgab, ihrer glücklichen
Muße teilhaftig zu werden, an der allein die
Werke des Genius reifen. Was hätte ich nicht um
zwei oder drei stille Jahre gegeben, die ich frei
von schiftstellerischer Arbeit bloß allein dem Stu-
dieren, bloß der Ausbildung meiner Begriffe, der
Zeitigung meiner Ideale hätte widmen können!
Zugleich die strengen Forderungen der Kunst zu
befriedigen und seinem schriftstellerischen Fleiß
auch nur die notwendige Unterstützung zu ver-
schaffen, ist in unserer deutschen literarischen
Welt, wie ich endlich weiß, unvereinbar. Zehen
Jahre habe ich mich angestrengt, beides zu vereinigen, aber es nur einigermaßen möglich zu
machen, kostete mir meine Gesundheit. Das Inter-

esse an meiner Wirksamkeit, einige schöne Blüten
des Lebens, die das Schicksal mir in den Weg
streute, verbargen mir diesen Verlust, bis ich zu
Anfang dieses Jahres—Sie wissen, wie— aus mei-
nem Traume geweckt wurde. Zu einer Zeit, wo
das Leben anfing, mir seinen ganzen Wert zu
zeigen, wo ich nahe dabei war, zwischen Vernunft
und Phantasie in mir ein zartes und ewiges Band
zu knüpfen, wo ich mich zu einem neuen Unter-
nehmen im Gebiete der Kunst [dem Wallenstein]
gürtete, nahte sich mir der Tod. . . ."

That the hardest blows of fate should coincide with
an unhoped-for offer of help was quite in keeping
with Schiller's belief that man is at the mercy of an
unpredictable, demonic fate—to which, however, he
must not bow—but also with his deep trust in a Providence that guides men through all hardships towards
its own goals. By a remarkable twist of fate, his illness
had brought that help without which he could not
have accomplished what he regarded as the mission
of his life.

From the experience of his illness he had realized
how far a human being can overcome his physical
nature and to what degree he can retain his spiritual
freedom in the face of natural sufferings. This line of
thought was also in accord with Kant's philosophy to
which Schiller had long wanted to devote a thorough
study. Now, with Danish help, he was in a position
to fulfill this wish.

When Schiller settled in Jena in 1787, it was the
center of Kantian philosophy. The general enthusiasm for Kant at that time is almost incomprehensible
in view of the difficulty of his subject matter and of
his style. The branch of learning that usually attracts

the least number of students suddenly became the most popular. Mature businessmen even turned over their affairs to other people in order to devote their time to the new doctrine of salvation. Professor Reinhold, Wieland's son-in-law and Schiller's friend, who lectured on Kant's philosophy in Jena, was not alone in his opinion that in a hundred years Kant would be as much revered as Jesus Christ.

No philosophy could have had more appeal to Schiller than that of Kant, whose premise was that the world of reason is more real than the sensual world and is superior to it. This is clearly expressed in many passages in his works and letters. It was the apostle of freedom in Schiller that was attracted by the principle that the human spirit is free and independent and that ideas are eternal principles which inspired men to spiritual heroism.

However, although Kant's formulation of the moral law made a deep impression on him, Schiller did not agree with its universal supremacy. Man has been given two natures, a sensual and a moral, and it cannot possibly be his duty to use one to repress the other. Only if the two natures act in union can man achieve harmony in his being. Schiller particularly disagreed with the idea that if a moral action is in accord with the inclination of an individual rather than against it, it loses its moral value. Demands such as these, which show a contempt for human nature and a lack of respect for its moral inclinations, inevitably lead to asceticism and a hostile attitude towards life. In many characters in Schiller's dramas, particularly in that of Queen Elizabeth in *Don Carlos*, Schiller has shown a natural, ingenuous morality which is spontaneous and quite independent of conscious reflection. Elizabeth does not have to repress her natural impulses in order

66

to act nobly. This is what Schiller calls "beautiful" or "perfect humanity."

In his essay *On Naive and Sentimental Poetry*, he introduces the idea of "pure nature" which is to be of basic significance in his entire work. In every human being there is a primary disposition that can be altered by the course of his life or even destroyed altogether. This primary nature of the human being which represents the union of sensuality and morality he calls the "naive," because it is present in every child. And it is the task of every human being to preserve in himself this originally pure human nature or, if it is destroyed by life, to restore it. The idea that this healing is necessary for modern, self-estranged man recurs in many passages throughout Schiller's work.

In the realm of aesthetics, too, Schiller found himself in basic disagreement with Kant. Kant was of the belief that taste, that is, the judgment of what is beautiful, is purely subjective. Schiller, on the other hand, was convinced of the existence of objective aesthetic laws. It was one of the first aims of his philosophical studies to explore these laws which he set down in the fourth of his so-called Kallias letters. His basic position is the following: Beauty can be evaluated according to an objective criterion. An object is beautiful when it appears free and independent of natural causes. A work of art is beautiful when all traces of the causes that have produced it have vanished: the raw material and the hand of the artist.

In a letter to Wilhelm von Humboldt written during the last year of his life, Schiller made a statement about this period of his life that may be regarded as definitive.

"Speculative philosophy, if ever I went for it, repelled me by its empty forms; I found in its

barren fields no quick water and no sustenance; but the profound fundamentals of ideal philosophy remain an eternal treasure, and for their sake alone we must deem ourselves fortunate to have lived in this age."

"Die spekulative Philosophie, wenn sie mich je gehabt hat, hat mich durch ihre hohle Formeln verscheucht; ich habe auf diesem kahlen Gefild keine lebendige Quelle und keine Nahrung für mich gefunden; aber die tiefen Grundideen der Idealphilosophie bleiben ein ewiger Schatz, und schon allein um ihretwillen muß man sich glücklich preisen, in dieser Zeit gelebt zu haben."

The fundamentals he had in mind while writing this passage were the principles of the independence and autonomy of the spirit of man.

In addition to the postulation of freedom, which is based on Kant's moral imperative, he makes a second demand which is characteristic of his own deepest nature. This is a call for union of the sensual and moral impulses, the marriage of "sensual happiness and peace of soul" which alone makes possible "perfect humanity."

The following is a quotation from "On Grace and Dignity."

"Man," he wrote, "should feel not only permitted but called upon to reconcile desire und duty; he should obey the dictates of his reason joyfully. A sensuous nature was wedded to his pure spiritual nature, not that he should cast it off as a burden or rid himself of it as of a coarse shell, but that he might accord it intimately with his higher being. When Nature made man a rational-sensual being, i.e., when she made him man, she implied for him the duty not to sever what she had combined, not to leave behind the sensual

68

part of his being even in the purest manifestations of his divine part, and not to build the
triumph of the latter on the suppression of the
first. When the morality of his thought emanates
from his total humanity as the combined effect
of both principles, when it has become natural for
him to think thus, then only is his morality
safely established, for as long as the moral principle in man applies coercion, so long the natural
drives are bound to be possessed of force to oppose
it. When the enemy has merely been downed, he
can arise again, but when he is reconciled, his
enmity is truly vanquished."

*"Der Mensch darf nicht nur, sondern soll Lust
und Pflicht in Verbindung bringen; er soll seiner
Vernunft mit Freuden gehorchen. Nicht um sie
wie eine Last wegzuwerfen oder wie eine grobe
Hülle von sich abzustreifen, nein, um sie aufs
innigste mit seinem höhern Selbst zu vereinbaren,
ist seiner reinen Geisternatur eine sinnliche bei-
gesellt. Dadurch schon, daß sie ihn zum vernünf-
tig sinnlichen Wesen, d.i. zum Menschen machte,
kündigte ihm die Natur die Verpflichtung an,
nicht zu trennen, was sie verbunden hat, auch in
den reinsten Äußerungen seines göttlichen Teiles
den sinnlichen nicht hinter sich zu lassen und
den Triumph des einen nicht auf Unterdrückung
des andern zu gründen. Erst alsdann, wenn sie
aus seiner gesamten Menschheit als die vereinigte
Wirkung beider Prinzipien hervorquillt, wenn sie
ihm zur Natur geworden ist, ist seine sittliche
Denkart geborgen; denn solange der sittliche Geist
noch Gewalt anwendet, so muß der Naturtrieb
ihm noch Macht entgegenzusetzen haben. Der
bloß niedergeworfene Feind kann wieder aufste-
hen, aber der versöhnte ist wahrhaft überwunden."*

Schiller's departure from Kant's doctrine on this

decisively important question amounts to a veritable break. The long years which Schiller had spent wrestling with the philosophy of Kant were not wasted. In the end he had achieved a new position which was peculiarly his own. It was this that made his friendship with Goethe possible.

In the summer of 1787, Schiller came to Weimar for a brief visit, seeking intellectual stimulation and hoping to make professional contacts. Since the Duke had bestowed on him the title of Councilor years before, it seemed quite possible that he might be given some position at court that would provide the economic basis for his literary work.

The little capital city of the tiny Duchy of Saxe-Weimar enjoyed a reputation out of all proportion to its size or political importance. Many of the most important authors and scholars of the time had come to live there, the first having been Wieland, who had been called to the court as tutor to the young Duke Karl August and his brother. Goethe arrived in 1775, having been invited for a short visit, and remained there for the rest of his life. He was followed by Herder, Wilhelm von Humboldt, and many other prominent men. Thus Weimar became a cultural center of the first order.

When Schiller arrived, Goethe was in Italy, and it was not known when or whether he would return. He made the acquaintance of Wieland and Herder and established especially with the former a most cordial relationship. But everywhere he met with traces of Goethe. To Körner he reported:

"The spirit of Goethe has molded all those who belong to his circle . . . Many (quite apart from Herder) mention the name of Goethe only with a kind of adoration and he is loved and admired

even more as a human being than as a writer. Herder ascribes to him a keen and all-inclusive intellect, the truest and most genuine feeling, and the greatest purity of heart. Everything he is, he is completely, and he can, like Julius Caesar, be many things at once."

"Goethens Geist hat alle Menschen, die sich zu seinem Zirkel zählen, gemodelt . . . Goethe wird von sehr vielen Menschen (auch außer Herdern) mit einer Art von Anbetung genannt und mehr noch als Mensch denn als Schriftsteller geliebt und bewundert. Herder gibt ihm einen klaren universalen Verstand, das wahrste und innigste Gefühl, die größte Reinheit des Herzens! Alles, was er ist, ist er ganz, und er kann, wie Julius Cäsar, vieles zugleich sein."

After his first great successes, the *Werther* and the *Götz,* Goethe had published no more literary works. Ten years older than Schiller, he had become the Duke's minister and was therefore the top-ranking government official. *Götz,* which was published when Schiller was still in the Karlsschule, had had a particularly strong influence on him, along with Shakespeare.

Upon his return from Italy, Goethe withdrew into a life of almost complete solitude. He was aware that he had experienced a kind of renaissance in Rome, but he felt that the best work he had done in Italy and since had been misunderstood and rejected. The fame Schiller was enjoying in Weimar seemed to him proof that his own entirely different kind of development had made him a stranger in his own home. And when in addition Schiller's philosophical essays appeared with their strong emphasis on Kant's demand that reason should rule nature, he felt that he must regard them as a direct attack on his own philosophical position.

Goethe's autobiography does not extend to this period in his life, but he did give us a brief account of his "First Encounter with Schiller," published originally in 1817 under the telling title of "Happy Event." In it, Goethe described his mood of discouragement when, upon his return from Italy, he found the literary scene in Germany dominated by productions as "repulsive" to him as Wilhelm Heinse's novel *Ardinghello* and Schiller's *The Robbers*.

> "I would gladly have abandoned," Goethe wrote, "every form of poetic work if that had been possible; for where was there a chance to outdo those productions of raving appeal and wild formlessness? Let the reader imagine the state of my mind! I tried to foster, and to impart to others, the purest conceptions, and I found myself wedged in between Ardinghello and Franz Moor."

With specific reference to Schiller, Goethe did not hesitate to state that at that time he found him odious and hateful because "his forceful but immature talent" poured out "a torrent of precisely the ethical and theatrical paradoxes" of which he, Goethe, had striven to rid himself. To justify his reaction to Schiller, Goethe formulated as the basic difference between them that he, Goethe, conceived of nature as an entity "independent and alive and ever productive in accordance with its own laws in all the depths and all the heights," while for Schiller nature was merely a welter of forces destined to be made "subject to the dominion of reason."

Goethe did not know that Schiller, if ever he had held such views, had long since outgrown them. Goethe did not know that Schiller's conception of nature had often come close to his own and that he had employed the Kantian philosophy primarily as a

tool of self-scrutiny from which he hoped to obtain a clarification of his unsolved problems. Still, as things looked outwardly, the two men seemed indeed to be "intellectual antipodes." "Agreement was unthinkable."

Schiller, however, had never given up hope. Since he regarded Goethe as the only man who could tell him the truth about himself and could really help him to advance his artistic development, he was intensely eager to win him over. That his hope was continually frustrated was a source of bitter disappointment to him. As so often in matters of profoundly personal concern, it is once again in Schiller's letters to Körner that we find the clearest expression of his mood at the time. He considered Goethe "incapable of either love or friendship." In a letter of February 2, 1789, he wrote summarily:

"Being with Goethe more often would make me unhappy. He never unbends—not for one moment, not to his closest friends. There is no way of getting hold of him. In fact, I do think he is an egotist to an extraordinary extent. He has the gift of making people feel beholden to him, of obligating them by minor and major favors. But as for himself, he always manages to keep aloof. He deigns to make his beneficent presence known, but only like a god and without getting involved. I take this to be a consistent and well-planned course of action, wholly designed to assure him the fullest enjoyment of his self-love. No one should tolerate such conditions around him. I hate him for it, although I love the greatness of his mind with all my heart and think of him highly. He reminds me of a priggish virgin whom one would like to get with child to humiliate her before the world. He has aroused in me a strange mixture of hate and love, a sensation not alto-

gether unlike that which Brutus and Cassius must have felt toward Caesar. I could kill that mind of his and again love it deep down in my heart."

"Öfters um Goethe zu sein, würde mich unglücklich machen: er hat auch gegen seine nächsten Freunde kein Moment der Ergießung, er ist an nichts zu fassen; ich glaube in der Tat, er ist ein Egoist in ungewöhnlichem Grade. Er besitzt das Talent, die Menschen zu fesseln und durch kleine sowohl als große Attentionen sich verbindlich zu machen; aber sich selbst weiß er immer frei zu behalten. Er macht seine Existenz wohltätig kund, aber nur wie ein Gott, ohne sich selbst zu geben,—dies scheint mir eine konsequente und planmäßige Handlungsart, die ganz auf den höchsten Genuß der Eigenliebe kalkuliert ist. Ein solches Wesen sollten die Menschen nicht um sich herum aufkommen lassen. Mir ist er dadurch verhaßt, ob ich gleich seinen Geist von ganzem Herzen liebe und groß von ihm denke. Ich betrachte ihn wie eine stolze Prüde, der man ein Kind machen muß, um sie vor der Welt zu demütigen. Eine ganz sonderbare Mischung von Haß und Liebe ist es, die er in mir erweckt hat, eine Empfindung, die derjenigen nicht ganz unähnlich ist, die Brutus und Cassius gegen Cäsar gehabt haben müssen; ich könnte seinen Geist umbringen und ihn wieder von Herzen lieben."

The ambivalence reflected in Schiller's hate-love for Goethe also manifests itself in his appraisal of Goethe's poetic powers as compared with his own: he admits he can never hope to reach Goethe's incontestable superiority, yet remains undaunted in his hope of creating something that will match Goethe's work. He wants to bar Goethe completely from his thoughts and his presence, and at the same time desires nothing more than to associate himself closely with Goethe.

"But with Goethe I cannot compete when he applies himself fully. His genius is much richer than mine, and so is his fund of knowledge. He has steadier senses and, in addition, an artistic sense refined and sublimated by a great store of information about all branches of art, and that is precisely what I lack, to a degree that borders on ignorance. . . . But I won't be discouraged, for the more I recognize what talents and requirements and how many I lack, the more I am convinced of the reality and strength of the one talent which, despite my shortcomings, made me advance to where I now am. For without a great talent on one side I could not have covered up so great a shortcoming on the other, as I actually did, and I certainly could not have advanced to a point where I exert an influence on minds that *are* minds . . . Of these powers I think I ought to be able to make good use, so as to get to where I need not fear to place a work of art of mine next to one of his."

"Aber mit Goethe messe ich mich nicht, wenn er seine ganze Kraft anwenden will. Er hat weit mehr Genie als ich und dabei weit mehr Reichtum an Kenntnissen, eine sicherere Sinnlichkeit und zu allem diesen einen durch Kunstkenntnis aller Art geläuterten und verfeinerten Kunstsinn; was mir in einem Grade, der ganz und gar bis zur Unwissenheit geht, mangelt. . . . Deswegen lasse ich mich aber nicht abschrecken; denn eben, je mehr ich empfinde, wie viele und welche Talente oder Erfordernisse mir fehlen, so überzeuge ich mich desto lebhafter von der Realität and Stärke desjenigen Talents, welches, jenes Mangels ungeachtet, mich so weit gebracht hat, als ich schon bin. Denn ohne ein großes Talent von der einen Seite hätte ich einen so großen Mangel von der anderen nicht so weit bedecken können, als geschehen ist, und es überhaupt nicht so weit brin-

gen können, um auf Köpfe *zu wirken. . . . Mit dieser Kraft muß ich doch etwas machen können, das mich soweit führt, ein Kunstwerk von mir neben eins von den seinigen zu stellen."*

As the highest official of the Duchy, Goethe had warmly endorsed the appointment of Schiller to a professorship at Jena, but he avoided every personal relationship although he and Schiller had many friends in common and although the vicinity of Jena to Weimar made the two men practically next-door neighbors. Schiller, too, mentioned the name of Goethe less and less frequently in the course of the following years. Yet the hour was to come that would bring them together.

Much later in life, Goethe said in his "Conversations with Eckermann":

"A daimonic power was clearly active in my contact with Schiller. We could have been led together sooner or we could have been led together later, but that this happened to us in precisely the epoch when my Italian journey was a thing of the past and when Schiller began to tire of philosophical speculation, was of importance and to both of us of the greatest consequence."

The publisher Cotta of Tübingen had interested Schiller in a new literary monthly, "Die Horen," and it was decided that apart from all the other outstanding German writers, Goethe, too, should be asked to collaborate. Goethe consented and even joined the Editorial Committee, but it seemed that a favorable constellation was needed to bring the two—Schiller and Goethe—really and permanently together.

One day in July, 1794, both men attended a meet-

ing of the Jena Society of Natural Philosophy. Both felt that the speaker's approach was narrow and too matter-of-fact. When they happened to leave together, Schiller remarked that he could not see how so disconnected a treatment of nature could possibly appeal to laymen. He made this statement as a historian whose prime endeavor had been to recognize meaningful patterns in the course of human events and who found it natural to demand that other disciplines practice a similar approach. Little could he know that his fortuitous remark was in a sense what Goethe had been waiting for all these years since his return from Italy.

In the previously cited autobiographical fragment of 1817, "First Encounter with Schiller," Goethe described the subsequent course of this memorable conversation in the following terms:

> "I replied that it [the speaker's disconnected approach to the study of nature] left the initiate perhaps equally ill at ease, and that after all there might be another way, one that would not take up nature separately and one by one but that would present her active and alive and driving from the whole to its parts. He wished to be enlightened on this but did not conceal his doubts. He could not admit that, as I asserted, the point was apparent from mere experience.
>
> "We reached his house. The discussion induced me to enter. Then I presented vividly the metamorphosis of plants, and with a few characteristic strokes of the pen I developed a symbolic plant for him to see. He heard and saw everything with great interest and obvious comprehension. But when I had finished, he shook his head and said: 'That is not experience, that is an idea.' I was taken aback, somewhat startled, for the point that separated us had thus been acutely stressed. . . .

The old resentment was coming up again, but I controlled myself and replied: 'I am delighted to hear that I have ideas without knowing about it and that I can even see them with my own eyes.'

"Schiller, whose tact and social skill were much greater than mine . . . replied as a well-trained Kantian, and when my obstinate realism occasioned numerous objections, there was a great deal of haggling and debating, and then we stopped. Neither could claim victory, both thought their positions impregnable. Statements like the following made me quite unhappy: 'How can an experience ever come about that would be adequate to an idea? For the specific quality of the latter is precisely that an experience can never be congruent with it.' If he took to be an idea what I stated as an experience, then there had to prevail between the two something to mediate and relate! In any event, the first step had been taken. The attraction of Schiller's personality was strong. All those who came near him felt they were his. I took an interest in his plans and promised to let him have for the "Horen" some of the things I had stored away . . . and so we sealed, through the greatest and possibly never composable contest of object and subject, an alliance which was to last uninterruptedly, working great good for us and others."

"Ich erwiderte darauf: daß sie den Einge-weihten selbst vielleicht unheimlich bleibe, und daß es doch wohl noch eine andere Weise geben könne, die Natur nicht gesondert und vereinzelt vorzunehmen, sondern sie wirkend und lebendig, aus dem Ganzen in die Teile strebend, darzustel-len. Er wünschte hierüber aufgeklärt zu sein, ver-barg aber seine Zweifel nicht; er konnte nicht eingestehen, daß ein solches, wie ich behauptete, schon aus der Erfahrung hervorgehe.

"Wir gelangten zu seinem Hause, das Gespräch
lockte mich hinein; da trug ich die Metamorphose
der Pflanzen lebhaft vor und ließ mit manchen
charakteristischen Federstrichen eine symbolische
Pflanze vor seinen Augen entstehen. Er vernahm
und schaute das alles mit großer Teilnahme, mit
entschiedener Fassungskraft; als ich aber geendet,
schüttelte er den Kopf und sagte: 'Das ist keine
Erfahrung, das ist eine Idee.' Ich stutzte, verdrieß-
lich einigermaßen: denn der Punkt, der uns trennte, war dadurch aufs strengste bezeichnet. . . . Der
alte Groll wollte sich regen, ich nahm mich aber
zusammen und versetzte: 'Das kann mir sehr lieb
sein, daß ich Ideen habe, ohne es zu wissen, und
sie sogar mit Augen sehe.'

"Schiller, der viel mehr Lebensklugheit und
Lebensart hatte als ich . . . erwiderte darauf als
ein gebildeter Kantianer; und als aus meinem
hartnäckigen Realismus mancher Anlaß zu leb-
haftem Widerspruch entstand, so ward viel gekämpft und dann Stillstand gemacht; keiner von
beiden konnte sich für den Sieger halten, beide
hielten sich für unüberwindlich. Sätze wie folgen-
der machten mich ganz unglücklich: 'Wie kann
jemals Erfahrung gegeben werden, die einer Idee
angemessen sein sollte? denn darin besteht eben
das Eigentümliche der letztern, daß ihr niemals
eine Erfahrung kongruieren könne.' Wenn er das
für eine Idee hielt, was ich als Erfahrung aus-
sprach, so mußte doch zwischen beiden irgend
etwas Vermittelndes, Bezügliches obwalten! Der
erste Schritt war jedoch getan. Schillers Anzie-
hungskraft war groß, er hielt alle fest, die sich
ihm näherten; ich nahm teil an seinen Absichten
und versprach, zu den Horen manches, was bei
mir verborgen lag, herzugeben; . . . und so besie-
gelten wir, durch den größten, vielleicht nie ganz
zu schlichtenden Wettkampf zwischen Objekt und
Subjekt, einen Bund, der ununterbrochen gedau-

ert und für uns und andere manches Gute ge-
wirkt hat."

This conversation Schiller used as the point of departure in his famous letter of August 23, 1794, by which he completed his conquest of Goethe. He showed in it how despite their differences, or because of them, their natures supplemented each other and how fertile this supplementation might be.

"The conversation I had with you the other day set the whole mass of my ideas in motion, for it concerned a subject which for several years has been of lively concern to me. Many points which I could not straighten out by myself were unexpectedly illuminated for me while I beheld the panoramic expanse of your thinking (for only thus can I describe the total impression I received from your ideas). There were several speculative ideas for which I lacked the object, the body, and you showed me where to look for it. Your observing eye, which rests so calmly, so chastely on the things before it, never lets you run the risk of going astray as speculation as well as arbitrary and purely self-directed imagination are apt to do. In your correct intuition, all the things are contained—and more completely by far—which analysis must painfully gather together, and only because it lies within you as one whole is your own wealth hidden from you; for unfortunately we know only what we dissect. A mind like yours realizes therefore but rarely how far it has progressed and how little reason there is for it to borrow from philosophy, which can only learn from you. Philosophy can take apart only what is given to it. The giving itself is not the business of the analyst but of the genius that reunites in accordance with objective laws under the occult but assured influence of pure reason.

"For a long time now, though rather from afar, I have been watching the progress of your mind and have noticed, in ever renewed admiration, the course you have charted for yourself. You seek necessity in nature, but you seek it by pursuing the most difficult path which any weaker power would wisely shun. You take all of nature together in order to cast light on the individual detail; in the totality of nature's phenomenal variations you look for the bases of explanation of the individual. From simple organization you go up step by step to more complex ones and finally construct the most complex of all, man, genetically out of the materials of the total structure of nature. You recreate him, as it were, after the model of nature, seeking thus to gain insight into his hidden mechanism. A great and truly heroic idea which shows amply how your mind is able to hold together in beautiful unity the abundant wealth of its conceptions. You cannot ever have hoped that your life would suffice to achieve such a goal, but to start out on such a course is worth more than to complete any other, and you have chosen, as Achilles chose in the Iliad between Phthia and immortality. If you had been born a Greek, or merely an Italian, and if from your cradle on an exquisite nature and an idealizing art had surrounded you, your way would have been greatly shortened or indeed been rendered completely superfluous. In your very first view of the things around you you would then have assimilated the form of the necessary, and with your first experiences the heroic style would have begun to evolve in you. But since you were born a German, since your Greek soul was cast in this nordic setting, you had no choice but that between either becoming yourself an artist of the North or providing your imagination with what reality denied it by calling upon the assistance of the power of

thought to bring forth from within, as it were, and by the devices of reason, a Greece of your own. At a time of life when the soul takes the world without to shape from it its own world within, you had—surrounded as you were by frustrated molds—imbued yourself with a savage nordic nature, when your undauntable genius, through its superiority over the material presented to it, discovered that lack from within, obtaining from without full confirmation of its find through your acquaintance with Greek nature. Now it was your task to correct the old, inferior nature that had previously been imposed upon your imagination, to correct it in the light of the superior model which your creative genius was fashioning, and that, evidently, is the kind of process that can be effected only by means of guiding principles. However, this logical orientation, which the mind must adopt when it wishes to reflect, is but arduously compatible with the aesthetic orientation which alone enables the spirit to create. So a new task was added to your program; for as you proceed from vision to abstraction, so you had to retrace your steps and transmute concepts to intuition and thoughts to emotions, since it is only the latter that enable the genius to produce.

"It is along these general lines that I conceive the history of your inner life to have progressed. Whether I am right, you yourself will know best. But what you can hardly know (since genius is to itself at all times the greatest mystery), is the existence of a perfect accord of your philosophical instinct with the absolute results of speculative reason. At first sight, to be sure, it may seem that no sharper contrast can be found than that between the speculative mind, which starts out from unity, and the intuitive spirit, which starts from multiplicity. If, however, the former seeks experience and does so chastely and faithfully, while the

82

latter seeks law and does so through the autonomously active and free power of thought, then it is surely a foregone conclusion that midway the two must meet. To be sure, the intuitive spirit deals only with individuals and the speculative mind only with species. But if the intuitive spirit is of the order of the genius and seeks in the empirical the character of necessity, it will produce still only individuals, but individuals with the character of the species; and if the speculative mind is of the order of the genius and does not abandon experience while rising above it, it will produce still only species but species with the possibility of life and with a well-founded reference to real objects.

"But I observe that in lieu of a letter I am about to write a treatise. I trust you will grant forgiveness for this to the lively interest which this topic arouses in me. And if you do not recognize yourself in this mirror, do not therefore, I beg you, avoid it."

"Die neulichen Unterhaltungen mit Ihnen haben meine ganze Ideenmasse in Bewegung gebracht; denn sie betrafen einen Gegenstand, der mich seit etlichen Jahren lebhaft beschäftigt. Über so manches, worüber ich mit mir selber nicht recht einig werden konnte, hat die Anschauung Ihres Geistes (denn so muß ich den Totaleindruck Ihrer Ideen auf mich nennen) ein unerwartetes Licht in mir angesteckt. Mir fehlte das Objekt, der Körper zu mehreren spekulativischen Ideen, und Sie brachten mich auf die Spur davon. Ihr beobachtender Blick, der so still und rein auf den Dingen ruht, setzt Sie nie in Gefahr, auf den Abweg zu geraten, in den sowohl die Spekulation als die willkürliche und bloß sich selbst gehorchende Einbildungskraft sich so leicht verirrt. In Ihrer richtigen Intuition liegt alles und weit vollständiger, was die Analyse mühsam sucht,

und nur weil es als ein Ganzes in Ihnen liegt,
ist Ihnen Ihr eigener Reichtum verborgen; denn
leider wissen wir nur das, was wir scheiden. Gei-
ster Ihrer Art wissen daher selten, wie weit sie
gedrungen sind, und wie wenig Ursache sie haben,
von der Philosophie zu borgen, die nur von Ihnen
lernen kann. Diese kann bloß zergliedern, was ihr
gegeben wird, aber das Geben selbst ist nicht die
Sache des Analytikers, sondern des Genies, wel-
ches unter dem dunkeln, aber sichern Einfluß
reiner Vernunft nach objektiven Gesetzen ver-
bindet.

"Lange schon habe ich, obgleich aus ziemlicher
Ferne, dem Gang Ihres Geistes zugesehen, und den
Weg, den Sie sich vorgezeichnet haben, mit immer
erneuerter Bewunderung bemerkt. Sie suchen das
Notwendige der Natur, aber Sie suchen es auf
dem schwersten Wege, vor welchem jede schwä-
chere Kraft sich wohl hüten wird. Sie nehmen die
ganze Natur zusammen, um über das Einzelne
Licht zu bekommen, in der Allheit ihrer Erschei-
nungsarten suchen Sie den Erklärungsgrund für
das Individuum auf. Von der einfachen Organi-
sation steigen Sie Schritt vor Schritt zu den mehr
verwickelten hinauf, um endlich die verwickeltste
von allen, den Menschen, genetisch aus den Mate-
rialien des ganzen Naturgebäudes zu erbauen. Da-
durch, daß Sie ihn der Natur gleichsam nacher-
schaffen, suchen Sie in seine verborgene Technik
einzudringen. Eine große und wahrhaft helden-
mäßige Idee, die zur Genüge zeigt, wie sehr Ihr
Geist das reiche Ganze seiner Vorstellungen in
einer schönen Einheit zusammenhält. Sie können
niemals gehofft haben, daß Ihr Leben zu einem
solchen Ziele zureichen werde, aber einen solchen
Weg auch nur einzuschlagen, ist mehr wert als
jeden anderen zu endigen,—und Sie haben ge-
wählt, wie Achill in der Ilias zwischen Phthia
und der Unsterblichkeit. Wären Sie als ein Grie-

*che, ja nur als ein Italiener geboren worden, und
hätte schon von der Wiege an eine auserlesene
Natur und eine idealisierende Kunst Sie umgeben,
so wäre Ihr Weg unendlich verkürzt, vielleicht
ganz überflüssig gemacht worden. Schon in die
erste Anschauung der Dinge hätten Sie dann die
Form des Notwendigen aufgenommen, und mit
Ihren ersten Erfahrungen hätte sich der große
Stil in Ihnen entwickelt. Nun, da Sie ein Deut-
scher geboren sind, da Ihr griechischer Geist in
diese nordische Schöpfung geworfen wurde, so
blieb Ihnen keine andere Wahl, als entweder
selbst zum nordischen Künstler zu werden oder
Ihrer Imagination das, was ihr die Wirklichkeit
vorenthielt, durch Nachhilfe der Denkkraft zu ersetzen und so gleichsam von innen heraus und auf
einem rationalen Wege ein Griechenland zu gebären. In derjenigen Lebensepoche, wo die Seele
sich aus der äußern Welt ihre innere bildet, von
mangelhaften Gestalten umringt, hatten Sie schon
eine wilde und nordische Natur in sich aufgenommen, als Ihr siegendes, seinem Material überle-
genes Genie diesen Mangel von innen entdeckte
und von außen her durch die Bekanntschaft mit
der griechischen Natur davon vergewissert wurde.
Jetzt mußten Sie die alte, Ihrer Einbildungskraft
schon aufgedrungene schlechtere Natur nach dem
besseren Muster, das Ihr bildender Geist sich erschuf, korrigieren, und das kann nun freilich
nicht anders als nach leitenden Begriffen vonstat-
ten gehen. Aber diese logische Richtung, welche
der Geist bei der Reflexion zu nehmen genötigt
ist, verträgt sich nicht wohl mit der ästhetischen,
durch welche allein er bildet. Sie hatten also eine
Arbeit mehr; denn so wie Sie von der Anschauung
zur Abstraktion übergingen, so mußten Sie nun
rückwärts Begriffe wieder in Intuitionen umsetzen
und Gedanken in Gefühle verwandeln, weil nur
durch diese das Genie hervorbringen kann.*

"So ungefähr beurteile ich den Gang Ihres Gei-
stes, und ob ich recht habe, werden Sie selbst am
besten wissen. Was Sie aber schwerlich wissen
können (weil das Genie sich immer selbst das
größte Geheimnis ist), ist die schöne Übereinstim-
mung Ihres philosophischen Instinktes mit den
reinsten Resultaten der spekulierenden Vernunft.
Beim ersten Anblick zwar scheint es, als könnte
es keine größeren Opposita geben, als den spekula-
tiven Geist, der von der Einheit, und den intui-
tiven, der von der Mannigfaltigkeit ausgeht. Sucht
aber der erste mit keuschem und treuem Sinn die
Erfahrung und sucht der letzte mit selbsttätiger
freier Denkkraft das Gesetz, so kann es gar nicht
fehlen, daß nicht beide einander auf halbem We-
ge begegnen werden. Zwar hat der intuitive Geist
nur mit Individuen und der spekulative nur mit
Gattungen zu tun. Ist aber der intuitive genialisch
und sucht er in dem Empirischen den Charakter
der Notwendigkeit auf, so wird er zwar immer
Individuen, aber mit dem Charakter der Gattung
erzeugen; und ist der spekulative Geist genialisch
und verliert er, indem er sich darüber erhebt,
die Erfahrung nicht, so wird er zwar immer nur
Gattungen, aber mit der Möglichkeit des Lebens
und mit begründeter Beziehung auf wirkliche Ob-
jekte erzeugen.

"Aber ich bemerke, daß ich anstatt eines Briefes
eine Abhandlung zu schreiben im Begriffe bin,—
verzeihen Sie es dem lebhaften Interesse, womit
dieser Gegenstand mich erfüllt hat; und sollten
Sie Ihr Bild in diesem Spiegel nicht erkennen, so
bitte ich sehr, fliehen Sie ihn darum nicht."

One point emerges with striking clarity from all
this: Both Schiller and Goethe had reached a point in
their development where the seemingly unbridgeable
gulf that separated subjective and objective reality
was their principal concern. Both were concerned to

establish in concrete form a truth that transcends the merely real and to do so by presenting the universal in the shape of the individual, raising the latter simultaneously to symbolic validity. This is what had been Goethe's preoccupation in his scientific work and forms the basis of his "idea" of the metamorphosis of plants. In terms more akin to Schiller's thinking the problem was the coincidence of the symbol, posited by autonomous reason and seeking concrete form, and the phenomenal multiplicity, existing in nature, which provides those forms for the symbol.

For quite a while it seemed to Schiller that he had found a tenable solution in the following argument: For the creative genius, he thought, the antagonism between speculative reason and free intuition cannot be valid. Since the creative genius possesses all human potentialities in congenital completeness, he bridges the gulf between subject and object, composing their conflict in a higher unity. The decisive characteristic of the creative genius is the power to combine, as contrasted with the merely analytical approach of the philosopher.

Here indeed lay an answer of inestimable value to Goethe, too. He sensed that, if Schiller regarded as an idea what he knew to be experience, there had to be a connection between the two, and Schiller now supplied the explanation that it is the prerogative of the creative genius to identify idea and experience in symbolic vision.

For a long time Goethe had been aware that he needed a new principle to bring order into the growing mass of his observations, and it had occurred to him that he might look for help among those who dealt in ideas. For this purpose he had tried to familiarize himself with Kant, but he had found this undertaking most distasteful. How welcome and also

how surprising it must have been for him that a man from whom he had thought himself poles apart proved able to grasp the essence of his spiritual nature and by deriving his scientific efforts as well as his poetry from the same ultimate bases gave promise to complement him in the precise area where he needed such complementation the most.

Goethe's reply to Schiller's opening letter was dated August 27, 1794. It shows with what wholehearted joy he accepted the hand proffered to him. We quote it in full:

"No pleasanter gift for my birthday, which will come round this week, could have been presented to me than your letter in which with a friendly hand you gave me a summing-up of my existence and encourage me by your interest to make a busier and livelier use of my powers.

"Full enjoyment and true benefit can only be mutual, and I look forward to the occasion that will permit me to explain to you what your conversation has meant to me, that I too count a new epoch from that day, and how pleased I am to have pursued my path without any particular encouragement, for it seems now that after so unexpected a meeting we must travel on together. I have always respected the honest and rare seriousness which is manifest in everything you have written and done, and now I have a right to claim that you yourself acquaint me with the progress of your thinking, especially during the last years. Once we have mutually explained to each other the points at which we have now arrived, we shall be able to work on together the more uninterruptedly.

"All about and within me I shall be delighted to share. For, since I am keenly aware that my venture surpasses by far the measure of human

powers and of their earthly duration, I wish to deposit this and that with you and thus preserve it not only but also give it new life.

"How great the benefit of your participation will be for me, you will soon realize, when—after a closer acquaintanceship—you come to discover in me a certain darkness and hesitation which I cannot master although I am very clearly aware of it. However, phenomena of that sort are not exceptional in our nature, by which we are after all pleased to be governed as long as it is not too much of a tyrant.

"I hope to spend some time with you soon. Let us use the occasion to discuss various matters."

"Zu meinem Geburtstag, der mir diese Woche erscheint, hätte mir kein angenehmer Geschenk werden können als Ihr Brief, in welchem Sie mit freundschaftlicher Hand die Summe meiner Existenz ziehen und mich durch Ihre Teilnahme zu einem emsigern und lebhafteren Gebrauch meiner Kräfte aufmuntern.

"Reiner Genuß und wahrer Nutzen kann nur wechselseitig sein, und ich freue mich, Ihnen gelegentlich zu entwickeln, was mir Ihre Unterhaltung gewährt hat, wie ich von jenem Tage an auch eine Epoche rechne und wie zufrieden ich bin, ohne sonderliche Aufmunterung auf meinem Wege fortgegangen zu sein, da es nun scheint, als wenn wir, nach einem so unvermuteten Begegnen, miteinander fortwandern müßten. Ich habe den redlichen und so seltenen Ernst, der in allem erscheint, was Sie geschrieben und getan haben immer zu schätzen gewußt, und ich darf nunmehr Anspruch machen, durch Sie selbst mit dem Gange Ihres Geistes, besonders in den letzten Jahren, bekannt zu werden. Haben wir uns wechselseitig die Punkte klar gemacht, wohin wir ge-

genwärtig gelangt sind, so werden wir desto un-
unterbrochener gemeinschaftlich arbeiten können.

"Alles was an und in mir ist, werde ich mit
Freuden mitteilen. Denn da ich sehr lebhaft fühle,
daß mein Unternehmen das Maß der menschli-
chen Kräfte und ihrer irdischen Dauer weit
übersteigt, so möchte ich manches bei Ihnen
deponieren und dadurch nicht allein erhalten,
sondern auch beleben.

"Wie groß der Vorteil Ihrer Teilnahme für
mich sein wird, werden Sie bald sehen, wenn Sie,
bei näherer Bekanntschaft, eine Art Dunkelheit
und Zaudern bei mir entdecken werden, über die
ich nicht Herr werden kann, wenn ich mich ihrer
gleich sehr deutlich bewußt bin. Doch dergleichen
Phänomene finden sich mehr in unsrer Natur,
von der wir uns denn doch gerne regieren lassen,
wenn sie nur nicht gar zu tyrannisch ist.

"Ich hoffe bald einige Zeit bei Ihnen zuzubrin-
gen, und dann wollen wir manches durchspre-
chen."

Schiller's next letter was written under date of August 31, 1794:

"Upon my return from Weissenfels, where I had gone to meet my friend Körner from Dresden, I received your next to last letter. Its content afforded me a double pleasure, for I infer from it that my conception of your character is in accord with your own feelings and also that the frankness with which I permitted my heart to speak to you did not arouse your displeasure. Our acquaintance —long overdue but inspiring in me many a beautiful hope—proves once again how much better it often is to let chance have its way than to try and get ahead of it by too much impatience and push. However urgently I desired to establish with you a closer relationship than that which is possible between the intentions of the writer and

his most attentive reader, I now understand perfectly that the so very different paths which you and I pursued could not advantageously bring us together at any time sooner than precisely the present. But now I may hope that we shall travel as companions whatever is left of the road ahead, and that the more profitably, since the last to meet in the course of a long journey are always the ones that have most to say to one another.

"Do not expect from me a ready abundance of ideas. That is what I shall find in you. My situation is such that I must strive to make much of little, and if at some future time it should come to pass that you get to know more closely my indigence in everything that is commonly called acquired knowledge, you will perhaps find that on occasion I made out fairly well. Since the circle of my thoughts is smaller, I simply run its course more quickly and more often. For just that reason I can employ my limited funds more profitably and produce in form the multiplicity which I lack in content. Your endeavor it is to simplify your vast holdings in ideas; I want variety for the little I own. You rule over a kingdom, I over no more than a fairly extended clan of notions which I would do anything to build up to a small world.

"Your mind proceeds intuitively to an extraordinary degree, and all your powers of thought seem to have agreed, as it were, to let imagination be their common representative. In the last analysis this is really the ultimate a man can make of himself, when he succeeds in generalizing his visions and in investing his sensations with legislative powers. That is your goal, and to what great extent have you not achieved it already! *My* mind proceeds, in a way, by symbolizing, and so I hover as a hybrid between concept and vision, between rule and sensation, between the technical thinker and the genius. It is this that gave me, especially

in my younger years, a rather awkward appearance in both the field of speculation and also of poetry; for usually the poet took over in me when I should have philosophized and the philosopher when I meant to poetize. Even now it happens often enough that imagination interferes with my abstractions and cold reason with my poetry. If I manage to master these two powers to a point where I can let my freedom determine their limits, I may look forward to a beautiful future. Unfortunately, since I have come to know and begun to use my moral powers as they are, illness threatens to undermine my physical powers. I hardly expect to have time to achieve in myself a great and general revolution of the spirit, but I shall do what I can; and when at last the building collapses, I may have succeeded in salvaging from the flames whatever is worth preserving.

"You wished me to talk about myself, and I have availed myself of this permission. Confidingly I lay before you these confessions, and I may hope that you will hear them in a spirit of charity . . ."

"Bei meiner Zurückkunft aus Weißenfels, wo ich mit meinem Freunde Körner aus Dresden eine Zusammenkunft gehabt, erhielt ich Ihren vorletzten Brief, dessen Inhalt mir doppelt erfreulich war. Denn ich ersehe daraus, daß ich in meiner Ansicht Ihres Wesens Ihrem eigenen Gefühl begegnete und daß Ihnen die Aufrichtigkeit, mit der ich mein Herz darin sprechen ließ, nicht mißfiel. Unsre späte, aber mir manche schöne Hoffnung erweckende Bekanntschaft ist mir abermals ein Beweis, wieviel besser man oft tut, den Zufall machen zu lassen, als ihm durch zu viele Geschäftigkeit vorzugreifen. Wie lebhaft auch immer mein Verlangen war, in ein näheres Verhältnis zu Ihnen zu treten, als zwischen dem Geist des Schriftstellers und seinem aufmerksamsten Leser

möglich ist, so begreife ich doch nunmehr voll-
kommen, daß die so sehr verschiedenen Bahnen,
auf denen Sie und ich wandelten, uns nicht wohl
früher als gerade jetzt mit Nutzen zusammenfüh-
ren konnten. Nun kann ich aber hoffen, daß wir,
soviel von dem Wege noch übrig sein mag, in
Gemeinschaft durchwandeln werden, und mit um-
so größerm Gewinn, da die letzten Gefährten auf
einer langen Reise sich immer am meisten zu
sagen haben.

"Erwarten Sie bei mir keinen großen materialen
Reichtum von Ideen; dies ist es, was ich bei Ihnen
finden werde. Mein Bedürfnis und Streben ist, aus
wenigem viel zu machen, und wenn Sie meine
Armut an allem, was man erworbene Erkenntnis
nennt, einmal näher kennen sollten, so finden Sie
vielleicht, daß es mir in manchen Stücken damit
mag gelungen sein. Weil mein Gedankenkreis
kleiner ist, so durchlaufe ich ihn eben darum
schneller und öfter und kann eben darum meine
kleine Barschaft besser nutzen und eine Mannig-
faltigkeit, die dem Inhalte fehlt, durch die Form
erzeugen. Sie bestreben sich, Ihre große Ideenwelt
zu simplifizieren, ich suche Varietät für meine
kleinen Besitzungen. Sie haben ein Königreich
zu regieren, ich nur eine etwas zahlreiche Fa-
milie von Begriffen, die ich herzlich gern zu einer
kleinen Welt erweitern möchte.

"Ihr Geist wirkt in einem außerordentlichen
Grade intuitiv, und alle Ihre denkenden Kräfte
scheinen auf die Imagination als ihre gemein-
schaftliche Repräsentantin gleichsam kompromit-
tiert zu haben. Im Grund ist dies das Höchste,
was der Mensch aus sich machen kann, sobald
es ihm gelingt, seine Anschauung zu generalisieren
und seine Empfindung gesetzgebend zu machen.
Darnach streben Sie, und in wie hohem Grade
haben Sie es schon erreicht! Mein Verstand wirkt
eigentlich mehr symbolisierend, und so schwebe

ich als eine Zwitterart zwischen dem Begriff und der Anschauung, zwischen der Regel und der Empfindung, zwischen dem technischen Kopf und dem Genie. Dies ist es, was mir, besonders in früheren Jahren, sowohl auf dem Felde der Spekulation als der Dichtkunst ein ziemlich linkisches Ansehen gegeben; denn gewöhnlich übereilte mich der Poet, wo ich philosophieren sollte, und der philosophische Geist, wo ich dichten wollte. Noch jetzt begegnet es mir häufig genug, daß die Einbildungskraft meine Abstraktionen und der kalte Verstand meine Dichtung stört. Kann ich dieser beiden Kräfte insoweit Meister werden, daß ich einer jeden durch meine Freiheit ihre Grenzen bestimmen kann, so erwartet mich noch ein schönes Los; leider aber, nachdem ich meine moralischen Kräfte recht zu kennen und zu gebrauchen angefangen, droht eine Krankheit meine physischen zu untergraben. Eine große und allgemeine Geistesrevolution werde ich schwerlich Zeit haben in mir zu vollenden, aber ich werde tun, was ich kann; und wenn endlich das Gebäude zusammenfällt, so habe ich doch vielleicht das Erhaltungswerte aus dem Brande geflüchtet.

"Sie wollten, daß ich von mir selbst reden sollte, und ich machte von dieser Erlaubnis Gebrauch. Mit Vertrauen lege ich Ihnen diese Geständnisse hin, und ich darf hoffen, daß Sie sie mit Liebe aufnehmen . . ."

Schiller was fully aware that he lacked the immediate sense for the naive and that he would never achieve fully the experience of what Goethe had termed the "daimon" to designate a certain mysterious interplay of destiny and character.

Goethe now invited Schiller to come and stay with him at Weimar for a prolonged visit so that they

might be able to clarify their thoughts further in oral discussions. When we read Schiller's letter of acceptance of September 7, 1794, we cannot escape an empathic awareness of the tragedy of the poet's personal life, for we know that the ailment he referred to with an almost medical matter-of-factness cast an ever lengthening shadow over the remaining fourteen years of his earthly existence.

"It is with great joy," Schiller wrote, "that I accept your kind invitation to come to Weimar, but I must beg you in all seriousness not to count on me in anything pertaining to your domestic routine, for it is an unfortunate fact that my cramps oblige me usually to sacrifice the entire forenoon to sleep because during the night they do not let me rest, and as a rule I do not feel well enough to be certain of any particular hour of the day. For these reasons you must allow me to comport myself in your home as a total stranger whom no one pays the slightest heed. If I can keep to myself, I shall escape the embarrassment of having others depend on the state of my health. The established order of things, which is a boon to other people, is my worst enemy; for no more is needed than that I *must* do a particular thing at a particular time to ensure that I shall not be able to do it.

"I apologize for these preliminaries which must needs be taken care of in advance if my presence in your house is to be at all possible. I ask no more than the dismal right to be ill while I am your guest . . ."

"Mit Freuden nehme ich Ihre gütige Einladung nach Weimar an, doch mit der ernstlichen Bitte, daß Sie in keinem einzigen Stück Ihrer häuslichen Ordnung auf mich rechnen mögen; denn leider nötigen mich meine Krämpfe gewöhnlich, den

ganzen Morgen dem Schlaf zu widmen, weil sie
mir des Nachts keine Ruhe lassen, und überhaupt
wird es mir nie so gut, auch den Tag über auf eine
bestimmte Stunde sicher zählen zu dürfen. Sie
werden mir also erlauben, mich in Ihrem Hause
als einen völlig Fremden zu betrachten, auf den
nicht geachtet wird, und dadurch, daß ich mich
ganz isoliere, der Verlegenheit zu entgehen, je-
mand anderes von meinem Befinden abhängen zu
lassen. Die Ordnung, die jedem andern Menschen
wohl macht, ist mein gefährlichster Feind; denn
ich darf nur in einer bestimmten Zeit etwas Be-
stimmtes vornehmen müssen, *so bin ich sicher,*
daß es mir nicht möglich sein wird.

"Entschuldigen Sie diese Präliminarien, die ich
notwendigerweise vorhergehen lassen mußte, um
meine Existenz bei Ihnen auch nur möglich zu
machen. Ich bitte bloß um die leidige Freiheit, bei
Ihnen krank sein zu dürfen . . ."

From this time on Schiller was always a welcome
guest at Goethe's home, and so was Goethe at Schiller's. Goethe had known Schiller's wife when she was
still a little girl and he had always been very fond of
her, which of course contributed greatly to providing
for the friendship of the two great men a setting of
natural ease. When external conditions prevented
them from seeing each other, they merely fell back on
exchanging letters at frequent intervals. For Schiller
Goethe's friendship became a fixed point around which
everything else in his life revolved, but to Goethe,
too, the relationship was of incomparable importance.
It was a working partnership of two great minds and
bore rich fruit for both.

Goethe asked Schiller to arrange his *Egmont* for the
stage, and Schiller was right when he called the version in which this play was first performed a joint
product of Goethe and himself. In the case of the

long series of distichs with which the two men delighted one another and which have come to be known as "Votive Tablets" and "Xenia," the original plan was actually that both Goethe and Schiller should incorporate them all in their collected poems and that the individual authorship should not be made known in any case. Scholars have succeeded, however, in identifying the author in each case with a fair degree of certainty. If we may dispense with further exemplifications of this extraordinary cooperation of two great poets, we must mention at least the influence which Schiller's fruitful and detailed criticism exerted on the final version of *Wilhelm Meister's Apprenticeship*, which Goethe was then completing. Schiller's suggestions and objections were largely heeded by Goethe, and at one time he even wanted his friend to give the concluding parts of the work the final shape which in his own opinion he had not as yet been able to find himself. How grateful Goethe was for Schiller's interest and advice is beautifully expressed in a letter of July, 7, 1796.

"I thank you warmly," Goethe wrote to his friend, "for your encouraging letter and for the report of what you felt and thought while reading the novel, especially Book Eight. If this latter meets with your approval, you will certainly not fail to see in it the traces of your own influence, for certainly, without our relationship I could not have completed the whole work, at least not in this way. A hundred times, while talking to you about theory and example, I was thinking of the situations which now lie before you and judged them by the principles on which we had agreed. Now again your friendly warning protects me from several obvious flaws. In a few instances, while reading your observations I knew immedi-

ately what had to be done and shall make use of it while doing the clean copy.

"How rarely do we find in the affairs and actions of ordinary life the interested concern which we desire on the part of others, but in this exalted case of aesthetic import there is hardly any hope for it at all, for how many people see the work of art as such, how many can see it as a whole, and then it is only love that can see all the things it contains and pure love that can see the things it lacks. What would I not have to add to express the unique situation in which I find myself with you . . ."

"Herzlich danke ich Ihnen für Ihren erquicken-den Brief und für die Mitteilung dessen, was Sie bei dem Roman, besonders bei dem achten Buche, empfunden und gedacht. Wenn dieses nach Ihrem Sinne ist, so werden Sie auch Ihren eigenen Einfluß darauf nicht verkennen, denn gewiß, ohne unser Verhältnis hätte ich das Ganze kaum, wenigstens nicht auf diese Weise zustande bringen können. Hundertmal, wenn ich mich mit Ihnen über Theorie und Beispiel unterhielt, hatte ich die Situationen im Sinne, die jetzt vor Ihnen liegen, und beurteilte sie im stillen nach den Grundsätzen, über die wir uns vereinigten. Auch nun schützt mich Ihre warnende Freundschaft vor ein paar in die Augen fallenden Mängeln, bei einigen Ihrer Bemerkungen habe ich das sogleich gefunden, wie zu helfen sei, und werde bei der neuen Abschrift davon Gebrauch machen.

"Wie selten findet man bei den Geschäften und Handlungen des gemeinen Lebens die gewünschte Teilnahme, und in diesem hohen ästhetischen Falle ist sie kaum zu hoffen, denn wie viele Menschen sehen das Kunstwerk an sich selbst, wie viele können es übersehen, und dann ist doch nur die Neigung, die alles sehen kann, was es enthält,

und die reine Neigung, die dabei noch sehen kann, was ihm mangelt. Und was wäre nicht noch alles hinzusetzen, um den einzelnen Fall auszudrücken, in dem ich mich nur mit Ihnen befinde . . ."

Nothing was of greater importance in Schiller's life than his friendship with Goethe, and if we have treated it in somewhat greater detail, we have done no more than give it its due. In a letter to Countess Schimmelmann, written on November 23, 1800, Schiller referred summarily to his acquaintance with Goethe as "the most beneficial occurrence" in his entire life. He stated explicitly that he was thinking not so much of the artist Goethe but rather of the man behind the artist. This he explained more fully in the following passage from the same letter:

"If it were not that, to me, he is of greater worth as a human being than anyone I ever knew, I would be content with admiring his genius from afar. I may say that in all the six years that I have lived together with him I never had reason to doubt the integrity of his character for one moment. There is exalted truth and uprightness in his nature and the highest seriousness for what is right and good. That is why prattlers, hypocrites and sophists never feel at ease in his company . . ."

"Wenn er nicht als Mensch für mich den größten Wert von allen hätte, die ich persönlich je habe kennen lernen, so würde ich sein Genie nur in der Ferne bewundern. Ich darf wohl sagen, daß ich in den sechs Jahren, die ich mit ihm zusammen lebte, auch nicht einen Augenblick an seinem Charakter irre geworden bin. Er hat eine hohe Wahrheit und Biederkeit in seiner Natur und den höchsten Ernst für das Rechte und Gute; darum haben sich Schwätzer und Heuchler und

*Sophisten in seiner Nähe immer übel befun-
den . . ."*

Ever since their paths first crossed, and—as we have
seen—for a long time before, Schiller had been ab-
sorbed in the vast complex of human problems that
Goethe represented for him. One great difference between the two men is apparent in the fact that
Goethe's life is replete with "experiences of the heart,"
of which all his poetic works show more or less evident
traces, while erotic forces play hardly any creative role
at all in Schiller's life. After some negligible involve-
ments during his early years, Schiller had settled
down to a solidly happy married life. It seems indeed
at times as though all the emotional tension and
passion that welled up in him did stem, vicariously
as it were, from his relationship with Goethe. Hatred
and love, hostility and admiration, wooing and frus--
tration, conquest and blissful possession—all the emotions that go with these experiences were often alive
in him with burning intensity. Much of this is expressed in his stirring elegy, "The Gifts of Fortune"
of 1798, which is perhaps Schiller's greatest poem.
Thomas Mann called it Schiller's "most deeply felt"
work, "in its sublime resignation his most beautiful"
poem, and he did not hesitate to assert that "nothing
more beautiful, more noble, more sacred is to be found
anywhere in the whole realm of emotion and of language." The poem is a fitting climax to our discussion
of the relationship of Goethe and Schiller.

THE GIFTS OF FORTUNE

Blest among men.—Yet unborn, the gods, the benevolent,
　　loved him.
　While he is still but a child, Venus holds him in her
　　arms.
Phoebus opens his eyes, his lips are untied by Hermes,
　And the emblem of might Zeus imprints on his brow.
Truly, sublime is his prospect. The fate that befell him
　　is godlike.
　His is the victor's crown long ere the fray has begun;
Long ere he starts on his journey, its goal is reckoned
　　accomplished;
　Ere he has proven his worth, safe he stands sheltered
　　in grace.

Great, to be sure, will I call the other who—self-made and
　　self-trained—
　Alters, by virtue's strength, even the Moira's decree.
Never the gifts of Fortune will thus be compelled. What
　　is given
　Only by grace must remain outside the pale of man's
　　will.
Earnest endeavor can help one to vanquish the powers
　　of evil,
　But the ultimate good unbidden descends from on
　　high.
Heaven bestows its gifts as love is bestowed by lovers:
　Favor rules Cupid's realm, likewise the realm of Zeus.

Think not the gods impartial. The curls of youth may
　　bewitch them.
　Gay in their hearts themselves, fain with the gay they
　　consort.
Not the keen-eyed observer is granted the bliss to behold
　　them;
　Only the unknowing blind witness their splendorous
　　light.

Often they choose for their gifts the simple soul of the
childlike,
Casting in humblest forms substance of heavenly kin.
Coming where least awaited, they foil him who proudly
expects them:
There is no magic, no spell potent to cast them in
bonds.
Whom the Father of men and Immortals has chosen his
minion
He bids his eagle seek out, carry to heavenly heights.
Guided by whim or fancy, the god finds the one among
many
Whom he decides to like, and with a loving hand
Crowns with laurels or fillet of power the head he has
chosen,
For, he himself wears his crown only by Fortune's
grace.

Smoothed is the path of the fortunate mortal by Phoebus
Apollo
And the subduer of hearts, Amor, the smiling god.
Neptune quiets the ocean before him, and blithely his
vessel—
"Caesar aboard and his luck"—follows his charted
course.
Gently the lion lies down at his feet, and the agile dolphin
Pushes its back into view, ready to serve as his mount.

Do not resent that the gods grant the favored few effort-
less triumphs
Or that whom Venus prefers safely she whisks from the
fight.
Worthy of praise deems the world whom the smiling
goddess has rescued,
Paying the other no heed whom she let sink to the
shades.
Do we account Achilles' glory impaired since Hephaestus
Fashioned his mighty shield and his destructive sword,

Since for this one mortal human all of Olympus is stir-
ring?
No, it glorifies him that he is loved by the gods,
That they would honor his wrath, and, for the sake of
his glory,
Plunge the flower of Greece into the Hadean night.
Do not resent that beauty's beauty stems from no merit,
That it is Venus's gift, free as the blossoms of Spring.
Let beauty enjoy its good fortune. Behold it and share
the enjoyment.
Undeserved are its charms. So is your power to see.
Let us rejoice that the gift of song has descended from
heaven,
That the poet, for us, sings what he learned from the
Muse.
Holding his fief from a god, he appears as a god to us
hearers,
Being by Fortune endowed, bliss he reflects upon us.
In the affairs of the market let Themis hold sway with
her balance.
There the weight of the toil measures by rights the
reward.
Not so with joy. It appears when a god has decreed its
appearance:
Only a miracle can conjure its warmth to men's hearts.

Everything human must slowly arise, must unfold, and
must ripen:
Ever from phase to phase plastic time leads it on.
But neither beauty nor fortune are ever born into being:
Perfect ere time began, perfect they face us today.
Every Venus on earth emerges, as did the divine one,
As an occult event from the infinite sea.
Perfect, like the divine Minerva, equipped with the aegis,
So every light-bearing thought springs from the Thun-
derer's head.

DAS GLÜCK

Selig, welchen die Götter, die gnädigen, vor der
    Geburt schon
   Liebten, welchen als Kind Venus im Arme
    gewiegt,
Welchem Phöbus die Augen, die Lippen Hermes
    gelöset
   Und das Siegel der Macht Zeus of die Stirne
    gedrückt!
Ein erhabenes Los, ein göttliches, ist ihm ge-
    fallen,
   Schon vor des Kampfes Beginn sind ihm die
    Schläfe bekränzt.
Ihm ist, eh er es lebte, das volle Leben gerechnet,
   Eh er die Mühe bestand, hat er die Charis er-
    langt.

Groß zwar nenn ich den Mann, der, sein eigner
    Bildner und Schöpfer,
   Durch der Tugend Gewalt selber die Parze be-
    zwingt;
Aber nicht erzwingt er das Glück, und was ihm
    die Charis
   Neidisch geweigert, erringt nimmer der streben-
    de Mut.
Vor Unwürdigem kann dich der Wille, der ernste,
    bewahren,
   Alles Höchste, es kommt frei von den Göttern
    herab.
Wie die Geliebte dich liebt, so kommen die himm-
    lischen Gaben,
   Oben in Jupiters Reich herrscht, wie in Amors,
    die Gunst.

Neigungen haben die Götter, sie lieben der grü-
    nenden Jugend
   Lockigte Scheitel, es zieht Freude die Fröhli-
    chen an.

Nicht der Sehende wird von ihrer Erscheinung
    beseligt,
  Ihrer Herrlichkeit Glanz hat nur der Blinde
    geschaut.
Gern erwählen sie sich der Einfalt kindliche Seele,
  In das bescheidne Gefäß schließen sie Göttli-
    ches ein.
Ungehofft sind sie da und täuschen die stolze
    Erwartung,
  Keines Bannes Gewalt zwinget die Freien herab.

Wem er geneigt, dem sendet der Vater der Men-
    schen und Götter
  Seinen Adler herab, trägt ihn zu himmlischen
    Höhn.
Unter die Menge greift er mit Eigenwillen, und
    welches
  Haupt ihm gefället, um das flicht er mit lie-
    bender Hand
Jetzt den Lorbeer und jetzt die herrschaftgebende
    Binde,
  Krönte doch selber den Gott nur das gewogene
    Glück.

Vor dem Glücklichen her tritt Phöbus, der py-
    thische Sieger,
  Und der die Herzen bezwingt, Amor, der lä-
    chelnde Gott.
Vor ihm ebnet Poseidon das Meer, sanft gleitet
    des Schiffes
  Kiel, das den Cäsar führt und sein allmächtiges
    Glück.
Ihm zu Füßen legt sich der Leu, das brausende
    Delphin
  Steigt aus den Tiefen, und fromm beut es den
    Rücken ihm an.

Zürne dem Glücklichen nicht, daß den leichten
    Sieg ihm die Götter

Schenken, daß aus der Schlacht Venus den Liebling entrückt.
Ihn, den die Lächelnde rettet, den Göttergeliebten
beneid ich,
Jenen nicht, dem sie mit Nacht deckt den ver-
dunkelten Blick.
War er weniger herrlich, Achilles, weil ihm He-
phästos
Selbst geschmiedet den Schild und das verderb-
liche Schwert,
Weil um den sterblichen Mann der große Olymp
sich beweget?
Das verherrlichet ihn, daß ihn die Götter geliebt,
Daß sie sein Zürnen geehrt und, Ruhm dem Liebling zu geben,
Hellas' bestes Geschlecht stürzten zum Orkus
hinab.

Zürne der Schönheit nicht, daß sie schön ist, daß
sie verdienstlos,
Wie der Lilie Kelch, prangt durch der Venus
Geschenk!
Laß sie die Glückliche sein—du schaust sie, du
bist der Beglückte,
Wie sie ohne Verdienst glänzt, so entzücket sie
dich.
Freue dich, daß die Gabe des Lieds vom Himmel
herabkommt,
Daß der Sänger dir singt, was ihn die Muse
gelehrt:
Weil der Gott ihn beseelt, so wird er dem Hörer
zum Gotte,
Weil er der Glückliche ist, kannst du der Selige
sein.
Auf dem geschäftigen Markt, da führe Themis
die Waage,
Und es messe der Lohn streng an der Mühe
sich ab;

Aber die Freude ruft nur ein Gott auf sterbliche
     Wangen,
  Wo kein Wunder geschieht, ist kein Beglückter
     zu sehn.
Alles Menschliche muß erst werden und wachsen
     und reifen,
  Und von Gestalt zu Gestalt führt es die bildende
     Zeit;
Aber das Glückliche siehest du nicht, das Schöne
     nicht werden,
  Fertig von Ewigkeit her steht es vollendet vor
     dir.
Jede irdische Venus ersteht, wie die erste des
     Himmels,
  Eine dunkle Geburt aus dem unendlichen Meer;
Wie die erste Minerva, so tritt, mit der Aegis
     gerüstet,
  Aus des Donnerers Haupt jeder Gedanke des
     Lichts.

How much Schiller and Goethe owed not only to
one another but also to the "special dispensation of
fortune" and "the workings of the daimon" which
brought them together, they both knew very well
and often stated in the letters they continued to exchange till Schiller's death parted them at last. On
July 2, 1796, Schiller wrote to Goethe:

"Among the most beautiful gifts of fortune I
count that I lived to see the completion of this
product [of *Wilhelm Meister's Apprenticeship*],
that it has occurred at a time when my powers are
still pressing forward, that I am still allowed to
drink at this limpid fountain, and the beautiful
relationship that exists between us makes it for
me a matter of religion to identify myself in this
matter with your cause, to nurse whatever is real
within me until it represents the purest mirror
of the spirit which lives in this body, and thus to

deserve the name of your friend in a higher sense.
How vividly have I not felt on this occasion, . . .
that in the face of the perfect there is no freedom
but love."

*"Ohnehin gehört es zu dem schönsten Glück
meines Daseins, daß ich die Vollendung dieses
Produkts* [Wilhelm Meisters Lehrjahre] *erlebte,
daß sie noch in die Periode meiner strebenden
Kräfte fällt, daß ich aus dieser reinen Quelle noch
schöpfen kann; und das schöne Verhältnis, das unter uns ist, macht es mir zu einer gewissen Religion, Ihre Sache hierin zu der meinigen zu machen,
alles, was in mir Realität ist, zu dem reinsten Spiegel des Geistes auszubilden, der in dieser Hülle
lebt, und so in einem höheren Sinne des Worts den
Namen Ihres Freundes zu verdienen. Wie lebhaft
habe ich bei dieser Gelegenheit erfahren, . . . daß
es dem Vortrefflichen gegenüber keine Freiheit
gibt als die Liebe."*

In a letter which Schiller addressed to Goethe on
June 18, 1797, we find this passage:

"Thanks to you I overcome more and more my
habitual tendency (which in all practical matters,
especially in matters poetic, is surely a bad habit)
to progress from the general to the individual.
Instead you lead me in the opposite direction from
individual occurrences to great laws. You are wont
to take your departure from a small and narrow
point, but this leads me far afield and thus does
me good in the depth of my being, while the other
road—the one which, left to my own devices, I
would be inclined to follow—takes me from afar to
the narrow, so that I have the unpleasant feeling
that I shall see myself poorer in the end than
when I started . . ."

*"Sie gewöhnen mir immer mehr die Tendenz
ab (die in allem Praktischen, besonders Poeti-*

schen, eine Unart ist), vom Allgemeinen zum In-
dividuellen zu gehen, und führen mich umgekehrt
von einzelnen Fällen zu großen Gesetzen fort. Der
Punkt ist immer klein und eng, von dem Sie aus-
zugehen pflegen, aber er führt mich ins Weite und
macht mir dadurch, in meiner Natur, wohl, an-
statt daß ich auf dem andern Weg, dem ich, mir
selbst überlassen, so gerne folge, immer vom Wei-
ten ins Enge komme und das unangenehme Ge-
fühl habe, mich am Ende ärmer zu sehen als am
Anfang . . ."

Goethe knew that he was indebted to Schiller for
a corresponding service in the opposite direction.

"If my nature," he wrote, "has the effect that
it draws back yours to within the limits of the
finite, then I derive from you the advantage that
from time to time I am drawn beyond my limits
or at least am prevented from clinging too long
to one narrow spot."

"Und wenn meine Natur die Wirkung hat, die
Ihrige ins Begrenzte zu ziehen, so habe ich durch
Sie den Vorteil, daß ich auch wohl manchmal
über meine Grenzen hinaus gezogen werde, wenig-
stens daß ich nicht so lange mich auf einem so
engen Fleck herumtreibe."

The most candid and therefore perhaps the most
beautiful expression of Schiller's recognition of his
debt to Goethe is found in a passage of the letter he
addressed to his friend under date of January 5, 1798.
The remarkable thing about this letter is the quite
unaccustomed candor with which Schiller described
the proud delight he had felt while reading a clean
copy of parts of his *Wallenstein*.

"Now," he wrote, "that I see my work neatly
written by another's hand and can look at it as
something detached from myself, it truly affords

me great pleasure. I find indeed that I have out-
done myself. That is the fruit of your companionship, for only the oft-repeated, the continuous
contact with a nature so objective and opposed to
mine, only my ardent endeavor to approach it and
the combined effort to see it and to think it could
enable me to expand my subjective limits to such
an extent . . . But it would be more proper that I
hear this from your mouth than that you learn
about it from me . . ."

*"Jetzt, da ich meine Arbeit von einer fremden
Hand reinlich geschrieben vor mir habe und sie
mir fremder ist, macht sie mir wirklich Freude.
Ich finde augenscheinlich, daß ich über mich
selbst hinausgegangen bin, welches die Frucht
unsers Umgangs ist; denn nur der vielmalige kon-
tinuierliche Verkehr mit einer so objektiv mir
entgegenstehenden Natur, mein lebhaftes Hin-
streben darnach und die vereinigte Bemühung,
sie anzuschauen und zu denken, konnte mich fähig machen, meine subjektiven Grenzen so weit
auseinanderzurücken . . . Doch es schickte sich
besser, daß ich das aus Ihrem Munde hörte, als
daß Sie es von mir erfahren . . ."*

To this Goethe replied the following day with a
warmth and spontaneity of feeling that is quite unusual in his letters:

"I congratulate you on your feeling of satisfaction with the finished portion of your work. Considering the clarity with which you see at once
all the demands you have to make upon yourself,
I do not doubt the validity of your verdict. The
favored meeting of our two natures has afforded
us many an advantage, and I trust this condition
shall remain in force unchanged and forever. If
I have served you as the representative of this
and that object, then you have led me back to

myself from too rigorous an observation of things outside and of the relations that exist between them. You have taught me to view more equitably the multifariousness of man's inner life; you have given me a new youth and have made me once again a poet, which I had long since as much as ceased to be . . ."

"Ich wünsche Ihnen Glück zu Ihrer Zufriedenheit mit dem fertigen Teil Ihres Werkes. Bei der Klarheit, mit der Sie die Forderungen übersehen, die Sie an sich zu machen haben, zweifle ich nicht an der völligen Gültigkeit Ihres Zeugnisses. Das günstige Zusammentreffen unserer beiden Naturen hat uns schon manchen Vorteil verschafft, und ich hoffe, dieses Verhältnis wird immer gleich fortwirken. Wenn ich Ihnen zum Repräsentanten mancher Objekte diente, so haben Sie mich von der allzustrengen Beobachtung der äußeren Dinge und ihrer Verhältnisse auf mich selbst zurückgeführt, Sie haben mich die Vielseitigkeit des innern Menschen mit mehr Billigkeit anzuschauen gelehrt, Sie haben mir eine zweite Jugend verschafft und mich wieder zum Dichter gemacht, welches zu sein ich so gut als aufgehört hatte . . ."

Schiller never forgot that he was a "sentimental" poet who approached a work of art from the ideal. Though the two men were always aware of the basic differences in their natures and each was to remain true to himself, they shared a common artistic aim. Each strove to create an art in which form and content were inseparably combined to produce the symbol of beauty, and to make the spiritual visible in the concrete. To be sure, the effect is achieved in different ways. In Goethe the idea shines out of the form, while in Schiller the idea creates the form, but essentially it is the same aim approached from different points of departure. Thus through close observation of Goethe's

nature and through the interchange of ideas, Schiller not only arrived at the final formulation of his ideas on the nature of poetry, but also at a deeper understanding of his own talent and vocation.

There is perhaps no simpler way to set off these matters in sharp relief than to juxtapose at this point Schiller's two major works in the field of theoretical aesthetics. The first of these, the *Letters on the Aesthetic Education of Man,* was written beginning in 1793, i.e., before the "happy encounter" of Schiller and Goethe. The other, *On Naive and Sentimental Poetry,* already referred to in our discussion of Schiller's relations with Kant, belongs in the year 1795 and has a title which we may very well translate into modern prose as *On Goethe and Schiller.* Neither of these works lays down a closed system; rather both show the development of Schiller's thinking on these subjects in such a way that we can see him in the process of arriving at new insights.

At the beginning of the aesthetic letters he explores the question of how man can be educated from a natural being into a rational being. For this, he believes, a transitional stage is necessary in which man is both at once. But the more deeply he delves into this intermediate form, the more it appears to him that it is not merely a means to a higher end. It no longer seems to him to be a transitional form, but a third nature of man which he calls "aesthetic humanity" and which is significant in its own right. He sees it as the spiritualization of man's sensual nature. As such it satisfies a demand which is also fulfilled in art, for art also represents the living union of nature and spirit.

The idea that the aim of man is to become a rational being was borrowed from Kant's concept of history. *Don Carlos* is still based on the idea that man

can be educated into a rational being by giving him political freedom and thereby eliminating the spiritual damage inflicted on him by absolutism. The French Revolution confirmed that the mere gaining of political freedom by no means converts men into rational beings. The state, which is responsible for the corruption of man, therefore cannot do this work of education.

It is art alone that is capable of bringing about the development of all of man's powers. Man, who is inwardly split and estranged from himself and from nature, can be made "complete" again by art. Schiller is not speaking here of art at its present stage of development, but, on the one hand, of a higher art of the future that is yet to be developed, and on the other, of Greek art, which to him represents the naive poetic world of humanity's childhood. Art sets men free because as creative imagination it deals freely with reality. By the free play of imagination it removes man from the seriousness and pressures of life. ("For life is stern, but art serenely joyous.") Art, however, should set man free not only while he is enjoying a real work of art, but throughout his life. This will become possible only if man remakes his own nature to match that of a genuine work of art where nature and spirit are united. Such freedom is possible only if man resolves the conflict between his two natures and unites them deeply and closely. If he does not succeed in doing this, either sensual nature will stifle the spirit, or the spirit will strangle the natural instincts. Aesthetic man alone possesses the freedom which Schiller calls "serenity" and which he praises as man's highest goal.

In his essay *On Naive and Sentimental Poetry* Schiller's thinking takes another decisive turn. The order of his values and objectives has been altered. The

113

starting point of human development is no longer "raw" human nature, which in the aesthetic letters was opposed to aesthetic culture. Nature is now held up as an image of the perfection to be realized through freedom. It supplants reason and represents both the origin and goal of history. This pure, original human nature, which is both sensuality and nature, he calls "naive." It is the nature with which man is endowed at birth. Although life may distort and repress it, mankind as a whole, as well as each individual, is called upon to regain it, to reestablish the union with nature and thus to find healing.

Every child, even in the modern world, is all nature, but it is the destiny of modern man to forfeit this state of oneness with nature, and this is where the great task of the poet comes in:

"Poets are everywhere, by definition, preservers of nature. Where they can no longer be that completely, having already experienced in themselves the destructive influence of arbitrary and artificial forms or been obliged to struggle with it, they appear as witnesses and avengers of nature. They either are nature or they seek nature when it has been lost. This accounts for the existence of two totally different poetic procedures which cover and circumscribe the whole area of poetry. All poets who really are poets belong, depending on the characteristics of the age in which they flourish or on the fortuitous circumstances which influence their intellectual format in general and their transitory state of mind, to the category of either the *naive* or the *sentimental*."

"*Die Dichter sind überall, schon ihrem Begriff nach, die Bewahrer der Natur. Wo sie dieses nicht ganz mehr sein können und schon in sich selbst den zerstörenden Einfluß willkürlicher und künst-*

licher Formen erfahren oder doch mit demselben
zu kämpfen gehabt haben, da werden sie als die
Zeugen und als die Rächer der Natur auftreten.
Sie werden entweder Natur sein, oder sie werden
die verlorene suchen. Daraus entspringen zwei ganz
verschiedene Dichtungsweisen, durch welche das
ganze Gebiet aer Poesie erschöpft und ausgemes-
sen wird. Alle Dichter, die es wirklich sind, wer-
den, je nachdem die Zeit beschaffen ist, in der sie
blühen, oder zufällige Umstände auf ihre allge-
meine Bildung und auf ihre vorübergehende Ge-
mütsstimmung Einfluß haben, entweder zu den
naiven oder zu den sentimentalischen gehören."

It is therefore the task of the poet to bring about
the restoration of pure human nature, for the essence
of poetry is rooted in the reunion of the spiritual with
the sensual. In Schiller's own words:

"This is what makes the poet, that he undoes in
himself what reminds of the world of artifice, that
he is able to restore in himself nature in its original unity."

"Eben das macht den Dichter aus, daß er alles
in sich aufhebt, was an eine künstliche Welt er-
innert, daß er die Natur in ihrer ursprünglichen
Einheit wieder in sich herstellt."

Schiller always attributed a high significance to the
role of luck and chance in human life, and this belief was strengthened by his own experiences. Genius,
however, is not only a miraculous gift, it also requires
congenial conditions in order to develop. But most
important of all is the free act of the struggling human
being. In the summer of 1795, when Schiller could
feel that the process of his renewal had been completed and that he was justified in returning to poetry,
he entered his period of mastery.

The Danish pension was about to terminate and Schiller was forced again to look around for some means of support. He therefore accepted the editorship of the new monthly periodical "Die Horen" (1795-1797) and that of the "Musenalmanach" (1796-1800). The long interlude of historical and philosophical studies was at an end—seven years had passed since his last poem, "The Artists"—and he returned to his poetic creation. His power of poetic expression quickly asserted itself.

One of the first poems, "The Ideal and Life," may be regarded as the pivotal core of Schiller's reflective poetry. Regrettably no translation has yet been produced to do full justice to this profound and noble poem. Its sublime ideality imbues it with a spirit of reassuring edification. It deplores the fate of modern man, but in doing so holds out hope for an eventual resolution of the conflict of man's dual nature:

"Would you be on earth like souls arisen,
Free while yet in death's prison . . ."

"*Wollt ihr schon auf Erden Göttern gleichen,
Frei sein in des Todes Reichen . . .*"

Freedom of spirit can be won despite the bondage of necessity. In his own life Schiller had not merely reached a new insight, he had arrived at a new feeling for life and could jubilantly proclaim his victory. Here, what he had worked out as abstract philosophy through years of hard work has been converted into poetry.

Aware that he had produced a poem unlike anything he had written before, Schiller sent it to Humboldt. The response is in its own way as unusual as the poem. Humboldt wrote:

"How shall I thank you, my dearest friend, for the indescribably high delight which your poem

116

has afforded me? Since the day when I received it, it has possessed me in the literal sense of the term . . . It simply cannot be compared to any of your earlier poetic works . . . It bears the full impress of your genius and its ultimate maturity and is a faithful reflection of your being. Now that I am familiar with it, I approach it with the same sensation which is aroused in me by your conversation at its most sacred moments. It emanates the same seriousness, the same dignity, the same tendency to combine all this in one, in a strange and as it were supernatural nature."

The man who responded with such devoted enthusiasm was a close friend of Schiller as well as of Goethe and Körner. Wilhelm von Humboldt, whose correspondence with Schiller is quoted frequently in this volume, stimulated the poet's intellectual and spiritual development in a fruitful exchange of ideas. Considered the actual founder of Berlin University, which he sought to endow with wide freedom of study and lecture, Humboldt later held high diplomatic office. He was the brother of the famous naturalist and geographer Alexander von Humboldt.

As a young man Humboldt served briefly on the legal staff of the Supreme Court of Justice in Berlin. Disgusted with the bureaucracy of the declining Prussian state, he soon withdrew from government service. Being a man of independent means, he then devoted himself entirely to the pursuit of his intellectual interests and self-development. He felt impelled, however, to write a treatise justifying his withdrawal from government service in which he claimed that enlightened despotism by its abusive practices suppressed all spontaneity in the people. His essays "Ideas on State Constitutions, Induced by the French

Revolution" and "Ideas on an Attempt to Determine the Limits of the Range of Action of a State" (1793?) (in the latter he posited the securing of personal freedom as the only task of the state) could be published, because of difficulties of censorship, only fragmentarily in periodicals, among others in the "New Thalia." Schiller's great interest in these concerns brought the two men so closely together that in 1793 Schiller suggested that Humboldt, who was eight years his junior, move to Jena.

Here in 1793-94 and 1795-96 the two families lived only a few doors apart, and the close association of the two men—Schiller and Humboldt saw one another twice a day and were often together until late into the night—was further encouraged by their wives, who had been intimate friends since girlhood.

Humboldt was a well-grounded scholar, at home in many fields, particularly in archeology, linguistics, and philosophy, and since his cultural ideal was similar to that of Schiller, he was able to respond to the latter's aesthetic-philosophical projects with enthusiasm and affection. He, too, was convinced that aesthetic culture was necessary in order to develop all the powers of the human being into a harmonious whole, and he shared Schiller's reverence for Greek culture, which, in the opinion of both, represented the purest development of man.

For Humboldt this exchange of ideas with Schiller was a delightful and unforgettable experience. Of all the many people who came under the spell of Schiller's magnetic personality none has described his charm as vividly as he. Here is his account of Schiller's way of conducting a conversation:

"He never went out of his way to look for an important topic of conversation, rather he left

it to chance to produce one. But from every subject he guided the conversation to a universal
point of view, and after a few interruptions one
would find oneself translated into the midst of
an intellectually stimulating discussion. He always treated a thought as a result to be arrived
at by common effort, seemed always to need the
other person, although the latter was aware that
he had received the idea only from him, and
never let him be idle. Schiller did not actually
speak beautifully. But his mind strove toward
a new intellectual gain in sharpness and definite-
ness; he controlled this effort and soared with
complete freedom above his subject. That is why
he used every association that happened to present itself with easy serenity, and that is why his
conversation was so rich in words that bear the
mark of happy inspirations of the moment. This
freedom, however, did not detract from the
course of the investigation. Schiller always kept
a firm hold on the thread that would lead to the
final point, and if the conversation did not happen to be disturbed, he did not break it off easily
until he had reached his goal."

Throughout his life Humboldt gratefully acknowledged that he owed the best that was in him to his
association with Schiller. Schiller, for his part, was
aware of his rare good fortune in having Humboldt
as a friend, and he relied on his advice when he was
completing his aesthetic-philosophical essays. Because
of Humboldt's pure and unselfish interest in his
friend and his friend's concerns, he was able to perform the most important service for which a critical
advisor can be called upon: to share with the most
sensitive and sympathetic understanding the moods
and thoughts that inspired the poet, and to assist
tirelessly in their stylistic perfection.

In April 1797 the Humboldts left Jena and saw Schiller again only during short visits in 1801 and 1802. Wanderlust and new duties called the younger man away. He accepted an appointment as Prussian Resident and later as ambassador plenipotentiary in Rome. His place in Schiller's life was never filled. Although the two continued to correspond, this was no substitute for the companionship they had had when they lived near one another. In Humboldt's last known letter to Schiller (Rome, October 22, 1803) he writes: "Remain to me, my dear good friend, what you are, and rest assured that whatever distance may separate us, my interest in you will forever be the same, and the smallest of your activities is of more importance to me than anything I myself could undertake." And after expressing his admiration for *The Bride of Messina*, he says in closing: "For you we need beg fate only for *life*. Youth and strength you have and will always possess." And in Schiller's last letter to Humboldt, dated April 2, 1805, he voiced his faith in the indestructibility of their friendship:

Our mutual understanding is independent of either time or space."

Für unser Einverständnis sind keine Jahre und keine Räume."

A lasting memorial to their friendship is their correspondence, which Humboldt assembled and published in 1830. The memoir prefacing the Humboldt-Schiller correspondence, "On Schiller and the Progress of His Thought," is the deepest testimonial to the uniqueness of Schiller's life and character and to his friend's devoted affection.

Zestfully Schiller had returned to poetry, but soon his first intense satisfaction with "The Ideal and Life"

began to diminish. Despite his extraordinary accomplishment in the field represented by this poem, he knew that it was not really possible to find concrete equivalents for such concepts as the ideal and inner freedom, and thus fuse object and idea, which was now his goal. He therefore felt impelled to follow Goethe's method and to start with the object instead of with the idea, to idealize the former, i.e., to reveal and portray the "pure and objective nature" in it. *Wilhelm Meister's Apprenticeship,* with which he was occupied almost every day and which was being written under his very eyes, undoubtedly influenced him here.

The first product of this new approach was "The Walk" (originally called "Elegy"). This poem shows very clearly the change that has taken place in Schiller's creative method. The objects with which the poet starts and which he has observed on his walk reveal to him their essence and meaning. On his journey through the ages he sees first the rural landscape and pastoral patterns of life of early man, the original state of happy innocence which in the dream of a golden age still survives. This early period of human culture is followed by periods when the world is expanding. Feudal and urban cultures pass before our eyes in a series of pictures and events. The concrete illustration is followed by the abstract idea in such a way that a perfect equilibrium is reached between concept and illustration.

The various modes of life evoked by the successive visions carry within them their own fate. The praise of culture that is the fruit of human freedom is followed by a lament for the abuse of this freedom which so offends nature that it destroys it, bringing chaos to the world.

"Freed from past bondage the overjoyed burgher
　　arises. If only
　　Breaking the fetters of fear broke not the bridle
　　　of shame!
'Liberty!' clamors Reason and 'Liberty!' beastliest
　　cravings
　　Which from Nature's restraint wantonly seek
　　　to escape.
Woe, in the storm the vessel is torn from the moor-
　　ing which safely
　　Held it ashore. The tide, furious in its pursuit,
Carries it off to boundless horizons. The coastline
　　has vanished,
　　High on the crests of the waves flounders dis-
　　　masted the boat.

"*Seine Fesseln zerbricht der Mensch, der Beglück-
　　te, zerriss' er*
　　*Mit den Fesseln der Furcht nur nicht den Zügel
　　　der Scham!*
*Freiheit ruft die Vernunft, Freiheit die wilde Be-
　　gierde,*
　　*Von der heil'gen Natur ringen sie lüstern sich
　　　los.*
*Ach, da reißen im Sturm die Anker, die an dem
　　Ufer*
　　*warnend ihn hielten, ihn faßt mächtig der flu-
　　　tende Strom.*
*Ins Unendliche reißt er ihn hin, die Küste ver-
　　schwindet,*
　　*Hoch auf der Fluten Gebirg wiegt sich ent-
　　　mastet der Kahn.*"

But the ages are conceived of as pursuing a cyclical
course. The end of the poem returns to its beginning.
Humanity moves toward an apocalyptic future, but it
is nature itself that contains within itself the power of
salvation. It is nature, which continually renews itself,

that gives man, who is subject to corruption and an-
nihilation, renewal and healing.

"Ever changes the will its purpose and mode.
In ever
Metamorphous design passes the pageant of
deeds.
But immutably youthful, eternally fresh in her
glory,
Constant Nature for aye honors the ancient
law."

*"Ewig wechselt der Wille den Zweck und die
Regel, in ewig
Wiederholter Gestalt wälzen die Taten sich
um;
Aber jugendlich immer, in immer veränderter
Schöne
Ehrst du, fromme Natur, züchtig das alte Ge-
setz."*

Schiller regarded "The Walk" as his best poem.
It is a powerful fresco and is particularly characteristic
of Schiller's view of life at the time. While he shows
what is good and meaningful in life he does not conceal its horrors.

In his essay "On Tragic Poetry" he wrote:

"And so we demand: Throw out this ill-con-
ceived pampering, these soft and effeminate pref-
erences which cast a veil over the stern face of
necessity in order to find favor with the senses,
which *lie* to us about the coincidence of well-
being and well-doing although the real world
shows no trace of it! Let the terror of fate come
up to us face to face. The solution for us lies not
in that we remain ignorant of the dangers that
surround us—for such ignorance will be shattered
in the end—but only in that we grow cognizant of
them."

"Also hinweg mit der falsch verstandenen Scho-
nung und dem schlaffen, verzärtelten Geschmack,
der über das ernste Angesicht der Notwendigkeit
einen Schleier wirft und, um sich bei den Sinnen
in Gunst zu setzen, eine Harmonie zwischen dem
Wohlsein und Wohlverhalten lügt, *wovon sich in*
der wirklichen Welt keine Spuren zeigen! Stirne
gegen Stirne zeige sich uns das böse Verhängnis.
Nicht in der Unwissenheit der uns umlagernden
Gefahren—denn diese muß doch endlich aufhö-
ren—, nur in der Bekanntschaft mit denselben ist
Heil für uns."

It is man's destiny to be aware of this dark aspect,
and his greatness derives from his ability to face it
without faltering. The chorus in *The Bride of Mes-*
sina expresses this as follows:

"But even from cloudless heights of air
The thunder can strike with its fires ablaze;
Therefore amid your cheerful days
Of Misfortune's treacherous presence beware!
Hang not your heart upon possessions
That adorn our life. Those who choose
To possess must also learn to lose.
In times of good fortune, make Sorrow's conces-
     sions."

"Aber auch aus entwölkter Höhe
Kann der zündende Donner schlagen,
Darum in deinen fröhlichen Tagen
Fürchte des Unglücks tückische Nähe!
Nicht an die Güter hänge dein Herz,
Die das Leben vergänglich zieren!
Wer besitzt, der lerne verlieren,
Wer im Glück ist, der lerne den Schmerz!"

Now, at the height of his powers, Schiller had won
through to a spiritual attitude that could not be

124

shaken by external fate. He called it serenity or freedom of mind, and, conscious of a strength within him capable of enduring reality and thus overcoming it, he did not need the support of faith.

Tragedy is thus the poetic realization of tragic humanity and it has a lofty moral purpose, that of inwardly overcoming the demonic power of fate. This is the school into which tragedy takes us. A passage from Schiller's posthumous papers reads as follows:

> "We are human; we are in the hands of fate; we are subject to the force of laws. Therefore a freer, more vital power must be aroused and exercised in us so that we may be able to restore ourselves."

> *"Wir sind Menschen, wir stehen unter dem Schicksal, wir sind unter dem Zwang von Gesetzen. Es muß also eine höhere, rüstigere Kraft in uns aufgeweckt und geübt werden, damit wir uns wieder herstellen können."*

Ours is indeed not a world where good fortune is meted out according to the merits of the individual. Even that which is perfect and beautiful has no claim to be spared. Aware that his own death was not far off, he wrote the moving elegy "Nenia" in which he mourns the destruction of the beautiful. Though the tragic disharmony of life inexorably demands the death of all living things, the lament for a loved one's death overcomes the law of death by extolling nobility and beauty in a final spiritual triumph. Even the perfection that was destroyed will live on in the impersonality of the song.

NENIA

Also the beautiful dies.—Its spell binds all men and immortals
   Save one: the Stygian Zeus. Armored in steel is his
     breast.

Once, only once did soften a lover the ruler of Hades.
   Yet, ere the threshold was reached, sternly he canceled
     his gift.

As Aphrodite stills not the gaping wounds of Adonis
   Which on the beautiful youth, hunted, the wild boar
     inflicts,

So the immortal Thetis saves not her divine son Achilles
   When at the Scaean Gate, falling, he meets with his
     fate.

But from the sea she arises with all the daughters of
   Nereus,
   And they intone their lament for her transfigured son.

Lo, all the gods now are weeping and weeping is every
     goddess
   That the beautiful wanes, that the perfect must die.

Glory is also to be a song of sorrow of loved ones,
   For, what is vulgar goes down songless to echoless
     depths.

NÄNIE

*Auch das Schöne muß sterben! Das Menschen und
      Götter bezwinget,
    Nicht die eherne Brust rührt es des stygischen
      Zeus.*

*Einmal nur erweichte die Liebe den Schattenbe-
      herrscher,
    Und an der Schwelle noch, streng, rief er
      zurück sein Geschenk.*

*Nicht stillt Aphrodite dem schönen Knaben die
      Wunde,*

*Die in den zierlichen Leib grausam der Eber
geritzt.*

*Nicht errettet den göttlichen Held die unsterb-
liche Mutter,
Wann er, am skäischen Tor fallend, sein
Schicksal erfüllt.*

*Aber sie steigt aus dem Meer mit allen Töchtern
des Nereus,
Und die Klage hebt an um den verherrlichten
Sohn.*

*Siehe! Da weinen die Götter, es weinen die Göt-
tinnen alle,
Daß das Schöne vergeht, daß das Vollkommene stirbt.*

*Auch ein Klaglied zu sein im Mund der Geliebten,
ist herrlich;
Denn das Gemeine geht klanglos zum Orkus
hinab.*

In his early dramas and in the "Aesthetic Letters"
he was as severe a critic of the weaknesses of his age as
he was of his own writings. Though it was his highest
aim to become a poet of the people, because this would
give him the opportunity to influence and educate his
age, he was not prepared to achieve popularity by
making concessions to the public taste. His attitude is
clearly expressed in a letter to Fichte written in 1795:

"Preserving my independence while noting what
others think and what they are prepared to flatter,
I accept only the rule of my nature or that of my
reason. . . . Virtually every line that has flowed
from my pen in the course of the last years bears
this imprint, and while it is true that external
considerations (which I share with more than one
other author) do not allow me to take no interest
in whether a large or a small public buys my
works, I at least pursued this goal following the

only course that is compatible with my individuality and my character, that is, not by trying to oblige the public through doing obeisance to the spirit of the age, but by endeavoring to surprise and arouse and stir it through a lively and bold presentation of *my* way of seeing things. That an author pursuing this path cannot become the darling of the public goes without saying."

"Unabhängig von dem, was um mich herum gemeint und geliebkoset wird, folge ich bloß dem Zwang entweder meiner Natur oder meiner Vernunft. . . . Beinahe jede Zeile, die seit den letzten Jahren aus meiner Feder geflossen ist, trägt dieses Gepräge, und wenn ich gleich aus äußeren Gründen, die ich mit noch mehr Schriftstellern gemein habe, nicht gleichgültig sein kann, ob mich ein großes oder kleines Publikum kauft, so habe ich mich wenigstens auf dem einzigen Wege darum beworben, der meiner Individualität und meinem Charakter entspricht,—nicht dadurch, daß ich mir durch Anschmiegung an den Geist der Zeit das Publikum zu gewinnen, sondern dadurch, daß ich es durch die lebhafte und kühne Aufstellung meiner Vorstellungsart zu überraschen, anzuspannen und zu erschüttern suchte. Daß ein Schriftsteller, welcher diesen Weg geht, nicht der Liebling seines Publikums werden kann, liegt in der Natur der Sache."

"Die Horen," by means of which, because of its high literary standards, Schiller had hoped to educate the taste of his public, was not as successful as he expected. The interest of its readers soon fell off, and the unfriendly and, at times, ignorant and spiteful comments in other periodicals cut down its circulation. In addition, he found himself deserted by many of his contributors with the result that he and Goethe had to provide most of the material themselves. The editing proved to be more and more of a thankless

task, and he would gladly have been released from the burden. But he had founded the periodical himself and felt obligated to continue the work because of the loyal support of his publisher, Cotta, as well as that of his remaining contributors. The real reason for the failure of "Die Horen" was that there was not a sufficient number of readers for a periodical of such a high literary level. So after three years of costly sacrifice—costly to the editor as well as to the publisher—it quietly perished.

While it was the hostile reception accorded to "Die Horen" which induced Schiller and Goethe to strike back, a still deeper reason was their desire to protest against the spirit of crass ignorance and arrogance. Inspired by his reading of the Xenia by the Roman poet Martial, Goethe proposed to Schiller that they write a series of polemic epigrams to be published in the "Musenalmanach." Schiller readily agreed. They planned at first to aim the epigrams at various German periodicals, but before long they added others leveled at certain authors and their works.

By the middle of 1796 they had got together four hundred and fourteen epigrams, a selection from an even larger number, under the title of "Xenia" (gifts to guests) and had launched them "into the land of the Philistines as foxes with burning tails." Most of them were intended as criticism and satire and have a sharp barb, but the positive natures of the two poets also asserted themselves, and a number of the epigrams aim higher and are more constructive in character. They are collected under the title of "Votive Tablets" and are excellent examples of aphoristic writing in perfect, classical form. The following sampling of specimens is representative of Schiller's contributions, except for the fact that it includes nothing of a purely polemical nature.

Your Own

Everyone shares in your thought. Your own are only your
feelings.
If you want God to be yours, feel Him Whom first
you but thought.

Das eigne Ideal

*Allen gehört, was du denkst; dein eigen ist nur, was du
fühlest.
Soll er dein Eigentum sein, fühle den Gott, den du
denkst.*

Dignity of Man

Stop now, I beg you. Stop talking. Let's feed him, provide him with shelter.
Once his Adam is clad, dignity comes by itself.

Würde des Menschen

*Nichts mehr davon, ich bitt' euch! Zu essen gebt ihm, zu
wohnen;
Habt ihr die Blöße bedeckt, gibt sich die Würde von
selbst.*

Light and Color

Dwell, you eternally one, in the realm of the one and
eternal.
Color, you changeful delight, gaily abide among men.

Licht und Farbe

*Wohne, du ewiglich Eines, dort bei dem ewiglich Einen!
Farbe, du wechselnde, komm freundlich zum Menschen
herab!*

Hallmark

Priests of Liberty, please stop pretending you did see the
goddess.
What you saw gnashing its teeth was neither free nor
divine.

Das Kennzeichen

Freiheitspriester! ihr habt die Göttin niemals gesehen,
Denn mit knirschendem Zahn zeigt sich die Göttliche
nicht.

Safety

Only the fiery steed, the courageous, can fall on the race
track.
Thoughtfully choosing his steps ambles the donkey
along.

Die Sicherheit

Nur das feurige Roß, das mutige, stürzt auf der Renn-
bahn,
Mit bedächtigem Paß schreitet der Esel daher.

The Master

Rightly we judge one a master by judging the things he
expresses.
Only the master of style proves himself when he omits.

Der Meister

Jeden andern Meister erkennt man an dem, was er aus-
spricht;
Was er weise verschweigt, zeigt mir den Meister des
Stils.

The Child in the Cradle

Fortunate child, to you now an infinite space is a cradle.
Coming of age you will find narrow the infinite world.

Das Kind in der Wiege

*Glücklicher Säugling! dir ist ein unendlicher Raum noch
die Wiege.
Werde Mann, und dir wird eng die unendliche Welt.*

Criterion for the Ideal Form of Government

That it provide for us all the means to think what is
rightful,
Not that it need to impose thoughts which it deems to
be right.

Die beste Staatsverfassung

*Diese nur kann ich dafür erkennen, die jedem erleichtert,
Gut zu denken, doch nie, daß er so denke, bedarf.*

The Epic of Raynard the Fox

Centuries back—I am to believe—some minstrel composed
this?
How could that be? What it says—all of it fits us today.

Reineke Fuchs

*Vor Jahrhunderten hätte ein Dichter dieses gesungen?
Wie ist das möglich? Der Stoff ist ja von gestern und
heut.*

The Good and the Great

Only two virtues are basic. Would they were always
united—
Always the Good also great, always the Great also good.

Güte und Größe

Nur zwei Tugenden gibt's—o wären sie immer vereinigt,
Immer die Güte auch groß, immer die Größe auch gut!

Everyone's Duty

Always strive for completeness, and if completion eludes
you,
Serve—as an integral part—something already complete.

Pflicht für jeden

Immer strebe zum Ganzen, und kannst du selber kein
Ganzes
Werden, als dienendes Glied schließ an ein Ganzes
dich an!

Dead Languages

Dead you call Pindar's language and dead the language
of Flaccus.
Yet from the two has come down all that is vital in
ours.

Tote Sprachen

Tote Sprachen nennt ihr die Sprachen des Flaccus und
Pindar,
Und von beiden nur kommt, was in der unsrigen lebt.

Scholarship

Some have enthroned it a goddess sublime and exacting,
while others
See in it Bessie the Cow, bounden to butter their bread.

Wissenschaft

Einem ist sie die hohe, die himmlische Göttin, dem
andern
Eine tüchtige Kuh, die ihn mit Butter versorgt.

To the Muse

No, I don't know what I would be without you, but
    surely I shudder
When I consider what lives millions, not knowing you,
    lead.

An die Muse

*Was ich ohne dich wäre, ich weiß es nicht—aber mir
    grauet,
Seh' ich, was ohne dich Hundert' und Tausende sind.*

The Key

If knowing yourself is your purpose, just watch what your
    neighbors are doing.
Knowledge of others you gain, probing within yourself.

Der Schlüssel

*Willst du dich selber erkennen, so sieh, wie die andern
    es treiben;
Willst du die andern verstehn, blick in dein eigenes
    Herz.*

My Faith

Do I profess a religion?—None, surely, of all you have
    mentioned.
Would you I told you why? All for religion's sake.

Mein Glaube

*Welche Religion ich bekenne? Keine von allen,
Die du mir nennst.—Und warum keine?—Aus Religion.*

The Homeric Hexameter

Ceaselessly surging its pulsating swell heaves you cease-
    lessly onward.
Aft you espy and fore nothing but ocean and sky.

Der epische Hexameter

Schwindelnd trägt er dich fort auf rastlos strömenden
  Wogen,
  Hinter dir siehst du, du siehst vor dir nur Himmel und
  Meer.

The Distich

In the hexameter rises the liquid song of the fountain,
  Which the pentameter then blithely returns to the
  pool.

Das Distichon

Im Hexameter steigt des Springquells flüssige Säule,
Im Pentameter drauf fällt sie melodisch herab.

Fatherhood

Forever alone you remain, regardless of all your achieve-
  ment,
  Till with a powerful bond nature links you to the
  Whole.

Der Vater

Wirke, soviel du willst, du stehest doch ewig allein da,
Bis an das All die Natur dich, die gewaltige knüpft.

The Ultimate

If it's the greatest, the highest you seek, the plant can
  direct you.
  Strive to become through your will what, without will,
  it is.

Das Höchste

Suchst du das Höchste, das Größte? Die Pflanze kann es
  dich lehren.
Was sie willenlos ist, sei du es wollend—das ist's!

St. Peter's Cathedral

If you expect of me awe beyond measure, I must dis-
  appoint you.
For, what is great in me makes greater yourself and not
  small.

Die Peterskirche

Suchst du das Unermeßliche hier, du hast dich geirret:
Meine Größe ist die, größer zu machen dich selbst.

Communication

Even in plainest garb the power of truth need not suffer.
If it's of beauty we speak, vessel and content are one.

Mitteilung

Aus der schlechtesten Hand kann Wahrheit mächtig noch
  wirken;
Bei dem Schönen allein macht das Gefäß den Gehalt.

Teleology

Great admiration is due the Creator who—thoughtful as
  always—
When he invented the cork, also provided the oak.

Der Teleolog

Welche Verehrung verdient der Weltenschöpfer, der
  gnädig
Als er den Korkbaum schuf, gleich auch den Stöpsel
  erfand!

What We Praise

Generics praise if you will. I can only praise the specific.
For in specifics alone can the generic appear.

Das Ehrwürdige

Ehret ihr immer das Ganze! Ich kann nur das Einzelne
achten:
Immer im Einzelnen nur hab' ich das Ganze erblickt.

Speech

Why cannot life be apparent to life by immediate
contact?
When the soul utters words, words are heard and not
soul.

Sprache

Warum kann der lebendige Geist dem Geist nicht er-
scheinen?
Spricht die Seele, so spricht, ach! schon die Seele nicht
mehr.

Immortality

Terror of death is upon you? You long to have life immortal?
Know that you are but a part. Know that the whole
cannot die.

Unsterblichkeit

Vor dem Tod erschrickst du? Du wünschest unsterblich
zu leben?
Leb' im Ganzen! Wenn du lange dahin bist, es bleibt.

Assignment

No one shall be like another, yet all shall equal the
highest.
How such a thing might be done? Each one perfect his
own self.

Aufgabe

Keiner sei gleich dem andern, doch gleich sei jeder dem
Höchsten!
Wie das zu machen? Es sei jeder vollendet in sich.

Truth

Truth is the same for us all, though to each it appears as
he sees it.
That it is one is what makes true its appearances too.

Wahrheit

Eine nur ist sie für alle, doch siehet sie jeder verschieden;
Daß es eines doch bleibt, macht das Verschiedene wahr.

The Age

Great is the age which for us the Father of Time has
engendered.
But in its greatness the age finds only men who are
small.

Der Zeitpunkt

Eine große Epoche hat das Jahrhundert geboren;
Aber der große Moment findet ein kleines Geschlecht.

[Tyrant and Tyranny]

Hate of a tyrant is well within grasp of souls that are
knavish.
Tyranny's hatred is more: Sign of the noble and great.

[Tyrann und Tyrannei]

Einen Tyrannen zu hassen vermögen auch knechtische
Seelen,
Nur wer die Tyrannei hasset, ist edel und groß.

Thingmongers

Naught is to you whatever one cannot measure in bushels,
  Pile up in warehouse and store, bundle in dozen and
    gross.

Die Sachmänner

*Euch ist alles ein Nichts, was man mit Scheffeln nicht
    misset,*
  *Was man in Bündeln nicht packt, was man in Spei-
    chern nicht häuft.*

Urn and Skeleton

Into their graves, the Greeks—who were human—took
  casts of the living.
We—insipidly—plant death in the midst of life.

Das Skelett und die Urne

*In das Grab hinein pflanzte der menschliche Grieche noch
    Leben,*
  *Und du, töricht Geschlecht, stellst in das Leben den
    Tod.*

Separation of Powers

Probers of truth must never be cast as agents of action,
  Nor must the makers of laws ever be called on to
    judge.

Verkehrter Beruf

*Forsche der Philosoph, der Weltmann handle! Doch weh
    uns,*
  *Handelt der Forscher, und gibt, der es vollzieht, das
    Gesetz!*

Achilles

While you were living, we paid you the honors befitting
  the godlike.
Now the immortal in you rules what is godlike in men.

Achilles

Vormals im Leben ehrten wir dich wie einen der Götter,
Nun du tot bist, so herrscht über die Geister dein Geist.

The Xenia were an immediate and great success, but no doubt because many of them attacked living writers. The serious poems also contained in the "Musenalmanach" could scarcely have accounted for the rise in its sales. As was to be expected, the epigrams brought forth violent counterattacks from their victims. Far from being disturbed by these, Goethe found them highly amusing, but they made Schiller extremely unhappy, as his nature was such that he could never bear an atmosphere of hostility. The two poets gave up any idea of replying to them and Goethe wrote to his friend: "After our mad venture with the Xenia we must take pains to work on only great and dignified works of art and shame all our adversaries by transforming our protean natures into noble forms."

No work occupied Schiller for so long a time as *Wallenstein*. From the beginning of 1791, when he first conceived the plan of the drama, to March 1799, when he finished it, he devoted most of his time to it. His knowledge of the subject went back still further. As early as 1786 his imagination had been stirred by Gustavus Adolphus and Wallenstein, the great figures of the Thirty Years' War which ravaged Germany in the seventeenth century. And his *History of the Thirty Years' War* had kept the subject present in his mind for years and gave him a very thorough knowledge of the period.

Wallenstein, who had created a mighty army out of virtually nothing, fought on the imperial, Catholic side. He had captured large sections of northern Ger-

many and had been made Duke of Mecklenburg by Emperor Ferdinand II. At the instigation of the Catholic party, which feared his power, he was removed from command of the army. The successes of the Protestants under Gustavus Adolphus forced the Emperor to recall Wallenstein, who since his dismissal, however, had become wholly obsessed with the thought of revenge. This retribution was to take the form of destroying the house of Habsburg, after which he himself planned to become ruler of the Empire. This he could do only if he were in control of the army, which in turn would depend on the Emperor's restoring his command. But in order to undermine the Emperor he needed to make an alliance with the Swedes. His treasonable negotiations were discovered by the Imperial Court. He was again dismissed and was assassinated in Eger in 1634. So much for the historical facts.

Wallenstein is Schiller's most important drama. The very difficulty and intractability of the material make it so. The subject was unsuitable to the kind of drama he had written before. Forcing him to put his hero through several transformations—as will be described in greater detail—in order to meet the changing demands of his dramatic-aesthetic views during the years when he was writing the play, *Wallenstein* brought him to the supreme degree of mastery that was to characterize the later dramas which followed in rapid succession.

In *Wallenstein* Schiller created something which had never before been attempted in a play. He brought to the stage a poetical work that has the basic characteristics of a novel. It shows the hero in relation to the various groups with which he was associated: the army, the generals, Max Piccolomini and Thekla. These serve not only to bring out all aspects of

141

Wallenstein himself—who remains in the background through much of the trilogy—but they are themselves portrayed with such breadth and vividness, and possess so much dramatic interest that they could well be the heroes of separate dramas.

The tremendous scope of the material contained in the tragedy makes it impossible to present in a single evening. In order to save it for the stage and to avoid drastic cuts, it was divided at Goethe's suggestion into two parts. An introductory play, *Wallenstein's Camp*, had already been included in the original plan.

There is no real action in the introductory piece. It consists of a series of pictures of camp life during the Thirty Years' War. All kinds of troops are represented, all nationalities and religions. The soldiers are fighting not for patriotic reasons but for pay and plunder. Nevertheless all these widely varied elements have been forged into a highly disciplined army. The secret of its unity is its general. The shadow of his powerful and mysterious personality seems to lower over the entire camp, he is constantly in the minds of his men.

The diction—Schiller uses doggerel—is intentionally archaic. This differentiates *The Camp* from the other two parts of the play. While it has no plot of its own, it reflects the happenings of the drama proper, and thus forms an explanatory background.

Schiller closes the fourth book of his *History of the Thirty Years' War* as follows:

"Thus Wallenstein, at the age of fifty years, ended his ever-active and extraordinary life, carried aloft by his quest for honor, cast down by lust for glory, with all his shortcomings still great and worthy of admiration, incomparable if he had kept within bounds. The virtues of the *ruler* and of the *hero*—wisdom, justice, firmness, and courage—are of colossal eminence in his character;

142

but he lacked the gentle virtues of the *human being* which adorn the hero and earn the ruler love."

"So endigte Wallenstein in einem Alter von fünfzig Jahren sein tatenreiches und außerordentliches Leben, durch Ehrgeiz emporgehoben, durch Ehrsucht gestürzt, bei allen seinen Mängeln noch groß und bewundernswert, unübertrefflich, wenn er Maß gehalten hätte. Die Tugenden des Herrschers *und* Helden, *Klugheit, Gerechtigkeit, Festigkeit und Mut, ragen in seinem Charakter kolossalisch hervor; aber ihm fehlten die sanften Tugenden des* Menschen, *die den Helden zieren und dem Herrscher Liebe erwerben."*

But even then Schiller questioned this characterization, and the passage which follows virtually amounts to a defense of Wallenstein's honor.

"The independence of his mind, the alertness of his reason raised him above the religious prejudices of his age, and the Jesuits never forgave him for having seen through their system and for regarding the Pope merely as the Bishop of Rome. . . . Through monkish intrigues he lost his command at Regensburg and his life at Eger; through monkish machinations he lost what is perhaps more than both, the honor of his name and his good reputation before posterity. For in the end it must be admitted, to give justice its due, that it was not the most trustworthy pens that have written for us the story of this extraordinary man and that his treachery and his designs upon the crown of Bohemia are not facts supported by incontrovertible proof but only surmises based on probability. As yet no document has been found that could uncover for us the secret motives of his actions with historical reliability, and among his deeds none is public and generally acknowledged

which might not after all have sprung from an innocent source. Many of his most frequently censured actions prove merely that he wanted peace and wanted it seriously; and most of his others are explained and excused by his justified distrust of the Emperor and his pardonable endeavor to maintain his standing. . . . If finally circumstances and despair made him act in a manner deserving indeed the judgment already passed against him while he was innocent, there still is nothing in that to justify the judgment itself. Wallenstein fell, not because he was a rebel, but he rebelled because he fell. It was a misfortune for him during his life that he had aroused the enmity of a victorious party, a misfortune after his death that the enemy survived him and wrote his history."

"Sein freier und heller Verstand erhob ihn über die Religionsvorurteile seines Jahrhunderts, und die Jesuiten vergaben es ihm nie, daß er ihr System durchschaute und in dem Papste nichts als einen römischen Bischof sah . . . Durch Mönchsintrigen verlor er zu Regensburg den Kommandostab und zu Eger das Leben; durch mönchische Künste verlor er vielleicht, was mehr war als beides, seinen ehrlichen Namen und seinen guten Ruf vor der Nachwelt. Denn endlich muß man zur Steuer der Gerechtigkeit gestehen, daß es nicht ganz treue Federn sind, die uns die Geschichte dieses außerordentlichen Mannes überliefert haben, daß die Verräterei des Herzogs und sein Entwurf auf die böhmische Krone sich auf keine streng bewiesene Tatsache, bloß auf wahrscheinliche Vermutungen gründen. Noch hat sich das Dokument nicht gefunden, das uns die geheimen Triebfedern seines Handelns mit historischer Zuverlässigkeit aufdeckte, und unter seinen öffentlichen, allgemein beglaubigten Taten ist keine, die nicht endlich aus einer unschuldigen Quelle könnte geflossen sein. Viele seiner

getadeltsten Schritte beweisen bloß seine ernst-
liche Neigung zum Frieden; die meisten andern
erklärt und entschuldigt das gerechte Mißtrauen
gegen den Kaiser und das verzeihliche Bestreben,
seine Wichtigkeit zu behaupten . . . Wenn end-
lich Not und Verzweiflung ihn antreiben, das Ur-
teil wirklich zu verdienen, das gegen den Un-
schuldigen gefällt war, so kann dieses dem Urteil
selbst nicht zu Rechtfertigung gereichen. So fiel
Wallenstein, nicht weil er Rebell war, sondern
er rebellierte, weil er fiel. Ein Unglück für den
Lebenden, daß er eine siegende Partei sich zum
Feinde gemacht hatte—ein Unglück für den To-
ten, daß ihn dieser Feind überlebte und seine
Geschichte schrieb."

This conception of the Wallenstein tragedy left open
the possibility of a new interpretation, an interpretation that would accord with the demands that Schiller
was learning to make of tragedy during these years of
aesthetic and philosophical study. In the first of the
passages quoted above Wallenstein is said to lack the
gentle virtues of the human being that adorn the hero
and earn the ruler love. However, according to Schiller's aesthetics, the character of the hero must be
"universally human," that is, his virtues and faults
must be understandable in terms of ordinary human
experience. A further requirement of genuine tragedy
is that the hero should not perish through his own
mistakes, but as a result of chance and fate. This requirement presented the most serious difficulty. Schiller wrote to Goethe on November 28, 1796:

"Too little of the hero's misfortune stems as yet
from what is really fate and too much from his
own fault. But in this I derive some consolation
from the example of *Macbeth* where fate is likewise to be blamed much less than the hero himself
for the fact that he perishes."

> *"Das eigentliche Schicksal tut noch zuwenig und der eigene Fehler des Helden noch zuviel zu seinem Unglück. Mich tröstet hier aber einigermaßen das Beispiel des* Macbeth, *wo das Schicksal ebenfalls weit weniger Schuld hat als der Mensch, daß er zugrunde geht."*

And finally the sharing of the hero's struggle under the blows of fate should call forth in the spectator the moral strength to endure his own fate. Schiller later gave the classic formulation of this demand in his poem, "Shakespeare's Shadow," where he spoke of the "great, gigantic fate that raises man up when it crushes man down." But the power of spiritual resistance should be aroused not only in the spectator, but also in the tragic hero, an idea which frequently recurs in Schiller's work and also occupies an important place in his posthumous writings. For the purposes of the tragedy, therefore, Wallenstein had to be raised from the great criminal of Schiller's historical work to a "sublime" figure. He must show that he is unbowed by the blows of fate and that he is superior to them.

The same day, November 28, 1796, Schiller devoted another lengthy letter almost exclusively to the problems of *Wallenstein*. It was addressed to Körner, and in it he wrote:

> "I am still brooding earnestly on my *Wallenstein*, but still the wretched work lies there before me, formless and endless. . . .
>
> "I think I may say that the subject is in the highest degree unmalleable for such a purpose; it has about it almost everything to make it unsuitable. Basically it is an action of state and from the standpoint of its poetic use it has all the vices a political string of events can have, an invisible, abstract object, small and countless devices, dispersed action, a timid progression, and—for the

poet's taste—an altogether dried out and cold pur-
posiveness, without, however, carrying this latter
to perfection and hence poetic greatness; for in
the end the plan goes wrong simply because it
was not handled skilfully enough. The foundation on which Wallenstein rests his enterprise is
his army, that is, from my point of view, an infinite expanse which I cannot present to the eye
and which it takes endless doing to conjure up
before the imagination. So then: I cannot show
the object on which he stands, but neither can I
show what makes him fall, for that is likewise the
mood of the army, the Imperial Court, the Emperor.—Also the passions themselves that move
him, revenge and ambition, are of the coldest
kind. And finally, his character is never noble and
may never be noble; and at all times he can
appear only terrible and never really great. If I
do not want to crush him, I must not confront
him with anything great; for that reason he necessarily holds me down."

"*Ich brüte noch immer ernstlich über dem*
Wallenstein, *aber noch immer liegt das unglück-
selige Werk formlos und endlos vor mir da.*
"*Der Stoff ist, ich darf wohl sagen, im höchsten
Grade ungeschmeidig für einen solchen Zweck;
er hat beinahe alles, was ihn davon ausschließen
sollte. Es ist im Grunde eine Staatsaktion und
hat in Rücksicht auf den poetischen Gebrauch
alle Unarten an sich, die eine politische Handlung nur haben kann, ein unsichtbares, abstrak-
tes Objekt, kleine und viele Mittel, zerstreute
Handlungen, einen furchtsamen Schritt, eine (für
den Vorteil des Poeten) viel zu kalte, trockene
Zweckmäßigkeit, ohne doch diese bis zur Vollendung und dadurch zu einer poetischen Größe
zu treiben; denn am Ende mißlingt der Entwurf
doch nur durch Ungeschicklichkeit. Die Base,
worauf Wallenstein seine Unternehmung grün-*

det, ist die Armee, mithin für mich eine unend-
liche Fläche, die ich nicht vors Auge und nur
mit unsäglicher Kunst vor die Phantasie bringen
kann: ich kann also das Objekt, worauf er ruht,
nicht zeigen und ebensowenig das, wodurch er
fällt; das ist ebenfalls die Stimmung der Armee,
der Hof, der Kaiser.—Auch die Leidenschaften
selbst, wodurch er bewegt wird, Rachsucht und
Ehrbegierde, sind von der kältesten Gattung.
Sein Charakter endlich ist niemals edel und darf
es nie sein, und durchaus kann er nur furchtbar,
nie eigentlich groß erscheinen. Um ihn nicht zu
erdrücken, darf ich ihm nichts Großes gegen-
überstellen; er hält mich dadurch notwendig
nieder."

The two aesthetic types of writing, as he explained
them in *On Naive and Sentimental Poetry,* he also
extended in the same essay to include two types of
human being, the realist and the idealist. Wallenstein,
as he emerges from the historical sources, is a realist,
and as a poet Schiller wanted to portray him objectively. The great difficulty was that Wallenstein like all
realists did not lend himself easily to poetic treatment;
still less so since his undertaking was not only morally
wrong, but also ended in failure. Schiller sums this up
as follows:

"In no part is he great, and in the whole he
loses out. His calculations are all concerned with
the final effect, and in this he fails. He cannot,
as the idealist does, withdraw within himself
and rise above matter, but he strives to subject
matter and won't succeed."

"Er ist im einzelnen nie groß, und im Ganzen
kommt er um seinen Zweck. Er berechnet alles
auf die Wirkung, und diese mißlingt. Er kann
sich nicht, wie der Idealist, in sich selbst einhül-

*len und sich über die Materie erheben, sondern
er will die Materie sich unterwerfen und erreicht
es nicht."*

As Schiller saw it now, the task of the writer consists in effecting a representation of pure objective
nature. He realized of course what this implied with
respect to his relationship with Goethe, who at this
time was deeply involved in revising and completing
Wilhelm Meister's Apprenticeship. Schiller watched
the growth of the novel with ever-increasing admiration. In his letter, dated July 2, 1796, he wrote to
Goethe:

> "Calm and profound, lucid and yet as incom-
> prehensible as nature, that is how it impresses the
> reader, that is how it stands before him, and
> everything in it—down to the last and least di-
> gression—breathes the beautiful spirit of equa-
> nimity from which it has sprung."

> *"Ruhig und tief, klar und doch unbegreiflich
> wie die Natur, so wirkt es, und so steht es da,
> und alles, auch das kleinste Nebenwerk, zeigt
> die schöne Gleichheit des Gemüts, aus welchem
> alles geflossen ist."*

In a letter to Körner written at about this time, he
wrote:

> "To be sure, the road I have taken leads me into
> Goethe's domain, and this obliges me to pit my
> strength against his. That I shall lose out in this,
> compared to him, is also certain. But since I still
> have something that is mine, something he cannot
> ever reach, his advantage will hurt neither me
> nor my work, and I feel hopeful that the reckon-
> ing will come out fairly even. In my moments of
> greatest courage I promise myself that while we
> shall be specified differently, our manners will not

be subordinated to each other but will be placed side by side under the same superior generic ideal."

"Daß ich auf deme Wege, den ich nun einschlage, in Goethes Gebiet gerate und mich mit ihm werde messen müssen, ist freilich wahr; auch ist es ausgemacht, daß ich hierin neben ihm verlieren werde. . . . Weil mir aber auch etwas übrig bleibt, was mein ist und was er nie erreichen kann, so wird sein Vorzug mir und meinem Produkt keinen Schaden tun, und ich hoffe, daß die Rechnung sich ziemlich heben soll. Man wird uns, wie ich in meinen mutvollsten Augenblicken mir verspreche, verschieden spezifizieren, aber unsere Arten einander nicht unterordnen, sondern unter einem höhern idealischen Gattungsbegriff einander koordinieren."

The artistic imagination, therefore, must transform the unsuitable subject matter into poetic action and out of the raw material of the historical sources create a drama of tragic power. Characters who are entangled in their fate must be so portrayed that we feel their fate as tragic and can sympathize with them as human beings. This attitude was fundamentally different from that which he entertained toward the heroes of his early dramas. Since in those early figures he had embodied a part of himself, he naturally took a lively interest in their destinies. But now, in reference to his work on *Wallenstein,* he could write to Goethe:

"As for the *spirit* in which I approach my work, I think you will be pleased with me. I seem to succeed fairly well in keeping the subject matter at arm's length and to add nothing that is no real part of it. I could almost say that the subject does not interest me at all, and I have never felt at

150

once so coolly detached from my theme and so
warmly involved in my work. The principal character and most of the secondary characters I have
been treating up until now with nothing but the
pure love of the artist. Only the one next to the
principal character, young Max Piccolomini, has
my interest because he has my sympathy, but this,
I am sure, shall promote the whole work rather
than detract from it."

*"In Rücksicht auf den Geist, in welchem ich
arbeite, werden Sie wahrscheinlich mit mir zufrieden sein. Es will mir ganz gut gelingen, meinen Stoff außer mir zu halten und nur den
Gegenstand zu geben. Beinahe möchte ich sagen,
das Sujet interessiert mich gar nicht, und ich
habe nie eine solche Kälte für meinen Gegenstand mit einer solchen Wärme für die Arbeit
in mir vereinigt. Den Hauptcharakter sowie die
meisten Nebencharaktere traktiere ich wirklich
bis jetzt mit der reinen Liebe des Künstlers;
bloß für den nächsten nach dem Hauptcharakter, den jungen Piccolomini bin ich durch meine
eigene Zuneigung interessiert, wobei das Ganze
übrigens eher gewinnen als verlieren soll."*

Thus he continued to struggle with the recalcitrant
material. Repeatedly he spoke of the "decisive crisis"
that "must take place in his poetic character." He
could not give up the artistic principles and aims that
he owed to his association with Goethe and his study
of the Greeks—the objectivity of the realistic approach
and Sophocles' theory that the seeds of the tragic development of a drama are contained in it from the
outset and that the pattern of events is dictated by an
inexorable fate—but he needed "to melt them down,"
as he put it, into his own nature.

Schiller's real problem was not so much how he was

to draw the character of Wallenstein, but how he was to give his drama unity in line with his aesthetic philosophy. And this brought him to the final transformation of Wallenstein. Here he applied to his hero the ideas regarding the onset of spiritual sickness and cure which he had worked out in his two great works on aesthetics. Wallenstein's originally pure nature had also been corrupted by the world. He had assembled an army for the Emperor in the time of greatest distress and thus probably prevented Ferdinand from losing his throne. The great general's dismissal at the Diet of Regensburg, which could only seem to him an act of ingratitude, shook the foundations of his humanity, turning him into a misanthrope and a power-seeking autocrat. Still, the spark of humanity has not been entirely extinguished in him, and so he becomes a split human being. This spark manifests itself as his conscience inspiring him to make far-reaching plans for a lasting peace. It leads him to put off his final act of treason. It is those counterforces in his nature that delay his action until it is too late, thus precipitating his own destruction, that arouse our sympathetic interest in his fate.

Whether or not this conception of Wallenstein's character is historically correct is beside the point. What is significant is that this development of spiritual sickness can always take place, indeed that, to a certain degree, it must take place. Thus in the transformation Wallenstein now undergoes he becomes universally human.

In *Wallenstein* Schiller created a drama which, both in form and content, was entirely his own. Goethe praised the "unique way" of "combining the illustrative with the speculative to form a unified whole," and described the drama as a gift of inestimable value to the German stage. Up to this time sentimental

family plays and at best middle-class tragedies had constituted the theatergoers' habitual fare. Now the audience was to be lifted from the narrow sphere of humdrum existence to an awareness of "mankind's higher purposes." The grandeur of Schiller's diction truly achieves classical stature in this work. The "Prologue," a model of nobility in style and content, is included in this volume, for its claim, that "a new era begins today upon this stage," has been endorsed by later generations.

Humboldt added his voice to the general acclaim in these words:

> "By those who really appreciate you you will always be called the creator of a new poetry. What you have done in every field has the stamp of greatness and depth that one does not find elsewhere. Your works live and move with all the freshness and reality of actual life, but in a purer, more ethereal element than others. They are produced and sustained by the strength of ideas which they generate in turn. Your poetry is not lacking in vividness and warmth, but it has more of the sublime."

Wallenstein represents a turning point in yet another respect. From the start Schiller had assumed that, like *Don Carlos*, it would be a book drama which would later be adapted for the stage. At Goethe's insistence, however, he decided to write it directly for the theater, and from now on he was to do this with all his dramas.

Work on *Wallenstein*, however, had to be interrupted once again because Schiller had to fill a new issue of the "Musenalmanach." For this purpose he employed the first ballads. To a certain extent he used them as practice pieces that were to help him with his big dramatic work. He tried to make these poems

as realistic as possible and to concentrate on the concrete illustration. Goethe, who was writing very few ballads at this time, gave him a good deal of material and assisted him with suggestions and criticism. "The Cranes of Ibycus," in particular, was a gift from Goethe who had already worked on the theme. This poem, "The Diver," "The Fight with the Dragon" and "The Guarantee" are probably Schiller's best-known ballads.

With the ballads Schiller finally achieved a truly objective mode of representation. In them thought is substance and substance thought. This explains their almost universal appeal. They have something to offer to every reader, whereas the reflective poems speak primarily to a select circle of like-minded admirers. "The Cranes of Ibycus" is included in this volume as an example of the ballads.

The pivotal element in this poem is the concept of the stage, which appears to be an entity endowed with all the functions of religion. The terrifying chorus of the Erinyes is, to be sure, an illusion, a mere stage effect, but as it imparts through word and motion an awareness of the power of Nemesis, it assumes the dimensions of a higher reality. Through it "the stage becomes a tribunal" and thus reveals that "moral order of the universe" which the listener misses all too often in the world of reality around him.

Although 1797 was meant to be the "ballad year," Schiller also wrote "The Maiden from Afar" that year. In it the maiden appears as a friendly genius who brings good fortune and blessings to all here below in this "vale of poor shepherds." The poem is a parable in verse, an idyllic fairy tale, and simultaneously an enigma. A single occurrence assumes vicariously the dimensions of a general truth.

154

THE MAIDEN FROM AFAR

Where humble shepherds had their dwelling,
A lonely vale, each new-born year,
As larks were winging, buds were swelling,
A lovely maiden would appear.

When spring awoke one day they'd find her,
From whence she came no one could tell.
The stranger left no trace behind her
And vanished when she said farewell.

Exalted by her blessed presence,
All hearts were gladdened, spirits rose.
Yet sensing there some lofty essence
No mortal dared to come too close.

She came with gifts of fruits and flowers
From far-off gardens known to none,
Which, watered by serener showers,
Had ripened in a happier sun.

With all alike she shared her treasure,
These fruits and flowers from distant lands.
Both young and old received full measure
And none went home with empty hands.

To everyone she gave her greeting,
But when she saw true lovers there
She most delighted in the meeting
And chose for them the flow'r most rare.

DAS MÄDCHEN AUS DER FREMDE

In einem Tal bei armen Hirten
Erschien mit jedem jungen Jahr,
Sobald die ersten Lerchen schwirrten,
Ein Mädchen, schön und wunderbar.

Sie war nicht in dem Tal geboren,
Man wußte nicht, woher sie kam,
Und schnell war ihre Spur verloren,
Sobald das Mädchen Abschied nahm.

Beseligend war ihre Nähe,
Und alle Herzen wurden weit,
Doch eine Würde, eine Höhe
Entfernte die Vertraulichkeit.

Sie brachte Blumen mit und Früchte,
Gereift auf einer andern Flur,
In einem andern Sonnenlichte,
In einer glücklichern Natur.

Und teilte jedem eine Gabe,
Dem Früchte, jenem Blumen aus,
Der Jüngling und der Greis am Stabe,
Ein jeder ging beschenkt nach Haus.

Willkommen waren alle Gäste,
Doch nahte sich ein liebend Paar,
Dem reichte sie der Gaben beste,
Der Blumen allerschönste dar.

It is the reader's task to solve the enigma in his own fashion. Could the miraculous girl who appears in the springtime of every passing year be poetry itself? In any case, she is what brings the highest joy and bliss to us poor shepherds.

After this interruption, Schiller completed *Wallenstein*. *The Camp* was performed in Weimar in October 1798, *The Piccolomini* and *Wallenstein's Death* in January and April 1799. For a year thereafter the trilogy was reserved for the theaters, which purchased their texts directly from Schiller. In June 1800 it was published in book form in an edition of four thousand

copies which were quickly sold—a remarkable success for the period.

Schiller had called 1797 the ballad year, and 1798, as he wrote, was to be the song year. In fact, all the remaining years of his life might be called song years. For now began, with "The Eleusinian Festival," the series of songs that was to be continued the following year through "The Song of the Bell" and led finally to the poems he wrote for Goethe's evening gatherings, which took place every other Wednesday in his house. Gracious and dignified social intercourse, regarded as an art of life, was to be judged as such by the criteria of true art. In these social songs, therefore, Schiller held himself to the highest standards of excellence.

While "The Walk" portrayed phases in the development of the state as a form of social organization, "The Song of the Bell" reflects a broadening of Schiller's interests in that it starts with the individual, showing the stages of his growth progressively as a member of his family, his local community, and finally of human society as a whole.

The making of the bell, from its beginning to its completion, becomes a simile of the development of the social organization of man in the family, the state, and the "loving community" of the future. The process of casting suggests comparative allusions to human life, whose development is surveyed by the poet. In every section of this clearly marked series the pious tone of the bell is sounded, and by relating each picture to the process of bell founding, the poet makes a framework which gives unity to the poem as a whole. The completed bell is meant to be a voice of the eternal and unchanging, as compared to man's changeable and transitory existence. It is a call for concord and love, accompanying with its ringing the ever-changing life of man.

"The Song of the Bell" is not only a song of songs of civic life, which it transfigures in days of toil and hours of festivity; it is also by virtue of its general human content a symphony of life itself, encompassing sensations and events in their deepest meaning, as they are universally experienced, and interpreting them in their relation to the eternal. Perfect unity of illustration and idea has been achieved here. Wilhelm von Humboldt calls it "the most wonderful testimony of what constitutes perfect poetic genius." "I do not know," he wrote, "of a poem in any language which, in such condensed form, reveals so wide a poetic orbit, covering the gamut of the deepest human emotions, and which, entirely in lyric style, depicts life and its most important phases and events as one epos surrounded by natural borders."

The political and military events of those years had revealed Germany's extreme weakness more and more plainly, and the Peace of Basel (1795) had made some of the tiny German states practically vassals of France; it even provided for the cession of the left bank of the Rhine to France. No ray of hope could be seen in Germany's political future. Schiller followed the developments with deepest interest. In the fragment "German Greatness" he raises the question:

"Can the German at this moment, when he emerges ingloriously from his tear-drenched war, when two overbearing nations crush him under an iron heel and the victor decrees his destiny —can he keep faith in himself? Can he take pride in his name and rejoice at being what he is? Can he carry his head high and claim with self-assurance his place in the family of nations?"

"Darf der Deutsche in diesem Augenblick, wo er ruhmlos aus seinem tränenvollen Kriege geht,

> *wo zwei übermütige Völker ihren Fuß auf sei-*
> *nen Nacken setzen und der Sieger sein Geschick*
> *bestimmt—darf er sich fühlen? Darf er sich seines*
> *Namens rühmen und freuen? Darf er sein Haupt*
> *erheben und mit Selbstgefühl auftreten in der*
> *Völker Reihe?"*

And Schiller himself supplies the answer:

> "Yes, he can! Hapless he emerges from the strug-
> gle, but that which makes his worth, that he did
> not lose."

> *"Ja, er darf's! Er geht unglücklich aus dem*
> *Kampf, aber das, was seinen Wert ausmacht, hat*
> *er nicht verloren."*

If the disease of the age was its treason against the spirit, if a cure could be found through the moral force of a free will, then the nation had no cause to be despondent, for the greatness of its past consisted precisely in the accomplishments of the spirit. Its great men—and these alone are a nation's true treasure and consolation—its great men, its Luther and Kant, its Lessing and Herder, its Winckelmann and Goethe, more than justified, they established and answered the nation's claim to a rank of equality in the civilized world; they inspired and upheld a patriotic pride more noble than any based merely on a position of external political power. What Schiller demands is that we put our lives in the service of the spirit, that we "help to build the eternal temple of human melio-ration and to preserve what past ages have brought forth," so that we may perfect in ourselves a general humanity and that "the most beautiful flowers which bloom in the gardens of the world may be gathered together in a single crown." Here the demand which Schiller had formulated in his *Letters on the Aesthetic Education of Man* appears again in the garb of an

159

expression of faith in the cultural contribution of his people.

"For in the end, when time has run its course —if at all the world has a plan and man's life a meaning—in the end reason and ethos must triumph, crude force succumb to form."

"Denn endlich an dem Ziel der Zeit, wenn anders die Welt einen Plan, wenn des Menschen Leben irgend nur Bedeutung hat, endlich muß die Sitte und die Vernunft siegen, die rohe Gewalt der Form erliegen."

At the end of 1799 Schiller moved to Weimar. It had become more and more necessary for him to be near Goethe. Since, as mentioned before, he was now writing his dramas directly for performance, he needed to be near the Weimar Theater. While *Wallenstein* was in rehearsal, the Duke had had a box built for Schiller in the proscenium, so that when he was suddenly indisposed he would not have to tax himself unduly. He now became extremely interested in theater production and was able to be of great assistance to Goethe, not only as a playwright but also as a director. Goethe even went so far as to propose that Schiller should substitute for him as director or even take over the position altogether, but the Duke rejected this suggestion. Goethe and Schiller, however, developed a kind of unofficial co-directorship with Schiller relieving Goethe from doing several adaptations and sometimes entire productions.

Goethe and Schiller worked out a style of performance in accord with their artistic principles which has been called "the classical style of the eighteenth century." Its basic requirement was that the actor, as well as the author, should portray not everyday reality, but higher truth. This called for a special style of delivery that often resembled an intense recita-

tive. Miming and grouping were based on the laws of the plastic art.

Schiller's dramatic writing profited greatly from his close association with the stage. The only regrettable result of his move to Weimar was that it brought his correspondence with Goethe virtually to an end. Goethe lived only a few doors away and the two men saw one another almost daily.

The repertory of the Weimar Theater consisted for the most part of mere entertainments. This was not a concession to the public taste, but was due rather to the lack of plays of sufficiently high standard which would be suitable for the new style of performance. The classical repertory had first to be laboriously created; it consisted almost entirely of products of the labors of Schiller and Goethe. These were not only their own plays, but also translations and free adaptations, of which Shakespeare's *Macbeth* and *Othello*, Voltaire's *Tancred*, Gozzi's *Turandot* and Lessing's *Nathan the Wise* were notable examples. But it was above all the dramas of Schiller's last period that were to enrich the Weimar Theater and the German stage in general.

Mary Stuart is the next drama after *Wallenstein*. This time Schiller was more fortunate in his choice of tragic material. He managed without difficulty to fit it into the framework of the five-act play, and he finished the tragedy in a little over a year. Both as a book and as a stage play it was an immediate success.

The play concerns the struggle for power between the Scotch Catholic and the English Protestant queens and the defeat of Mary. It is dominated dramatically by the middle act, the powerful fourth scene of which is included in this volume. The climax of the tragedy, however, is the death of Mary, which alone provides the key to its understanding.

161

Besides the external action there is an internal drama which culminates in the moral victory of the heroine. Condemned to death, she becomes transfigured and so emerges victorious over Elizabeth, who for her part has been condemned by a higher tribunal. Despised and forsaken, Elizabeth stands before us with nothing left but naked power.

Schiller based the play on historical sources that make Mary guilty of a number of crimes, the gravest being her participation in the murder of her husband. He ascribes them to her upbringing at the corrupt court of Catherine de Medici. In this drama, however, she is innocent of the charge of participating in the conspiracy against the English Queen.

Of all of Schiller's tragedies, *Mary Stuart* is the most tightly constructed, and the characters are the most objectively portrayed. The individual acts are carefully balanced and divided between the two chief characters. The requirement of unity of time, place and action is observed very consistently. Since from the start Mary's death is a foregone conclusion—what takes place is simply the consequence of previous events, and delaying moments are introduced which, however, only serve to hasten the catastrophe—the entire action takes place in three days.

It is at the meeting of the two queens, when Mary intends to renounce the throne and plead for freedom and her life, that the Scottish queen seals her doom. Elizabeth, wishing to humiliate her, succeeds only in arousing Mary's regal pride. Mary then hurls in her face the unforgivable insult:

"A bastard has profaned the throne of England,
The noble-hearted British people has
Been cheated by a crafty, cheap impostor.
If right prevailed, you would be lying in
The dust before me, for *I* am your King."

"Der Thron von England ist durch einen Bastard
Entweiht, der Briten edelherzig Volk
Durch eine listge Gauklerin betrogen.
Regierte Recht, so läget Ihr vor mir
Im Staube jetzt, denn ich bin Euer König."

The attempt of Mortimer and Leicester to save Mary is a final deceptive hope that only hastens the end. But Mary transforms her inevitable fate by accepting it. As one who thus "casts off the shackles of the world," she acts as a free spirit. Death imposed on her is no longer an object of terror but a merciful dispensation of fate:

"God grants that by this death, which I do not
    deserve,
I shall atone for early grievous bloodguilt."

"Gott würdigt mich, durch diesen unverdienten
    Tod
Die frühe schwere Blutschuld abzubüßen."

She feels:

". . . man is ennobled,
However low he sinks, by his last fate."

". . . den Menschen adelt,
Den tiefstgesunkenen, das letzte Schicksal."

Here as elsewhere, Schiller requires of tragedy not only that it move men deeply and shock them out of their emotional indifference, but also that it awaken in them an urge for freedom which makes them superior to their earthly fate. This was Schiller's own great achievement in his maturity. It is this that gives Mary the strength to face death calmly and to rise above her earthly trials. Schiller's message is that man indeed has a divine nature which can be restored to its original purity.

Schiller's next drama, *The Maid of Orleans,* was the only one of the later plays which did not receive its first performance in Weimar. The Duke was dubious about the choice of subject, because Voltaire's satiric epic, *La Pucelle d'Orléans,* had ridiculed Joan of Arc to such an extent that he feared a scandal. Voltaire's profanation seemed to have destroyed forever the charm of the subject.

It may well be that Schiller chose the subject just because, as he later remarked, he did not want to see the noble picture of man treated with such contempt. The first performance took place in the Leipzig Theater. Schiller himself, who was just returning from his last visit to his friend Körner, was present. The occasion turned into an enthusiastic tribute to the poet by the academic youth.

Schiller departs widely from historical tradition. Instead of dying at the stake after having been condemned as a witch, Joan meets death in a triumphant apotheosis. The figure of Joan is stylized in a mythical fashion, so that she seems remote, strange and superhuman. This is explained by the fact that after she has been assigned her heavenly mission she no longer has a home on earth. This mission was not undertaken voluntarily, it was ruthlessly imposed upon her. She must abandon entirely her human nature, but the deity does not release her from her human emotions. As a result, she inevitably commits a sin which can be expiated only by suffering and penance. At the end she says:

"Now there is peace within me. Come what may,
I am aware now of no further weakness."

*"In mir ist Friede. Komme, was da will,
Ich bin mir keiner Schwachheit mehr bewußt."*

To be weak is the lot of man. But she has already entered into the kingdom of the spirit. The transformation of the human being into a god has already taken place. Thus the final scene is not a martydom, but a transfiguration. Joan has been imprisoned by the English and, bound hand and foot, is forced to look on at the battle from the high watchtower. All seems lost for France until a miracle once more takes place. She bursts her chains, rushes into the midst of the battle and leads the French to victory.

At the close the tragedy is transformed into a religious pageant. Death loses its power through the strength of the human soul which has been called to its mission by heaven itself.

The poet placed his heroine between the divine and the earthly. Through her "the noble image of humanity" is to be raised to immortality.

"But what has happened! Light clouds bear me
        up.
My heavy armor has become wing'd raiment.
Upwards—upwards.—Earth is rushing back.
Brief is the pain, and joy is everlasting."

*"Wie wird mir—leichte Wolken heben mich,
Der schwere Panzer wird zum Flügelkleide.
Hinauf—hinauf—die Erde flieht zurück.
Kurz ist der Schmerz und ewig ist die Freude!"*

Through the fall of 1801 into late summer of 1802, Schiller was too ill to undertake any big work. A few poems, such as, "To My Friends," "The Four Ages," and "Longing" are the only fruits of this period. He also hesitated between various dramatic subjects which had interested him for some time; the subject he finally chose was *The Bride of Messina*.

This drama is the creative expression of his deep

admiration for Greek tragedy and for antiquity. Since 1788, when he devoted his summer in Rudolstadt to the reading of Homer and the Greek tragedians, it had been his plan to write a tragedy in the Greek manner. What he particularly admired in this style was its great simplicity and clarity. He found in it one means to achieve the goal of self-perfection in overcoming the faults of his own early writing. But the chorus used in ancient tragedy also came to seem more and more important to him.

The story of the two hostile brothers, on which the *Bride* is based, is Schiller's own invention. The tragedy is the drama of a family that has a fateful curse hanging over it, as in the *Oedipus* of Sophocles. At the beginning of the play, the two hostile brothers have become reconciled, but they fall passionately in love with the same unknown woman who turns out to be their sister. These human beings, enmeshed in guilt, can only succeed in atoning by voluntary death. From the stage, as from a place of devotion, the chorus speaks the closing words:

> "Of all possessions life is not the highest,
> The worst of evils is, however, guilt."

> *"Das Leben ist der Güter höchstes nicht,
> Der Übel größtes aber ist die Schuld."*

On March 19, 1803, in celebration of the birthday of the Duke of Meiningen, the play was performed in Weimar and the author received expressions of enthusiastic admiration. In a letter to Körner he writes:

> "I for one, may say that it was during the performance of *The Bride of Messina* that I had for the first time the impression of a true tragedy. The chorus held it all beautifully together, and an exalted, awe-inspiring solemnity prevailed through all phases of the action. Goethe had the same feel-

ing. He thinks this contribution consecrated the
boards of the stage to something higher."

*"Was mich betrifft, so kann ich wohl sagen, daß
ich in der Vorstellung der* Braut von Messina *zum
ersten Mal den Eindruck einer wahren Tragödie
bekam. Der Chor hielt das Ganze trefflich zusammen, und ein hoher, furchtbarer Ernst waltete
durch die ganze Handlung. Goethen ist es auch so
ergangen; er meint: der theatralische Boden wäre
durch diese Erscheinung zu etwas Höherem ein-
geweiht worden."*

The book edition of *The Bride of Messina* has an
introductory essay, "On the Use of the Chorus in Tragedy." In it Schiller examines and justifies all the requirements of the new style of dramatic writing.

"That art alone is genuine which provides the
highest enjoyment. The highest enjoyment, however, is freedom of the spirit in the vivacious play
of all its powers.

"From the arts of the imaginative faculties
everyone expects a certain liberation from the
limitations of reality, he wants to delight in the
possible and give free rein to his fancy. The man
with the least expectations still wants to forget
his business, his everyday life, his individual self;
he wants to feel himself in extraordinary situations, to revel in the odd vagaries of chance. If
he is of a more serious nature, he wants to find
on the stage that moral government of the world
which he misses in actual life. Yet he himself
knows perfectly well that he is only carrying on
a pointless game, that in the last analysis he is
only indulging in dreams, and when he comes
back again from the stage into the actual world
the latter will once again beset him with all its
oppressive constriction; he will be the world's victim as before, for that has remained what it was

and nothing in him has been altered. Nothing has been gained thereby but a pleasing illusion of the moment which will vanish upon awakening. . . .

"Genuine art, on the other hand, does not have as its object a mere transitory game. Its serious purpose is not merely to translate the human being into a momentary dream of freedom, but actually to *make* him free. It accomplishes this by awakening a power within him, by using and developing this power to remove to a distance of objectivity the sensory world, which otherwise only weighs us down as raw material and oppresses us as a blind force, to transform the sensory world into a free creation of our spirit, and to control the material world through ideas.

"Precisely because genuine art aims at something real and objective, it cannot be satisfied with the mere appearance of truth. Upon truth itself, on the solid bedrock of nature it rears its ideal structure.

"But how art can and shall be at once ideal and yet in the profoundest sense real—how it can and shall totally abandon actuality and at the same time conform most exactly to nature—this is what few people understand. . . .

"With the introduction of metrical speech one has already been brought a large step nearer to poetic tragedy. . . . The introduction of the chorus would be the final and decisive step—and if it served no other purpose than to declare war openly and honestly on naturalism in art, it would be a living wall that tragedy draws about itself in order to shut itself definitely away from the actual world and preserve for itself its ideal ground and its poetic freedom. . . ."

"*Die rechte Kunst ist nur diese, welche den höchsten Genuß verschafft. Der höchste Genuß*

aber ist die Freiheit des Gemüts in dem lebendigen Spiel aller seiner Kräfte.

"*Jeder Mensch zwar erwartet von den Künsten der Einbildungskraft eine gewisse Befreiung von den Schranken des Wirklichen, er will sich an dem Möglichen ergötzen und seiner Phantasie Raum geben. Der am wenigsten erwartet, will doch sein Geschäft, sein gemeines Leben, sein Individuum vergessen, er will sich in außerordentlichen Lagen fühlen, sich an den seltsamen Kombinationen des Zufalls weiden; er will, wenn er von ernsthafter Natur ist, die moralische Weltregierung, die er im wirklichen Leben vermißt, auf der Schaubühne finden. Aber er weiß selbst recht gut, daß er im eigentlichen Sinn sich nur an Träumen weidet, und wenn er von dem Schauplatz wieder in die wirkliche Welt zurückkehrt, so umgibt ihn diese wieder mit ihrer ganzen drückenden Enge, er ist ihr Raub wie vorher, denn sie selbst ist geblieben, was sie war, und an ihm ist nichts verändert worden. Dadurch ist also nichts gewonnen als ein gefälliger Wahn des Augenblicks, der beim Erwachen verschwindet ...*

"*Die wahre Kunst aber hat es nicht bloß auf ein vorübergehendes Spiel abgesehen; es ist ihr Ernst damit, den Menschen nicht bloß in einen augenblicklichen Traum von Freiheit zu versetzen, sondern ihn wirklich und in der Tat frei zu machen, und dieses dadurch, daß sie eine Kraft in ihm erweckt, übt und ausbildet, die sinnliche Welt, die sonst nur als ein roher Stoff auf uns lastet, als eine blinde Macht auf uns drückt, in eine objektive Ferne zu rücken, in ein freies Werk unseres Geistes zu verwandeln und das Materielle durch Ideen zu beherrschen.*

"*Und eben darum, weil die reale Kunst etwas Reelles und Objektives will, so kann sie sich nicht bloß mit dem Schein der Wahrheit begnügen;*

auf der Wahrheit selbst, auf dem festen und tie-
fen Grunde der Natur errichtet sie ihr ideales
Gebäude.

"Wie aber nun die Kunst zugleich ganz ideell
und doch im tiefsten Sinne reell sein—wie sie
das Wirkliche ganz verlassen und doch aufs ge-
nauste mit der Natur übereinstimmen soll und
kann, das ist's was wenige fassen. . . .

"Durch Einführung einer metrischen Sprache ist
man indes der poetischen Tragödie schon um
einen großen Schritt näher gekommen. Die Ein-
führung des Chors wäre der letzte, der entschei-
dende Schritt—und wenn derselbe auch nur dazu
diente, dem Naturalism in der Kunst offen und
ehrlich den Krieg zu erklären, so sollte er uns
eine lebendige Mauer sein, die die Tragödie
um sich herumzieht, um sich von der wirklichen
Welt rein abzuschließen, und sich ihren idealen
Boden, ihre poetische Freiheit zu bewahren . . ."

In this drama metrical speech was to surpass the
splendor it displays in his other dramas.

"The tragic poet surrounds his strictly delimited
action and the sharp delineations of his characters with a weft of lyrical splendor in which,
as in a far-flung purple drapery, the acting personages move free and noble with dignified restraint and lofty serenity."

"[Es] umgibt der tragische Dichter seine streng
abgemessene Handlung und die festen Umrisse
seiner handelnden Figuren mit einem lyrischen
Prachtgewebe, in welchem sich, wie in einem
weitgefalteten Purpurgewand, die handelnden
Personen frei und edel mit einer gehaltenen Wür-
de und hoher Ruhe bewegen."

And we do indeed encounter here lines which may
be reckoned among the finest of Schiller's later lyric
verse, among the finest in the German language.

"The chorus abandons the narrow circle of the action to discourse on past and future, distant ages and peoples, the entire range of things human, in order to draw the great conclusions of life and to pronounce the teachings of wisdom. But it does this with the full power of the imagination, with a bold lyric freedom that marches with the pace of gods about the high peaks of human affairs—and it does so to the accompaniment of the entire sensual power of rhythm and of music in tone and gesture. . . .

Just as the chorus brings life to language, so does it bring calm into action—but the beautiful and lofty calm which must be the character of a noble work of art. For the spectator's feelings must retain their freedom even amid the most vehement passion; they must not be the victim of impressions, but rather they must come away serene and clear from the agitations sustained. What common judgment finds objectionable in the chorus, namely, that it breaks the illusion and interferes with the force of the affects, is just what serves as its highest recommendation. For it is precisely this blind power of affects that the true artist avoids, it is precisely this illusion that he scorns to arouse. If the blows with which tragedy afflicts our hearts were to follow one upon another uninterruptedly, affliction would prevail over activity. We would be confused amid the subject matter and no longer float above it. The chorus, by holding the parts separate and by intervening between the passions with its calming observations, gives us back our freedom, which would otherwise be lost in the storm of emotional agitation. The tragic persons likewise have need of this respite, this calm, to collect themselves, for they are not real beings that merely obey the force of the moment and represent mere individuals, but ideal personages and representatives

of their class, who pronounce upon the profound in mankind."

"Der Chor verläßt den engen Kreis der Handlung, um sich über Vergangenes und Künftiges, über ferne Zeiten und Völker, über das Menschliche überhaupt zu verbreiten, um die großen Resultate des Lebens zu ziehen und die Lehren der Weisheit auszusprechen. Aber er tut dieses mit der vollen Macht der Phantasie, mit einer kühnen lyrischen Freiheit, welche auf den hohen Gipfeln der menschlichen Dinge wie mit Schritten der Götter einhergeht—und er tut es, von der ganzen sinnlichen Macht des Rhythmus und der Musik in Tönen und Bewegungen begleitet . . .

So wie der Chor in die Sprache Leben bringt, so bringt er Ruhe in die Handlung—aber die schöne und hohe Ruhe, die der Charakter eines edlen Kunstwerkes sein muß. Denn das Gemüt des Zuschauers soll auch in der heftigsten Passion seine Freiheit behalten; es soll kein Raub der Eindrücke sein, sondern sich immer klar und heiter von den Rührungen scheiden, die es erleidet. Was das gemeine Urteil an dem Chor zu tadeln pflegt, daß er die Täuschungen aufhebe, daß er die Gewalt der Affekte breche, das gereicht ihm zu seiner höchsten Empfehlung; denn eben diese blinde Gewalt der Affekte ist es, die der wahre Künstler vermeidet, diese Täuschung ist es, die er zu erregen verschmäht. Wenn die Schläge, womit die Tragödie unser Herz trifft, ohne Unterbrechung aufeinander folgten, so würde das Leiden über die Tätigkeit siegen. Wir würden uns mit dem Stoffe vermengen und nicht mehr über demselben schweben. Dadurch daß der Chor die Teile auseinanderhält und zwischen die Passionen mit seiner beruhigenden Betrachtung tritt, gibt er uns unsere Freiheit zurück, die im Sturm der Affekte verloren gehen würde. Auch die tragischen Personen selbst bedürfen dieses Anhalts, dieser Ruhe,

um sich zu sammeln; denn sie sind keine wirkli-
chen Wesen, die bloß der Gewalt des Moments
gehorchen und bloß ein Individuum darstellen,
sondern ideale Personen und Repräsentanten
ihrer Gattung, die das Tiefe der Menschheit aus-
sprechen . . ."

It was Schiller's belief that singing, instrumental
music and dancing, forming part of a composite work
of art of cultic significance, were necessary in order
for classical tragedy to achieve its full effect. He and
Goethe had expected their friend Zelter to provide
the music. When their hopes were disappointed, they
decided to have the lines of the chorus recited, as they
still are today, by alternate speakers in a solemn ele-
vated style. The chorus of the *Bride* has never been
performed in such a way as to bring out its full effectiveness. For this, as Schiller resignedly expressed it,
it would have to be "translated from the possible
stage (that is, the one that is available to us) to a
real stage (that is, the ideal)." The real stage, as we
know, has moved still further from what Schiller desired.

After the *Bride* was finished there came a slight
pause in Schiller's creative activity. He translated two
comedies from the French, Picard's *The Sponger (Mé-
diocre et rampant)* and *The Nephew as Uncle (Encore
des ménechmes)*. These were intended to enlarge the
repertory of the theater and to bring in some money.
And now at the end of his career, Schiller was to present the Germans with their great folk play, *William
Tell.*

The reason for his choice of subject is interesting.
It had been rumored that he was working on a William Tell play, and as a result he received more and
more inquiries about it. It was this that decided him

to look into the subject and study the sources (Johannes von Müller's *Stories of the Swiss Confederation* and Ägidius Tschudi's *Helvetian Chronicle*).

As early as 1797, Goethe had been working on the plan for a William Tell epic, but he abandoned it for the sake of his friend and put at his disposal the knowledge he had gleaned from his trips to Switzerland. In August 1802 Schiller's imagination became so fired by the story that he set to work on the play and finished it in less than six months, although the material did not lend itself easily to dramatic treatment. The action is widely separated, both temporally and geographically, and is for the most part political.

While he was still at work on the play Schiller became convinced that the subject would arouse a great deal of interest, and not merely because of current political events—Swiss freedom had been drastically curtailed by the interference of the French. *William Tell* proved to be his most popular play. It enjoyed more popularity than any of his previous dramas, as it has to the present day.

The plot is based on the revolt of the three Swiss cantons Uri, Schwyz and Unterwalden, against Austrian oppression in the person of Gessler, the Bailiff, and on Gessler's persecution of William Tell and Tell's retaliation. The tyranny of the Bailiff is the link between the two actions.

In striking contrast to all Schiller's other plays, which have only the briefest stage directions, the first scene begins with a full description of the landscape:

"The high rocky shore of Lake Lucerne opposite Canton Schwyz. The lake forms a bay in the coast; a hut stands not far from the shore; a fisher lad is rowing about in a boat. Beyond the lake may be seen the green meadows, villages, and farmsteads of Schwyz lying in bright sunshine. To the spectator's left are visible the peaks of the

Haken surrounded by clouds; to the right, in the far distance icecapped mountains can be seen. Even before the curtain goes up there is heard the cow-calling song and also the melodious tones of the cowbells, which continue for some time after the curtain has gone up."

"*Hohes Felsenufer des Vierwaldstättersees, Schwyz gegenüber. Der See macht eine Bucht ins Land, eine Hütte is unweit dem Ufer. Fischerknabe fährt sich in einem Kahn. Über den See hinweg sieht man die grünen Matten, Dörfer und Höfe von Schwyz im hellen Sonnenschein liegen. Zur Linken des Zuschauers zeigen sich die Spitzen des Haken, mit Wolken umgeben; zur Rechten im fernen Hintergrund sieht man die Eisgebirge. Noch ehe der Vorhang aufgeht, hört man den Kuhreigen und das harmonische Geläut der Herdenglocken, welches sich auch bei eröffneter Szene noch eine Zeit lang fortsetzt.*"

And soon after that:

"The landscape is altered; a muffled roar is heard from the mountains, shadows of clouds hurry across the scene."

"*Die Landschaft verändert sich, man hört ein dumpfes Krachen von den Bergen, Schatten von Wolken laufen über die Gegend.*"

The description of the landscape is, however, not confined to the stage directions. It is constantly present in the lines of the play, which tell of towering cliffs, glaciers and avalanches, of quiet lakes and sudden storms. It is astonishing that Schiller, who never visited Switzerland, was able to paint from his imagination so vivid and accurate a picture. That he brings in so many natural sights and spectacles indicates his intention to have nature play an active role in the story. This is especially evident in the close of the Rütli scene, where the attention of the audience

is focused entirely on the spectacle of the sun rising over the snowcapped mountains. The sudden storm that overtakes Gessler in the boat after he has committed his crime suggests the indignant fury of nature itself. The emphasis on the landscape, however, is also intended to show the dependence upon nature of simple, primitive people. The songs of the fishermen, shepherds and hunters, which are sung to the cowherd's melody, the old folk tune of the Alpine shepherds, serve the same purpose. The use of music also shows a widening of Schiller's range of theatrical resources.

The opening scene is extraordinarily effective. It shows the peaceful landscape and the harmonious life of the shepherd and peasant folk. But soon disaster descends upon them. The oppression of the people by the brutal tyranny of the Emperor's Bailiff is vividly illustrated in the following scenes, which, like a symbolic prelude, anticipate all of the action to come.

The Swiss people see the traditional rights granted them by the Emperor threatened, but they are averse to violence and endure patiently until the last possible moment. It is not until an appalling crime is committed—old Melchtal is blinded as punishment for a small misdemeanor of his son—that the three cantons form an alliance on the Rütli to free the country from foreign tyranny.

William Tell, the hero who was forced by the Bailiff to shoot an apple off the head of his own child in order to save himself and the child, commits the act that arouses the entire people to rise up in revolt. Yet he acts only as a father and husband. He is no more concerned with a political ideology than are the Confederates, who are primarily taking up arms against oppression. To call *William Tell* a national drama is completely to distort the facts. Nor should it be interpreted as an indication of Schiller's sympathy for the

French Revolution. The play's dedication to Karl Theodor von Dalberg contrasts the Confederates' fight for freedom with the French Revolution and clearly sides with the former.

"When savage forces hostilely contend
And blinded fury feeds the flames of war;
When in the strife of parties without end
The voice of Justice can be heard no more;
When all the vices are set free to rend,
When despots' whims profane what men adore
And hoist the anchor on which states rely,
That is no theme for joyous songs to try.

"But when a people, pasturing its herds,
Contented, coveting no alien gain,
Casts off restraint ignoble beyond words,
Yet in its anger honors the humane,
Humble with all that victory affords,
That is immortal, fit for poet's strain.
I show you such a picture in my play.
You know it: greatness is your innate way."

*"Wenn rohe Kräfte feindlich sich entzweien,
Und blinde Wut die Kriegesflamme schürt;
Wenn sich im Kampfe tobender Parteien
Die Stimme der Gerechtigkeit verliert;
Wenn alle Laster schamlos sich befreien,
Wenn freche Willkür an das Heilge rührt,
Den Anker löst, an dem die Staaten hängen—
Das ist kein Stoff zu freudigen Gesängen.*

*"Doch wenn ein Volk, das fromm die Herden
weidet,
Sich selbst genug, nicht fremden Guts begehrt,
Den Zwang abwirft, den es unwürdig leidet,
Doch selbst im Zorn die Menschlichkeit noch
ehrt,
Im Glücke selbst, im Siege sich bescheidet:
Das ist unsterblich und des Liedes wert.*

177

Und solch ein Bild darf ich dir freudig zeigen.
Du kennst's, denn alles Große ist dein eigen."

William Tell differs from all of Schiller's other plays in that it does not have a tragic ending. Nor is there any tragic guilt to be expiated. While the motives of Tell's deed are originally purely personal, the deed works for the good and the salvation of his people. The folk play thus becomes a hymn to the "limits of a tyrant's power." While it has dramatic climaxes that are extremely effective it is more in the nature of a pageant, a heroic idyll, especially in its culmination in the Rütli scene. It is performed in Switzerland even today with large crowds of people participating, and is a highly colorful panorama.

The world that the poet portrays is a healthy world, a world in which idea and reality seem to have been reconciled. This reflects Schiller's own state of mind.

Schiller lived for only a year after he had finished *William Tell*. It was a year of painful physical suffering. All his last dramas were written in the intervals between attacks, which followed one another more and more closely.

Although fully aware that he might not have long to live, he thought that he would still have time to strike out in a new direction. If he could live to the age of fifty, as he often observed to his friends, he would at least have provided for his children's education.

It was for these reasons that he accepted the invitation of Iffland, the intendant of the Berlin Theater, to visit him in Berlin. Queen Louise was anxious to keep him there permanently. While he was tempted by the higher income he would have had there and the lively intellectual life of the big city, he finally decided not to stay because he could not bring himself to leave Weimar and Goethe.

After his return from Berlin he had a new attack,

more painful and violent than any before. It was only after some months that he was able to do any work at all. In March 1804, with death staring him in the face, he decided to write a play called *Demetrius*. He chose this subject after long hesitation instead of Warbeck, a figure which had interested him for years. This time, he said, he hoped to surpass all his previous dramas. The character of the hero and the action of the play —the first act and the major part of the second act are in nearly final form—indicate that in all probability he would have realized his ambition. The plans have been preserved in full, which is not the case with Schiller's other dramas, and they provide excellent insight into his method of work. The 442 pages in folio contain excerpts from books on Russia, thoughts on the construction of the plot, outlines and sketches.

The starting point of the tragedy is the hero's belief that he is of royal blood and is therefore the rightful claimant to the Russian throne. At the height of his power he learns that he has been only a tool in the hands of a schemer, and with frightful suddenness a change comes over him. A profound split takes place in his being, and the gay self-confidence to which he owes his rise to power is destroyed. Deprived of belief in himself and his right to the throne, he stands on ground that crumbles beneath him. But he cannot stop. Too many people believe in him and have made his cause their own. A victim of deception himself, he must now resort to lies and intrigue. He cannot avoid the use of tyrannical power, ultimately stirring up resistance which finally leads to his downfall.

On the last days of Schiller's life we have a report by his sister-in-law Caroline, who wrote in her biography *Schiller's Life*:

"Schiller's physical strength had visibly declined since the attack in Jena. His complexion had

changed, turning gray, which often frightened me. But his mind remained strong and alert. Who is ready to give his belief to the worst? In all extremities, hope survives in the recesses of our hearts, guarding its delicate sprig so the first breath of mild air may draw from it a promise of new life. So it was with us. Schiller himself seemed to give thought to everything that might alleviate his condition and prolong his life. He thought riding might do him good. He had bought a gentle horse from a friend and was looking forward to taking it out come spring. Some time ago we had induced him to keep a horse in Jena, but he very soon sold it again. He could not enjoy it, he said, for this was an expense for him alone, and his family did not share the enjoyment.

"During his last years he often longed to travel and see more of the world's wonders. We enjoyed making plans and talked about the best way of getting near the ocean which he would have liked very much to see, but we never went beyond planning, and within a few days the habit of quiet endeavor and the joy of creative work would again win the upper hand. The last spring of his life, he had the ever-recurring desire to visit Switzerland and compare the land of Tell with his own description of it. We seized upon this and began to discuss various plans. He listened, but more than once he said: 'Any project involving me must not extend beyond two years.'

"To see Bauerbach again, where he had spent his first days of freedom, was likewise a recurrent wish of his last years. The little green valley in its wooded surroundings was a pleasant sight in his reminiscent imagination. But our worry lest a sudden attack of his illness might befall him far from all possibility of proper care, as well as other practical difficulties, prevented us from carrying out this plan.

"The last winter, the life we led was particu-

larly rich in things to remember. An unspeakable mellowness pervaded Schiller's entire being and was manifest in all his opinions and reactions. A veritable *pax Dei* reigned in his soul. I was reading Livy at the time, and Roman history was a frequent topic of conversation for us. Once he observed: Since the splendor and the grandeur of life, which can flourish only among free men, had declined with the Roman Republic, something new had needs to arise. It was Christianity that led to a new exaltation of the life of the spirit and cast humanity in a new mold by opening up a higher perspective for the soul.

"On Herder's *Ideas Relating to the History of Mankind* we had often disagreed in the past. He respected the book, but my lively appreciation of it he could not fully accept. 'I don't know what it is,' he told me in the early days of his last spring, 'but now this book speaks to me in a very different way, and it is very dear to me.' I still remember a conversation about death and how Schiller summed it up in the beautiful words: 'Death can be no evil; it is so universal.'

"He gave much thought to the education of his boys. He watched their progress painstakingly and worked out plans for their future existence in accordance with the distinctive character of each. On the last walk I took with him through the park he said: 'If only I could put aside enough for the children to save them from depending on others. That thought is unbearable to me!'

"A few weeks before his last illness he heard Mademoiselle Schmalz sing at my home. Her soulful recital moved him deeply. She sang Zingarelli's beautiful aria from *Romeo and Juliet,* 'Ombra adorata aspetta,' and Schiller confessed to me that no song had ever stirred him as deeply as this. It seemed that imminent dissolution had sharpened all the organs of his heart and of his soul.

"The last time we rode together to the theater—

it was a play by Schröder that was given that night
—he remarked that something very strange was
going on inside him; on his left side, which had
not been free from pain in years, he now felt
nothing at all. The autopsy revealed his left lung
to be completely destroyed.

"On May 1, Schiller's last illness began with the
usual symptoms of one of his frequent episodes
of catarrhal fever. He did not seem to feel more
seriously ill than on similar occasions in the past.
He received some friends in his room and clearly
enjoyed their conversation. Herr von Cotta called,
passing through Weimar on his way to Leipzig,
and Schiller was delighted to see him. All matters
of business that were pending between them were
to be taken care of at the time of his return.

"Since Schiller's cough grew worse when he
talked, we tried to keep him quiet. And then, he
liked best to see only my sister and myself near
him. Good old Heinrich Voss offered to stay with
him nights; but Schiller preferred to be alone with
his faithful servant.

"*Demetrius* was constantly on his mind. The
interruption of this work distressed him. The physician we had called had never before treated him
for a similar illness. In such situations Schiller
had always been under the care of Dr. Stark, but
he had accompanied the Grand Duchess to Leipzig. The physician tried to put our minds at ease,
assuring us that all the prescriptions were correct
and that his treatment followed Stark's method in
every detail.

"Till the sixth day Schiller's head was entirely
clear. He himself did not seem to believe that
his illness was unusually dangerous. He even remarked that he had given a great deal of thought
to his condition in the course of the last few days
and that he thought he had devised a method
that would improve matters. It did not enter his

mind that he might make arrangements for the future of his family once he had departed. My husband was with the Grand Duchess at Leipzig. Schiller was eagerly waiting for his return. It is possible that he wished to discuss with him various matters of a practical nature.

"On May 6, toward nightfall, he began to speak disconnectedly, but he never lost consciousness. His perception remained clear. Everything incongruous had to be removed. A copy of Kotzebue's periodical had somehow got into his room. 'Please take it away,' he asked, 'so that I can truthfully say I never saw it. Give me fairy tales and stories of knights. That is where the material for everything great and beautiful lies.'

"When I went to see him the night of May 7, he wished to start a conversation of the accustomed sort on suitable subjects for tragedies and the ways and means by which the higher forces in men must be stimulated. In my replies I did not show my normal eagerness, for I meant to keep him quiet. He felt this and said: 'Well, if no one understands me any more, if I too don't understand myself any more, I think I had better stop talking.' Soon afterwards he dozed off, but he spoke a great deal in his sleep. 'Is that your hell, is that your heaven?' he exclaimed before he awoke. Then he looked up with a gentle smile as though a consoling apparition were beckoning to him. He took some soup, and when I took leave of him he said: 'I expect to sleep well this night, God willing.'

"The morning hours of May 8 he spent in comparative comfort, quiet and often half sleeping. When I arrived toward evening, standing by the side of his bed and asking how he felt, he pressed my hand and said: 'All the time better and more cheerful.' I sensed that he was not talking about his physical condition. Those were his last words

to me, the last words I heard from his cherished lips. He indicated that he wanted me to open the curtains. He wished to see the sun. With serenity in his eyes he looked into the beautiful evening light, and nature received his last farewell. He rarely asked to see his children. His youngest daughter, who had been taken to his bedside in the early hours of May 8, he had watched with pleasure and joy. His good servant, who spent the nights with him, said that he had spoken a great deal, mostly about *Demetrius,* from which he had recited whole scenes. A few times he had implored God to save him from a slow death. His prayer was heard. In the morning of May 9 he fell unconscious. He uttered only disconnected words, mostly Latin.

"The bath that had been prescribed for him he did not seem to like, but in all things concerned with his care he was cooperative and patient. The physician had thought necessary to make him take a glass of champagne to stimulate his sinking energies. It was the last thing he drank. The pressure in his chest was apparently not very painful. When he felt it coming, he sank back into his pillows and looked around, but he did not seem to recognize us.

"By three o'clock he was completely passive; his respiration was irregular. My sister knelt at his bedside. She said he pressed her hand. I stood at the foot of the bed and with the physician put warmed pillows over his feet. Something like an electric discharge flashed through the features of his face. His head sank back. The most perfect calm reigned in his expression. His features were those of one restfully asleep. It was Thursday morning, May 9, 1805."

Marfa's monologue from Act Two of *Demetrius* was found on Schiller's desk. We have in it his last lines. Their vibrant diction and loftiness of thought

belie our knowledge that he who wrote them felt the hand of death already on his shoulder. They are Schiller's farewell, the final testimony of his searching will to freedom and fulfillment.

"He was taken from the world in the fullness of his powers," wrote Wilhelm von Humboldt in his essay "On Schiller and the Progress of His Thought." "His goal was so exalted that he could never reach the end, and the ever-active drive of his intellect would have allowed no fear lest he reach a standstill. For a long time to come he might have enjoyed the bliss of poetic creation. His life ended before completing its due course, but while it lasted he was concerned—exclusively and unremittingly—with matters in the realm of the ideas and the imagination. Of no one could we say more truthfully that 'he had cast away the fears of earthly things, leaving behind the dungeon of life and taking refuge in the domains of the ideal.' He lived surrounded only by the highest ideas and the most brilliant imagery that man is able to absorb or can produce. Who departs thus is truly in possession of the gifts of fortune."

The following account of Schiller's burial is taken from the concluding chapter of Ludwig Bellermann's biography of the poet.

"It was the custom in Weimar to dispose of burials in the quiet of night without any pomp. The right to carry the dead for a fee rotated among the guilds. Schiller's burial was to take place in this manner the night of May 11. It happened to be the tailors' turn. There was no one to take care of these practical matters. Lotte was overwhelmed with grief and had asked Councilor of the Consistory Günther to attend to everything. Goethe was ill, Wolzogen not home, the Court away. A young admirer of Schiller, the later

185

Burgomaster of Weimar, Schwabe, sensed the impropriety of such a funeral and succeeded (against considerable resistance) in making the last-minute change that instead of the tailors' carrying the remains of the great man for money to his final resting place, this duty of honor was to be assumed by twenty young men from the upper classes, including scholars, artists, and civil servants, with Schwabe himself in the lead. But the established hour could not be changed. In profound silence the little procession moved through the streets. It was a beautiful night. 'Never,' said Caroline, 'have I heard so persistent and full-sounding a song of nightingales as then.' At the cemetery, Schiller's brother-in-law, Wolzogen, joined the nocturnal procession. Upon receiving the sad news in Naumburg, he had hurried home on horseback.

"The following afternoon a memorial service was held at St. James's Church. It began and ended with songs from Mozart's *Requiem*, and Superintendent General Voigt (Herder's successor) spoke the funeral oration. The body was laid to rest in the so-called *Landschaftskassengewölbe*. Twenty years later the vault was opened, and a great many coffins were found, all badly decomposed. One of these was Schiller's. But it was still possible to single out his bones. Upon the Grand Duke's wish, the skull was preserved in the pedestal of Schiller's bust at the library. Subsequently it was reunited with the other bones and taken to a dignified resting place in the Princes' Vault. There Karl August now lies with his two poets.

"Throughout those difficult days, Goethe was prevented by his own illness from participating in the events. During the preceding period he had been extremely depressed and sensed the imminence of his great loss. Once Voss found him weeping in his garden, and when he talked to him about Schiller's ill-

ness, Goethe said only: 'Fate is inexorable, and man is small.' When death had come, no one dared tell him. Heinrich Meyer was with him when the news was received. He was called out, but he had not the heart to go in again, and he left without taking leave. The loneliness in which Goethe now found himself, the confusion which he read in the faces of those around him, the eagerness with which everyone seemed to avoid him, all these things affected him deeply. 'I sense,' he said finally, 'Schiller must be very ill,' and the rest of the evening he was completely withdrawn in himself. During the night he was heard weeping. The following morning he could bear it no longer and said to Christiane: 'It is true, is it not, Schiller was *very* ill yesterday.' The way he stressed the word 'very' was too much for her; she lost control of herself, and instead of replying she sobbed loudly. 'He is dead?' Goethe now asked with a firm voice. 'You spoke the word yourself,' she answered. Then he just repeated, 'He is dead,' turned away, and covered his eyes with both hands. In a letter to Zelter he wrote a few days later: 'I thought I was about to lose myself, and now I lose a friend and with him half my existence.'

"In Goethe's *Day and Year Books* we read that his first thought upon 'getting hold of himself' was to complete the *Demetrius*, the outline of which was as clear to his mind as it had been to Schiller's. 'I had the burning desire to continue our intercourse in spite of death, to show our traditional collaboration in this at its ultimate climax. His loss seemed replaced if I continued his life.' But there were obstacles in the way of this plan, and it was never carried out. The same holds true for a great memorial celebration that was planned for the stage. It was to have been a solemn symbolic act: The god of death, Thanatos, was to appear; and choruses of young men and women, of

warriors, and of old people—and, joining them, 'the Wife' and 'the Friend'—were to express their love, their prayer for salvation, their pain. Zelter promised to provide the music. But nothing beyond a hasty sketch was done. Reading it we regret sorely that no more was accomplished, even if we think only of these two lines spoken by the chorus of young men:

> 'And his nights of sleepless hours
> Cast new light in our days.'

> *'Seine durchgewachten Nächte*
> *Haben unsern Tag erhellt.'*

"We cannot help being saddened by the fact that Goethe carried out neither of these projects and likewise that in those days he did not have the strength to impart form and dignity to the funeral ceremony. But we must not chide the great man for what he did not do because his soul was suffocated with pain. For he did give his sorrow form and word, mightier and more dignified than anyone before or after. For the memorial celebration on August 10, 1805, in which the 'Song of the Bell' was dramatized on the Lauchstädt stage, Goethe wrote the 'Epilogue to Schiller's Song of the Bell.' No more glorious words were ever sounded in the German language. Like the majestic surge of the waves in the ocean, so these immortal lines roll along, borne by friendship and poetry, presenting the innermost being of the departed lovingly and thoughtfully in sublime and in friendly pictures and setting in manly resignation a limit to mourning death's having taken him who deserved to live:

> 'For he was ours. Proudly said, this word
> Shall echo far beyond all plaintive mourning.'"

> *'Denn er war unser! Mag das stolze Wort*
> *Den lauten Schmerz gewaltig übertönen!'"*

For the survivor the image of his departed friend became transfigured into one of purest piety. "No one is worthy of Schiller unless he honors and reveres him," Goethe cried to his daughter-in-law, Ottilie. "All of you are much too trivial and worldly for him." His admiration for Schiller's spiritual and moral greatness inspired him to write the verses in his "Epilogue to Schiller's Song of the Bell":

"Behind him lay, in waning haze reflected,
The coarse-grained stuff that keeps us all
    subjected."

*"Und hinter ihm, in wesenlosem Scheine,
Lag, was uns alle bändigt, das Gemeine."*

There was in him "an innate Christ-like tendency," Goethe wrote to Zelter on November 30, 1830: "He never touched anything common without ennobling it." This elevating and lofty quality is the result of the forceful determination with which he stipulates that human existence has an absolute meaning: even in the prison of circumstance man can preserve his inner freedom, can determine his own fate and, "as the great task of his life," can realize "the pure, idealistic human being" which everyone "by disposition and destiny" bears within him. Man must not expect to find greatness and worth already present in life; it is up to him to create his world.

"Verily, a noble soul
Does not seek in life for greatness
But puts greatness into it."

*"Wisset, ein erhabener Sinn
Legt das Große in das Leben
Und er sucht es nicht darin."*

No intellectual history of Europe can pass over Schiller's influence. To consider his message outmoded

is a dangerous fallacy reflecting the misguided belief that what is universally human can ever become obsolete and must give way to "the wave of the future."

What could be more timely today than Schiller's appeal, written some 160 years ago, that men "work quietly at establishing better concepts, nobler principles, and purer morals, since in the end it is upon these that all improvements of social conditions depend"?

To trace the path of Schiller's spirit and take possession anew of the great legacy he left to all those coming after him is an intellectual and ethical experience of unique power.

In the words of Hugo von Hofmannsthal, who in this gave voice to the mood of the élite of the early twentieth century and, unwittingly, to our mood as well:

> "We who have come to share the fate of being citizens of a sorely harassed world turn to the memory of the great of the past, not to enjoy but to learn by what means to achieve a renascence. Beyond the reach of the phantoms of the age we seek the great ideas to guide us in the endeavor. With other secular fears we cast off the fears of the age. More and more our present is but a veil, and the awareness of a sublimer present emerges. In it the light of Schiller greets us like a lodestar of the ages."

What Hugo von Hofmannsthal here means to convey is akin to what Goethe expressed in his deeply felt words of farewell at the end of his "Epilogue to Schiller's Song of the Bell":

> "Beyond us, comet-wise, he soars, aspiring,
> With his own light unfathomed light acquiring."

> *"Er schwebt uns vor wie ein Komet entschwindend,*
> *Unendlich Licht mit seinem Licht verbindend."*

PART TWO

DIE GESETZGEBUNG DES LYKURGUS UND SOLON
LYKURGUS

UM den Lykurgischen Plan gehörig würdigen zu können, muß man auf die damalige politische Lage von Sparta zurücksehen und die Verfassung kennen lernen, worin er Lacedämon fand, als er seinen neuen Entwurf zum Vorschein brachte. Zwei Könige, beide mit gleicher Gewalt versehen, standen an der Spitze des Staats; jeder eifersüchtig auf den andern, jeder geschäftig, sich einen Anhang zu machen und dadurch die Gewalt seines Throngehilfen zu beschränken. Diese Eifersucht hatte sich von den zwei ersten Königen Prokles und Eurysthen auf ihre beiderseitigen Linien bis auf Lykurg fortgeerbt, daß Sparta während dieses langen Zeitraums unaufhörlich von Faktionen beunruhigt wurde. Jeder König suchte durch Bewilligung großer Freiheiten das Volk zu bestechen, und diese Bewilligungen führten das Volk zur Frechheit und endlich zum Aufruhr. Zwischen Monarchie und Demokratie schwankte der Staat hin und wider und ging mit schnellem Wechsel von einem Extrem auf das andre über. Zwischen den Rechten des Volks und der Gewalt der Könige waren noch keine Grenzen gezeichnet, der Reichtum floß in wenigen Familien zusammen. Die reichen Bürger tyrannisierten die armen, und die Verzweiflung der letztern äußerte sich in Empörung.

Von innerer Zwietracht zerrissen, mußte der schwache Staat die Beute seiner kriegrischen Nachbarn werden oder in mehrere kleinere Tyrannien zerfallen. So fand Lykurgus Sparta: unbestimmte Grenzen der königlichen und Volksgewalt, ungleiche Austeilung der Glücksgüter unter den Bürgern, Mangel an Gemeingeist und Eintracht und eine gänzliche politische Entkräftung waren die Übel, die sich dem Gesetzgeber am dringendsten darstellten, auf die er also bei seiner Gesetzgebung vorzüglich Rücksicht nahm.

Als der Tag erschien, wo Lykurgus seine Gesetze bekannt machen wollte, ließ er dreißig der vornehmsten Bürger, die er vorher zum Besten seines Planes gewonnen hatte, bewaffnet auf dem Marktplatz erscheinen, um denen, die sich etwa widersetzen würden, Furcht einzujagen. Der König

THE LEGISLATION
OF
LYCURGUS AND SOLON

LYCURGUS

In order properly to appreciate the plan of Lycurgus, we must take a look at the political situation in Sparta at that period and study the constitution that existed when he came forward with his new proposal. Two kings, each having equal power, were at the head of the government; each jealous of the other, each endeavoring to build up a following of his own and thereby to limit the power of his associate. This jealousy had been handed down by the two first kings, Procles and Eurysthenes, to their respective descendants until the time of Lycurgus, with the result that during this long period Sparta was continually disturbed by factions. Each king sought to bribe the people by granting extraordinary liberties, and these concessions finally made the people insolent and rebellious. The state fluctuated back and forth between monarchy and democracy, passing rapidly from one extreme to the other. No fixed lines of demarcation has as yet been drawn between the rights of the people and the powers of royalty. Wealth accumulated in a few families. The rich citizens tyrannized over the poor and the despair of the latter expressed itself in rebellion.

Torn by internal discord, the feeble republic had either to become the prey of its warlike neighbors or split up into several small tyrannies. It was in this condition that Lycurgus found Sparta: with ill-defined limits to royal and popular powers, with an unequal distribution of property among its citizens, lacking in public spirit and unity and in a state of complete political exhaustion. These were the evils that most urgently claimed the attention of the legislator and which he had, therefore, chiefly to consider in framing his laws.

On the day that Lycurgus wished to promulgate his laws, he had thirty of the most prominent citizens, whom he had previously won over to his cause, appear in the marketplace. They were armed in order to instil fear in those who might oppose him. King Charilaus, frightened

Charilaus, von diesen Anstalten in Schrecken gesetzt, entfloh in den Tempel der Minerva, weil er glaubte, daß die ganze Sache gegen ihn gerichtet sei. Aber man benahm ihm diese Furcht und brachte ihn sogar dahin, daß er selbst den Plan des Lykurgus tätig unterstützte.

Die erste Einrichtung betraf die Regierung. Um künftig auf immer zu verhindern, daß die Republik zwischen königlicher Tyrannei und anarchischer Demokratie hin und her geworfen würde, legte Lykurgus eine dritte Macht als Gegengewicht in die Mitte: er gründete einen *Senat*. Die Senatoren, 28 an der Zahl und also 30 mit den Königen, sollten auf die Seite des Volks treten, wenn die *Könige* ihre Gewalt mißbrauchten, und, wenn im Gegenteil die Gewalt des Volks zu groß werden wollte, die Könige gegen dasselbe in Schutz nehmen. Eine vortreffliche Anordnung, wodurch Sparta auf immer allen den gewaltsamen innern Stürmen entging, die es bisher erschüttert hatten. Dadurch ward es jedem Teile unmöglich gemacht, den andern unter die Füße zu treten; gegen Senat und Volk konnten die Könige nichts ausrichten, und ebenso wenig konnte das Volk das Übergewicht erhalten, wenn der Senat mit den Königen gemeine Sache machte.

Aber einem dritten Fall hatte Lykurgus nicht begegnet — wenn nämlich der Senat selbst seine Macht mißbrauchte. Der Senat konnte sich als ein Mittelglied, ohne Gefahr der öffentlichen Ruhe, gleich leicht mit den Königen wie mit dem Volk verbinden, aber ohne große Gefahr des Staats durften sich die Könige nicht mit dem Volk gegen den Senat vereinigen. Dieser letzte fing daher bald an, diese vorteilhafte Lage zu benutzen und einen ausschweifenden Gebrauch von seiner Gewalt zu machen, welches um so mehr gelang, da die geringe Anzahl der Senatoren es ihnen leicht machte, sich mit einander einzuverstehen. Der Nachfolger des Lykurgus ergänzte deswegen diese Lücke und führte die Ephoren ein, welche der Macht des Senats einen Zaum anlegten.

Gefährlicher und kühner war die zweite Anordnung, welche Lykurgus machte. Diese war: das ganze Land in gleichen Teilen unter den Bürgern zu verteilen und den Un-

by these moves, fled to the temple of Minerva, believing that the whole affair was directed against him. But his fears were allayed and he was even prevailed upon to give active support to Lycurgus' plan.

The first innovation concerned the government. In order to prevent the republic in future from wavering between royal tyranny and anarchical democracy, Lycurgus created a third power to counterbalance the other two. He established a *senate*. The senators, of whom there were twenty-eight, making thirty with the kings, were to side with the people if the kings abused their power. On the other hand, if the people were to become too powerful, the senators would side with the kings and protect them from the people. An excellent arrangement by means of which Sparta was permanently relieved of all the violent, internal commotions that had previously convulsed it. By this means each party was prevented from trampling on the other. Opposed by both senate and people, the kings were powerless to perpetrate anything; nor could the people arrogate the power if the senate and the kings joined forces against them.

But Lycurgus had overlooked a third contingency: that the senate itself might abuse its power. As an intermediary agent, the senate could easily join with either the kings or the people without imperiling the public peace, but the kings could not unite with the people against the senate without greatly endangering the safety of the state. The senate soon began to make use of its advantageous position in an extravagant manner. In this it succeeded all the more readily since the small number of senators made it easy for them to reach an agreement among themselves. Lycurgus' successor filled this gap by introducing the ephors who were to keep the power of the senate in check.

The second innovation made by Lycurgus was bolder and more dangerous. This was to divide the entire country into equal portions between the citizens and to abolish

terschied zwischen Reichen und Armen auf immerdar aufzuheben. Ganz Lakonien wurde in 30000 Felder, der Acker um die Stadt Sparta selbst in 9000 Felder geteilt, jedes groß genug, daß eine Familie reichlich damit auskommen konnte. Sparta gab jetzt einen schönen reizenden Anblick, und Lykurgus selbst weidete sich an diesem Schauspiel, als er in der Folge das Land durchreiste. "Ganz Lakonien", rief er aus, "gleicht einem Acker, den Brüder brüderlich unter sich teilten."

Ebenso gerne wie die Äcker hätte Lykurgus auch die beweglichen Güter verteilt, aber diesem Vorhaben sellten sich unüberwindliche Schwierigkeiten entgegen. Er versuchte also durch Umwege zu diesem Ziele zu gelangen und das, was er nicht durch ein Machtwort aufheben konnte, von sich selbst fallen zu machen.

Er fing damit an, alle goldnen und silbernen Münzen zu verbieten und an ihrer Statt eiserne einzuführen. Zugleich gab er einem großen und schweren Stück Eisen einen sehr geringen Wert, daß man einen großen Raum brauchte, um eine kleine Geldsumme aufzubewahren, und viele Pferde, um sie fortzuschaffen. Ja, damit man nicht einmal versucht werden möchte, dieses Geld des *Eisens* wegen zu schätzen und zusammenzuscharren, so ließ er das Eisen, welches dazu genommen wurde, vorher glühend in Essig löschen und härten, wodurch es zu jedem andern Gebrauch untüchtig wurde. Wer sollte nun stehlen oder sich bestechen lassen oder Reichtümer aufzuhäufen trachten, da der kleine Gewinn weder verhehlt noch genutzt werden konnte?

Nicht genug, daß Lykurg seinen Mitbürgern dadurch die *Mittel* zur Üppigkeit entzog—er rückte ihnen auch die *Gegenstände* derselben aus den Augen, die sie dazu hätten reizen können. Spartas eiserne Münze konnte kein fremder Kaufmann brauchen, und eine andre hatten sie ihm nicht zu geben. Alle Künstler, die für den Luxus arbeiteten, verschwanden jetzt aus Lakonien, kein auswärtiges Schiff erschien mehr in seinen Häfen; kein Abenteurer zeigte sich mehr, sein Glück in diesem Lande zu suchen, kein Kaufmann kam, die Eitelkeit und Wollust zu brandschatzen, denn sie konnten nichts mit sich hinwegnehmen als eiserne

forever the disinction between rich and poor. All of Laconia was divided into thirty thousand shares, the land around the city of Sparta itself into nine thousand, each sufficient to provide abundant support for a family. Sparta now became a beautiful and charming sight to behold, and Lycurgus delighted in the spectacle when he traveled through the country. "All Laconia," he exclaimed, "is like a field which brothers have shared with one another as brothers."

Lycurgus would also have liked to distribute movable property, but invincible obstacles prevented him from carrying out this measure. He therefore tried to achieve this end by a circuitous route and to cause what he had been unable to abolish by decree to disappear of its own accord.

He began by prohibiting the use of all gold and silver coins and introducing iron coins in their stead. At the same time he assigned a trifling value to a large and heavy lump of iron, so that considerable space was required to keep a small sum of money and a large number of horses to move it. In order that no one should be tempted to set store by this money because of the iron, he had the iron used for this purpose fired to red heat and cooled and hardened in vinegar which rendered it unfit for any other use.

Who now would be tempted to steal or to accept bribes or to accumulate riches when the small profit could neither be concealed or used?

Lycurgus was not content with depriving his fellow citizens of the *means* of luxury. He also removed from sight the *objects* that could have aroused their desire for it. No foreign merchant had any use for Sparta's iron coin and there was no other kind to offer him. Artists who worked to gratify luxurious tastes now disappeared from Laconia. No foreign ship appeared in Spartan ports. No adventurous traveler appeared to seek his fortune in that country. No merchant came to exploit the vanity and voluptuousness of the Spartans, for he could take away nothing but iron coin which was despised in every

Münzen, die in allen andern Ländern verachtet wurden. Der Luxus hörte auf, weil niemand da war, der ihn unterhalten hätte.

Lykurg arbeitete noch auf eine andre Art der Üppigkeit entgegen. Er verordnete, daß alle Bürger an einem öffentlichen Orte in Gemeinschaft zusammen speisen und alle *dieselbe* vorgeschriebene Kost mit einander teilen sollten. Es war nicht erlaubt, zu Hause der Weichlichkeit zu dienen und sich durch eigne Köche kostbare Speisen zurichten zu lassen. Jeder mußte monatlich eine gewisse Summe an Lebensmitteln zu der öffentlichen Mahlzeit geben, und dafür erhielt er die Kost von dem Staat. Fünfzehn speisten gewöhnlich an einem Tische zusammen, und jeder Tischgenosse mußte alle übrigen Stimmen für sich haben, um an die Tafel aufgenommen zu werden. Wegbleiben durfte keiner ohne eine gültige Entschuldigung; dieses Gebot wurde so strenge gehalten, daß selbst Agis, einer der folgenden Könige, als er aus einem rühmlich geführten Kriege nach Sparta zurückkam und mit seiner Gemahlin allein speisen wollte, eine abschlägige Antwort von den Ephoren erhielt. Unter den Speisen der Spartaner ist die schwarze Suppe berühmt: ein Gericht, zu dessen Lobe gesagt wurde, die Spartaner hätten gut tapfer sein, weil es kein so großes Übel wäre, zu sterben, als ihre schwarze Suppe zu essen. Ihre Mahlzeit würzten sie mit Lustigkeit und Scherz, denn Lykurg selbst war so sehr ein Freund der geselligen Freude, daß er dem Gott des Lachens in seinem Hause einen Altar errichtete.

Durch die Einführung dieser gemeinschaftlichen Speisung gewann Lykurgus für seinen Zweck sehr viel. Aller Luxus an kostbarem Tafelgeräte hörte auf, weil man an dem öffentlichen Tisch keinen Gebrauch davon machen konnte. Der Schwelgerei wurde auf immer Einhalt getan; gesunde und starke Körper waren die Folge dieser Mäßigkeit und Ordnung, und gesunde Väter konnten dem Staate starke Kinder zeugen. Die gemeinschaftliche Speisung gewöhnte die Bürger, mit einander zu leben und sich als Glieder desselben Staatskörpers zu betrachten—nicht einmal zu gedenken, daß eine so gleiche Lebensweise auch auf die gleiche Stimmung der Gemüter Einfluß haben mußte.

other country. Luxury vanished because there was no one to keep it up.

Lycurgus worked in yet another way to counteract luxury. He ordered all citizens to eat together in a public place and to partake of the same prescribed fare. It was unlawful to cultivate effeminate habits at home and to have costly viands prepared by special cooks. Every month each citizen had to provide a certain quantity of foodstuffs for the public table and in return the state furnished him with the food he required. There were generally fifteen persons at a table and each person had to receive the unanimous vote of the others to be allowed to sit at the table. No one was allowed to absent himself without a valid excuse. This rule was so strictly enforced that even King Agis, one of the later kings, was refused by the ephors the privilege of dining alone with his wife after his return from a victorious campaign. Famous among Spartan dishes was the black soup. It was said in its praise that it was not difficult for the Spartans to be brave since to die was no greater misfortune than to eat their black soup. They seasoned their meals with mirth and fun, for Lycurgus was so fond of gayety that he erected an altar to the god of laughter in his own house.

By introducing the custom of common meals Lycurgus accomplished a great deal for his purpose. People no longer went in for expensive tableware since it could not be used at the public table. Excesses were prevented forever. This moderate and regulated living resulted in strong, healthy bodies, and healthy parents were able to beget robust children for the state. Eating together accustomed the citizens to living with one another and to looking upon themselves as members of the same political body. What is more, so uniform a mode of life inevitably served to produce a uniform attitude of mind.

Ein ander Gesetz verordnete, daß kein Haus ein andres Dach haben durfte, als welches mit der Axt verfertigt worden, und keine andre Türe, als die bloß mit Hilfe einer Säge gemacht worden sei. In ein so schlechtes Haus konnte sich niemand einfallen lassen kostbare Meublen zu schaffen; alles mußte sich harmonisch zu dem Ganzen stimmen.

Lykurgus begriff wohl, daß es nicht damit getan sei, Gesetze für seine Mitbürger zu schaffen; er mußte auch Bürger für diese Gesetze erschaffen. In den Gemütern der Spartaner mußte er seiner Verfassung die Ewigkeit sichern, in *diesen* mußte er die Empfänglichkeit für fremde Eindrücke ertöten.

Der wichtigste Teil seiner Gesetzgebung daher die Erziehung, und durch diese schloß er gleichsam den Kreis, in welchem der spartanische Staat sich um sich selbst bewegen sollte. Die Erziehung war ein wichtiges Werk des Staats, und der Staat ein fortdauerndes Werk dieser Erziehung.

Seine Sorgfalt für die Kinder erstreckte sich bis auf die Quellen der Zeugung. Die Körper der Jungfrauen wurden durch Leibesübungen gehärtet, um starke gesunde Kinder leicht zu gebären. Sie gingen sogar unbekleidet, um alle Unfälle der Witterung auszuhalten. Der Bräutigam mußte sie rauben und durfte sie auch nur des Nachts und verstohlen besuchen. Dadurch blieben beide in den ersten Jahren der Ehe einander immer noch fremd, und ihre Liebe blieb neu und lebendig.

Aus der Ehe selbst wurde alle Eifersucht verbannt. Alles, auch die Schamhaftigkeit, ordnete der Gesetzgeber seinem Hauptzweck unter. Er opferte die weibliche Treue auf, um gesunde Kinder für den Staat zu gewinnen.

Sobald das Kind geboren war, gehörte es dem Staat. — Vater und Mutter hatten es verloren. Es wurde von den Ältesten besichtigt; wenn es stark und wohlgebildet war, übergab man es einer Wärterin; war es schwächlich und mißgestaltet, so warf man es in einen Abgrund an dem Berge Taygetus.

Die spartanischen Wärterinnen wurden wegen der harten Erziehung, die sie den Kindern gaben, in ganz Griechenland berühmt und in entfernte Länder berufen. Sobald ein

Another law decreed that no house could have a roof not made with an axe and no door but one made only with a saw. No one dreamed of furnishing so crude a house with expensive furniture; every part of the house must be in harmony with the whole.

Lycurgus saw clearly that it was not enough to make laws for his fellow citizens; that he also had to create citizens for these laws. He had to secure perpetuity for his constitution in the minds of the Spartans; he also had to deaden their susceptibility to foreign impressions.

The most important part of his legislation was the education of children. This closed, as it were, the circle within which the Spartan republic was to revolve as a self-sufficient unit. Education was an important task of the state and the state was a continuous product of education.

His concern for future generations extended even to the fountainhead of procreation. The bodies of young females were hardened by exercise so that they would easily bear sound, robust offspring. They even went without clothes in order to become inured to all kinds of weather. The bridegroom had to abduct his bride and was permitted to visit her only at night and in secret. This prevented the man and wife from becoming too intimate with one another during the first years of their marriage and kept their love fresh and alive.

Jealously was entirely banished from the marriage relationship. The lawgiver subordinated everything to his main object, even female modesty. He sacrificed matrimonial fidelity in order to procure healthy children for the state.

As soon as the child was born it became the property of the state. It no longer belonged to its father and mother. It was examined by the elders: if it was strong and well-formed it was put in the care of a nurse; if it was weak and misshapen it was thrown from a high cliff on Mount Taygetus.

The Spartan nurses, famous throughout Greece for their rigid upbringing of the children, were called into distant countries. As soon as a boy reached his seventh year, he

Knabe das siebente Jahr erreicht hatte, wurde er ihnen genommen und mit Kindern seines Alters gemeinschaftlich
erzogen, ernährt und unterrichtet. Frühe lehrte man ihn Be-
schwerlichkeiten Trotz bieten und durch Leibesübungen
eine Herrschaft über seine Glieder erlangen. Erreichten sie
die Jünglingsjahre, so hatten die edelsten unter ihnen Hoffnung, Freunde unter den Erwachsenen zu erhalten, die durch
eine begeisterte Liebe an sie gebunden waren. Die Alten
waren bei ihren Spielen zugegen, beobachteten das auf-
keimende Genie und ermunterten die Ruhmbegierde durch
Lob oder Tadel. Wenn sie sich satt essen wollten, so mußten sie die Lebensmittel dazu stehlen, und wer sich ertappen
ließ, hatte eine harte Züchtigung und Schande zu erwarten.
Lykurgus wählte dieses Mittel, um sie frühe an List und
Ränke zu gewöhnen—Eigenschaften, die er für den kriegrischen Zweck, zu dem er sie bildete, ebenso wichtig glaubte
als Leibesstärke und Mut. Wir haben schon oben gesehen,
wie wenig gewissenhaft Lykurgus im Betreff der Sittlichkeit
war, wenn es darauf ankam, seinen politischen Zweck zu
verfolgen. Übrigens muß man in Betrachtung ziehen, daß
weder die Entweihung der Ehen noch dieser befohlene Diebstahl in Sparta den *politischen* Schaden anrichten konnten,
den sie in jedem andern Staate würden zur Folge gehabt
haben. Da der Staat die Erziehung der Kinder übernahm,
so war sie unabhängig von dem Glück und der Reinigkeit
der Ehen; da in Sparta wenig Wert auf dem Eigentum ruhte
und fast alle Güter gemeinschaftlich waren, so war die Sicherheit des Eigentums kein so wichtiger Punkt, und ein Angriff
darauf—besonders wenn der Staat selbst ihn lenkte und Absichten dadurch erreichte—kein bürgerliches Verbrechen.
Den jungen Spartanern war es verboten, sich zu schmücken,
ausgenommen wenn sie in das Treffen oder in sonst eine
große Gefahr gingen. Dann erlaubte man ihnen, ihre Haare
schön aufzuputzen, ihre Kleider zu schmücken und Zieraten
an den Waffen zu tragen. Das Haar, sagte Lykurgus, mache
schöne Leute schöner und häßliche fürchterlich. Es war gewiß ein feiner Kunstgriff des Gesetzgebers, etwas Lachen-
des und Festliches mit Gelegenheiten der Gefahr zu verbinden und ihnen dadurch das Schreckliche zu benehmen.

was taken from them and was then raised, fed and instructed with other children of the same age. Early in life he was taught to endure hardship and to acquire mastery of his body through physical exercise. When the boys grew to manhood, the noblest of them could hope to find friends among the older citizens with whom they established bonds of warm, enthusiastic affection. The old were present at the games, watched the rising genius and spurred the ambition of the young men with praise of censure. If a youth wanted a full meal, he had to steal the food, and if anyone was caught doing this, he might expect severe punishment and public disgrace. Lycurgus chose this method of teaching them to resort to cunning and intrigue at an early age. These qualities he considered as important for the warlike purpose for which he developed them as physical strength and courage. We have already pointed out how unscrupulous Lycurgus was about morality when it was a question of serving his political ends. However, we must remember that neither the profanation of marriage nor this legitimatized theft could do as much political damage in Sparta as it would have in any other state. As the state took charge of the education of children, education was independent of the happiness or purity of the marriage. Since little value was attached to possession and almost all goods were public property, security of ownership was of no great importance. An attack on property—especially when directed by the state for a definite political end—was no crime in the eyes of the law.

The young Spartans were forbidden to adorn themselves except when going to battle or to meet some other danger. At such times they were permitted to adorn their hair, to ornament their garments and arms. Lycurgus used to say that hair made handsome people more handsome and ugly people hideous. It was undoubtedly a fine trick on the part of the Lawgiver to associate festivity and mirth with dangerous ordeals and thus to eliminate the element of dread. He went still further. In time of war he some-

Er ging noch weiter. Er ließ im Kriege von der strengen Disziplin etwas nach; die Lebensart war dann freier, und Vergehungen wurden weniger hart geahndet. Daher kam es, daß der Krieg den Spartanern allein eine Art von Erholung war und daß sie sich darauf wie auf eine fröhliche Gelegenheit freuten. Rückte der Feind an, so ließ der spartanische König das Kastorische Lied anstimmen, die Soldaten rückten in festgeschlossenen Reihen unter Flötengesang fort und gingen freudig und unerschrocken, nach dem Klange der Musik, der Gefahr entgegen.

Der Plan des Lykurgus brachte es mit sich, daß die Anhänglichkeit an das Eigentum der Anhänglichkeit an das Vaterland durchaus nachstand und daß die Gemüter, durch keine Privatsorge zerstreut, nur dem Staate lebten. Darum fand er für gut und notwendig, seinen Mitbürgern auch die Geschäfte des gewöhnlichen Lebens zu ersparen und diese durch Fremdlinge verrichten zu lassen, damit auch nicht einmal die Sorge der Arbeit oder die Freude an häuslichen Geschäften ihren Geist von dem Interesse des Vaterlands abzöge. Die Äcker und das Haus wurden deswegen von Sklaven besorgt, die in Sparta dem Vieh gleich geachtet wurden. Man nennt sie Heloten, weil die ersten Sklaven der Spartaner Einwohner der Stadt Helos in Lakonien gewesen, die sie bekriegt und zu Gefangenen gemacht hatten. Von diesen Heloten führten nachher alle spartanischen Sklaven, die sie in ihren Kriegen erbeuteten, den Namen.

Abscheulich war der Gebrauch, den man in Sparta von diesen unglücklichen Menschen machte. Man betrachtete sie als ein Geräte, von dem man zu politischen Absichten, wie man wollte, Gebrauch machen könnte, und die Menschheit wurde auf eine wirklich empörende Art in ihnen verspottet. Um der spartanischen Jugend ein abschreckendes Bild von der Unmäßigkeit im Trinken zu geben, zwang man diese Heloten, sich zu betrinken, und stellte sie dann in diesem Zustand öffentlich zur Schau aus. Man ließ sie schändliche Lieder singen und lächerliche Tänze tanzen; die Tänze der Freigebornen waren ihnen verboten.

Man gebrauchte sie zu einer noch weit unmenschlichern Absicht. Es war dem Staat darum zu tun, den Mut seiner

what relaxed the severe discipline; the mode of living was a little more liberal and transgressions were punished less rigorously. Hence war became a sort of recreation for the Spartans and they anticipated it with delight like an occasion for merrymaking. At the approach of the enemy, Lycurgus ordered the Castorean hymn to be sung, and, accompanied by the music of flutes, the soldiers marched out in serried ranks to meet the danger, joyous and unafraid.

Lycurgus' legislation had the effect of subordinating attachment to private property to attachment to the national interest; relieved of personal cares, the Spartan lived exclusively for the state. He therefore considered it advisable to save his fellow citizens the trouble of attending to the ordinary business of life and to have it performed by foreigners so that their minds should not be distracted from the national interest by business worries or domestic pleasures. The labor in house and field was therefore done by slaves whose position in Sparta was on a par with that of cattle. They were called Helots because the first Spartan slaves were inhabitants of the Lacedemonian city of Helos whom the Spartans had conquered and taken prisoner. The name Helots was afterward given to all Spartan slaves who were taken in battle.

The treatment which these unhappy people endured in Sparta was inhuman. They were regarded as mere chattels to be used for political purposes as their owners pleased. In them humanity was degraded in a shocking fashion. In order to illustrate to the Spartan youths the evil effects of alcoholic liquor, these Helots were compelled to become drunk and were shown in public in this condition. They were made to sing scandalous songs and to dance grotesque dances. They were forbidden to perform the dances of the free citizens.

They were used for still more inhuman purposes. The state wished to put the courage of its boldest youths to

kühnsten Jünglinge auf schwere Proben zu setzen und sie durch blutige Vorspiele zum Kriege vorzubereiten. Der Senat schickte also zu gewissen Zeiten eine Anzahl dieser Jünglinge auf das Land; nichts als ein Dolch und etwas Speise wurde ihnen auf die Reise mitgegeben. Am Tage war ihnen auferlegt, sich verborgen zu halten; bei Nachtzeit aber zogen sie auf die Straßen und schlugen die Heloten tot, die ihnen in die Hände fielen. Diese Anstalt nannte man die Kryptia oder den Hinterhalt; aber ob Lykurgus der Stifter derselben war, ist noch im Zweifel. Wenigstens folgt sie ganz aus seinem Prinzip. Wie die Republik Sparta in ihren Kriegen glücklich war, so vermehrte sich auch die Anzahl dieser Heloten, daß sie anfingen, der Republik selbst gefährlich zu werden, und auch wirklich, durch eine so barbarische Behandlung zur Verzweiflung gebracht, Empörungen entspannen. Der Senat faßte einen unmenschlichen Entschluß, den er durch die Notwendigkeit entschuldigt glaubte. Unter dem Vorwand, ihnen die Freiheit zu schenken, wurden einmal während des peloponnesischen Kriegs 2000 der tapfersten Heloten versammelt und, mit Kränzen geschmückt, in einer feierlichen Prozession in den Tempel begleitet. Hier aber verschwanden sie plötzlich, und niemand erfuhr, was mit ihnen geworden war. So viel ist übrigens gewiß und in Griechenland zum Sprichwort geworden, daß die spartanischen Sklaven die unglückseligsten aller andern Sklaven, so wie die spartanischen freien Bürger die freiesten aller Bürger gewesen.

Weil den letztern alle Arbeiten durch die Heloten abgenommen waren, so brachten sie ihr ganzes Leben müßig zu; die Jugend übte sich in kriegerischen Spielen und Geschicklichkeiten, und die Alten waren die Zuschauer und Richter bei diesen Übungen. Einem spartanischen Greis gereichte es zur Schande, von dem Ort wegzubleiben, wo die Jugend erzogen wurde. Auf diese Art kam es, daß jeder Spartaner mit dem Staat lebte; alle Handlungen wurden dadurch *öffentliche* Handlungen. Unter den Augen der Nation reifte die Jugend heran und verblühte das Alter. Unaufhörlich hatte der Spartaner Sparta vor Augen und Sparta ihn. Er war Zeuge von allem, und alles war Zeuge seines

severe tests and to prepare them for war by bloody practices. For this purpose, at certain times of year, the Senate would send a number of young men into the country provided with nothing but a dagger and some food. They were ordered to conceal themselves by day, but at night they went out on the public roads and killed the Helots who fell into their hands. This was called Cryptia or ambush, but there is some doubt as to whether it was originated by Lycurgus. In any event, it is entirely in keeping with his system. As a result of successful wars, the number of Helots grew so considerable that they became a source of danger to the state. Driven to despair by this barbarous treatment, they incited rebellions. The Senate hit upon an inhuman expedient which it justified on the grounds of necessity. Proclaiming that it would grant them their liberty, the Senate assembled two thousand of the bravest Helots on a certain occasion during the Pelopennesian War, and, adorned with wreaths, they were conducted to the temples in solemn procession. Here they suddenly vanished and nobody ever knew what had become of them. This much is certain, and it became a common saying among the Greeks that Spartan slaves were the most miserable of all slaves and Spartan citizens the freest of all citizens.

Since all labor was performed by the Helots, the citizens passed their lives in idleness. The young men spent the time in warlike games and skills and the elders acted as spectators and judges on these occasions. It was considered disgraceful in Sparta for an old man to stay away from the place where the young were being trained. In this way, every Spartan became identified with the state; all his acts became *public* acts. Youth matured and old age declined under the eyes of the nation. The Spartan kept his eye constantly on Sparta and Sparta kept its eye on him. He witnessed everything that took place and his

Lebens. Die Ruhmbegierde erhielt einen immerwährenden Sporn, der Nationalgeist eine unaufhörliche Nahrung; die Idee von *Vaterland* und *vaterländischem Interesse* verwuchs mit dem innersten Leben aller seiner Bürger. Noch andre Gelegenheiten, diese Triebe zu entflammen, gaben die öffentlichen Feste, welche in dem müßigen Sparta sehr zahlreich waren. Kriegrische Volkslieder wurden dabei gesungen, welche den Ruhm der fürs Vaterland gefallenen Bürger oder Ermunterungen zur Tapferkeit zum gewöhnlichen Inhalt hatten. Sie erschienen an diesen Festen in drei Chören, nach dem Alter eingeteilt. Das Chor der Alten fing an, zu singen: *"In der Vorzeit waren wir Helden."* Das Chor der Männer anwortete: *"Helden sind wir jetzt! Komme wer will, es zu erproben!"* Das dritte Chor der Knaben fiel ein: *"Helden werden wir einst und euch durch Taten verdunkeln."* Werfen wir einen bloß flüchtigen Blick auf die Gesetzgebung des Lykurgus, so befällt uns wirklich ein angenehmes Erstaunen. Unter allen ähnlichen Instituten des Altertums ist sie unstreitig die vollendetste, die mosaische Gesetzgebung ausgenommen, der sie in vielen Stücken und vorzüglich in dem Prinzipium gleicht, das ihr zum Grund liegt. Sie ist wirklich in sich selbst vollendet; alles schließt sich darin an einander an, eines wird durch alles und alles durch eins gehalten. Bessere Mittel konnte Lykurgus wohl nicht wählen, den Zweck zu erreichen, den er vor Augen hatte, einen Staat nämlich, der, von allen übrigen isoliert, sich selbst genug und fähig wäre, durch innern Kreislauf und eigne lebendige Kraft sich selbst zu erhalten. Kein Gesetzgeber hat je einem Staate diese Einheit, dieses Nationalinteresse, diesen Gemeingeist gegeben, den Lykurgus dem seinigen gab. Und wodurch hat Lykurgus dieses bewirkt?—Dadurch, daß er die Tätigkeit seiner Mitbürger in den Staat zu leiten wußte und ihnen alle andern Wege zuschloß, die sie hätten davon abziehen können.

Alles, was Menschenseelen fesselt und Leidenschaften entzündet, alles außer dem politischen Interesse hatte er durch seine Gesetzgebung entfernt. Reichtum und Wollüste, Wissenschaft und Kunst hatten keinen Zugang zu den Gemütern der Spartaner. Durch die gleiche gemeinschaftliche

own life was witnessed by all of his compatriots. The love of glory was continually stimulated, the national spirit continually fed. The idea of *country* and *patriotic interest* was implanted in the innermost life of every citizen. The public festivals, of which there were many in idle Sparta, afforded further opportunities for kindling the national enthusiasm. Warlike folksongs were sung which usually celebrated the glory of citizens who had died in battle for their country or inspired men to acts of bravery. At these festivals the citizens were arranged in three choruses according to age. The chorus of elders began by singing: "In past ages we were heroes." The men's chorus replied: "We are heroes now! Come who may to try us!" The third chorus of boys concluded: "Heroes we shall be; we shall obscure you by our deeds."

If we cast merely a superficial glance at Lycurgus' legislation, we indeed experience a pleasant surprise. Among all similar institutions of antiquity, this is undoubtedly the most perfect, with the sole exception of the Mosaic law, which it resembles in many respects and especially in its fundamental principles. It is really complete in itself. Every part ties in with every other, each being dependent upon the whole, and the whole upon each part. Lycurgus could have chosen no better means to accomplish the aim he had in view, namely to found a state, isolated from all others, self-sufficient and capable of maintaining itself by its own cycle of activity and vital force. No lawgiver has ever imparted to a state the unity, the interest in the national welfare and public spirit that Lycurgus developed in the Spartans. And how did he achieve this? By concentrating the activities of his countrymen on the state and closing off every avenue that might have diverted their attention elsewhere.

By his legislation Lycurgus had removed all that can enthrall the human heart or inflame the passions except political interests. The Spartans were given no opportunity to know the appeal of wealth and pleasure, the sciences and the arts. Universal poverty eliminated differ-

Armut fiel die Vergleichung der Glücksumstände weg, die in den meisten Menschen die Gewinnsucht entzündet; der Wunsch nach Besitztümern fiel mit der Gelegenheit hinweg, sie zu zeigen und zu nutzen. Durch die tiefe Unwissenheit in Kunst und Wissenschaft, welche alle Köpfe in Sparta auf gleiche Art verfinsterte, verwahrte er es vor Eingriffen, die ein erleuchteter Geist in die Verfassung getan haben würde; eben diese Unwissenheit, mit dem rauhen Nationaltrotz verbunden, der jedem Spartaner eigentümlich war, stand ihrer Vermischung mit andern griechischen Völkern unaufhörlich im Wege. In der Wiege schon waren sie zu Spartanern gestempelt, und je mehr sie andern Nationen entgegen stießen, desto fester mußten sie an ihrem Mittelpunkt halten. Das Vaterland war das erste Schauspiel, das sich dem spartanischen Knaben zeigte, wenn er zum Denken erwachte. Er erwachte im Schoß des Staats; alles, was um ihn lag, war Nation, Staat und Vaterland. Es war der erste Eindruck in seinem Gehirne, und sein ganzes Leben war eine ewige Erneuerung dieses Eindrucks.

Zu Hause fand der Spartaner nichts, das ihn hätte fesseln können; alle Reize hatte der Gesetzgeber seinen Augen entzogen. Nur im Schoße des Staats fand er Beschäftigung, Ergötzung, Ehre, Belohnung; alle seine Triebe und Leidenschaften waren nach diesem Mittelpunkt hingeleitet. Der Staat hatte also die ganze Energie, die Kraft aller seiner einzelnen Bürger, und an dem Gemeingeiste, der alle zusammen entflammte, mußte sich der Nationalgeist jedes einzelnen Bürgers entzünden. Daher ist es kein Wunder, daß die spartanische Vaterlandstugend einen Grad von Stärke erreichte, der uns unglaublich scheinen muß. Daher kam es, daß bei dem Bürger dieser Republik gar kein Zweifel stattfinden konnte, wenn es darauf ankam, zwischen Selbsterhaltung und Rettung des Vaterlands eine Wahl zu treffen.

Daher ist es begreiflich, wie sich der spartanische König Leonidas mit seinen 300 Helden die Grabschrift verdienen konnte, die schönste ihrer Art und das erhabenste Denkmal politischer Tugend: "Erzähle, Wandrer, wenn du nach Sparta kommst, daß wir, seinen Gesetzen gehorsam, hier gefallen sind."

ences in circumstance which ordinarily arouse envy. The desire for possessions disappeared with the opportunity to display and use them. The deep ignorance in the arts and sciences that clouded every Spartan mind protected the constitution from the attacks to which it might have been exposed by enlightened intellects. This same ignorance, coupled with the crude national pride peculiar to every Spartan, was a constant barrier to any intermingling with other Greek peoples. From the cradle the citizens were stamped as Spartans and the more they opposed other nations, the more attached they became to their own orbit. His country was the first sight that greeted the Spartan boy when his mental faculties began to develop. He awoke in the bosom of the state. He was surrounded by nothing but the nation, national concerns, his native land. These were the first impressions his brain received and all his life long the same impressions were constantly renewed.

In his home the Spartan found nothing to attract him. The lawgiver had removed all temptations from his sight. It was only in the bosom of the state that he found occupation, delight, honor, reward. All of his impulses and passions were directed toward this center. The state owned the energy and powers of all its citizens. The common spirit that inflamed all hearts must kindle the national spirit of every individual citizen. It is no wonder, therefore, that Spartan patriotism attained a degree of intensity that must seem incredible to us. For this reason, if the citizens of his state were called upon to choose between self-preservation and the defense of their country there was no doubt as to where the choice would lie.

All this will enable us to understand how it was possible for the Spartan King Leonidas and his three hundred heroes to earn the following epitaph, the most beautiful of its kind and the most sublime monument to political virtue: "Say of us, Wanderer, when you arrive in Sparta, that we have fallen here in obedience to its laws."

Man muß also eingestehen, daß nichts Zweckmäßigers, nichts durchdachter sein kann als diese Staatsverfassung, daß sie in ihrer Art ein vollendetes Kunstwerk vorstellt und, in ihrer ganzen Strenge befolgt, notwendig auf sich selbst hätte ruhen müssen. Wäre aber meine Schilderung hier zu Ende, so würde ich mich eines sehr großen Irrtums schuldig gemacht haben. Diese bewundrungswürdige Verfassung ist im höchsten Grade verwerflich, und nichts Traurigers könnte der Menschheit begegnen, als wenn alle Staaten nach diesem Muster wären gegründet worden. Es wird uns nicht schwer fallen, uns von dieser Behauptung zu überzeugen.

Gegen seinen eignen Zweck gehalten, ist die Gesetzgebung des Lykurgus ein Meisterstück der Staats- und Menschenkunde. Er wollte einen mächtigen, in sich selbst gegründeten unzerstörbaren Staat; politische Stärke und Dauerhaftigkeit waren das Ziel, wornach er strebte, und dieses Ziel hat er so weit erreicht, als unter seinen Umständen möglich war. Aber hält man den Zweck, welchen Lykurgus sich vorsetzte, gegen den Zweck der Menschheit, so muß eine tiefe Mißbilligung an die Stelle der Bewunderung treten, die uns der erste flüchtige Blick abgewonnen hat. Alles darf dem Besten des Staats zum Opfer gebracht werden, nur dasjenige nicht, dem der Staat selbst nur als ein Mittel dient. Der Staat selbst ist niemals Zweck, er ist nur wichtig als eine Bedingung, unter welcher der Zweck der Menschheit erfüllt werden kann, und dieser Zweck der Menschheit ist kein andrer als Ausbildung aller Kräfte des Menschen, Fortschreitung. Hindert eine Staatsverfassung, daß alle Kräfte, die im Menschen liegen, sich entwickeln, hindert sie die Fortschreitung des Geistes, so ist sie verwerflich und schädlich, sie mag übrigens noch so durchdacht und in ihrer Art noch so vollkommen sein. Ihre Dauerhaftigkeit selbst gereicht ihr alsdann viel mehr zum Vorwurf als zum Ruhme — sie ist dann nur ein verlängertes Übel; je länger sie Bestand hat, um so schädlicher ist sie.

Überhaupt können wir bei Beurteilung politischer Anstalten als eine Regel festsetzen, daß sie nur gut und lobenswürdig sind, insofern sie alle Kräfte, die im Menschen liegen, zur

It must be admitted, therefore, that nothing could be more carefully conceived or more adequate to the purpose than this constitution, that it is a perfect masterpiece of its kind and, if rigidly enforced, would necessarily maintain itself indefinitely. But I would be making a grave mistake if I were to conclude my description here. This admirable constitution deserves our severest condemnation and nothing more disastrous could befall the human race than to have all states patterned after it. We shall not find it difficult to persuade ourselves of the truth of this assertion.

Considered in the light of what he wished to accomplish, the legislation of Lycurgus is a masterpiece of political science and human psychology. He wanted to establish a powerful, self-sustaining, indestructible state. Political strength and durability were his aim, and this aim he accomplished insofar as circumstances permitted. The admiration aroused by a superficial glance at his achievement must give way to strong condemnation when his aims are compared with those of humanity. Everything may be sacrificed to the best interests of the state except the end which the state itself is designed to serve. The state is not an end in itself. It is important only as a means to the realization of an end which is no other than the development of all the faculties of man and cultural progress. If a constitution hinders this development, if it hinders intellectual progress, it is harmful and worthless, no matter how ingeniously it is conceived and how perfectly it may function in its own way. Its durability is to be regretted rather than admired. It is only a prolongation of evil. The longer such a state exists the more detrimental it becomes.

In judging the value of political institutions, we may follow the general rule that they are to be commended only insofar as they favor or, at any rate, do not inter-

Ausbildung bringen, insofern sie Fortschreitung der Kultur befördern oder wenigstens nicht hemmen. Dieses gilt von Religions- wie von politischen Gesetzen: beide sind verwerflich, wenn sie eine Kraft des menschlichen Geistes fesseln, wenn sie ihm in irgend etwas einen Stillstand auferlegen. Ein Gesetz z. B., wodurch eine Nation verbunden würde, bei dem Glaubensschema beständig zu verharren, das ihr in einer gewissen Periode als das vortrefflichste erschienen, ein solches Gesetz wäre ein Attentat gegen die Menschheit, und keine noch so scheinbare Absicht würde es rechtfertigen können. Es wäre unmittelbar gegen das höchste Gut, gegen den höchsten Zweck der Gesellschaft gerichtet.

Mit diesem allgemeinen Maßstab versehen, können wir nicht lange zweifelhaft sein, wie wir den Lykurgischen Staat beurteilen sollen.

Eine einzige Tugend war es, die in Sparta mit Hintansetzung aller andern geübt wurde: Vaterlandsliebe.

Diesem künstlichen Triebe wurden die natürlichsten, schönsten Gefühle der Menschheit zum Opfer gebracht.

Auf Unkosten aller sittlichen Gefühle wurde das politische Verdienst errungen und die Fähigkeit dazu ausgebildet. In Sparta gab es keine ehliche Liebe, keine Mutterliebe, keine kindliche Liebe, keine Freundschaft—es gab nichts als Bürger, nichts als bürgerliche Tugend. Lange Zeit hat man jene spartanische Mutter bewundert, die ihren aus dem Treffen entkommenen Sohn mit Unwillen von sich stößt und nach dem Tempel eilt, den Göttern für den gefallenen zu danken. Zu einer solchen unnatürlichen Stärke des Geistes hätte man der Menschheit nicht Glück wünschen sollen. Eine zärtliche Mutter ist eine weit schönere Erscheinung in der moralischen Welt als ein heroisches Zwittergeschöpf, das die natürliche Empfindung verleugnet, um eine künstliche Pflicht zu befriedigen.

Welch schöneres Schauspiel gibt der rauhe Krieger Cajus Marius in seinem Lager vor Rom, der Rache und Sieg aufopfert, weil er die Tränen der Mutter nicht fließen sehen kann!

Dadurch daß der Staat der Vater seines Kindes wurde, hörte

fere with, the development of the useful powers of humanity and the progress of culture. This applies to religious as well as to political laws. Both are to be condemned if they fetter the human mind and impose a standstill on man in any respect. A law, for instance, which compelled a nation to adhere forever to a dogma that at one time seemed excellent would be a violation of the rights of humanity which is never justifiable on any grounds, however plausible. It would be directly opposed to the highest good, to the highest objective of society.

Armed with this general criterion, we cannot hesitate to pronounce judgment on the republic of Lycurgus.

One virtue was practiced in Sparta to the exclusion of all the rest: this was patriotism.

To this artificial sentiment the most natural and beautiful affections of the human heart were sacrificed.

Political service was achieved and the ability to perform it was developed by sacrificing all moral sensibilities. Sparta knew nothing of conjugal love, maternal affection, filial piety, friendship. It recognized only citizens and civic virtues. The Spartan mother has long been admired who indignantly repulsed the son returning from battle and rushed to the temple to thanks the gods for the son who had met his death. Humanity is not to be congratulated for such unnatural strength of mind. In the moral world a tender mother is a much more beautiful phenomenon than a heroic monster who denies her natural feelings in order to perform an artificial duty.

How much more beautiful is the spectacle of the rough warrior, Caius Marius, in his camp before Rome who sacrifices vengeance and victory because he cannot bear the sight of his mother's tears.

Since the state became the father of the child, the natural father did not perform this role. The child never learned

der natürliche Vater desselben auf, es zu sein. Das Kind lernte nie seine Mutter, seinen Vater lieben, weil es, schon in dem zärtesten Alter von ihnen gerissen, seine Eltern nicht an ihren Wohltaten, nur von Hörensagen erfuhr.

Auf eine noch empörendere Art wurde das allgemeine Menschengefühl in Sparta ertötet, und die Seele aller Pflichten, die Achtung gegen die Gattung, ging unwiederbringlich verloren. Ein Staatsgesetz machte den Spartanern die Unmenschlichkeit gegen ihre Sklaven zur Pflicht; in diesen unglücklichen Schlachtopfern wurde die Menschheit beschimpft und mißhandelt. In dem spartanischen Gesetzbuche selbst wurde der gefährliche Grundsatz gepredigt, Menschen als Mittel und nicht als Zwecke zu betrachten— dadurch wurden die Grundfesten des Naturrechts und der Sittlichkeit gesetzmäßig eingerissen. Die ganze Moralität wurde preisgegeben, um etwas zu erhalten, das doch nur als ein Mittel zu dieser Moralität einen Wert haben kann.

Kann etwas widersprechender sein, und kann ein Widerspruch schrecklichere Folgen haben als diese? Nicht genug, daß Lykurgus auf den Ruin der Sittlichkeit seinen Staat gründete, er arbeitete auf eine andre Art gegen den höchsten Zweck der Menschheit, indem er durch sein fein durchdachtes Staatssystem den Geist der Spartaner auf derjenigen Stufe festhielt, worauf er ihn fand, und auf ewig alle Fortschreitung hemmte.

Aller Kunstfleiß war aus Sparta verbannt, alle Wissenschaften wurden vernachlässigt, aller Handelsverkehr mit fremden Völkern verboten, alles Auswärtige wurde ausgeschlossen. Dadurch wurden alle Kanäle gesperrt, wodurch seiner Nation helle Begriffe zufließen konnten; in einer ewigen Einförmigkeit, in einem traurigen Egoismus sollte sich der spartanische Staat ewig nur um sich selbst bewegen.

Das Geschäft aller seiner vereinigten Bürger war, sich zu erhalten, was sie besaßen, und zu bleiben, was sie waren, nichts Neues zu bewerben, nicht auf eine höhere Stufe zu steigen. Unerbittliche Gesetze mußten darüber wachen, daß keine Neuerung in das Uhrwerk des Staates griff, daß selbst der Fortschritt der Zeit an der Form der Gesetze

to love its father or mother because, having been taken from them in earliest infancy, it knew its parents only by hearsay, not by the benefits it had received from them.

Ordinary human feelings were eradicated in Sparta in a still more revolting manner, and respect for the human race which is the essence of duty, was irretrievably lost. A state law required the inhuman treatment of slaves. In these hapless victims mankind itself was insulted and mistreated. In the Spartan code the dangerous principle was laid down that men were to be considered as a means, not as an end, thus demolishing by law the foundations of natural rights and morality. All morality was sacrificed to achieve an end which can be valuable only as a means to the establishment of this morality.

Could anything be more contradictory, and could the contradiction be followed by more frightful consequences? Not only did Lycurgus found his state upon the legalized ruin of morality, he also thwarted the highest purpose of humanity by arresting the minds of the Spartans at the level where he found them and by preventing all possibility of progress forever.

All industry was banished from Sparta, all sciences were neglected, all commerce with other countries was prohibited and everything foreign was excluded. Thus all channels through which enlightened ideas could flow into the nation were closed. The Spartan state was to revolve only about its own center in perpetual monotony and gloomy egotism.

It was the common aim of the citizens to preserve what they possessed, to remain as they were and not to strive for anything new and elevate themselves to a higher level of culture. Inexorable laws had to guard the government machinery from being tampered with by any innovation, even by changes of legal form that normally come about

nichts veränderte. Um diese lokale, diese temporäre Verfassung dauerhaft zu machen, mußte man den Geist des Volks auf derjenigen Stelle festhalten, worauf er bei ihrer Gründung gestanden.

Wir haben aber gesehen, daß Fortschreitung des Geistes das Ziel des Staats sein soll.—

Der Staat des Lykurgus konnte nur unter der einzigen Bedingung fortdauern, wenn der Geist des Volks stille stünde; er konnte sich also nur dadurch erhalten, daß er den höchsten und einzigen Zweck eines Staats verfehlte. Was man also zum Lobe des Lykurgus angeführt hat, daß Sparta nur so lange blühen würde, als es dem Buchstaben seines Gesetzes folgte, ist das Schlimmste, was von ihm gesagt werden konnte. Eben dadurch, daß es die alte Staatsform nicht verlassen durfte, die Lykurg ihm gegeben, ohne sich dem gänzlichen Untergang auszusetzen, daß es bleiben mußte, was es war, daß es stehen mußte, wo ein einziger Mann es hingeworfen, eben dadurch war Sparta ein unglücklicher Staat—und kein traurigeres Geschenk hätte ihm sein Gesetzgeber machen können als diese gerühmte ewige Dauer einer Verfassung, die seiner wahren Größe und Glückseligkeit so sehr im Wege stand.

Nehmen wir dies zusammen, so verschwindet der falsche Glanz, wodurch die einzige hervorstechende Seite des spartanischen Staats ein unerfahrnes Auge blendet—wir sehen nichts mehr als einen schülerhaften unvollkommnen Versuch—das erste Exerzitium des jugendlichen Weltalters, dem es noch an Erfahrung und hellen Einsichten fehlte, die wahren Verhältnisse der Dinge zu erkennen. So fehlerhaft dieser erste Versuch ausgefallen ist, so wird und muß er einem philosophischen Forscher der Menschengeschichte immer sehr merkwürdig bleiben. Immer war es ein Riesenschritt des menschlichen Geistes, dasjenige als ein Kunstwerk zu behandeln, was bis jetzt dem Zufall und der Leidenschaft überlassen gewesen war. Unvollkommen mußte notwendig der erste Versuch in der schwersten aller Künste sein, aber schätzbar bleibt er immer, weil er in der wichtigsten aller Künste angestellt worden ist. Die Bildhauer fingen mit Hermessäulen an, ehe sie sich zu der vollkomm-

with the passage of time. In order to ensure the permanence of this local and temporary legislation, the minds of the people had to be kept at the level where the lawgiver found them.

We have seen, however, that intellectual progress should be the aim of the state.

The republic of Lycurgus could endure only if the mental development of the people was arrested, and thus it could maintain its existence only if it failed to fulfill the highest and only true purpose of political government. Therefore, what has been said in praise of Lycurgus, namely that Sparta would prosper only as long as it followed his laws to the letter, is the worst that could be said of them. What made Sparta an unhappy state was the very fact that it could not relinquish the old form of government without exposing itself to complete ruin; that it had to remain what it was; that it had to stand where a single man had placed it. Its lawgiver could not have made it a more disastrous gift than this much vaunted perpetual constitution which was such an obstacle to its true greatness and happiness.

If we look at the total picture, the false splendor which emanates from the only prominent feature of the Spartan republic and which dazzles the inexperienced eye, vanishes at once. We see nothing more than the imperfect attempt of a novice, the first political exercise of a young age that still lacked the experience and clear vision to recognize the relations of things. But for all the imperfection of this first attempt, it cannot fail to excite the interest of a philosophical student of human history. It was always a gigantic step for the human mind to treat as a work of art what had hitherto been left to chance and passion. The first attempt in the most difficult of all arts must necessarily have been imperfect, but since it is also the most important of arts, the attempt is nonetheless of value. Sculptors began with the columns of Hermes before they attempted to chisel the perfect form

nen Form eines Antinous, eines vatikanischen Apolls er-
huben; die Gesetzgeber werden sich noch lange in rohen
Versuchen üben, bis sich ihnen endlich das glückliche
Gleichgewicht der gesellschaftlichen Kräfte von selbst darbietet.

Der Stein leidet geduldig den bildenden Meißel, und die
Saiten, die der Tonkünstler anschlägt, antworten ihm, ohne
seinem Finger zu widerstreben.

Der Gesetzgeber allein bearbeitet einen selbsttätigen wider-
strebenden Stoff—die menschliche Freiheit. Nur unvollkommen kann er das Ideal in Erfüllung bringen, das er in
seinem Gehirne noch so rein entworfen hat; aber hier ist
der Versuch allein schon alles Lobes wert, wenn er mit un-
eigennützigem Wohlwollen unternommen und mit Zweckmäßigkeit vollendet wird.

SOLON

Von der Gesetzgebung des Lykurgus in Sparta war die
Gesetzgebung Solons in Athen fast durchaus das Wider-
spiel—und da die beiden Republiken Sparta und Athen
die Hauptrolle in der griechischen Geschichte spielen, so
ist es ein anziehendes Geschäft, ihre verschiedenen Staats-
verfassungen neben einander zu stellen und ihre Gebrechen
und Vorzüge gegen einander abzuwägen.

Nach dem Tode des Kodrus wurde die königliche Würde in Athen abgeschafft und einer Obrigkeit, die den Namen *Archon* führte, die höchste Gewalt auf *lebenslang* übertragen. In einem Zeitraum von mehr als 300 Jahren herrschten dreizehn solcher Archonten in Athen, und aus diesem
Zeitraum hat uns die Geschichte nichts Merkwürdiges von
der neuen Republik aufbehalten. Aber der Geist der Demokratie, der den Atheniensern schon zu Homers Zeiten
eigentümlich war, regte sich am Schluß dieser Periode
wieder. Eine lebenslängliche Dauer des Archontats war
ihnen doch ein allzu lebhaftes Bild der königlichen Würde,
und vielleicht hatten die vorhergegangenen Archonten ihre
große und dauerhafte Macht mißbraucht. Man setzte also die
Dauer der Archonten auf *zehen Jahre.* Ein wichtiger Schritt
zur künftigen Freiheit; denn dadurch, daß es alle zehen Jahre

of an Antinous, of an Apollo of Belvedere. Lawgivers will have to continue their rude experiments for a long time before the happy balance of social forces automatically presents itself.

Stone bears patiently the blows of the chisel and the strings that the musician causes to vibrate respond to his touch without resistance.

The lawgiver alone works on a self-active, refractory material: human freedom. He can realize only imperfectly the ideal sketched in his brain in ever so pure a form. But the mere attempt is praiseworthy if it is undertaken with disinterested benevolence and carried out with practical wisdom.

SOLON

Solon's legislation in Athens was almost the direct opposite of that of Lycurgus in Sparta. Inasmuch as these two republics, Sparta and Athens, played the chief roles in Greek history, it is interesting to compare their constitutions and to weigh their respective defects and virtues.

After the death of Codrus, the office of king was abolished and the highest power was conferred *for life* on a magistrate called an *archon*. For a period of three hundred years thirteen of these archons ruled in Athens. History has recorded nothing remarkable about the young republic during this time. But the democratic spirit, which was peculiar to the Athenians even in Homer's time, again became active at the close of the period. The archon with his lifelong tenure was an all too vivid reminder of royalty, and some of the later archons may have abused their great power. The term of office was therefore limited to *ten years*. This was an important step toward liberty; for by electing a new ruler every ten

einen neuen Beherrscher wählte, erneuerte das Volk den Aktus seiner Souveränität; es nahm alle zehen Jahre seine weggegebene Gewalt zurück, um sie nach Gutbefinden von neuem wegzugeben. Dadurch blieb ihm immer in frischem Gedächtnis, was die Untertanen erblicher Monarchien zuletzt ganz vergessen, daß es selbst die Quelle der höchsten Gewalt, daß der Fürst nur das Geschöpf der Nation ist.

300 Jahre hatte das atheniensische Volk einen lebenslänglichen Archon über sich geduldet, aber die zehenjährigen Archonten wurde es schon im 70. Jahre müde. Dies war ganz natürlich; denn während dieser Zeit hatte es siebenmal die Archontenwahl erneuert, es war also siebenmal an seine Souveränität erinnert worden. Der Geist der Freiheit hatte sich also in der zweiten Periode weit lebhafter regen müssen, weit schneller entwickeln müssen als in der ersten.

Der siebente der zehenjährigen Archonten war auch der letzte von dieser Gattung. Das Volk wollte alle Jahre den Genuß seiner Obergewalt haben, es hatte die Erfahrung gemacht, daß eine auf zehen Jahre verliehene Gewalt noch immer lang genug daure, um zum Mißbrauch zu verführen. Künftig also war die Archontenwürde auf ein einziges Jahr eingeschränkt, nach dessen Verfluß eine neue Wahl vorgenommen wurde. Es tat noch einen Schritt weiter. Weil auch eine noch so kurz dauernde Gewalt in den Händen eines einzigen der Monarchie schon sehr nahe kommt, so schwächte es diese Gewalt, indem es dieselbe unter neun Archonten verteilte, die zugleich regierten.

Drei dieser neun Archonten hatten Vorzüge vor den sechs übrigen. Der erste, *Archon Eponymos* genannt, führte den Vorsitz bei der Versammlung; sein Name stand unter den öffentlichen Akten; nach ihm nannte man das Jahr. Der zweite, *Basileus* oder König genannt, hatte über die Religion zu wachen und den Gottesdienst zu besorgen; dies war aus frühern Zeiten beibehalten, wo die Aufsicht über den Gottesdienst ein wesentliches Stück der Königswürde gewesen. Der dritte, *Polemarch*, war Anführer im Kriege. Die sechs übrigen führten den Namen *Thesmotheten*, weil sie die Konstitution zu bewahren und die Gesetze zu erhalten und auszulegen hatten.

years, the people exercised their sovereignty afresh. They resumed their power every ten years in order to give it away again as they saw fit. In this way the Athenian people were constantly reminded of what in the end the subjects of hereditary monarchs entirely forget, namely that they, the people, are the source of supreme power, that the prince is merely the creature of the nation.

For three hundred years the Athenians had tolerated archons with lifelong tenure of office, but they became weary of the ten-year archons after seventy. This was quite natural, for they had elected their archons seven times and thus had been reminded of their sovereignty seven times. The spirit of freedom was called upon to be far more active, to develop far more rapidly in the second period than in the first.

The seventh of the ten-year archons was the last of his kind. The people wanted to enjoy the exercise of their authority every year. They had discovered that ten years of power was still long enough to lead to abuses. Henceforth the archon's term of office was limited to one year, at the end of which time a new election took place. The Athenians even went a step further. Since so much power in the hands of one man, even for so short a period, was very like a monarchy, they weakened this power by dividing it between nine archons who ruled together.

Three of these nine archons had privileges the other six did not possess. The first, called *archon eponymos,* presided over the assembly. His signature appeared on official documents. The year was named after him. The second, called *archon basileus* or king, was to supervise religion and religious worship. This had been carried over from former times when the supervision of worship had been an essential function of the crown. The third, *archon polemarchos,* commanded the army in time of war. The six remaining archons were called *thesmothetae* because it was their duty to protect the constitution and to interpret the laws.

Die Archonten wurden aus den vornehmsten Familien gewählt, und in spätern Zeiten erst drangen sich auch Personen aus dem Volk in diese Würde. Die Verfassung war daher einer Aristokratie weit näher als einer Volksregierung, und das letzte hatte also noch nicht sehr viel dabei gewonnen.

Die Anordnung, daß jedes Jahr neun neue Archonten gewählt wurden, hatte neben ihrer gute Seite—nämlich Mißbrauch der höchsten Gewalt zu verhüten—auch eine sehr schlimme, und diese war: daß sie Faktionen im Staat hervorbrachte. Denn nun gab es viele Bürger im Staat, welche die höchste Gewalt bekleidet und wieder abgegeben hatten. Mit Niederlegung ihrer Würde konnten sie nicht so leicht auch den Geschmack an dieser Würde, nicht so leicht das Vergnügen am Herrschen ablegen, das sie zu kosten angefangen hatten. Sie wünschten also wieder zu werden, was sie waren, sie machten sich also einen Anhang, sie erregten innere Stürme in der Republik. Die schnellere Abwechselung und die größere Anzahl der Archonten machten ferner jedem angesehenen und reichen Athenienser Hoffnung, zum Archontat zu gelangen, eine Hoffnung, die er vorher, als nur *einer* diese Würde bekleidete und nicht so bald wieder darin abgelöst wurde, wenig oder nicht gekannt hatte. Diese Hoffnung wurde endlich bei ihnen zur Ungeduld, und diese Ungeduld führte sie zu gefährlichen Anschlägen. Beide also, sowohl die, welche schon Archonten gewesen, als die, welche sich sehnten, es zu werden, wurden der bürgerlichen Ruhe auf gleiche Art gefährlich.

Das Schlimmste dabei war, daß die obrigkeitliche Macht durch Verteilung unter mehrere und durch ihre kurze Dauer mehr als jemals gebrochen war. Es fehlte daher an einer starken Hand, die Faktionen zu bändigen und die aufrührerischen Köpfe im Zaum zu halten. Mächtige und verwegene Bürger stürzten den Staat in Verwirrung und strebten nach Unabhängigkeit.

Man warf endlich, um diesen Unruhen zu steuern, die Augen auf einen unbescholtenen und allgemein gefürchteten Bürger, dem die Verbesserung der Gesetze, die bis jetzt nur in mangelhaften Traditionen bestanden, übertragen ward.

The archons were chosen from the noblest families, and it was not until later that members of the lower classes became eligible for the office. This constitution, therefore, was an aristocratic rather than a democratic form of government. The people had not gained very much by the change.

In addition to its good side—namely, that it prevented the abuse of power—the arrangement whereby nine archons were elected every year had the great disadvantage that it gave rise to factions. There were now many citizens who had possessed and in turn relinquished the highest power. When they retired from office they did not find it so easy, once having had a taste of it, to relinquish the enjoyment of power and authority. Wishing to become again what they had been, they collected a following and stirred up storms within the republic. The more rapid turnover and the greater number of archons gave every rich and distinguished Athenian the hope of achieving that dignity, a hope which previously, when only one man had the office and retained it for a fairly long time, he had scarcely known if at all. Finally hope would transform itself into impatience and this impatience gave rise to dangerous plots. Both groups, therefore, those who had already been archons and those who desired to become archons, became equally dangerous to civil peace.

The worst of it was that the governing power, being divided among several men and being retained for so short a time, was very much weakened. A strong hand was needed to control the factions and to keep rebellious spirits in rein. Bold and powerful citizens plunged the republic into confusion and strove for independence.

At last, in order to put an end to the unrest, a blameless and universally feared citizen was commissioned to reform the laws which heretofore had been based on unsound traditions. The name of this citizen was Draco, a

225

Drako hieß dieser gefürchtete Bürger — ein Mann ohne
Menschengefühl, der der menschlichen Natur nichts Gutes
zutraute, alle Handlungen bloß in dem finstern Spiegel seiner eignen trüben Seele sah und ganz ohne Schonung war
für die Schwächen der Menschheit: ein schlechter Philosoph und ein noch schlechterer Kenner der Menschen, mit
kaltem Herzen, beschränktem Kopf und unbiegsam in seinen Vorurteilen. Solch ein Mann war vortrefflich, Gesetze
zu *vollziehen;* aber sie zu *geben,* konnte man keine schlim-
mere Wahl treffen.

Es ist uns wenig von den Gesetzen des Drako übrig geblieben, aber dieses wenige schildert uns den Mann und
den Geist seiner Gesetzgebung. Alle Verbrechen strafte er
ohne Unterschied mit dem Tode, den Müßiggang wie den
Mord, den Diebstahl eines Kohls oder eines Schafs wie
den Hochverrat und die Mordbrennerei. Als man ihn daher fragte, warum er die kleinen Vergehungen eben so streng
bestrafe als die schwersten Verbrechen, so war seine Antwort: "Die kleinsten Verbrechen sind des Todes würdig;
für die größten weiß ich keine andre Strafe als den Tod
darum muß ich beide gleich behandeln."

Drakos Gesetze sind der Versuch eines Anfängers in der
Kunst, Menschen zu regieren. *Schrecken* ist das einzige Instrument, wodurch er wirkt. Er straft nur begangenes Übel,
er verhindert es nicht, er bekümmert sich nicht darum, die
Quelle desselben zu verstopfen und die Menschen zu ver-
bessern. Einen Menschen aus den Lebendigen vertilgen, weil
er etwas Böses begangen hat, heißt ebenso viel als einen
Baum umhauen, weil *eine* seiner Früchte faul ist.

Seine Gesetze sind doppelt zu tadeln, weil sie nicht allein
die heiligen Gefühle und Rechte der Menschheit wider sich
haben, sondern auch, weil sie auf das Volk, *dem* er sie gab,
nicht berechnet waren. War ein Volk in der Welt unge-
schickt, durch *solche* Gesetze zu gedeihen, so war es das
atheniensische. Die Sklaven der Pharaonen oder des Königs der Könige würden sich endlich vielleicht darein gefunden haben — aber wie konnten Athenienser unter ein solches Joch sich beugen!

Auch blieben sie kaum ein halbes Jahrhundert in Kraft, ob

226

man with no human feeling, who thought human nature incapable of any good, who viewed all actions in the gloomy mirror of his own dark soul; a man wholly devoid of compassion for the weakness of humanity; a poor philosopher, with little understanding of men, a cold heart, a limited mentality and rigid prejudices. Such a man would have been excellent at *enforcing* laws, but a worse person to make them could scarcely have been chosen.

Very little of Draco's legislation has come down to us, but this little gives us a picture of the man and the character of his laws. All crimes were punished indiscriminately by death: idleness and murder, the theft of a cabbage or a sheep, high treason and arson. When asked why he punished trifling transgressions as severely as the gravest crimes, he replied: "The slightest violations of the law are worthy of death. I know of no more severe punishment for the greater offenses than death, therefore I must mete out the same punishment for both."

Draco's laws are the attempt of a beginner in the art of governing men. *Terror* is his only means of attaining his end. He merely punishes transgressions, he does not prevent them. He makes no effort to stop up the sources of evil and to improve men. To take the life of a man because he has done something wrong is like chopping down a tree because it has produced one bad fruit.
His laws are to be condemned on two scores: not only because they violate the sacred feelings and rights of mankind, but also because they were not adapted to the people for whom they were intended. If ever there was a people in the world unlikely to prosper under such laws, it was the Athenian. The slaves of the pharaohs or of the king of kings might eventually have accommodated themselves to such laws, but how could Athenians be expected to bend their necks beneath such a yoke?

Nor did they remain in force more than half a century,

er ihnen gleich den unbescheidnen Titel *unwandelbarer Gesetze* gab.

Drako hatte also seinen Auftrag sehr schlecht erfüllt, und anstatt zu nützen, schadeten seine Gesetze. Weil sie nämlich nicht befolgt werden konnten und doch keine andre sogleich da waren, ihre Stelle zu ersetzen, so war es ebenso viel, als wenn Athen gar kein Gesetz gehabt hätte, und die traurigste Anarchie riß ein.

Damals war der Zustand des atheniensischen Volks äußerst zu beklagen. *Eine* Klasse des Volks besaß alles, die *andre* hingegen gar nichts; die Reichen unterdrückten und plünderten aufs unbarmherzigste die Armen. Es entstand eine unermeßliche Scheidewand zwischen beiden. Die Not zwang die ärmern Bürger, zu den *Reichen* ihre Zuflucht zu nehmen: zu eben den Blutigeln, die sie ausgesogen hatten; aber sie fanden nur eine grausame Hilfe bei diesen. Für die Summen, die sie aufnahmen, mußten sie ungeheure Zinsen bezahlen und, wenn sie nicht Termin hielten, ihre Ländereien selbst an die Gläubiger abtreten. Nachdem sie nichts mehr zu geben hatten und doch leben mußten, waren sie dahin gebracht, ihre eigene Kinder als Sklaven zu verkaufen, und endlich, als auch diese Zuflucht erschöpft war, borgten sie auf ihren eigenen Leib und mußten sich gefallen lassen, von ihren Kreditoren als Sklaven verkauft zu werden. Gegen diesen abscheulichen Menschenhandel war noch kein Gesetz in Attika gegeben, und nichts hielt die grausame Habsucht der reichen Bürger in Schranken. So schrecklich war der Zustand Athens. Wenn der Staat nicht zu Grunde gehen sollte, so mußte man dieses zerstörte Gleichgewicht der Güter auf eine gewaltsame Art wieder herstellen.

Zu diesem Ende waren unter dem Volk drei Faktionen entstanden. Die *eine*, welcher die armen Bürger besonders beitraten, forderte eine *Demokratie*, eine gleiche Verteilung der Äcker, wie sie Lykurgus in Sparta eingeführt hatte; die *andre*, welche die Reichen ausmachten, stritt für die *Aristokratie*.

Die *dritte* wollte beide Staatsformen mit einander verbunden wissen und setzte sich den beiden andern entgegen, daß keine durchdringen konnte.

although he gave them the arrogant title of *inalterable* laws.

Draco had, therefore, performed his task very badly. Instead of benefiting the republic, his laws were detrimental to it. Because the laws could not be obeyed and there were no other laws to take their place, it was actually as though there were no laws at all in Athens, and the saddest anarchy prevailed.

At that time the situation of the Athenian people was indeed deplorable. One class of citizens owned everything, the other nothing. The poor were oppressed and exploited most unmercifully by the rich. The classes were separated by an impassable gulf. Want compelled the poor to appeal for help to the rich, to the very people who, like leeches, had sucked them dry. But the help they received was of a very cruel sort. For the money they borrowed they had to pay an enormous rate of interest and if they did not pay by the time stipulated, their property was forfeited to their creditors. Having exhausted their means and still being obliged to go on living, they were forced to sell their children as slaves. Finally, when even this resource failed them, they borrowed on their own bodies and had to permit their creditors to sell them as slaves. There was as yet no law in Attica prohibiting this abominable traffic in human flesh and no way of curbing the cruel rapacity of the rich. So frightful was the situation in Athens that, if the state was not to be ruined, the equilibrium which had been destroyed by the unequal distribution of property had to be restored by violent means.

To this end, three parties had arisen among the people, all of which proposed to remedy the situation. One party, made up of the poor citizens, demanded a democratic government, an equal distribution of the land such as Lycurgus had introduced in Sparta. Another, representing the rich, pressed for the establishment of an aristocracy.

The third party wanted to combine both forms of government and, by opposing the other two, prevented either from prevailing.

Es war keine Hoffnung, diesen Streit auf eine ruhige Art beizulegen, so lange man nicht einen Mann fand, dem sich alle drei Parteien auf gleiche Weise unterwarfen und ihn zum Schiedsrichter über sich anerkannten.

Glücklicherweise fand sich ein solcher Mann, und seine Verdienste um die Republik, sein sanfter billiger Charakter und der Ruf seiner Weisheit hatte längst schon die Augen der Nation auf ihn gezogen. Dieser Mann war Solon, von königlicher Abkunft wie Lykurgus, denn er zählte den Kodrus unter seinen Ahnherrn. Solons Vater war ein sehr reicher Mann gewesen, aber durch Wohltun hatte er sein Vermögen geschwächt, und der junge Solon mußte in seinen ersten Jahren die Kaufmannschaft ergreifen. Durch Reisen, welche ihm diese Lebensart notwendig machte, und durch den Verkehr mit auswärtigen Völkern bereicherte sich sein Geist, und sein Genie entwickelte sich im Umgang mit fremden Weisen. Frühe schon legte er sich auf die Dichtkunst, und die Fertigkeit, die er darin erlangte, kam ihm in der Folge sehr gut zu statten, moralische Wahrheiten und politische Regeln in dieses gefällige Gewand zu kleiden. Sein Herz war empfindlich für Freude und Liebe; einige Schwachheiten seiner Jugend machten ihn um so nachsichtiger gegen die Menschheit und gaben seinen Gesetzen das Gepräge von Sanftmut und Milde, das sie von den Satzungen des Drako und Lykurgus so schön unterscheidet. Er war ferner noch ein tapfrer Heerführer gewesen, hatte der Republik den Besitz der Insel Salamine erworben und noch andere wichtige Kriegsdienste geleistet. Damals war das Studium der Weisheit noch nicht wie jetzt von politischer und kriegrischer Wirksamkeit getrennt; der Weise war der beste Staatsmann, der erfahrenste Feldherr, der tapferste Soldat; seine Weisheit floß in alle Geschäfte seines bürgerlichen Lebens. Solons Ruf war durch ganz Griechenland erschollen, und in die allgemeine Angelegenheiten des Peloponnes hatte er einen sehr großen Einfluß.

Solon war der Mann, der allen Parteien in Athen gleich lieb war. Die Reichen hatten große Hoffnungen von ihm, weil er selbst ein begüterter Mann war. Die Armen vertrauten ihm, weil er ein rechtschaffner Mann war. Der verständige

There was no hope of settling this dispute in a peaceful manner unless a man could be found to whose judgment all three parties would be willing to bow and whom they would all accept as their arbiter.

Fortunately there was such a man, a man whose services to the republic, whose gentleness and reasonableness and whose reputation for wisdom had attracted the attention of the nation for a long time. This man was Solon, like Lycurgus of royal descent, for he numbered Codrus among his ancestors. Solon's father had been a very rich man, but had reduced his means by his good works, and young Solon was forced to go into commerce during the first years of his citizenship. Since he had had to travel extensively for business reasons, his mind had been enriched by contact with foreign peoples and his genius cultivated through association with foreign sages. He devoted himself to poetry at an early age and the skill he developed in this art was afterward of great use to him in clothing moral truths and political rules in this attractive garb. His heart was susceptible to joy and love. The foibles of his youth made him all the more lenient toward humanity and gave his laws the mild and gentle character that made them so beautiful in comparison with the statutes of Draco and Lycurgus. What is more, he had been a brave general and had rendered many important military services to the republic, including the conquest of the island of Salamine. At that time the study of philosophy was not yet separated as it is now from that of political and military activity. The philosopher was the best statesman, the most experienced general, the bravest soldier. His wisdom was applied to every department of civil life. Solon's reputation had spread throughout all of Greece and he had a very great influence in Peloponnesian affairs.

Solon was equally suitable to all parties in Athens. The rich had high hopes of him because he himself was a man of property. The poor trusted him because he was an honest man. The more intelligent Athenians wanted

231

Teil der Athenienser wünschte sich ihn zum *Herrscher,* weil die Monarchie das sicherste Mittel schien, die Faktionen zu unterdrücken; seine Verwandten wünschten dieses gleichfalls, aber aus eigennützigen Absichten, um die Herrschaft mit ihm zu teilen. Solon verschmähte diesen Rat: die Monarchie, sagte er, sei ein schöner Wohnplatz, aber er habe keinen Ausgang.

Er begnügte sich, sich zum Archon und Gesetzgeber ernennen zu lassen, und übernahm dieses große Amt ungern, und nur aus Achtung für das Wohl der Bürger.

Das erste, womit er sein Werk eröffnete, war das berühmte Edikt, *Seisachtheia* oder Erledigung genannt, wodurch alle Schulden aufgehoben und zugleich verboten wurde, daß künftig keiner dem andern auf seinen Leib etwas leihen durfte. Dieses Edikt war allerdings ein gewaltsamer Angriff auf das Eigentum, aber die höchste Not des Staats machte einen gewaltsamen Schritt notwendig. Er war unter zwei Übeln das kleinere, denn die Klasse des Volks, welche dadurch litt, war weit geringer als die, welche dadurch glücklich wurde.

Durch dieses wohltätige Edikt wälzte er auf einmal die schweren Lasten ab, welche die arme Bürgerklasse seit Jahrhunderten niedergedrückt hatten: die Reichen aber machte er dadurch nicht elend, denn er ließ ihnen, was sie hatten; er nahm ihnen nur die Mittel, ungerecht zu sein. Nichtsdestoweniger erntete er von den Armen so wenig Dank als von den Reichen. Die Armen hatten auf eine völlig gleiche Länderteilung gerechnet, davon in Sparta das Beispiel gegeben war, und murrten deswegen gegen ihn, daß er ihre Erwartung hintergangen hatte. Sie vergaßen, daß der Gesetzgeber den Reichen ebenso gut als den Armen *Gerechtigkeit* schuldig sei und daß die Anordnung des Lykurgus eben darum nicht nachahmungswürdig sei, weil sie sich auf eine Unbilligkeit gründete, die zu vermeiden gewesen wäre.

Der Undank des Volks preßte dem Gesetzgeber eine bescheidene Klage aus. "Ehmals", sagte er, "rauschte mir von allen Seiten mein Lob entgegen; jetzt schielt alles mit feindlichen Blicken auf mich." Bald aber zeigten sich in Attika die wohltätigen Folgen seiner Verfügung. Das Land, das

him as their ruler because monarchy seemed to them the surest way of suppressing the factions. His relatives shared this desire, but for selfish motives. They hoped to have a part in the government. Solon rejected this advice. "Monarchy," he said, "is a beautiful dwelling, but it has no exit."

He was content to allow himself to be appointed archon and lawgiver. He undertook this great work unwillingly and only out of respect for the welfare of his fellow citizens.

His first act was to issue the celebrated edict called *seisachtheia* or settlement. According to this all debts were canceled and no one in future was permitted to lend anything to another on his body. Strictly speaking, this edict represented a violent attack on property, but the critical state of the nation made violent measures necessary. It was the lesser of two evils, for the class that suffered from this edict was far smaller than the class that benefited by it.

By this beneficient edict he at once relieved the poor of the heavy burden that had oppressed them for centuries. Nor were the rich reduced to poverty, for they retained what they already possessed. He merely took from them the means of being unjust. Nevertheless, he earned no more gratitude from the poor than from the rich. The poor had hoped for an equal distribution of land, of which an example was given in Sparta, and grumbled because he had disappointed their expectations. They forgot that the lawgiver is under obligation to mete out justice to both the rich and the poor, and that it was not desirable to imitate Lycurgus' measure because it was based on an injustice which should have been avoided.

The ingratitude of the people wrung a modest complaint from the lawgiver. "Formerly," he said, "everyone sang my praises. Now everyone leers at me with hostile eyes." Soon, however, the beneficial results of his decree became evident in Attica. The land that formerly

vorher Sklavendienste tat, war jetzt frei; der Bürger bearbeitete den Acker jetzt als sein Eigentum, den er vorher als Tagelöhner für seinen Kreditor bearbeitet hatte. Viele ins Ausland verkaufte Bürger, die schon angefangen hatten, ihre Muttersprache zu verlernen, sahen als freie Menschen ihr Vaterland wieder.

Das Vertrauen in den Gesetzgeber kehrte zurück. Man übertrug ihm die ganze Reformation des Staats und unumschränkte Gewalt, über das Eigentum und die Rechte der Bürger zu verfügen. Der erste Gebrauch, den er davon machte, war, daß er alle Gesetze des Drako abschaffte—diejenigen ausgenommen, welche gegen den Mord und Ehebruch gerichtet waren.

Nun übernahm er das große Werk, der Republik eine neue Konstitution zu geben.

Alle atheniensischen Bürger mußten sich einer Schätzung des Vermögens unterwerfen, und nach dieser Schätzung wurden sie in vier Klassen oder Zünfte geteilt.

Die erste begriff diejenigen in sich, welche jährlich 500 Maß von trocknen und flüssigen Dingen Einkommen hatten.

Die zweite enthielt diejenigen, welche 300 Maß Einkommen hatten und ein Pferd halten konnten.

Die dritte diejenigen, welche nur die Hälfte davon hatten, und wo also immer zwei zusammentreten mußten, um diese Summe herauszubringen. Man nannte sie deswegen die Zweigespannten.

In der vierten waren die, welche keine liegenden Gründe besaßen und bloß von ihrer Handarbeit lebten, Handwerker, Taglöhner und Künstler.

Die drei ersten Klassen konnten öffentliche Ämter bekleiden; die aus der letzten waren davon ausgeschlossen, doch hatten sie bei der Nationalversammlung eine Stimme wie die übrigen, und dadurch allein genossen sie einen großen Anteil an der Regierung. Vor die Nationalversammlung, *Ecclesia* genannt, wurden alle große Angelegenheiten gebracht und durch dieselbe entschieden: die Wahl der Obrigkeiten, die Besetzung der Ämter, wichtige Rechtshändel, Finanzangelegenheiten, Krieg und Frieden. Da ferner die Solonischen Gesetze mit einer gewissen Dunkelheit behaftet

had toiled in slave labor was now free. The citizen now cultivated as his own property the field in which he had been obliged to work as a day laborer for his creditor. Many citizens who had been sold to foreigners and had already begun to forget their own language returned to their native land as free men.

Confidence in the lawgiver was restored. The entire reformation of the state was entrusted to him and he was given unlimited power over the property and rights of the citizens. The first use he made of his power was to abolish all the laws of Draco except those directed against murder and adultery.

After this he undertook the great task of giving the republic a new constitution.

All Athenian citizens had to submit to an estimate of their income and on the basis of this they were divided into four classes or guilds.

The first class was made up of those who had a yearly income of five hundred measures of dry and liquid property.

The second was made up of those who had three hundred measures and were able to keep a horse.

The third comprised those who owned only half of this amount and who therefore had to join up with another man in order to produce it. For this reason they were called a two-horse team.

The fourth class included those who possessed no land and earned their living by manual labor: artisans, day laborers and artists.

The first three classes could hold public office. Those belonging to the fourth class were not eligible. But in the national assembly they voted like the rest and this secured them a large share in the government. All important matters were brought before the national assembly, called the *ecclesia*, and were decided by it: the selection of authorities, the distribution of offices, important litigations, financial transactions, war and peace. Furthermore, the text of the Solonian law being somewhat obscure, every time the judge was in doubt as to the

waren, so mußte in jedem Fall, wo der Richter über ein Gesetz, das er auszulegen hatte, zweifelhaft war, an die Ecclesia appelliert werden, welche dann in letzter Instanz entschied, wie das Gesetz zu verstehen sei. Von allen Tribunalen konnte man an das Volk appellieren. Vor dem dreißigsten Jahr hatte niemand Zutritt zur Nationalversammlung; aber sobald einer das erforderliche Alter hatte, so konnte er ungestraft nicht mehr wegbleiben, denn Solon haßte und bekämpfte nichts so sehr als Lauigkeit gegen das gemeine Wesen.

Athens Verfassung war auf diese Art in eine vollkommene Demokratie verwandelt; im strengsten Verstande war das Volk *souverän*, und nicht bloß durch Repräsentanten herrschte es, sondern in eigner Person und durch sich selbst. Bald aber zeigten sich nachteilige Folgen dieser Einrichtung. Das Volk war zu schnell mächtig geworden, um sich dieses Vorrechts mit Mäßigung zu bedienen; Leidenschaft mischte sich in die öffentliche Versammlung, und der Tumult, den eine so große Volksmenge erregte, erlaubte nicht immer, reif zu überlegen und weise zu entscheiden. Diesem Übel zu begegnen, schuf Solon einen Senat, zu welchem aus jeder der vier Zünfte 100 Mitglieder genommen wurden. Dieser Senat mußte sich vorher über die Punkte beratschlagen, welche der Ecclesia vorgelegt werden sollten. Nichts, was nicht vorher vom Senat in Überlegung genommen worden, durfte vor das Volk gebracht werden, aber das Volk allein behielt die Entscheidung. War eine Angelegenheit von dem Senat dem Volk *vorgetragen*, so traten die *Redner* auf, die Wahl desselben zu lenken. Diese Menschenklasse hat sich in Athen sehr viel Wichtigkeit erworben und durch den Mißbrauch, den sie von ihrer Kunst und dem leicht beweglichen Sinn der Athenienser machte, der Republik ebenso viel geschadet, als sie ihr hätte nützen können, wenn sie, von Privatabsichten rein, das *wahre* Interesse des Staats immer vor Augen gehabt hätte. Alle Kunstgriffe der Beredsamkeit bot der Redner auf, dem Volk diejenige Seite einer Sache annehmlich zu machen, wozu er es gerne bringen wollte; und verstand er seine Kunst, so waren alle Herzen in seinen Händen. Durch diese Redner wurde dem Volk eine sanfte und er-

meaning, appeal had to be made as a last resort to the ecclesia which then decided how it was to be interpreted. Appeal could be made to the people from any tribunal. No one could be a member of the national assembly before the age of thirty, but once he had arrived at the legal age he could not stay away from a session without becoming liable to punishment. There was nothing that Solon opposed and detested more than indifference to the affairs of state.

Thus the Athenian constitution was transformed into a complete democracy. The people were sovereign in the strictest sense of the term. They ruled not merely through representatives, but directly in their own names.

Soon, however, this system led to unpleasant consequences. The people had come to power too rapidly to exercise their privilege with moderation. There were outbreaks of passion in the public assembly and the tumult that arose in so large a crowd did not always permit of calm deliberation and wise decisions.

To remedy this evil, Solon created a senate made up of one hundred members from each of the four guilds. This senate was to deliberate on each point before laying it before the ecclesia. Nothing that had not been considered by the senate could be brought before the people, but the final decision was reserved for the people alone.

After the matter had been laid before the people, orators delivered speeches for the purpose of influencing the vote. These orators acquired considerable importance in Athens. By misusing their ability to sway the highly susceptible minds of the Athenians, they harmed the republic as much as they could have benefited it if they had always kept their eyes on the true interests of the state. The orator resorted to all the tricks of eloquence to make the point he wished to carry attractive to the people. If he was skillful, the hearts of the people were in his hands. The orators bound the people by gentle and legitimate

laubte Fessel angelegt. Sie herrschten durch Überredung, und ihre Herrschaft war darum nicht weniger groß, weil sie der freien Wahl etwas übrig ließ. Das Volk behielt völlige Freiheit, zu wählen und zu verwerfen; aber durch die Kunst, womit man ihm die Dinge vorzulegen wußte, lenkte man diese Freiheit. Eine vortreffliche Einrichtung, wenn die Funktion der Redner immer in reinen und treuen Händen geblieben wäre. Bald aber wurden aus diesen Rednern Sophisten, die ihren Ruhm darein setzten, das Schlimme gut und das Gute schlimm zu machen. Mitten in Athen war ein großer öffentlicher Platz, von Bildsäulen der Götter und Helden umgeben, das *Prytaneum* genannt. Auf diesem Platz war die Versammlung des Senats, und die Senatoren erhielten davon den Namen der Prytanen. Von einem Prytanen wurde ein untadelhaftes Leben verlangt. Keinem Verschwender, keinem, der seinem Vater unehrerbietig begegnet, keinem, welcher sich nur einmal betrunken hatte, durfte es in den Sinn kommen, sich zu diesem Amte zu melden.

Als sich in der Folge die Bevölkerung in Athen vermehrte und anstatt der vier Zünfte, welche Solon eingeführt hatte, zehen Zünfte gemacht wurden, wurde auch die Anzahl der Prytanen von 400 bis 1000 gesetzt. Aber von diesen 1000 Prytanen waren jährlich nur 500 in Funktion, und auch diese 500 nie auf einmal. Funfzig derselben regierten immer fünf Wochen lang, und zwar so, daß in jeder Woche nur 10 im Amte standen. So war es ganz unmöglich, willkürlich zu verfahren, denn jeder hatte ebenso viele Zeugen und Hüter seiner Handlungen, als er Amtsgenossen hatte, und der nachfolgende konnte immer die Verwaltung seines Vorgängers mustern. Alle fünf Wochen wurden vier Volksversammlungen gehalten, die außerordentlichen nicht mit gerechnet—eine Einrichtung, wodurch es ganz unmöglich gemacht ward, daß eine Angelegenheit lange unentschieden blieb und der Gang der Geschäfte verzögert wurde.

Außer dem Senat der Prytanen, den er neu erschuf, brachte Solon auch den *Areopagus* wieder in Ansehen, den Drako erniedrigt hatte, weil er ihm zu menschlich dachte. Er machte ihn zum obersten Aufseher und Schutzgeist der Gesetze und befestigte, wie Plutarch sagt, an diesen beiden Gerich-

chains. They ruled by persuasion and their rule was no less powerful because it left the people a margin of free choice. The people were quite free to adopt or to reject a proposal, but this freedom was controlled by the cunning way in which issues were presented. This would have been an excellent system if the orators had always been animated by pure and honest motives. But soon the art of oratory became perverted by sophists who prided themselves on their ability to make evil look like good and good like evil.

In the center of Athens there was a large public square called the Prytaneum which was surrounded by statues of gods and heroes. The senate held its sessions on this square for which reason the senators were called *prytanes*. A prytanis was expected to lead a blameless life. No spendthrift, no one who had treated his father with disrespect, no one who had ever been intoxicated could think of being elected to this office.

Later on, when the population of Athens had increased and there were ten guilds instead of the four introduced by Solon, the number of prytanes was also increased from four hundred to one thousand. But of the thousand only five hundred were on active duty each year and not all of the five hundred at one time. Fifty of them governed for five weeks and in such a way that only ten of them were in office each week. Thus it became quite impossible to rule in an arbitrary manner, for each had as many witnesses to his acts as he had colleagues and his successor could always reexamine them. Four popular assemblies were held every five weeks, not counting extraordinary convocations. By this system, delay was rendered impossible and business was transacted with despatch.

Besides creating the senate, Solon also restored the *areopagus* whose authority had been curtailed by Draco because he considered it too humane. He made it the supreme guardian of the law and, as Plutarch says, fastened

ten, dem Senat nämlich und dem Areopagus, wie an zwei
Ankern die Republik.

Diese zwei Gerichtshöfe waren eingesetzt, über die Erhaltung des Staats und seiner Gesetze zu wachen. Zehen andere Tribunale beschäftigten sich mit Anwendung der Gesetze, mit der Gerechtigkeitspflege. Über Mordtaten erkann-
ten vier Gerichtshöfe, das Palladium, das Delphinium, die
Phreattys und Heliäa. Die zwei erstern bestätigte Solon nur,
sie waren schon unter den Königen gestiftet. Unvorsätzliche
Mordtaten wurden vor dem *Palladium* gerichtet. Vor dem
Delphinium stellten sich die, welche sich zu einem für erlaubt gehaltenen Totschlag bekannten. Das Gericht *Phre-*
attys wurde eingesetzt, um über diejenigen zu erkennen, welche eines vorsätzlichen Totschlags wegen angeklagt wurden,
nachdem sie bereits eines unvorsätzlichen Mordes wegen
außer Landes geflüchtet waren. Der Beklagte erschien auf
einem Schiffe, und am Ufer standen seine Richter. War er
unschuldig, so kehrte er ruhig an seinen Verbannungsort zurück, in der fröhlichen Hoffnung, einst wieder heimkehren
zu dürfen. Wurde er schuldig befunden, so kehrte er zwar
auch unversehrt zurück, aber sein Vaterland hatte er auf
ewig verloren.

Das vierte Kriminalgericht war die *Heliäa*, die ihren Namen
von der Sonne hatte, weil sie sich gleich nach Aufgang der
Sonne und an einem Orte, den die Sonne bestrahlt, zu ver-
sammeln pflegte. Die Heliäa war eine außerordentliche Kommission der andern großen Tribunale; ihre Mitglieder waren
zugleich Richter und Magistrate. Sie hatten nicht bloß Gesetze anzuwenden und zu vollziehen, sondern auch zu ver-
bessern und ihren Sinn zu bestimmen. Ihre Versammlung
war feierlich, und ein furchtbarer Eid verband sie zur Wahrheit.

Sobald ein Todesurteil gefällt war, und der Beklagte hatte
sich nicht durch eine freiwillige Verbannung demselben entzogen, so überlieferte man ihn den *Eilf Männern*; diesen
Namen führte die Kommission, wozu jede der zehen Zünfte einen Mann hergab, die mit dem Blutrichter eilf ausmachten. Diese Eilf Männer hatten die Aufsicht über die
Gefängnisse und vollzogen die Todesurteile. Der Todes-

the republic to these two tribunals, the senate and the areopagus, as to two anchors.

These two tribunals had been instituted for the purpose of watching over the preservation of the state and its laws. Ten other tribunals had charge of the application of the laws; they constituted the ordinary judiciary. Murder cases were tried before four courts, the *palladium*, *delphinium*, *phreattys* and *heliaea*. The first two were merely confirmed by Solon; they had been instituted by the kings. Unintentional homicide was tried by the palladium. Those who confessed to killing, but for a justifiable cause, presented themselves before the delphinium. The phreattys was established for the trial of those who had been accused of deliberate murder after they had already fled the country on the charge of unintentional homicide. The accused appeared on board a ship and his judges stood on the shore. If he was innocent, he quietly returned to his place of exile in the joyous hope of being allowed to return at some future time. If he was found guilty, he also returned unmolested but was permanently exiled from his country.

The fourth criminal court, the heliaea, derived its name from the sun because it met immediately after sunrise at a place shone upon by the sun. This court was an extraordinary commission of the other three tribunals. Its members were both magistrates and judges. Its function was not merely to apply and execute laws, but also to improve and interpret them. These men met in solemn conclave and were bound by a terrible oath to speak the truth.

As soon as sentence of death had been pronounced, if the accused had not evaded it by going into voluntary exile, he was delivered over to the Eleven. This was the name assigned to a commission to which each of the ten guilds furnished one man, thus making eleven with the executioner. These eleven men supervised the prisons and executed the death sentence. The Athenians had three

arten, welche man den Verbrechern in Athen zuerkannte, waren dreierlei. Entweder man stürzte ihn in einen Schlund, auch in das Meer hinunter, oder man richtete ihn mit dem Schwert hin oder gab ihm Schierling zu trinken.

Zunächst der Todesstrafe kam die Verweisung. Diese Strafe ist schrecklich in glückseligen Ländern; es gibt Staaten, aus denen es kein Unglück ist verwiesen zu werden. Daß es die Verweisung zunächst an die Todesstrafe und, wenn sie ewig war, dieser letztern gleich setzte, ist ein schönes Selbstgefühl des atheniensischen Volks. Der Athenienser, der sein Vaterland verloren, konnte in der ganzen übrigen Welt kein Athen mehr finden.

Die Verbannung war mit einer Konfiskation aller Güter verbunden, den Ostracismus allein ausgenommen.

Bürger, welche durch außerordentliche Verdienste oder Glück zu einem größern Einfluß und Ansehen gelangt waren, als sich mit der republikanischen Gleichheit vertrug, und die also anfingen, der bürgerlichen Freiheit gefährlich zu werden, verbannte man zuweilen—ehe sie diese Verbannung verdienten. Um den Staat zu retten, war man unrecht gegen einen einzelnen Bürger. Die Idee, welche diesem Gebrauche zum Grund liegt, ist an sich zu loben: aber das Mittel, welches man erwählte, zeugt von einer kindischen Politik. Man nannte diese Art der Verbannung den *Ostracismus*, weil die Vota auf Scherben geschrieben wurden. Sechstausend Stimmen waren nötig, einen Bürger mit dieser Strafe zu belegen. Der Ostracismus mußte seiner Natur nach meistens den verdientesten Bürger treffen; er ehrte also mehr, als er schändete—aber darum war er doch nicht weniger ungerecht und grausam, denn er nahm dem Würdigsten, was ihm das Teuerste war, die Heimat.

Eine vierte Art von Strafen bei Kriminalverbrechen war die Strafe der Säule. Die Schuld des Verbrechers wurde auf eine Säule geschrieben, und dies machte ihn ehrlos mit seinem ganzen Geschlechte.

Geringere bürgerliche Händel zu entscheiden, waren sechs Tribunale eingesetzt, die aber niemals wichtig wurden, weil dem Verurteilten von allen die Appellation an die höhern Gerichte und an die Ecclesia offen stand. Jeder führte seine

242

ways of putting criminals to death. The guilty man was either hurled down a precipice or into the ocean, decapitated or given hemlock to drink.

Exile ranked second to the death penalty. This is a terrible punishment in happy countries, but there are states from which it is no misfortune to be exiled. The fact that the Athenian people ranked exile second to the death penalty and, if it was permanent, considered it equal to the latter, is a fine testimonial to their national pride. An Athenian who had lost his country could not find another Athens anywhere in the world.

Exile, with the exception of ostracism, was accompanied by the confiscation of property.

Citizens who, because of extraordinary services or good fortune, had acquired more influence and authority than was compatible with republican equality and so were becoming dangerous to republican liberty were sometimes exiled—even before they had actually deserved to be. An individual citizen had to suffer injustice in order to save the state. The idea underlying this is laudable in itself, but the means chosen to carry it out is evidence of political childishness. This sort of exile was called ostracism because votes were written on pieces of pottery. Six thousand votes were required to inflict this punishment. By its nature ostracism was usually inflicted on the most deserving citizens. Therefore it was more of an honor than a disgrace, but it was nonetheless cruel and unjust, for it deprived the most worthy of what was most precious to him, his native land.

A fourth kind of punishment for crime was the punishment of columns. The crime of which a man was guilty was inscribed on a column and this disgraced him together with his entire family.

Less significant disputes were brought before six tribunals that never gained importance because the condemned parties always had the right to appeal to the higher courts and the ecclesia. Every citizen pleaded his own cause ex-

Sache selbst, Weiber, Kinder und Sklaven ausgenommen. Eine Wasseruhr bestimmte die Dauer von seiner und seines Anklägers Rede. Die wichtigsten bürgerlichen Händel mußten in 24 Stunden entschieden sein.

So viel von den bürgerlichen und politischen Anordnungen Solons; aber darauf allein schränkte sich dieser Gesetzgeber nicht ein. Es ist ein Vorzug, den die alten Gesetzgeber vor den neuern haben, daß sie ihre Menschen den Gesetzen zubilden, die sie ihnen erteilen, daß sie auch die Sittlichkeit, den Charakter, den gesellschaftlichen Umgang mitnehmen und den Bürger nie von dem Menschen trennen wie wir. Bei uns stehen die Gesetze nicht selten in direktem Widerspruch mit den Sitten. Bei den Alten standen Gesetze und Sitten in einer viel schöneren Harmonie. Ihre Staatskörper haben daher auch eine so lebendige Wärme, die den unsrigen ganz fehlt; mit unzerstörbaren Zügen war der Staat in die Seelen der Bürger gegraben.

Indessen muß man auch hier in Anpreisung des Altertums sehr behutsam sein. Fast durchgängig kann man behaupten, daß die *Absichten* der alten Gesetzgeber weise und lobenswürdig waren, daß sie aber in den *Mitteln* fehlten. Diese Mittel zeugen oft von unrichtigen Begriffen und einer einseitigen Vorstellungsart. Wo wir zu weit zurückbleiben, eilten sie zu weit vor. Wenn unsre Gesetzgeber Unrecht getan haben, daß sie moralische Pflichten und Sitten ganz vernachlässigten, so hatten die Gesetzgeber der Griechen darin Unrecht, daß sie moralische Pflichten mit dem Zwang der Gesetze einschärften. Zur moralischen Schönheit der Handlungen ist Freiheit des Willens die erste Bedingung, und diese Freiheit ist dahin, sobald man moralische Tugend durch gesetzliche Strafen erzwingen will. Das edelste Vorrecht der menschlichen Natur ist, sich selbst zu bestimmen und das Gute um des Guten willen tun. Kein bürgerliches Gesetz darf Treue gegen den Freund, Großmut gegen den Feind, Dankbarkeit gegen Vater und Mutter zwangsmäßig gebieten; denn sobald es dieses tut, wird eine freie moralische Empfindung in ein Werk der Furcht, in eine sklavische Regung verwandelt.

Aber wieder auf unsern Solon zurückzukommen.

244

cept women, children and slaves. The duration of the speeches made by defendant and plaintiff was regulated by a water clock. The most important civil suits had to be decided in twenty-four hours.

So much for the civil and political institutions of Solon, but the lawgiver did not stop here. Ancient lawgivers enjoyed the privilege of shaping man in accordance with their laws, concerning themselves with morality, the formation of character and social intercourse, and did not differentiate, as we do, between the man and the citizen. With us laws are not infrequently in direct opposition to customs. In antiquity a much more beautiful harmony prevailed between laws and customs. This is why the body politic was animated by a warm and lively zeal that is lacking in our institutions. The state was indelibly engraved on the souls of the citizens.

Here too, however, we must be cautious in our praise of antiquity. It may be said that the intentions of the ancient lawgivers, almost without exception, were wise and praiseworthy, but they did not always employ the best means of executing them. There is frequently evidence in them of wrong conceptions and one-sidedness. They went too far where we do not go far enough. If our lawmakers are wrong in entirely neglecting moral duties and customs, the Greeks too were wrong in enforcing moral duties by law. Freedom of will is the first condition of moral beauty and this freedom is destroyed if moral virtue is enforced by legal penalties. It is the noblest privilege of human nature to determine its own conduct and to do good for its own sake. No law should exact loyalty to a friend, generosity toward an enemy, gratitude to father and mother. If this is done, a free moral sentiment is transformed into the product of fear, a slavish emotion.

But to return to Solon.

Ein Solonisches Gesetz verordnet, daß jeder Bürger die Beleidigung, die einem andern widerführe, als sich selbst angetan betrachten und nicht ruhen solle, bis sie an dem Beleidiger gerochen sei. Das Gesetz ist vortrefflich, wenn man seine Absicht dabei betrachtet. Seine Absicht war, jedem Bürger warmen Anteil an allen übrigen einzuflößen und alle mit einander daran zu gewöhnen, sich als Glieder eines zusammenhängenden Ganzen anzusehen. Wie angenehm würden wir überrascht werden, wenn wir in ein Land kämen, wo uns jeder Vorübergehende ungerufen gegen einen Beleidiger in Schutz nähme. Aber wie sehr würde unser Vergnügen verlieren, wenn uns zugleich dabei gesagt würde, daß er so schön habe handeln *müssen*.

Ein andres Gesetz, welches Solon gab, erklärt denjenigen für ehrlos, der bei einem bürgerlichen Aufruhr neutral bleibe. Auch bei diesem Gesetz lag eine unverkennbare gute Absicht zum Grunde. Dem Gesetzgeber war es darum zu tun, seinen Bürgern das innigste Interesse an dem Staat einzuflößen. Kälte gegen das Vaterland war ihm das Hassenswürdigste an einem Bürger. Neutralität kann oft eine Folge dieser Kälte sein; aber er vergaß, daß oft das feurigste Interesse am Vaterland diese Neutralität *gebietet*—alsdann nämlich, wenn beide Parteien Unrecht haben und das Vaterland bei beiden gleichviel zu verlieren haben würde.

Ein andres Gesetz des Solon verbietet, von den Toten übel zu reden; ein andres, an öffentlichen Örtern, wie vor Gericht, im Tempel oder im Schauspiel, einem Lebenden Böses nachzusagen. Einen Bastard spricht er von kindlichen Pflichten los, denn der Vater, sagt er, habe sich schon durch die genossene sinnliche Lust bezahlt gemacht; ebenso sprach er den Sohn von der Pflicht frei, seinen Vater zu ernähren, wenn dieser ihn keine Kunst hätte lernen lassen. Er erlaubte, Testamente zu machen und sein Vermögen nach Willkür zu verschenken, denn Freunde, die man sich wählt, sagte er, sind mehr wert als bloße Verwandte. Die Aussteuer schaffte er ab, weil er wollte, daß die Liebe, und nicht der Eigennutz Ehen stiftete. Noch ein schöner Zug von Sanftmut in seinem Charakter ist, daß er

One of his laws decrees that every citizen must regard an insult received by another as directed against himself and must not rest until the offender is punished. The law is excellent when viewed in the light of its underlying purpose. Its purpose was to inspire everyone with a warm interest in his neighbor and to accustom him to look upon himself as part of a consistent whole What a pleasant surprise it would be for us to arrive in a country where every passer-by, without a word from us, would protect us from insults. But how much less pleasure we would derive from this if we were told that this protection was compulsory.

Another law instituted by Solon states that it is dishonorable for anyone to remain neutral during a rebellion. The underlying purpose of this law was also undoubtedly a good one. The lawmaker was anxious to inspire in his fellow citizens a lively interest in the affairs of state. For a citizen to be indifferent to his country he regarded as a most detestable attitude. Neutrality is often the result of indifference. Bu he forgot that the most intense patriotic devotion frequently demands just such neutrality; in a case, for instance, where both parties are in the wrong and the country would suffer if either were to prevail.

Another of Solon's laws forbids a man to speak ill of the dead. Still another forbids him to indulge in malicious talk about the living in public places such as the courts, the temple, the theater. He absolves bastards of all filial duties toward the father who, he said, has already been repaid by the sensual pleasure he has enjoyed. He likewise absolved the son from the obligation to support his father if the latter has neglected to have his son taught a trade. He permitted a man to make a will and to dispose of his property as he wished, for friends of one's own choosing, he said, are worth more than mere relatives. He abolished dowries because he wished to make love rather than interest the basis of marriage. Further evidence of his gentle character is the fact that he called odious things

247

verhaßten Dingen mildere Namen gab. Abgaben hießen Beiträge, Besatzungen Wächter der Stadt, Gefängnisse Gemächer, und die Schuldenvernichtung nannte er Erleichterung. Den Aufwand, zu dem der athenienische Geist sich so sehr neigte, mäßigte er durch weise Verordnungen; strenge Gesetze wachten über die Sitten des Frauenzimmers, über den Umgang beider Geschlechter und die Heiligkeit der Ehen.

Diese Gesetze, verordnete er, sollten nur auf 100 Jahre gültig sein—wie viel weiter sah er als Lykurgus! Er begriff, daß Gesetze nur Dienerinnen der Bildung sind, daß Nationen in ihrem männlichen Alter eine andere Führung nötig haben als in ihrer Kindheit. Lykurg verewigte die Geistes-Kindheit der Spartaner, um dadurch seine Gesetze bei ihnen zu verewigen, aber sein Staat ist verschwunden mit seinen Gesetzen. Solon hingegen versprach den seinigen nur eine hundertjährige Dauer, und noch heutigestages sind viele derselben im römischen Gesetzbuche in Kraft. Die Zeit ist eine gerechte Richterin aller Verdienste.

Man hat dem Solon zum Vorwurf gemacht, daß er dem Volk zu große Gewalt gegeben habe, und dieser Vorwurf ist nicht ungegründet. Indem er eine Klippe, die *Oligarchie*, zu sehr vermied, ist er einer andern, der *Anarchie*, zu nahe gekommen—aber doch auch nur nahe gekommen, denn der Senat der Prytanen und das Gericht des Areopagus waren starke Zügel der demokratischen Gewalt. Die Übel, welche von einer Demokratie unzertrennlich sind, tumultuarische und leidenschaftliche Entscheidungen und der Geist der Faktion, konnten freilich in Athen nicht vermieden werden—aber diese Übel sind doch weit mehr der Form, die er wählte, als dem Wesen der Demokratie zuzuschreiben. Er fehlte darin sehr, daß er das Volk nicht durch Repräsentanten, sondern in Person entscheiden ließ, welches wegen der starken Menschenmenge nicht ohne Verwirrung und Tumult und wegen der überlegenen Anzahl der unbemittelten Bürger nicht immer ohne Bestechung abgehen konnte. Der Ostracismus, wobei 6000 Stimmen zum wenigsten erfordert wurden, läßt uns abnehmen, wie stürmisch es bei dergleichen Volksversammlung mag zugegangen sein.

by milder names. Taxes were called contributions, garrisons were guardians of the city, prisons, apartments, and the cancellation of debts was called relief. He tempered by wise regulations the extravagant behavior to which Athenians were prone. Rigid laws governed the morals of women, the association of the two sexes and the sanctity of marriage.

These laws, he decreed, were to be valid only for one hundred years. How much more farsighted he was than Lycurgus! He understood that laws are merely the servants of culture, that nations in their maturity require a different kind of guidance from that required by nations in their infancy. Lycurgus perpetuated the mental infancy of the Spartans in order to perpetuate his laws. But both his state and his laws have vanished. Solon, on the other hand, made his laws binding for only one hundred years, and many of them are to be found in the Roman code to this very day. Time is a righteous judge of all merits.

Solon has been reproached for giving too much power to the people and this reproach is not unwarranted. In attempting to avoid one cliff, *oligarchy,* he came too near another, *anarchy*; but he only approached it, for the senate and the areopagus kept strong reins on popular power. The evils, which are inseparable from democratic government, tumultuous and passionate debates could not, it is true, be avoided in Athens. But these evils are to be attributed to the form he chose rather than to the essential nature of democracy. He erred in allowing the people to make decisions in person rather than through representatives. Because of the vast number of people involved, discussions could not very well take place without confusion and tumult and, owing to the large proportion of poor citizens, bribery was unavoidable. The sentence of ostracism, which required at least six thousand votes, shows us how stormy such popular assemblies

Wenn man aber auf der andern Seite bedenkt, wie gut auch der gemeinste Athenienser mit dem gemeinen Wesen bekannt war, wie mächtig der Nationalgeist in ihm wirkte, wie sehr der Gesetzgeber dafür gesorgt hatte, daß dem Bürger das Vaterland über alles ging, so wird man einen bessern Begriff von dem politischen Verstand des atheniensischen Pöbels bekommen und sich wenigstens hüten, von dem gemeinen Volke bei *uns* voreilig auf *jenes* zu schließen. Alle große Versammlungen haben immer eine gewisse Gesetzlosigkeit in ihrem Gefolge—alle kleinere aber haben Mühe, sich von aristokratischem Despotismus ganz rein zu erhalten. Zwischen beiden eine glückliche Mitte zu treffen, ist das schwerste Problem, das die kommenden Jahrhunderte erst auflösen sollen. Bewundernswert bleibt mir immer der Geist, der den Solon bei seiner Gesetzgebung beseelte, der Geist der gesunden und echten Staatskunst, die das Grundprinzipium, worauf alle Staaten ruhen müssen, nie aus den Augen verlor: sich selbst die Gesetze zu geben, denen man gehorchen soll, und die Pflichten des Bürgers aus Einsicht und aus Liebe zum Vaterland, nicht aus sklavischer Furcht vor der Strafe, nicht aus blinder und schlaffer Ergebung in den Willen eines Obern zu erfüllen.

Schön und trefflich war es von Solon, daß er Achtung hatte für die menschliche Natur und nie den Menschen dem Staat, nie den Zweck dem Mittel aufopferte, sondern den Staat dem Menschen dienen ließ. Seine Gesetze waren laxe Bänder, an denen sich der Geist der Bürger frei und leicht nach allen Richtungen bewegte und nie empfand, daß sie ihn lenkten; die Gesetze des Lykurgus waren eiserne Fesseln, an denen der kühne Mut sich wund rieb, die durch ihr drückendes Gewicht den Geist niederzogen. Alle mögliche Bahnen schloß der atheniensische Gesetzgeber dem Genie und dem Fleiß seiner Bürger auf; der spartanische Gesetzgeber vermauerte den seinigen alle bis auf eine einzige—das politische Verdienst. Lykurg befahl den Müßiggang durch Gesetze, Solon strafte ihn strenge. Darum reiften in Athen alle Tugenden, blühten alle Gewerbe und Künste, regten sich alle Sehnen des Fleißes; darum wurden alle Felder des Wissens dort bearbeitet. Wo findet man in Sparta ei-

may have been. On the other hand, if we consider how well even the common man was acquainted with the business of the republic, how strongly he was imbued with the national spirit, how much care the lawgiver had taken to make love of country the foremost sentiment in the hearts of the citizens, we shall have a better understanding of the political intelligence of the Athenian mob and at least shall not make the mistake of placing them on the same level as the common people of our age.

All large assemblies lead to a certain amount of lawlessness, but smaller assemblies have difficulty in keeping altogether free of aristocratic despotism. To hit the right mean between these two extremes is the most difficult problem and will only be solved by future generations. I shall always admire the spirit that animated Solon, the spirit of healthy and genuine statesmanship that never loses sight of the fundamental principle on which all governments must be based: the principle that the people themselves must make the laws they are to obey and that the duties of a citizen must be discharged out of rational conviction and patriotism, not out of slavish fear of punishment or a blind and passive submission to the will of a master.

Solon gave a fine account of himself in showing a respect for human nature, and never sacrificing the human being for the state, nor the end for the means, but saw to it that the state served man. His laws were loose reins within which the minds of the citizens could move freely and easily in all directions without feeling that they were being guided. The laws of Lycurgus were iron fetters against which the bold spirit chafed until it sank bleeding beneath the heavy weight. The Athenian lawgiver opened up every possible avenue to the genius and industry of his fellow citizens. The Spartan lawgiver blocked up every avenue but one, political service. Lycurgus imposed idleness by law, Solon punished it severely. Hence all virtues came to maturity in Athens, all trades and arts flourished, all of the sinews of industry were flexed, all fields of knowledge were cultivated.

nen Sokrates, einen Thukydides, einen Sophokles una Plato? Sparta konnte nur Herrscher und Krieger—keine Künstler, keine Dichter, keine Denker, keine Weltbürger erzeugen. Beide, Solon wie Lykurg, waren große Männer, beide waren rechtschaffne Männer, aber wie verschieden haben sie gewirkt, weil sie von entgegengesetzten Prinzipien ausgingen. Um den atheniensischen Gesetzgeber steht die Freiheit und die Freude, der Fleiß und der Überfluß—stehen alle Künste und Tugenden, alle Grazien und Musen herum, sehen dankbar zu ihm auf und nennen ihn ihren Vater und Schöpfer. Um den Lykurgus sieht man nichts als Tyrannei und ihr schreckliches Gegenteil, die Knechtschaft, die ihre Ketten schüttelt und dem Urheber ihres Elends flucht.

Der Charakter eines ganzen Volks ist der treueste Abdruck seiner Gesetze und also auch der sicherste Richter ihres Werts oder Unwerts. Beschränkt war der Kopf des Spartaners und unempfindlich sein Herz. Er war stolz und hochfahrend gegen seine Bundsgenossen, hart gegen seine Überwundenen, unmenschlich gegen seine Sklaven und knechtisch gegen seine Obern; in seinen Unterhandlungen war er ungewissenhaft und treulos, in seinen Entscheidungen despotisch, und seiner Größe, seiner Tugend selbst fehlte es an der gefälligen Anmut, welche allein die Herzen gewinnt. Der Athenienser hingegen war weichmütig und sanft im Umgang, höflich aufgeweckt im Gespräch, leutselig gegen den Geringen, gastfrei und gefällig gegen den Fremden. Er liebte zwar Weichlichkeit und Putz, aber dies hinderte nicht, daß er im Treffen nicht wie ein Löwe kämpfte. Gekleidet in Purpur und mit Wohlgerüchen gesalbt, brachte er die Millionen des Xerxes und die rauhen Spartaner auf gleiche Weise zum Zittern. Er liebte die Vergnügungen der Tafel und konnte nur schwer dem Reiz der Wollust widerstehen; aber Völlerei und schamloses Betragen machten ehrlos in Athen. Delikatesse und Wohlanständigkeit wurden bei keinem Volke des Altertums so getrieben als bei diesem: in einem Kriege mit dem mazedonischen Philipp hatten die Athenienser einige Briefe des Königs aufgefangen, unter denen auch einer an seine Gemahlin war; die übrigen

Where in Sparta could one find a Socrates, a Thucydides, a Sophocles, a Plato? Sparta could produce only rulers and warriors, no artists, no poets, no thinkers, no citizens of the world. Solon and Lycurgus were both great men, both were honest men. But how different was their influence because they started from opposite principles. The Athenian lawgiver is surrounded by liberty and joy, industry and abundance; all the arts and virtues, all the graces and muses look up to him with gratitude and call him their father and creator. Lycurgus is surrounded only by tyranny and its horrid opposite, bondage that rattles its chains and curses the author of its misery.

The character of an entire people is the most faithful expression of its laws and the most reliable criterion of its worth or worthlessness. The Spartan mind was limited, the Spartan heart unfeeling. The Spartan was proud and over-bearing with his allies, cruel toward the vanquished, inhuman to his slaves, servile with his superiors. He was unscrupulous and perfidious in his negotiations and his virtues lacked the pleasing charm that alone wins hearts. The Athenian, on the other hand, was gentle and meek in his dealings with his fellow man, polite and lively in conversation, affable with his inferiors, hospitable and obliging with strangers. He was fond of comfort and fashionable clothes, but this did not prevent him from fighting like a lion in battle. Clad in purple and scented with perfumes, he caused the millions of Xerxes and even the rough Spartans to tremble. He loved the pleasures of the table and found it difficult to resist the delights of sensuality, but gluttony and shameless conduct were looked upon as disgraceful in Athens. Delicacy and propriety were more highly cultivated by the Athenians than by any other nation of antiquity. In a war against Philip of Macedonia, the Athenians captured some letters belonging to the King, among which was one to his wife. All

alle wurden geöffnet, diesen einzigen schickten sie unerbrochen zurück. Der Athenienser war großmütig im Glücke, und im Unglücke standhaft—*dann* kostete es ihn nichts, für das Vaterland alles zu wagen. Seine Sklaven behandelte er menschlich, und der mißhandelte Knecht durfte seinen Tyrannen verklagen. Selbst die Tiere erfuhren die Großmut dieses Volk; nach vollendetem Bau des Tempels Hekatonpedon wurde verordnet, alle Lasttiere, welche dabei geschäftig gewesen, frei zu lassen und auf ihr ganzes künftiges Leben auf den besten Weiden umsonst zu ernähren. Eins dieser Tiere kam nachher von freien Stücken zur Arbeit und lief mechanisch vor den übrigen her, welche Lasten zogen. Dieser Anblick rührte die Athenienser so sehr, daß sie verordneten, dieses Tier auf Unkosten des Staats inskünftige besonders zu unterhalten.

Indessen bin ich es der Gerechtigkeit schuldig, auch die Fehler der Athenienser nicht zu verschweigen, denn die Geschichte soll keine Lobrednerin sein. Dieses Volk, das wir seiner feinen Sitten, seiner Sanftmut, seiner Weisheit wegen bewundert haben, befleckte sich nicht selten mit dem schändlichsten Undank gegen seine größten Männer, mit Grausamkeit gegen seine überwundenen Feinde. Durch die Schmeicheleien seiner Redner verdorben, trotzig auf seine Freiheit und auf so viele glänzende Vorzüge eitel, drückte es seine Bundsgenossen und Nachbarn oft mit unerträglichem Stolze und ließ sich bei öffentlichen Beratschlagungen von einem leichtsinnigen Schwindelgeist leiten, der oft die Bemühungen seiner weisesten Staatsmänner zu nichte machte und den Staat an den Rand des Verderbens riß. Jeder einzelne Athenienser war lenksam und weichmütig; aber in öffentlichen Versammlungen war er der vorige Mann nicht mehr. Daher schildert uns Aristophanes seine Landsleute als vernünftige Greise zu Hause und als Narren in Versammlungen. Die Liebe zum Ruhme und der Durst nach Neuheit beherrschte sie bis zur Ausschweifung; an den Ruhm setzte der Athenienser oft seine Glücksgüter, sein Leben und nicht selten—seine Tugend. Eine Krone von Ölzweigen, eine Inschrift auf einer Säule, die sein Verdienst verkündigte, war ihm ein feurigerer Sporn zu großen

were opened except this which was returned to him intact. The Athenian was generous in prosperity, steadfast in adversity—at which time he gladly risked everything for his country. He treated his slaves humanely; an ill-treated servant was permitted to bring suit against his master. Even animals were generously treated by this people. After the completion of the temple Hekatonpedon, it was decreed that all the animals that had assisted in the work should be relieved of any further labor and should be allowed for the rest of their lives to pasture in the richest meadows. Afterwards one of these animals returned to work of its own accord, running mechanically in front of the others that were pulling loads. This spectacle so touched the people that the order was given that the animal should in future be given special care at the public expense.

In the interests of justice, however, I must not conceal the faults of the Athenians, for history must not be a flatterer. This people, whom we have admired for its fine manners, its gentleness, its wisdom, was not infrequently guilty of the most shameful ingratitude toward its greatest men and of cruelty toward its vanquished enemies. Spoiled by their freedom and vain of their brilliant achievements, they were often intolerably proud in their dealings with their allies and neighbors. In public debates, they allowed themselves to be governed by a spirit of frivolity and levity which frequently frustrated the efforts of their wisest statesmen and brought the republic to the brink of ruin. The individual Athenian was gentle and malleable; but he was a changed man at public meetings. This is why Aristophanes portrays his countrymen as sensible old men at home and as fools at the assembly. They were governed by an excessive love of glory and thirst for novelty. For the sake of glory, the Athenian risked his life, his property and not infrequently his virtue. A crown of olive branches, an inscription on a column proclaiming his merits spurred him more keenly

Taten als dem Perser alle Schätze des großen Königs. So sehr das atheniensische Volk seinen Undank übertrieb, so ausschweifend war es wieder in seiner Dankbarkeit. Von einem solchen Volke im Triumph aus der Versammlung heimbegleitet zu werden, es auch nur *einen* Tag zu beschäftigen, war ein höherer Genuß für die Ruhmsucht des Atheniensers und auch ein wahrerer Genuß, als ein Monarch seinen geliebtesten Sklaven gewähren kann; denn es ist ganz etwas anders, ein ganzes stolzes, zart empfindendes Volk zu rühren, als einem einzigen Menschen zu gefallen. Der Athenienser mußte in immerwährender Bewegung sein; unaufhörlich haschte sein Sinn nach neuen Eindrücken, neuen Genüssen. Dieser Sucht nach Neuheit mußte man täglich neue Nahrung reichen, wenn sie sich nicht gegen den Staat selbst kehren sollte. Darum rettete ein Schauspiel, das man zu rechter Zeit gab, oft die öffentliche Ruhe, welche der Aufruhr bedrohte—darum hatte oft ein Usurpator gewonnen Spiel, wenn er nur diesem Hange des Volks durch eine Reihe von Lustbarkeiten opferte. Aber eben darum wehe dem verdientesten Bürger, wenn er die Kunst nicht verstand, täglich *neu* zu sein und sein Verdienst zu verjüngen!

Der Abend von Solons Leben war nicht so heiter, als sein Leben es verdient hätte. Um den Zudringlichkeiten der Athenienser zu entgehen, die ihn täglich mit Fragen und Vorschlägen heimsuchten, machte er, sobald seine Gesetze im Gange waren, eine Reise durch Kleinasien, nach den Inseln und nach Aegypten, wo er sich mit den Weisesten seiner Zeit besprach, den königlichen Hof des Krösus in Lydien und den zu Sais in Aegypten besuchte. Was von seiner Zusammenkunft mit Thales von Milet und mit Krösus erzählt wird, ist zu bekannt, um hier noch wiederholt zu werden. Bei seiner Zurückkunft nach Athen fand er den Staat von drei Parteien zerrüttet, welche zwei gefährliche Männer, Megakles und Pisistratus, zu Anführern hatten. Megakles machte sich mächtig und furchtbar durch seinen Reichtum, Pisistratus durch seine Staatsklugheit und sein Genie. Dieser Pisistratus, Solons ehemaliger Liebling und der Julius Cäsar von Athen, erschien einsmals bleich auf seinem Wagen ausgestreckt vor der Volksversammlung und

to great deeds than all the treasures of the Great King ever spurred on the Persian. Athenians were as extravagant in their gratitude as in their ingratitude. To be borne home in triumph from the assembly by such a people, to attract their attention if only for a day, afforded the vainglorious Athenian a higher and truer delight than a monarch could bestow on his greatest favorites; for it is one thing to please one man and quite another to touch a proud and sensitive people. The Athenian had to be in a constant state of excitement; he was continually striving after new impressions, new pleasures. This quest for novelty had to be rewarded with fresh satisfactions every day if it was not to become a source of trouble to the state. For this reason a spectacle presented at the strategic moment often preserved the public peace when it was threatened with an insurrection. For the same reason a usurper frequently won the game only because he knew how to cater to this passion for novelty by presenting a series of amusements. But woe to even the most meritorious citizen if he had not learned the art of being new each day and of rejuvenating his own merit.

The evening of Solon's life was less cheerful than he deserved. To escape the importunities of the Athenians who plagued him daily with questions and proposals, he left Athens as soon as his laws were in operation and journeyed to Asia Minor, to the islands and to Egypt where he conversed with the wisest men of his age. He also visited the court of King Croesus of Lydia and that of Sais in Egypt. What is recorded concerning his interview with Thales of Miletus and with Croesus is too well known to be repeated here.

Upon his return to Athens he found the republic torn by three factions led by two dangerous men, Megacles and Pisistratus. Megacles was powerful and formidable because of his wealth, Pisistratus, by reason of his political shrewdness and genius. This Pisistratus, Solon's erstwhile favorite, the Julius Caesar of Athens, appeared one day before the ecclesia stretched out on his chariot, pale

bespritzt mit dem Blut einer Wunde, die er sich selbst in den Arm geritzt hatte. "So", sagte er, "haben mich meine Feinde um eurentwillen mißhandelt. Mein Leben ist in ewiger Gefahr, wenn ihr nicht Anstalten trefft, es zu schützen." Alsbald trugen seine Freunde, wie er sie selbst unterrichtet hatte, darauf an, daß ihm eine Leibwache gehalten würde, die ihn begleiten sollte, so oft er öffentlich ausging. Solon erriet den betrügerischen Sinn dieses Vorschlags und setzte sich eifrig, aber fruchtlos dagegen. Der Vorschlag ging durch, Pisistratus erhielt eine Leibwache, und nicht sobald sah er sich an ihrer Spitze, als er die Zitadelle von Athen in Besitz nahm. Jetzt fiel die Decke von den Augen des Volks, aber zu spät. Der Schrecken ergriff Athen; Megakles und seine Anhänger entwichen aus der Stadt und überließen sie dem Usurpator. Solon, der sich allein nicht hatte täuschen lassen, war jetzt auch der einzige, der den Mut nicht verlor; so viel er angewandt hatte, seine Mitbürger von ihrer Übereilung zurückzuhalten, als es noch Zeit war, so viel wandte er jetzt an, ihren sinkenden Mut zu beleben. Als er nirgends Eingang fand, ging er nach Hause, legte seine Waffen vor seine Haustüre und rief: "Nun hab ich getan, was ich konnte zum Besten des Vaterlands." Er dachte auf keine Flucht, sondern fuhr fort, die Torheit der Athenienser und die Gewissenlosigkeit des Tyrannen heftig zu tadeln. Als ihn seine Freunde fragten, was ihn so mutig mache, dem Mächtigen zu trotzen, so antwortete er: "Mein Alter gibt mir diesen Mut." Er starb, und seine letzten Blicke sahen sein Vaterland nicht frei.

Aber Athen war in keines Barbaren Hände gefallen. Pisistratus war ein edler Mensch und ehrte die Solonischen Gesetze. Als er in der Folge zweimal von seinem Nebenbuhler vertrieben und zweimal wieder Meister von der Stadt wurde, bis er endlich im ruhigen Besitz seiner Herrschaft blieb, machte er seine Usurpation durch wahre Verdienste um den Staat und glänzende Tugenden vergessen. Niemand bemerkte unter ihm, daß Athen nicht mehr frei war, so gelind und still floß seine Regierung, und nicht er, sondern Solons Gesetze herrschten. Pisistratus eröffnete das goldne Alter von Athen; unter ihm dämmerte der schöne Morgen

and covered with blood from a wound that he himself had scratched on his arm. "This," he said, "is how my enemies have mistreated me for your sakes. My life is in constant danger unless you take steps to protect it."

Thereupon his friends, in accordance with his instructions made a motion that a bodyguard should be formed to accompany him whenever he went out in public. Solon guessed the treacherous motive behind this proposal and vigorously opposed it, but in vain. The proposal was adopted, Pisistratus was given a bodyguard and no sooner was he at its head that he took possession of the citadel of Athens. Now the people's eyes were opened, but too late. Terror seized Athens. Megacles and his friends escaped from the city, abandoning it to the usurper.

Solon, who alone had not been deceived by the usurper's wiles, was now the only man who did not lose heart. He now expended as much energy upon raising their sinking spirits as he had previously expended upon preventing them from committing the rash act for which they were paying the price. When no one would listen to him, he went home, laid down his arms in front of his door and cried: "Now I have done all I can for the welfare of my country." He never thought of taking flight, but continued his outspoken and strong censure of the Athenians and the unscrupulousness of the tyrant. When asked by his friends what gave him the courage to defy the powerful tyrant, he replied: "My age gives me the courage." He did not live to see his country's freedom.

But Athens had not fallen into the hands of a barbarian. Pisistratus was a noble-hearted man with a profound respect for Solon's laws. Having been twice expelled by his rival and having twice recaptured the government of the city, he made the people forget his usurpation by his real services to the republic and his brilliant virtues. No one noticed the loss of liberty in Athens, so mild and peaceful was the flow of his reign; it was not he, but Solon's law that was ruling. Pisistratus ushered in the golden age of Athens. The beautiful dawn of Greek art

der griechischen Künste auf. Er starb, wie ein Vater bedauert.

Sein angefangenes Werk wurde von seinen Söhnen Hipparch und Hippias fortgesetzt. Beide Brüder regierten mit Eintracht, und gleiche Liebe zur Wissenschaft beseelte beide. Unter ihnen blühten schon Simonides und Anakreon, und die Akademie wurde gestiftet. Alles eilte dem herrlichen Zeitalter des Perikles entgegen.

began to appear in his time. He died, mourned like a father.

The work he had begun was continued by his sons, Hippias and Hipparchus. The two brothers governed harmoniously, both animated by the same love of knowledge. Under them, Simonides and Anacreon were already flourishing, and the Academy was founded. Everything moved rapidly toward the glorious age of Pericles.

DIE SCHAUBÜHNE ALS EINE MORALISCHE
ANSTALT BETRACHTET

EIN allgemeiner unwiderstehlicher Hang nach dem Neu-
en und Außerordentlichen, ein Verlangen, sich in einem
leidenschaftlichen Zustande zu fühlen, hat, nach Sulzers
Bemerkung, der Schaubühne die Entstehung gegeben. Erschöpft von den höhern Anstrengungen des Geistes, ermattet von den einförmigen, oft niederdrückenden Geschäften
des Berufs und von Sinnlichkeit gesättigt mußte der Mensch
eine Leerheit in seinem Wesen fühlen, die dem ewigen Trieb
nach Tätigkeit zuwider war. Unsre Natur, gleich unfähig,
länger im Zustande des Tiers fortzudauern, als die feinern
Arbeiten des Verstandes fortzusetzen, verlangte einen mitt-
leren Zustand, der beide widersprechende Enden vereinigte,
die harte Spannung zu sanfter Harmonie herabstimmte und
den wechselsweisen Übergang eines Zustandes in den andern erleichterte. Diesen Nutzen leistet überhaupt nun der
ästhetische Sinn oder das Gefühl für das Schöne. Da aber
eines weisen Gesetzgebers erstes Augenmerk sein muß, unter zwei Wirkungen die höchste herauszulesen, so wird er
sich nicht begnügen, die Neigungen seines Volks nur ent-
waffnet zu haben; er wird sie auch, wenn es irgend nur möglich ist, als Werkzeuge höherer Plane gebrauchen und in
Quellen von Glückseligkeit zu verwandeln bemüht sein, und
darum wählte er vor allen andern die Bühne, die dem nach
Tätigkeit dürstenden Geist einen unendlichen Kreis eröff-
net, jeder Seelenkraft Nahrung gibt, ohne eine einzige zu
überspannen, und die Bildung des Verstandes und des Herzens mit der edelsten Unterhaltung vereinigt.
Derjenige, welcher zuerst die Bemerkung machte, daß eines
Staats festeste Säule *Religion* sei—daß ohne sie die Gesetze
selbst ihre Kraft verlieren, hat vielleicht, ohne es zu wollen
oder zu wissen, die Schaubühne von ihrer edelsten Seite ver-
teidigt. Eben diese Unzulänglichkeit, diese schwankende
Eigenschaft der politischen Gesetze, welche dem Staat die
Religion unentbehrlich macht, bestimmt auch den sittlichen
Einfluß der Bühne. Gesetze, wollte er sagen, drehen sich
nur um verneinende Pflichten—Religion dehnt ihre Forderungen auf wirkliches Handeln aus. Gesetze hemmen nur
Wirkungen, die den Zusammenhang der Gesellschaft auf-

THE STAGE CONSIDERED AS A
MORAL INSTITUTION

The stage owes its origin to the irresistible attraction of things new and extraordinary, to man's desire for passionate experience, as Sulzer has observed. Exhausted by the higher efforts of the mind, wearied by the monotonous and frequently depressing duties of his profession, satiated with sensuality, man must have felt an emptiness in his nature that was at odds with his desire for constant activity. Human nature, incapable either of remaining forever in an animal state or of devoting itself exclusively to the more subtle work of the intellect, demanded a middle condition which would unite these two contradictory extremes; a condition that would ease the hard tension between them and produce a gentle harmony, thereby facilitating the mutual transition from one to the other. This function is performed by the aesthetic sense or the appreciation of beauty.

Since it must be the first aim of the wise legislator, when faced with two effects, to choose the higher, he will not be content merely to have disarmed the impulses of his people. He will aslo endeavor, if possible, to use these tendencies as instruments for higher plans and convert them into sources of happiness. To this end he selected the stage as the best means of opening an endless sphere to the spirit thirsting for action, of feeding all spiritual powers without straining any, and of combining the cultivation of the mind and the emotions with the noblest entertainment.

The man who first made the statement that *religion* is the strongest pillar of the state; that without religion law itself would be deprived of its force, has, perhaps, unknowingly supplied the stage with its noblest defense. The very inadequacy and unreliability of political laws that make religion indispensable to the state also determine the moral influence of the stage. This man meant to imply that, while laws revolve around negative duties, religion extends her demands to positive acts. Laws merely impede actions that might cause the disintegration of society. Religion prescribes actions that tend to consolidate the structure of society. Laws control only

lösen—Religion befiehlt solche, die ihn inniger machen. Jene herrschen nur über die offenbaren Äußerungen des Willens, nur Taten sind ihnen untertan—diese setzt ihre Gerichtsbarkeit bis in die verborgensten Winkel des Herzens fort und verfolgt den Gedanken bis an die innerste Quelle. Gesetze sind glatt und geschmeidig, wandelbar wie Laune und Leidenschaft—Religion bindet streng und ewig. Wenn wir nun aber auch voraussetzen wollten, was nimmermehr ist— wenn wir der Religion diese große Gewalt über jedes Menschenherz einräumen, wird sie oder kann sie die ganze Bildung vollenden?—Religion (ich trenne hier ihre politische Seite von ihrer göttlichen), Religion wirkt im ganzen mehr auf den sinnlichen Teil des Volks—sie wirkt vielleicht durch das Sinnliche allein so unfehlbar. Ihre Kraft ist dahin, wenn wir ihr dieses nehmen—und wodurch wirkt die Bühne? Religion ist dem größern Teile der Menschen nichts mehr, wenn wir ihre Bilder, ihre Probleme vertilgen, wenn wir ihre Gemälde von Himmel und Hölle zernichten— und doch sind es nur Gemälde der Phantasie, Rätsel ohne Auflösung, Schreckbilder und Lockungen aus der Ferne. Welche Verstärkung für Religion und Gesetze, wenn sie mit der Schaubühne in Bund treten, wo Anschauung und lebendige Gegenwart ist, wo Laster und Tugend, Glückseligkeit und Elend, Torheit und Weisheit in tausend Gemälden faßlich und wahr an dem Menschen vorübergehen, wo die Vorsehung ihre Rätsel auflöst, ihren Knoten vor seinen Augen entwickelt, wo das menschliche Herz auf den Foltern der Leidenschaft seine leisesten Regungen beichtet, alle Larven fallen, alle Schminke verfliegt und die Wahrheit unbestechlich wie Rhadamanthus Gericht hält.

Die Gerichtsbarkeit der Bühne fängt an, wo das Gebiet der weltlichen Gesetze sich endigt. Wenn die Gerechtigkeit für Gold verblindet und im Solde der Laster schwelgt, wenn die Frevel der Mächtigen ihrer Ohnmacht spotten und Menschenfurcht den Arm der Obrigkeit bindet, übernimmt die Schaubühne Schwert und Wage und reißt die Laster vor einen schrecklichen Richterstuhl. Das ganze Reich der Phantasie und Geschichte, Vergangenheit und Zukunft stehen ihrem Wink zu Gebot. Kühne Verbrecher, die längst schon

the external manifestations of the will; actions alone are subject to them. Religion extends her jurisdiction to the remotest corners of the heart and traces thought to its deepest source. Laws are smooth and flexible, as changeable as mood and passion. The bonds of religion are stern and eternal.

Even if we assume, as indeed we cannot, that religion possesses this great power over every human heart, will it, or can it bring to perfection all of human culture? On the whole, religion (I am separating here the political aspect from the divine) acts mainly on the sensual part of the people. It probably has an infallible effect only by way of the senses. It loses its power if we take this away. And how does the stage achieve its effect? Religion ceases to be anything for most men if we remove its images, its problems, if we destroy its pictures of heaven and hell. And yet they are only fantasy pictures, riddles without a solution, terrifying phantoms and distant allurements.

What strength religion and law can gain when they are allied with the stage, where reality can be viewed as living presence, where vice and virtue, happiness and misery, folly and wisdom pass in review before man in thousands of true and concrete pictures, where Providence solves her riddles, ties her knots before our eyes; where the human heart, on the rack of passion, confesses its subtlest stirrings; where every mask is dropped, every painted cheek is faded, and truth, like Rhadamanthus, sits incorruptibly in judgment.

The jurisdiction of the stage begins where the domain of secular law comes to an end. When justice is blinded by gold and revels in the wages of vice; when the crimes of the mighty scorn her impotence and the dread of human power has tied the hands of legal authority, then the stage takes up the sword and the scales and drags vice before a dreadful tribunal. The entire realm of fantasy and history, the past and the future are at its beck and call. Bold criminals, who have long since turned to dust,

265

im Staub vermodern, werden durch den allmächtigen Ruf der Dichtkunst jetzt vorgeladen und wiederholen zum schauervollen Unterricht der Nachwelt ein schändliches Leben. Ohnmächtig, gleich den Schatten in einem Hohlspiegel, wandeln die Schrecken ihres Jahrhunderts vor unserm Augen vorbei, und mit wollüstigem Entsetzen verfluchen wir ihr Gedächtnis. Wenn keine Moral mehr gelehrt wird, keine Religion mehr Glauben findet, wenn kein Gesetz mehr vorhanden ist, wird uns Medea noch anschauern, wenn sie die Treppen des Palastes herunter wankt, und der Kindermord jetzt geschehen ist. Heilsame Schauer werden die Menschheit ergreifen, und in der Stille wird jeder sein gutes Gewissen preisen, wenn Lady Macbeth, eine schreckliche Nachtwandlerin, ihre Hände wäscht und alle Wohlgerüche Arabiens herbeiruft, den häßlichen Mordgeruch zu vertilgen. So gewiß sichtbare Darstellung mächtiger wirkt als toter Buchstab und kalte Erzählung, so gewiß wirkt die Schaubühne tiefer und dauernder als Moral und Gesetze.

Aber hier *unterstützt* sie die weltliche Gerechtigkeit nur— ihr ist noch ein weiteres Feld geöffnet. Tausend Laster, die jene ungestraft duldet, straft sie; tausend Tugenden, wovon jene schweigt, werden von der Bühne empfohlen. Hier begleitet sie die Weisheit und die Religion. Aus dieser reinen Quelle schöpft sie ihre Lehren und Muster und kleidet die strenge Pflicht in ein reizendes lockendes Gewand. Mit welch herrlichen Empfindungen, Entschlüssen, Leidenschaften schwellt sie unsere Seele, welche göttliche Ideale stellt sie uns zur Nacheiferung aus! — Wenn der gütige August dem Verräter Cinna, der schon den tödlichen Spruch auf seinen Lippen zu lesen meint, groß wie seine Götter, die Hand reicht: "Laß uns Freunde sein, Cinna!"—wer unter der Menge wird in *dem* Augenblick nicht gern seinem Todfeind die Hand drücken wollen, dem göttlichen Römer zu gleichen?—Wenn Franz von Sickingen, auf dem Wege, einen Fürsten zu züchtigen und für fremde Rechte zu kämpfen, unversehens hinter sich schaut und den Rauch aufsteigen sieht von seiner Feste, wo Weib und Kind hilflos zurückblieben, und *er*— weiter zieht, Wort zu halten—wie groß wird mir da der

are summoned to appear before us by the all-powerful voice of poetry and to reenact their shameful lives for the instruction of a horrified posterity. Like impotent shadow figures in a concave mirror, they unfold before our eyes the terrors of their own century, and we heap imprecations upon their memory in an ecstasy of horror. Even when morality is no longer taught, even when there is no longer any faith in religion, even when law has ceased to exist, we will still shudder at the sight of Medea as she staggers down the palace steps, the murder of her children having taken place. Humanity will tremble with wholesome horror and each man will secretly congratulate himself on his own good conscience when he sees that frightful sleepwalker, Lady Macbeth, washing her hands and hears her challenge all the perfumes of Arabia to obliterate the loathsome smell of murder. As surely as a visual representation has a more powerful effect than a dead text or a cold narrative, so the stage exercises a more profound and lasting influence than morality and law.

Here, however, the stage merely assists human justice. A still wider field is open to it. A thousand vices that are tolerated by justice are punished in the theater. A thousand virtues ignored by human law are recommended on the stage. Here it serves as a companion to wisdom and religion. It draws its teachings and examples from this pure source and clothes stern duty in a charming and alluring garb. What glorious emotions, resolutions, passions well up in our souls, and with what godlike ideals it challenges our ambitions! When gracious Augustus, magnanimous like his gods, holds out his hand to the traitor Cinna who already imagines he sees the death sentence on his lips, and says: "Let us be friends, Cinna," —who among us, at this moment, would not gladly clasp the hand of his mortal enemy in order to emulate the divine Roman? When Franz von Sickingen, on his way to punish a prince and to fight for alien rights, happens to look back and see the smoke rising from the castle occupied by his helpless wife and children, continues on his journey to keep his word—then, how great man rises

Mensch, wie klein und verächtlich das gefürchtete unüberwindliche Schicksal!

Ebenso häßlich, als liebenswürdig die Tugend, malen sich die Laster in ihrem furchtbaren Spiegel ab. Wenn der hilflose kindische Lear in Nacht und Ungewitter vergebens an das Haus seiner Töchter pocht, wenn er sein weißes Haar in die Lüfte streut und den tobenden Elementen erzählt, wie unnatürlich seine Regan gewesen, wenn sein wütender Schmerz zuletzt in den schrecklichen Worten von ihm strömt: "Ich gab euch alles!"—wie abscheulich zeigt sich uns da der Undank? wie feierlich geloben wir Ehrfurcht und kindliche Liebe!—

Aber der Wirkungskreis der Bühne dehnt sich noch weiter aus. Auch da, wo Religion und Gesetze es unter ihrer Würde achten, Menschenempfindungen zu begleiten, ist *sie* für unsere Bildung noch geschäftig. Das Glück der Gesellschaft wird ebenso sehr durch Torheit als durch Verbrechen und Laster gestört. Eine Erfahrung lehrt es, die so alt ist als die Welt, daß im Gewebe menschlicher Dinge oft die größten Gewichte an den kleinsten und zärtesten Fäden hangen und, wenn wir Handlungen zu ihrer Quelle zurückbegleiten, wir zehenmal lächeln müssen, ehe wir uns einmal entsetzen. Mein Verzeichnis von Bösewichtern wird mit jedem Tage, den ich älter werde, kürzer, und mein Register von Toren vollzähliger und länger. Wenn die ganze moralische Verschuldung des einen Geschlechtes aus einer und eben der Quelle hervorspringt, wenn alle die ungeheuren Extreme von Laster, die es jemals gebrandmarkt haben, nur veränderte Formen, nur höhere Grade einer Eigenschaft sind, die wir zuletzt alle einstimmig belächeln und lieben, warum sollte die Natur bei dem andern Geschlechte nicht die nämliche Wege gegangen sein? Ich kenne nur *ein* Geheimnis, den Menschen vor Verschlimmerung zu bewahren, und dieses ist—sein Herz gegen Schwächen zu schützen.

Einen großen Teil dieser Wirkung können wir von der Schaubühne erwarten. Sie ist es, die der großen Klasse von Toren den Spiegel vorhält und die tausendfachen Formen derselben mit heilsamem Spott beschämt. Was sie oben durch Rührung und Schrecken wirkte, leistet sie hier (schneller viel-

before me, how small and contemptible the dread power of insuperable destiny!

Vice, as reflected in the mirror of the stage, is made as hideous as virtue is made desirable. When the helpless, childish Lear, out in a stormy night, knocks in vain on his daughters' door; when, his white hair streaming in the wind, he describes the unnatural conduct of his daughter Regan to the raging elements; when at last he pours out his unbearable suffering in the words: "I gave you everything!": how abominable ingratitude seems to us, how solemnly we promise respect and filial love!

But the sphere of influence of the stage extends still farther. The theater continues to work for our development even in those areas where religion and law will not stoop to follow human sentiments. The happiness of society is as much disturbed by folly as by crime and vice. Experience as old as the world teaches us that in the web of human events, the heaviest weights are often suspended by the most delicate threads; and in tracing actions to their source, we have to smile ten times before revolting in horror once. My list of criminals grows shorter every day of my life, but my list of fools becomes more complete and longer. If the moral guilt of one class of people stems from one and the same source; if the appalling extremes of vice that have stigmatized it are merely altered forms, higher degrees of a quality which in the end provokes only smiles and sympathy, why should not nature have adopted the same course in the case of the other class? I know of only one method of guarding man against depravity, and that is to guard his heart against weaknesses.

We can expect the stage to serve this function to a considerable degree. It is the stage that holds the mirror up to the great class of fools and shames the manifold forms of their folly with wholesome ridicule. The effect it produced before by means of terror and pity, it achieves

269

leicht und unfehlbarer) durch Scherz und Satire. Wenn wir es unternehmen wollten, Lustspiel und Trauerspiel nach dem Maß der erreichten Wirkung zu schätzen, so würde vielleicht die Erfahrung dem ersten den Vorrang geben. Spott und Verachtung verwunden den Stolz des Menschen empfindlicher, als Verabscheuung sein Gewissen foltert. Vor dem Schrecklichen verkriecht sich unsre Feigheit, aber eben diese Feigheit überliefert uns dem Stachel der Satire. Gesetz und Gewissen schützen uns *oft* für Verbrechen und Lastern— Lächerlichkeiten verlangen einen eigenen feinern Sinn, den wir nirgends mehr als vor dem Schauplatze üben. Vielleicht, daß wir einen Freund bevollmächtigen, unsre Sitten und unser Herz anzugreifen, aber es kostet uns Mühe, ihm ein einziges Lachen zu vergeben. Unsre Vergehungen ertragen einen Aufseher und Richter, unsre Unarten kaum einen Zeugen.—Die Schaubühne allein kann unsre Schwächen belachen, weil sie unsrer Empfindlichkeit schont und den schuldigen Toren nicht wissen will—Ohne rot zu werden, sehen wir unsre Larve aus ihrem Spiegel fallen und danken insgeheim für die sanfte Ermahnung.

Aber ihr großer Wirkungskreis ist noch lange nicht geendigt. Die Schaubühne ist mehr als jede andere öffentliche Anstalt des Staats eine Schule der praktischen Weisheit, ein Wegweiser durch das bürgerliche Leben, ein unfehlbarer Schlüssel zu den geheimsten Zugängen der menschlichen Seele. Ich gebe zu, daß Eigenliebe und Abhärtung des Gewissens nicht selten ihre beste Wirkung vernichten, daß sich noch tausend Laster mit frecher Stirne vor ihrem Spiegel behaupten, tausend gute Gefühle vom kalten Herzen des Zuschauers fruchtlos zurückfallen—ich selbst bin der Meinung, daß vielleicht Molières Harpagon noch keinen Wucherer besserte, daß der Selbstmörder Beverley noch wenige seiner Brüder von der abscheulichen Spielsucht zurückzog, daß Karl Moors unglückliche Räubergeschichte die Landstraßen nicht viel sicherer machen wird—aber wenn wir auch diese große Wirkung der Schaubühne einschränken, wenn wir so ungerecht sein wollen, sie gar aufzuheben —wie unendlich viel bleibt noch von ihrem Einfluß zurück? Wenn sie die Summe der Laster weder tilgt noch vermin-

here (and perhaps more speedily and infallibly) by wit and satire. If we were to judge comedy and tragedy on the basis of their effectiveness, experience would probably decide in favor of the former. Loathing may torture a man's conscience, but he suffers more keenly when his pride is wounded by derision and contempt. Our cowardice causes us to recoil from what is frightening, but this very cowardice exposes us to the sting of satire. Law and conscience often protect us from crime and vice; the ludicrous demands a peculiarly fine perception which we exercise nowhere more than in front of the stage. We may allow a friend to attack our morals and our emotions, but we find it hard to forgive him a single laugh at our expense. Our transgressions may tolerate a mentor and judge, our bad habits hardly a witness. The stage alone is permitted to ridicule our weaknesses because it spares our sensibilities and does not care to know who is the guilty fool. Without blushing we can see our own mask reflected in its mirror and are secretly grateful for the gentle rebuke.

But the stage's broad scope by no means comes to an end here. The stage, more than any other public institution, is a school of practical wisdom, a guide through social life, an infallible key to the most secret passages of the human soul. Self-love and a callous conscience, admittedly, often neutralize its effect. A thousand vices brazenly persist despite its castigations. A thousand good feelings meet with no response from the cold heart of the spectator. I myself am of the opinion that perhaps Molière's Harpagon has never reformed a single usurer, that the suicide of Beverley has saved very few of his brothers from the abominable addiction to gambling, that Karl Moor's unfortunate brigands' story will not make the highroads safer for travelers. But even if we set limits to *this effect* of the stage, even if we are so unjust as to discount it altogether, is not what remains of its influence still vast enough? Even if the stage neither augments nor diminishes the total number of

271

dert, hat sie uns nicht mit denselben bekannt gemacht?—
Mit diesen Lasterhaften, diesen Toren müssen wir leben.
Wir müssen ihnen ausweichen oder begegnen; wir müssen
sie untergraben oder ihnen unterliegen. Jetzt aber überraschen sie uns nicht mehr. Wir sind auf ihre Anschläge vorbereitet. Die Schaubühne hat uns das Geheimnis verraten,
sie ausfündig und unschädlich zu machen. *Sie* zog dem Heuchler die künstliche Maske ab und entdeckte das Netz, womit uns List und Kabale umstrickten. Betrug und Falsch-
heit riß sie aus krummen Labyrinthen hervor und zeigte ihr
schreckliches Angesicht dem Tag. Vielleicht, daß die ster-
bende Sara nicht *einen* Wollüstling schreckt, daß alle Gemälde gestrafter Verführung seine Glut nicht erkälten, und
daß selbst die verschlagene Spielerin diese Wirkung ernstlich zu verhüten bedacht ist—glücklich genug, daß die arg-
lose Unschuld jetzt seine Schlingen kennt, daß die Bühne
sie lehrte seinen Schwüren mißtrauen und vor seiner Anbetung zittern.
Nicht bloß auf Menschen und Menschencharakter, auch auf
Schicksale macht uns die Schaubühne aufmerksam und lehrt
uns die große Kunst, sie zu ertragen. Im Gewebe unsers
Lebens spielen *Zufall* und *Plan* eine gleich große Rolle; den
letztern lenken *wir*, dem erstern müssen wir uns blind unterwerfen. Gewinn genug, wenn unausbleibliche Verhäng-
nisse uns nicht ganz ohne Fassung finden, wenn unser Mut,
unsre Klugheit sich einst schon in ähnlichen übten und unser
Herz zu dem Schlag sich gehärtet hat. Die Schaubühne führt
uns eine mannigfaltige Szene menschlicher Leiden vor. Sie
zieht uns künstlich in fremde Bedrängnisse und belohnt uns
das augenblickliche Leiden mit wollüstigen Tränen und einem
herrlichen Zuwachs an Mut und Erfahrung. Mit ihr folgen
wir der verlassenen Ariadne durch das widerhallende Naxos, steigen mit ihr in den Hungerturm Ugolinos hinunter,
betreten mit ihr das entsetzliche Blutgerüste und behorchen
mit ihr die feierliche Stunde des Todes. Hier hören wir, was
unsre Seele in leisen Ahnungen fühlte, die überraschte Natur laut und unwidersprechlich bekräftigen. Im Gewölbe des
Towers verläßt den betrogenen Liebling die Gunst seiner
Königin.—Jetzt, da er sterben soll, entfliegt dem geängstig-

vices, has it not acquainted us with them? We have to live with these profligates and fools. We must either avoid them or put up with them, undermine their influence or succumb to it. But now they no longer surprise us. We are prepared for their assaults. The stage has revealed to us the secret of finding them out and rendering them harmless. It is the stage that has lifted the mask from the hypocrite's face and exposed the net in which cunning and cabal have entangled us. It has dragged deception and falsehood from their labyrinthine dens and made them show their horrid countenances to the light of day. The dying Sarah may not frighten a single debauchee. All the pictures of the dreadful fate in store for the seducer may not quench his fire. The artful actress herself may be contriving to prevent her artistry from having this effect. Nevertheless we can be thankful that his snares have been revealed to unsuspecting innocence, and that it has been taught by the stage to mistrust his promises and tremble at his vows of love.

The stage not only makes us aware of men and human character, but also of the grim power of destiny, and teaches us the great art of bearing it. In the web of life chance and design play an equal role. The latter we can direct, to the former we must submit blindly. We have already gained much if an inevitable fate does not find us wholly unprepared, if our courage and our prudence have already been exercised in similar circumstances and if our hearts have been steeled for the blow. The stage presents us with many varied scenes of human woe. It involves us artificially in the troubles of strangers and rewards us for the momentary pain with pleasurable tears and a magnificent increase of courage and experience. It escorts us with the forsaken Ariadne through the echoing passages of Naxos. It descends with us to Ugolino's tower of starvation. In its company we ascend the steps of the frightful scaffold and witness the solemn hour of death. What we have experienced in our souls only as a vague presentiment, we hear on the stage loudly and incontrovertibly corroborated by nature taken by surprise. In the Tower dungeon the queen withdraws her favor from the deceived favorite. In the face of death,

273

ten Moor seine treulose sophistische Weisheit. Die Ewigkeit entläßt einen Toten, Geheimnisse zu offenbaren, die kein Lebendiger wissen kann, und der sichere Bösewicht verliert seinen letzten gräßlichen Hinterhalt, weil auch Gräber noch ausplaudern.

Aber nicht genug, daß uns die Bühne mit Schicksalen der Menschheit bekannt macht, sie lehrt uns auch gerechter gegen den Unglücklichen sein und nachsichtsvoller über ihn richten. Dann nur, wenn wir die Tiefe seiner Bedrängnisse ausmessen, dürfen wir das Urteil über ihn aussprechen. Kein Verbrechen ist schändender als das Verbrechen des Diebs —aber mischen wir nicht alle eine Träne des Mitleids in unsern Verdammungsspruch, wenn wir uns in den schrecklichen Drang verlieren, worin Eduard Ruhberg die Tat vollbringt?—Selbstmord wird allgemein als Frevel verabscheut; wenn aber, bestürmt von den Drohungen eines wütenden Vaters, bestürmt von Liebe, von der Vorstellung schrecklicher Klostermauern, Mariane den Gift trinkt, wer von uns will der erste sein, der über dem beweinenswürdigen Schlachtopfer einer verruchten Maxime den Stab bricht?—Menschlichkeit und Duldung fangen an, der herrschende Geist unsrer Zeit zu werden; ihre Strahlen sind bis in die Gerichtssäle und noch weiter—in das Herz unsrer Fürsten gedrungen. Wie viel Anteil an diesem göttlichen Werk gehört unsern Bühnen? Sind *sie* es nicht, die den Menschen mit dem Menschen. bekannt machten und das geheime Räderwerk aufdeckten, nach welchem er handelt?

Eine merkwürdige Klasse von Menschen hat Ursache, dankbarer als alle übrigen gegen die Bühne zu sein. Hier nur hören die Großen der Welt, was sie nie oder selten hören —Wahrheit; was sie nie oder selten sehen, sehen sie hier —den Menschen.

So groß und vielfach ist das Verdienst der bessern Bühne um die sittliche Bildung; kein geringeres gebührt ihr um die ganze Aufklärung des Verstandes. Eben hier in dieser höhern Sphäre weiß der große Kopf, der feurige Patriot sie erst ganz zu gebrauchen.

Er wirft einen Blick durch das Menschengeschlecht, vergleicht Völker mit Völkern, Jahrhunderte mit Jahrhunderten

274

the treacherous sophistry of the frightened Moor deserts him. Eternity releases a dead man in order to reveal secrets which cannot be known to the living. The confident villain loses his last ghastly refuge because even the tomb can speak.

But the stage not only familiarizes us with the fate of mankind, it also teaches us to be more just toward the unfortunate and to judge him more leniently; for it is only when we know the full measure of his suffering that we are permitted to pronounce sentence upon him. No crime is more dishonorable than that of a thief, but, even as we condemn him, can we refrain from shedding a tear of compassion for Eduard Ruhberg when we have shared with him the dreadful agony that drives him to commit the deed? Suicide is usually regarded as a crime; but when Mariana, overwhelmed by the threats of an irate father, by her unhappy love and by the terrifying prospect of the convent walls, drains the poisoned cup, who would be the first to condemn this victim of an infamous maxim? Humanity and tolerance are becoming the ruling principles of our age. Their rays have penetrated to our courts of justice and even to the hearts of our princes. How great a share in this divine work belongs to our theaters? Is it not the theater that makes man known to man and discloses the secret mechanism that controls his conduct?

One noteworthy class of men has more cause to be grateful to the stage than any other. It is only here that the great of the world hear what they rarely if ever hear elsewhere: the truth. Here they see what they scarcely ever see: man.

While man's moral development has greatly benefited, and in a variety of ways, from the higher order of drama, his intellectual enlightenment is no less indebted to it. It is in this higher realm that the great mind, the warm-hearted patriot uses it to the best advantage.

Surveying the human race as a whole, comparing nations with nations, centuries with centuries, he sees how the

und findet, wie sklavisch die größere Masse des Volks an Ketten des Vorurteils und der Meinung gefangen liegt, die seiner Glückseligkeit ewig entgegenarbeiten—daß die reinern Strahlen der Wahrheit nur wenig *einzelne* Köpfe beleuchten, welche den kleinen Gewinn vielleicht mit dem Aufwand eines ganzen Lebens erkauften. Wodurch kann der weise Gesetzgeber die Nation derselben teilhaftig machen?

Die Schaubühne ist der gemeinschaftliche Kanal, in welchen von dem denkenden bessern Teile des Volks das Licht der Weisheit herunterströmt und von da aus in milderen Strahlen durch den ganzen Staat sich verbreitet. Richtigere Begriffe, geläuterte Grundsätze, reinere Gefühle fließen von hier durch alle Adern des Volks; der Nebel der Barbarei, des finstern Aberglaubens verschwindet, die Nacht weicht dem siegenden Licht. Unter so vielen herrlichen Früchten der bessern Bühne will ich nur zwo auszeichnen. Wie allgemein ist nur seit wenigen Jahren die Duldung der Religionen und Sekten geworden?—Noch ehe uns Nathan der Jude und Saladin der Sarazene beschämten und die göttliche Lehre uns predigten, daß Ergebenheit in Gott von unserm Wähnen über Gott so gar nicht abhängig sei—ehe noch Joseph der Zweite die fürchterliche Hyder des frommen Hasses bekämpfte, pflanzte die Schaubühne Menschlichkeit und Sanftmut in unser Herz, die abscheulichen Gemälde heidnischer Pfaffenwut lehrten uns Religionshaß vermeiden—in diesem schrecklichen Spiegel wusch das Christentum seine Flecken ab. Mit ebenso glücklichem Erfolge würden sich von der Schaubühne Irrtümer der *Erziehung* bekämpfen lassen; das Stück ist noch zu hoffen, wo dieses merkwürdige Thema behandelt wird. Keine Angelegenheit ist dem Staat durch ihre Folgen so wichtig als diese, und doch ist keine so preisgegeben, keine dem Wahne, dem Leichtsinn des Bürgers so uneingeschränkt anvertraut, wie es diese ist. Nur die Schaubühne könnte die unglücklichen Schlachtopfer vernachlässigter Erziehung in rührenden erschütternden Gemälden an ihm vorüberführen; hier könnten unsre Väter eigensinnigen Maximen entsagen, unsre Mütter vernünftiger lieben lernen. Falsche Begriffe führen das beste Herz des Erziehers irre; desto schlimmer, wenn

majority of people are chained like slaves to prejudice and opinion which forever deter them from finding happiness, and that the pure rays of truth illumine only a few isolated minds which had perhaps expended their entire lives in order to purchase their little gain. How can a wise legislator enable his people to share in these benefits?

The stage is the common channel in which from the thinking, better part of the people the light of wisdom flows down, diffusing from there in milder rays through the entire state. More correct ideas, purified principles and feelings flow from thence through all the vein of all the people. The mists of barbarism, of gloomy superstition disappear. Night yields to victorious light.

Among the many magnificent fruits of the better stage, I would like to single out two. How universal has the tolerance of religious sects become in recent years! Even before Nathan the Jew and Saladin the Saracen shamed us and preached the divine doctrine that submission to the will of God is not dependent upon our misconceptions of Him; even before Joseph II battled with the dreadful hydra of pious hatred, the stage was engaged in planting the seeds of humanity and gentleness in our hearts. The shocking pictures of heathenish, priestly fanaticism taught us to avoid religious hatred. In this frightful mirror Christianity cleansed itself of its stains.

Errors in *education* might be combated in the stage with equal success. We are still awaiting the play that will deal with this significant subject. Because of its effects, no subject is of more importance to the state than this, and yet no institution is so at the mercy of the illusions and caprices of the citizenry as education. The stage alone could pass in review the unfortunate victims of careless education in a series of moving, upsetting pictures. Our fathers might learn to abandon their foolish maxims; our mothers might learn to love more wisely. The best-hearted teachers are led astray by false ideas.

sie sich noch mit *Methode* brüsten und den zarten Schöß-
ling in Philanthropinen und Gewächshäusern systematisch
zugrund richten.

Nicht weniger ließen sich—verstünden es die Oberhäupter
und Vormünder des Staats—von der Schaubühne aus die
Meinungen der Nation über Regierung und Regenten zu-
rechtweisen. Die gesetzgebende Macht spräche hier durch
fremde Symbole zu dem Untertan, verantwortete sich gegen
seine Klagen, noch ehe sie laut werden, und bestäche seine
Zweifelsucht, ohne es zu scheinen. Sogar Industrie und Er-
findungsgeist könnten und würden vor dem Schauplatze
Feuer fangen, wenn die Dichter es der Mühe wert hielten,
Patrioten zu sein, und der Staat sich herablassen wollte, sie
zu hören.

Unmöglich kann ich hier den großen Einfluß übergehen,
den eine gute stehende Bühne auf den Geist der Nation
haben würde. Nationalgeist eines Volks nenne ich die Ähn-
lichkeit und Übereinstimmung seiner Meinungen und Neigungen bei Gegenständen, worüber eine andere Nation anders meint und empfindet. Nur der Schaubühne ist es möglich, diese Übereinstimmung in einem hohen Grad zu be-
wirken, weil sie das ganze Gebiet des menschlichen Wissens
durchwandert, alle Situationen des Lebens erschöpft und
in alle Winkel des Herzens hinunter leuchtet; weil sie alle
Stände und Klassen in sich vereinigt und den gebahntesten
Weg zum Verstand und zum Herzen hat. Wenn in allen
unsern Stücken *ein* Hauptzug herrschte, wenn unsre Dichter
unter sich einig werden und einen festen Bund zu diesem
Endzweck errichten wollten—wenn strenge Auswahl ihre
Arbeiten leitete, ihr Pinsel nur Volksgegenständen sich weihte
—mit einem Wort, wenn wir es erlebten, eine Nationalbühne
zu haben, so würden wir auch eine Nation. Was kettete
Griechenland so fest aneinander? Was zog das Volk so un-
widerstehlich nach seiner Bühne?—Nichts anders als der
vaterländische Inhalt der Stücke, der griechische Geist, das
große überwältigende Interesse des Staats, der besseren
Menschheit, das in denselbigen atmete.

Noch ein Verdienst hat die Bühne—ein Verdienst, das ich
jetzt um so lieber in Anschlag bringe, weil ich vermute, daß

It is still worse when they pride themselves on a certain method and systematically ruin the tender young plant in philanthropinums and hothouses.

Likewise the chiefs and guardians of the state—if they knew how to do it—could use the stage to correct and enlighten popular opinion of government and the governing class. The legislating power might speak to those subject to it in foreign symbols, might defend its actions before they had time to utter a complaint, might silence their doubts without appearing to do so. Even industry and inventiveness might draw inspiration from the stage if the poets thought it worth while to be patriotic and if princes would condescend to hear them.

I cannot possibly overlook the great influence that a good permanent theater would exercise on the spirit of a nation. By national spirit I mean opinions and tendencies which are common to the people of one nation and differ from those of other nationalities. Only the stage can produce this accord to so great a degree because it takes all human knowledge as its province, exhausts all situations of life, and sheds light into every corner of the human heart; because it unites all sorts and conditions of people and commands the most popular road to the heart and understanding.

If a single characteristic predominated in all of our plays; if all of our poets were in accord and were to form a firm alliance to work for this end; if their work were governed by strict selection; if they were to devote their paintbrushes to national subjects; in a word, if we were to see the establishment of a national theater: then we would become a nation. What linked the Greek states so firmly together? What drew the people so irresistibly to the stage? It was the patriotic subjects of their plays. It was the Greek spirit, the great and consuming interest in the republic and in a better humanity that pervaded them.

The stage has another merit which I especially delight in mentioning, because the stage now seems to have won

ihr Rechtshandel mit ihren Verfolgern ohnehin schon gewonnen sein wird. Was bis hieher zu beweisen unternommen worden, daß sie auf Sitten und Aufklärung wesentlich wirke, war zweifelhaft——daß sie unter allen Erfindungen des Luxus und allen Anstalten zur gesellschaftlichen Ergötzlichkeit den Vorzug verdiene, haben selbst ihre Feinde gestanden. Aber was sie hier leistet, ist wichtiger, als man gewohnt ist zu glauben.

Die menschliche Natur erträgt es nicht, ununterbrochen und ewig auf der Folter der Geschäfte zu liegen; die Reize der Sinne sterben mit ihrer Befriedigung. Der Mensch, überladen von tierischem Genuß, der langen Anstrengung müde, vom ewigen Triebe nach Tätigkeit gequält, dürstet nach bessern auserlesenern Vergnügungen, oder stürzt zügellos in wilde Zerstreuungen, die seinen Hinfall beschleunigen und die Ruhe der Gesellschaft zerstören. Bacchantische Freuden, verderbliches Spiel, tausend Rasereien, die der Müßiggang ausheckt, sind unvermeidlich, wenn der Gesetzgeber diesen Hang des Volks nicht zu lenken weiß. Der Mann von Geschäften ist in Gefahr, ein Leben, das er dem Staat so großmütig hinopferte, mit dem unseligen Spleen abzubüßen——der Gelehrte zum dumpfen Pedanten herabzusinken——der Pöbel zum Tier. Die Schaubühne ist die Stiftung, wo sich Vergnügen mit Unterricht, Ruhe mit Anstrengung, Kurzweil mit Bildung gattet, wo keine Kraft der Seele zum Nachteil der andern gespannt, kein Vergnügen auf Unkosten des Ganzen genossen wird. Wenn Gram an dem Herzen nagt, wenn trübe Laune unsre einsamen Stunden vergiftet, wenn uns Welt und Geschäfte anekeln, wenn tausend Lasten unsre Seele drücken und unsre Reizbarkeit unter Arbeiten des Berufs zu ersticken droht, so empfängt uns die Bühne——in dieser künstlichen Welt träumen wir die wirkliche hinweg, wir werden uns selbst wieder gegeben, unsre Empfindung erwacht, heilsame Leidenschaften erschüttern unsre schlummernde Natur und treiben das Blut in frischeren Wallungen. Der Unglückliche weint hier mit fremdem Kummer seinen eigenen aus——der Glückliche wird nüchtern und der Sichere besorgt. Der empfindsame Weichling härtet sich zum Manne, der rohe Unmensch fängt hier zum

its case against its persecutors. The influence upon morals and enlightenment that we have so far claimed for it has been doubted. But even its enemies have admitted that it is to be preferred to all other luxuries and forms of public entertainment. Its services in this respect, however, are more important than is usually conceded.

Human nature cannot bear the constant, unrelenting grind of business. Sensual delight dies with gratification. Man, surfeited with animal pleasures, weary of long exertion, tormented by an unceasing desire for activity, thirsts for better and finer amusement. If he does not find it, he will plunge headlong into debauchery which hastens his ruin and destroys the peace of society. Bacchanalian carousings, the ruinous games of chance, a thousand revelries hatched by idleness become inevitable unless the legislator knows how to guide these tendencies in his people. The businessman is in danger of becoming a miserable hypochondriac in return for a life he has generously devoted to the state. The scholar is likely to sink into dull pedantry, the common man becomes a brute.

The stage is an institution where pleasure is combined with instruction, rest with exertion, amusement with culture. Not a single faculty is strained to the detriment of another, no pleasure is enjoyed at the expense of the whole. When grief gnaws at our hearts, when melancholy poisons our solitary hours, when the world and business have become repulsive to us, when our souls are oppressed by a thosuand burdens and the drudgery of our profession threatens to deaden our sensibilities, the stage welcomes us to her bosom. In the dreams of this artificial world, we can forget the real one. We find ourselves once more. Our feeling reawakens. Wholesome passions stir our slumbering nature and the blood begins to circulate in our veins with renewed vigor. Here the unhappy man dispels his sorrow in weeping over that of another. The happy become more sober and the overconfident more cautious. The sensitive weakling learns to stand up to the tough demands of manhood. The

erstenmal zu empfinden an. Und dann endlich—welch ein Triumph für dich, Natur!—so oft zu Boden getretene, so oft wieder auferstehende Natur!—wenn Menschen aus allen Kreisen und Zonen und Ständen, abgeworfen jede Fessel der Künstelei und der Mode, herausgerissen aus jedem Drange des Schicksals, durch *eine* allwebende Sympathie verbrüdert, in *ein* Geschlecht wieder aufgelöst, ihrer selbst und der Welt vergessen und ihrem himmlischen Ursprung sich nähern. Jeder einzelne genießt die Entzückungen aller, die verstärkt und verschönert aus hundert Augen auf ihn zurückfallen, und seine Brust gibt jetzt nur *einer* Empfindung Raum—es ist diese: ein *Mensch* zu sein.

unfeeling brute experiences human feeling for the first time.

And finally, what a triumph for you, oh nature—nature so often trampled underfoot, who has just as often risen again—when men from all corners of the earth and every walk of life, having shed their shackles of affectation and fashion, torn away from the insistent pressure of fate, united by the all-embracing bond of brotherly sympathy, resolved in one human race again, oblivious of themselves and of the world, come closer to their divine origin. Each enjoys the raptures of all, which are reflected on him from a hundred eyes in heightened beauty and intensity, and in his breast there is room for only one sensation: the awareness that he is a human being.

EINLEITUNG

EINE der merkwürdigsten Staatsbegebenheiten, die das
sechzehnte Jahrhundert zum glänzendsten der Welt gemacht haben, dünkt mir die Gründung der niederländischen Freiheit. Wenn die schimmernden Taten der Ruhmsucht und einer verderblichen Herrschbegierde auf unsere
Bewunderung Anspruch machen, wie viel mehr eine Begebenheit, wo die bedrängte Menschheit um ihre edelsten
Rechte ringt, wo mit der guten Sache ungewöhnliche Kräfte
sich paaren und die Hilfsmittel entschloßner Verzweiflung
über die furchtbaren Künste der Tyrannei in ungleichem
Wettkampf siegen. Groß und beruhigend ist der Gedanke,
daß gegen die trotzigen Anmaßungen der Fürstengewalt
endlich noch eine Hilfe vorhanden ist, daß ihre berechnet-
sten Plane an der menschlichen Freiheit zu Schanden werden, daß ein herzhafter Widerstand auch den gestreckten
Arm eines Despoten beugen, heldenmütige Beharrung seine
schrecklichen Hilfsquellen endlich erschöpfen kann. Nirgends durchdrang mich diese Wahrheit so lebhaft als bei
der Geschichte jenes denkwürdigen Aufruhrs, der die vereinigten Niederlande auf immer von der spanischen Krone
trennte—und darum achtete ich es des Versuches nicht unwert, dieses schöne Denkmal bürgerlicher Stärke vor der
Welt aufzustellen, in der Brust meines Lesers ein fröhliches
Gefühl seiner selbst zu erwecken und ein neues unverwerf-
liches Beispiel zu geben, was Menschen wagen dürfen für die
gute Sache und ausrichten mögen durch Vereinigung.
Es ist nicht das Außerordentliche oder Heroische dieser Begebenheit, was mich anreizt, sie zu beschreiben. Die Jahr-
bücher der Welt haben uns ähnliche Unternehmungen aufbewahrt, die in der Anlage noch kühner, in der Ausführung
noch glänzender erscheinen. Manche Staaten stürzten mit
einer prächtigern Erschütterung zusammen, mit erhabene-
rem Schwunge stiegen andere auf. Auch erwarte man hier
keine hervorragende, kolossalische Menschen, keine der
staunenswürdigen Taten, die uns die Geschichte vergange-
ner Zeiten in so reichlicher Fülle darbietet. Jene Zeiten sind
vorbei, jene Menschen sind nicht mehr. Im weichlichen
Schoß der Verfeinerung haben wir die Kräfte erschlaffen
284

INTRODUCTION
TO THE REVOLT IN THE NETHERLANDS

Among the noteworthy political events that make the
sixteenth century the most brilliant period of history
appears to me to be the establishment of freedom in the
Netherlands. If even the glittering exploits of ambition
and of a pernicious lust for power claim our admiration,
how much more deeply are we stirred by a situation in
which oppressed humanity struggled for its noblest
rights, in which extraordinary powers were enlisted in
the service of a good cause and the resources of resolute
despair triumphed in unequal contest over the dreadful
machinations of tyranny.

It is an inspiring thought that resources exist which can
be called upon to combat the arrogant usurpations of
despotic power, that the most cleverly devised plans to
destroy the liberty of mankind can be frustrated; that
resolute resistance can weaken even the long arm of a
despot; and that heroic perseverance can at last exhaust
its terrible resources.

Never was this truth brought home to me so vividly as
by the history of that memorable rebellion which sev-
ered forever the United Netherlands from the Spanish
Crown. For this reason I have thought it worth while
to attempt to present to the world this magnificent testimonial to civilian fortitude, to awaken in the breast of
my reader an exhilarating consciousness of his own
powers, and to place before him a fresh and irrefutable
example of what men may risk in a good cause and of
what they may accomplish when united.

It is not the extraordinary or heroic features of this episode that have inspired me to describe it. The annals
of history record many similar enterprises even bolder
in conception and more brilliant in execution. Nations
have fallen after a more noble struggle, others have risen
more gloriously. Nor must we expect to find men of
colossal stature or those marvelous exploits of which
there are so many examples in the history of past ages.
Those days are over; such men no longer exist. In the
soft lap of refinement we have allowed the powers to

lassen, die jene Zeitalter übten und notwendig machten. Mit niedergeschlagener Bewunderung staunen wir jetzt diese Riesenbilder an, wie ein entnervter Greis die mannhaften Spiele der Jugend. Nicht so bei vorliegender Geschichte. Das Volk, welches wir hier auftreten sehen, war das friedfertigste dieses Weltteils und weniger als alle seine Nachbarn jenes Heldengeists fähig, der auch der geringfügigsten Handlung einen höhern Schwung gibt. Der Drang der Umstände überraschte es mit seiner eigenen Kraft und nötigte ihm eine vorübergehende Größe auf, die es nie haben sollte und vielleicht nie wieder haben wird. Es ist also gerade der Mangel an heroischer Größe, was diese Begebenheit eigentümlich und unterrichtend macht, und wenn sich andere zum Zweck setzen, die Überlegenheit des Genies über den Zufall zu zeigen, so stelle ich hier ein Gemälde auf, wo die Not das Genie erschuf und die Zufälle Helden machten.

Wäre es irgend erlaubt, in menschliche Dinge eine höhere Vorsicht zu flechten, so wäre es bei dieser Geschichte; so widersprechend erscheint sie der Vernunft und allen Erfahrungen. Philipp der Zweite, der mächtigste Souverän seiner Zeit, dessen gefürchtete Übermacht ganz Europa zu verschlingen droht, dessen Schätze die vereinigten Reichtümer aller christlichen Könige übersteigen, dessen Flotten in allen Meeren gebieten; ein Monarch, dessen gefährlichen Zwecken zahlreiche Heere dienen, Heere, die, durch lange und blutige Kriege und eine römische Mannszucht gehärtet, durch einen trotzigen Nationalstolz begeistert und erhitzt durch das Andenken erfochtener Siege, nach Ehre und Beute dürsten und sich unter dem verwegenen Genie ihrer Führer als folgsame Glieder bewegen—dieser gefürchtete Mensch, einem hartnäckigen Entwurf hingegeben, *ein* Unternehmen die rastlose Arbeit seines langen Regentenlaufs, alle diese furchtbaren Hilfsmittel auf einen einzigen Zweck gerichtet, den er am Abend seiner Tage unerfüllt aufgeben muß— Philipp der Zweite, mit wenigen schwachen Nationen im Kampfe, den er nicht endigen kann!

Und gegen welche Nationen? Hier ein friedfertiges Fischer- und Hirtenvolk, in einem vergessenen Winkel Europens, den es noch mühsam der Meeresflut abgewann; die See sein

degenerate which men displayed in former times and which were necessary for survival. Now we can only gaze with awe and admiration at those gigantic figures as a feeble old man looks back on the athletic feats of youth.

But this chapter of history is different. The people who play the chief role in it were the most peaceful on this continent and less endowed than their neighbors with the heroic spirit that imparts a lofty character to even the most insignificant actions. The pressure of circumstances surprised them with its peculiar power and forced upon them a temporary greatness which they could never have been expected to possess and which they may never again display. It is this very lack of heroic grandeur that makes this event remarkable and instructive. And while others make it their purpose to show the superiority of genius over chance, the picture I shall paint is one in which necessity created genius and chance forged heroes.

If ever it is permissible to see the intervention of Providence in human affairs, this episode would be a case in point. So contrary to reason and experience was the course of events. Philip II is the most powerful sovereign of his time, a sovereign whose dreaded supremacy threatens the independence of all of Europe; whose treasures exceed the combined wealth of all the monarchs of Christendom; whose fleets dominate the seas. His ambitious projects are backed by numerous armies, armies hardened by long and bloody wars and a Roman discipline; troops fired with stubborn national pride and the memory of past victories. Thirsting for glory and spoil, they are wholly obedient to the daring genius of their leaders.

Philip, this dreaded potentate, obstinately pursues a single plan, a single purpose, devoting to it the untiring efforts of a long reign, concentrating all those terrible resources upon a single aim, only to be forced in the evening of his life to abandon it. Philip II finds himself locked in battle with a few weak nations, a battle he is unable to terminate.

And with what nations? One is a peaceful people, fishermen and shepherds, inhabiting a forgotten corner of Europe which they are still laboriously wresting from

Gewerbe, sein Reichtum und seine Plage, eine freie Armut sein höchstes Gut, sein Ruhm, seine Tugend. Dort ein gutartiges gesittetes Handelsvolk, schwelgend von den üppigen Früchten eines gesegneten Fleißes, wachsam auf Gesetze, die seine Wohltäter waren. In der glücklichen Muße des Wohlstandes verläßt es der Bedürfnisse ängstlichen Kreis und lernt nach höherer Befriedigung dürsten. Die neue Wahrheit, deren erfreuender Morgen jetzt über Europa hervorbricht, wirft einen befruchtenden Strahl in diese günstige Zone, und freudig empfängt der freie Bürger das Licht, dem sich gedrückte traurige Sklaven verschließen. Ein fröhlicher Mutwille, der gerne den Überfluß und die Freiheit begleitet, reizt es an, das Ansehen verjährter Meinungen zu prüfen und eine schimpfliche Kette zu brechen. Die schwere Zuchtrute des Despotismus hängt über ihm, eine willkürliche Gewalt droht die Grundpfeiler seines Glücks einzureißen, der Bewahrer seiner Gesetze wird sein Tyrann. Einfach in seiner Staatsweisheit wie in seinen Sitten, erkühnt es sich, einen veralteten Vertrag aufzuweisen und den Herrn beider Indien an das Naturrecht zu mahnen. Ein Name entscheidet den ganzen Ausgang der Dinge. Man nannte Rebellion in Madrid, was in Brüssel nur eine gesetzliche Handlung hieß; die Beschwerden Brabants forderten einen staatsklugen Mittler; Philipp der Zweite sandte ihm einen Henker, und die Losung des Kriegs war gegeben. Eine Tyrannei ohne Beispiel greift Leben und Eigentum an. Der verzweifelnde Bürger, dem zwischen einem zweifachen Tode die Wahl gelassen wird, erwählt den edleren auf dem Schlachtfeld. Ein wohlhabendes üppiges Volk liebt den Frieden, aber es wird kriegerisch, wenn es arm wird. Jetzt hört es auf, für ein Leben zu zittern, dem alles mangeln soll, warum es wünschenswürdig war. Die Wut des Aufruhrs ergreift die entferntesten Provinzen; Handel und Wandel liegen darnieder; die Schiffe verschwinden aus den Häfen, der Künstler aus seiner Werkstätte, der Landmann aus den verwüsteten Feldern. Tausende fliehen in ferne Länder, tausend Opfer fallen auf dem Blutgerüste, und neue Tausende drängen sich hinzu; denn

the sea. The sea is their profession, their wealth and their plague; poverty and freedom their greatest blessing, their glory, their virtue. The other is a nation of good-natured, highly civilized tradesmen, revelling in the abundant fruits and blessings of their industry, strict guardians of the law which has proved to be their benefactor. Enjoying the leisure of affluence, they abandon their anxious preoccupation with immediate needs and learn to thirst for nobler satisfactions.

The joyous dawn of the new truth then breaking over Europe sheds a fruitful ray on this favored region. The free burgher gladly welcomes the light which oppressed and miserable slaves refuse to admit. A daring exuberance which frequently comes with freedom and prosperity, spurs this people on to question the authority of antiquated opinions and to burst their ignominious chains.

The heavy rod of despotism hangs over their heads; an arbitrary power threatens to tear down the strong pillars of their happiness; the guardian of their laws becomes their tyrant. Simple in their political concepts as well as in their manners, they dare to appeal to ancient treaties and to remind the lord of both Indies of the natural rights of man.

The entire course of events is determined by the name applied to this behavior. What in Madrid was called a rebellion was termed in Brussels lawful conduct. The complaints of Brabant required a politically shrewd mediator. But Philip sent an executioner and this was the signal for war. An unexampled tyranny attacks life and property. The despairing citizens, left only with a choice of two deaths, choose the nobler, death on the battlefield. A wealthy, luxury-loving people is fond of peace, but it becomes warlike when threatened with poverty. Then it ceases to tremble for a life deprived of everything that had made it desirable. The rage of rebellion seizes the most remote provinces. Trade and commerce come to a standstill. Ships disappear from the harbors. The artisan abandons his workshop, the farmer his ravaged fields. Thousands flee to distant lands. Thousands of victims fall on the scaffold and thousands more press on to the

göttlich muß eine Lehre sein, für die so freudig gestorben werden kann. Noch fehlt die letzte vollendende Hand— der erleuchtete unternehmende Geist, der diesen großen politischen Augenblick haschte und die Geburt des Zufalls zum Plane der Weisheit erzöge.

Wilhelm der Stille weiht sich, ein zweiter Brutus, dem großen Anliegen der Freiheit. Über eine furchtsame Selbstsucht erhaben, kündigt er dem Throne strafbare Pflichten auf, entkleidet sich großmütig seines fürstlichen Daseins, steigt zu einer freiwilligen Armut herunter und ist nichts mehr als ein Bürger der Welt. Die gerechte Sache wird gewagt auf das Glücksspiel der Schlachten; aber zusammengeraffte Mietlinge und friedliches Landvolk können dem furchtbaren Andrang einer geübten Kriegsmacht nicht Stand halten. Zweimal führt er seine mutlosen Heere gegen den Tyrannen, zweimal verlassen sie ihn, aber nicht sein Mut. Philipp der Zweite sendet so viele Verstärkungen, als seines Mittlers grausame Habsucht Bettler machte. Flüchtlinge, die das Vaterland auswarf, suchen sich ein neues auf dem Meere, und auf den Schiffen ihres Feindes Sättigung ihrer Rache und ihres Hungers. Jetzt werden Seehelden aus Korsaren, aus Raubschiffen zieht sich eine Marine zusammen, und eine Republik steigt aus Morästen empor. Sieben Provinzen zerreißen zugleich ihre Bande; ein neuer jugendlicher Staat, mächtig durch Eintracht, seine Wasserflut und Verzweiflung. Ein feierlicher Spruch der Nation entsetzt den Tyrannen des Thrones, der spanische Name verschwindet aus allen Gesetzen.

Jetzt ist eine Tat getan, die keine Vergebung mehr findet; die Republik wird fürchterlich, weil sie nicht mehr zurück kann. Faktionen zerreißen ihren Bund; selbst ihr schreckliches Element, das Meer, mit ihrem Unterdrücker verschworen, droht ihrem zarten Anfang ein frühzeitiges Grab. Sie fühlt ihre Kräfte der überlegenen Macht des Feindes erliegen und wirft sich bittend vor Europens mächtigste Throne, eine Souveränität wegzuschenken, die sie nicht mehr beschützen kann. Endlich und mühsam—so verächtlich begann dieser Staat, daß selbst die Habsucht fremder Könige seine junge

fray. A doctrine must indeed be divine for men to lay down their lives for it so joyously. All that is lacking is the hand to provide the finishing touch, the enlightened, enterprising spirit to seize on this great political moment and convert what was born of chance into the plan of wisdom.

William the Silent, like a second Brutus, dedicates himself to the great cause of liberty. Rising above selfish fear, he renounces offensive duties assigned him by the throne, magnanimously divests himself of his princely dignity and descends to a state of voluntary poverty, becoming a mere citizen of the world. The cause of justice is staked on the hazardous game of war. But the hastily recruited army of mercenaries and peaceable farmers is unable to withstand the fearful might of an experienced military force. Twice William leads his dispirited troops against the tyrant. Twice he is abandoned by them, but not by his courage.

Philip II sends as many reinforcements as there are people made beggars by the cruel greed of his governor. Fugitives, cast off by their native lands, seek a new home on the sea and satisfy both their thirst for vengeance and their hunger on the ships of the enemy. Corsairs are now transformed into naval heroes; pirate ships band together to make a navy; a republic rises out of the morasses. Seven provinces break their shackles simultaneously to form a new young nation relying for its strength on its waters, its unity and its despair. A solemn decree deposes the tyrant and the Spanish name is expunged from all its laws.

This is the act for which there is no forgiveness. The republic becomes formidable because it can no longer retreat from its position. Within, it is torn by factions; without, that terrible element, the sea, is in league with its oppressors and threatens the infant state with a premature grave. Feeling that it is about to succumb to the superior force of the enemy, it prostrates itself before the most powerful thrones of Europe, beseeching them to accept a sovereignty which no longer protects it.

At last, after many rebuffs—the state was so despised in its early infancy that even the greediest monarchs

Blüte verschmähte—einem Fremdling endlich dringt sie ihre gefährliche Krone auf. Neue Hoffnungen erfrischen ihren sinkenden Mut, aber einen Verräter gab ihr in diesem neuen Landesvater das Schicksal, und in dem drangvollen Zeitpunkt, wo der unerbittliche Feind vor den Toren schon stürmet, tastet Karl von Anjou die Freiheit an, zu deren Schutz er gerufen worden. Eines Meuchelmörders Hand reißt noch den Steuermann von dem Ruder, ihr Schicksal scheint vollendet, mit Wilhelm von Oranien alle ihre rettenden Engel geflohen—aber das Schiff fliegt im Sturme, und die wallenden Segel bedürfen des Ruderers Hilfe nicht mehr.

Philipp der Zweite sieht die Frucht einer Tat verloren, die ihm seine fürstliche Ehre und wer weiß ob nicht den heimlichen Stolz seines stillen Bewußtseins kostet. Hartnäckig und ungewiß ringt mit dem Despotismus die Freiheit; mörderische Schlachten werden gefochten; eine glänzende Heldenreihe wechselt auf dem Felde der Ehre; Flandern und Brabant war die Schule, die dem kommenden Jahrhundert Feldherrn erzog. Ein langer verwüstender Krieg zertritt den Segen des offenen Landes, Sieger und Besiegte verbluten, während daß der werdende Wasserstaat den fliehenden Fleiß zu sich lockte und auf den Trümmern seines Nachbars den herrlichen Bau seiner Größe erhub. Vierzig Jahre dauerte ein Krieg, dessen glückliche Endigung Philipps sterbendes Auge nicht erfreute, der ein Paradies in Europa vertilgte und ein neues aus seinen Ruinen erschuf—der die Blüte der kriegerischen Jugend verschlang, einen ganzen Weltteil bereicherte und den Besitzer des goldreichen Peru zum armen Manne machte. Dieser Monarch, der, ohne sein Land zu drücken, neunmalhundert Tonnen Goldes verschwenden durfte, der noch weit mehr durch tyrannische Künste erzwang, häufte eine Schuld von hundertundvierzig Millionen Dukaten auf sein entvölkertes Land. Ein unversöhnlicher Haß der Freiheit verschlang alle diese Schätze und verzehrte fruchtlos sein königliches Leben; aber die Reformation gedeihte unter den Verwüstungen seines Schwerts, und die neue Republik hob aus Bürgerblut ihre siegende Fahne.

Diese unnatürliche Wendung der Dinge scheint an ein Wunder zu grenzen; aber vieles vereinigte sich, die Gewalt dieses Königs zu brechen und die Fortschritte des jungen Staats

spurned it—it forces the precarious throne on a stranger. New hopes begin to revive its failing courage. But in this new father of his country fate has given it a traitor, and at the critical moment when the inexorable foe is storming its gates, Charles of Anjou violates the liberties he had been called upon to protect. The assassin's hand snatches the pilot from the helm. The career of the republic appears to have come to an end. Its guardian angels appear to have fled at the death of William of Orange. But the ship continues to ride the storm, its swelling sails no longer require the pilot's hand.

Philip II fails to reap the fruits of a deed which cost him his royal honor, and perhaps also the secret pride of his silent consciousness. Stubbornly and uncertainly liberty struggles with despotism. Murderous battles are fought. A brilliant array of heroes succeed one another on the field of glory, and Flanders and Brabant become the training ground for generals of the next century. A long and devastating war tramples down the rich yield of the open country. Victor and vanquished alike bleed to death, while the rising republic of the waters attracts the fleeing industriousness and erects the noble edifice of its greatness on the ruins of its neighbor.

The war went on for forty years. Its successful termination brought no gladness to the dying Philip. It destroyed one paradise in Europe and created another on the ruins. It consumed the finest flower of military youth, and while it enriched an entire continent it turned the possessor of golden Peru into a poor man.

This monarch, who could spend nine hundred tons of gold without oppressing his people, who extorted far more by tyrannical methods, heaped on his depopulated country a debt of one hundred and forty million ducats. An implacable hatred of liberty swallowed up all these treasures and fruitlessly consumed his royal life. But the Reformation prospered amidst the devastations of his sword, and the banner of the new republic floated victorious over the blood of its citizens.

This unnatural turn of events seems nothing short of miraculous. Many factors, however, combined to break the power of this king to favor the progress of the infant

zu begünstigen. Wäre das ganze Gewicht seiner Macht auf die vereinigten Provinzen gefallen, so war keine Rettung für ihre Religion, ihre Freiheit. Sein eigner Ehrgeiz kam ihrer Schwäche zu Hilfe, indem er ihn nötigte, seine Macht zu teilen. Die kostbare Politik, in jedem Kabinett Europens Verräter zu besolden, die Unterstützungen der Ligue in Frankreich, der Aufstand der Mauren in Grenada, Portugals Eroberung und der prächtige Bau vom Escurial erschöpften endlich seine so unermeßlich scheinenden Schätze und untersagten ihm, mit Lebhaftigkeit und Nachdruck im Felde zu handeln. Die deutschen und italienischen Truppen, die nur die Hoffnung der Beute unter seine Fahnen gelockt hatte, empörten sich jetzt, weil er sie nicht bezahlen konnte, und verließen treulos ihre Führer im entscheidenden Moment ihrer Wirksamkeit. Diese fürchterlichen Werkzeuge der Unterdrückung kehrten jetzt ihre gefährliche Macht gegen ihn selbst und wüteten feindlich in den Provinzen, die ihm treu geblieben waren. Jene unglückliche Ausrüstung gegen Britannien, an die er, gleich einem rasenden Spieler, die ganze Kraft seines Königreichs wagte, vollendete seine Entnervung; mit der Armada ging der Tribut beider Indien und der Kern der spanischen Heldenzucht unter.

Aber in eben dem Maße, wie sich die spanische Macht erschöpfte, gewann die Republik frisches Leben. Die Lücken, welche die neue Religion, die Tyrannei der Glaubensgerichte, die wütende Raubsucht der Soldateska und die Verheerungen eines langwierigen Kriegs ohne Unterlaß in die Provinzen Brabant, Flandern und Hennegau rissen, die der Waffenplatz und die Vorratskammer dieses kostbaren Krieges waren, machten es natürlicherweise mit jedem Jahre schwerer, die Armeen zu unterhalten und zu erneuern. Die katholischen Niederlande hatten schon eine Million Bürger verloren, und die zertretenen Felder nährten ihre Pflüger nicht mehr. Spanien selbst konnte wenig Volk mehr entraten. Diese Länder, durch einen schnellen Wohlstand überrascht, der den Müßiggang herbeiführte, hatten sehr an Bevölkerung verloren und konnten diese Menschenversendungen nach der neuen Welt und den Niederlanden nicht lange aushalten. Wenige unter diesen sahen ihr Vaterland wieder: diese wenigen hatten es als Jünglinge verlassen und kamen nun

state. Had the entire weight of his power fallen on the United Provinces, there would have been no salvation for their religion or for their liberty. His own ambition, which compelled him to divide his power, came to the aid of their weakness. The costly policy of maintaining traitors in every cabinet of Europe, the support of the League in France, the revolt of the Moors in Granada, the conquest of Portugal and the construction of the magnificent Escurial: all these finally drained his seemingly inexhaustible treasury and prevented him from conducting the war with spirit and vigor.

The German and Italian troops, drawn to his banner only by the hope of gain, mutinied when he could no longer pay them and faithlessly deserted their leaders at the crucial moment. These terrible instruments of oppression now turned against him and vindictively ravaged the provinces that remained faithful to him. The unfortunate expedition against England, on which, like a desperate gambler, he staked the entire strength of his kingdom, completed his ruin. The wealth of the two Indies and the flower of Spanish chivalry went down with the Armada.

But as the Spanish power declined the republic gained fresh vigor. The new religion, the tyranny of the Inquisition, the savage greed of the soldiery and the devastations of long and ceaseless warfare made tremendous inroads on the provinces of Brabant, Flanders and Hainault, which were the arsenals and the magazines of this costly contest. With every year it naturally became more difficult to recruit and support the royal armies. The Catholic Netherlands had already lost a million citizens and the trampled fields could not longer support the plowmen.

By now Spain itself had few men to spare. That country, surprised by a sudden prosperity which had brought idleness and leisure, had lost much of its population and could not long endure the continual drafts of men required both for the New World and the Netherlands. Few of these conscripts ever saw their country again, and they, having left as youths, returned old and infirm.

als entkräftete Greise zurück. Das gemeiner gewordene Gold machte den Soldaten immer teurer; der überhandnehmende Reiz der Weichlichkeit steigerte den Preis der entgegengesetzten Tugenden. Ganz anders verhielt es sich mit den Rebellen. Alle die Tausende, welche die Grausamkeit der königlichen Statthalter aus den südlichen Niederlanden, der Hugenottenkrieg aus Frankreich und der Gewissenszwang aus andern Gegenden Europens verjagten, alle gehörten ihnen. Ihr Werbeplatz war die ganze christliche Welt. Für sie arbeitete der Fanatismus der Verfolger, wie der Verfolgten. Die frische Begeisterung einer neu verkündigten Lehre, Rachsucht, Hunger und hoffnungsloses Elend zogen aus allen Distrikten Europens Abenteurer unter ihre Fahnen. Alles, was für die neue Lehre gewonnen war, was von dem Despotismus gelitten oder noch künftig von ihm zu fürchten hatte, machte das Schicksal dieser neuen Republik gleichsam zu seinem eigenen. Jede Kränkung, von einem Tyrannen erlitten, gab ein Bürgerrecht in Holland. Man drängte sich nach einem Lande, wo die Freiheit ihre erfreuende Fahne aufsteckte, wo der flüchtigen Religion Achtung und Sicherheit und Rache an ihren Unterdrückern gewiß war. Wenn wir den Zusammenfluß aller Völker in dem heutigen Holland betrachten, die beim Eintritt in sein Gebiet ihre Menschenrechte zurück empfangen, was muß es damals gewesen sein, wo noch das ganze übrige Europa unter einem traurigen Geistesdruck seufzte, wo Amsterdam beinahe der einzige Freihafen aller Meinungen war? Viele hundert Familien retteten ihren Reichtum in ein Land, das der Ozean und die Eintracht gleich mächtig beschirmten. Die republikanische Armee war vollzählig, ohne daß man nötig gehabt hätte, den Pflug zu entblößen. Mitten unter dem Waffengeräusch blühten Gewerbe und Handel, und der ruhige Bürger genoß im voraus alle Früchte der Freiheit, die mit fremdem Blut erst erstritten wurden. Zu eben der Zeit, wo die Republik Holland noch um ihr Dasein kämpfte, rückte sie die Grenzen ihres Gebiets über das Weltmeer hinaus und baute still an ihren ostindischen Thronen.

Noch mehr. Spanien führte diesen kostbaren Krieg mit totem unfruchtbarem Golde, das nie in *die* Hand zurückkehrte, die es weggab, aber den Preis aller Bedürfnisse in Europa

Gold which had become more common made soldiers proportionally dearer. The increasing charm of soft living raised the price of the opposite virtues.

But the situation of the rebels was quite different. All of the thousands driven from the southern Netherlands by the cruelty of the viceroy, from France by the Huguenots' war, from other parts of Europe by intolerance, all joined the insurgents. The entire Christian world was their recruiting ground. The fanaticism of the persecutor and the persecuted worked in their behalf. The fresh enthusiasm inspired by a new doctrine, revenge, hunger and hopeless misery drew to their standards adventurers from every quarter of Europe. All who had become converted to the new doctrine, all who had suffered from or had reason to fear despotism linked their fortunes with those of the new republic. Anyone who had suffered injury at the hands of a tyrant had a right to citizenship in Holland. Men flocked to a country where liberty raised her inspiring banner, where a persecuted religion was assured of respect and security and of revenge on the oppressor.

If we consider the conflux of people in present-day Holland who sought by entering it to regain their rights as men, what must it have been when all the rest of Europe was groaning under the heavy pressure of intolerance, when Amsterdam was virtually the only free port for all shades of opinion?

Many hundreds of families sought refuge for their wealth in a land protected both by the ocean and domestic unity. The republican army maintained its full complement without stripping the farm of plowmen. Trade and industry flourished amid the clash of arms and peaceful citizens enjoyed in advance the fruits of liberty which were to be purchased for them by foreign blood. At the very time when the republic of Holland was battling for her life, she extended her dominions beyond the ocean and was quietly occupied in founding her East Indian Empire.

What is more, Spain conducted this war with dead, barren gold which never returned to the hand that gave it, while this same gold raised the price of all necessities in

erhöhte. Die Schatzkammer der Republik waren Arbeitsamkeit und Handel. Jenes verminderte, diese vervielfältigte die Zeit. In eben dem Maße, wie sich die Hilfsquellen der Regierung bei der langen Fortdauer des Kriegs erschöpften, fing die Republik eigentlich erst an, ihre Ernte zu halten. Es war eine gesparte dankbare Aussaat, die spät, aber hundertfältig wiedergab; der Baum, von welchem Philipp sich Früchte brach, war ein umgehauener Stamm und grünte nicht wieder.

Philipps widriges Schicksal wollte, daß alle Schätze, die er zum Untergang der Provinzen verschwendete, sie selbst noch bereichern halfen. Jene ununterbrochenen Ausflüsse des spanischen Goldes hatten Reichtum und Luxus durch ganz Europa verbreitet; Europa aber empfing seine vermehrten Bedürfnisse größtenteils aus den Händen der Niederländer, die den Handel der ganzen damaligen Welt beherrschten und den Preis aller Waren bestimmten. Sogar während dieses Kriegs konnte Philipp der Republik Holland den Handel mit seinen eignen Untertanen nicht wehren, ja er konnte dieses nicht einmal wünschen. Er selbst bezahlte den Rebellen die Unkosten ihrer Verteidigung: denn eben der Krieg, der sie aufreiben sollte, vermehrte den Absatz ihrer Waren. Der ungeheure Aufwand für seine Flotten und Armeen floß größtenteils in die Schatzkammer der Republik, die mit den flämischen und brabantischen Handelsplätzen in Verbindung stand. Was Philipp *gegen* die Rebellen in Bewegung setzte, wirkte mittelbar *für* sie. Alle die unermeßlichen Summen, die ein vierzigjähriger Krieg verschlang, waren in die Fässer der Danaiden gegossen und zerrannen in einer bodenlosen Tiefe.

Der träge Gang dieses Kriegs tat dem König von Spanien ebenso viel Schaden, als er den Rebellen Vorteile brachte. Seine Armee war größtenteils aus den Überresten jener siegreichen Truppen zusammengeflossen, die unter Karln dem Fünften bereits ihre Lorbeern gesammelt hatten. Alter und lange Dienste berechtigten sie zur Ruhe; viele unter ihnen, die der Krieg bereichert hatte, wünschten sich ungeduldig nach ihrer Heimat zurück, ein mühevolles Leben gemächlich zu enden. Ihr vormaliger Eifer, ihr Heldenfeuer und

Europe. The treasury of the republic was industriousness and commerce. Time drained the one as it filled the other. And as the resources of the Spanish government became exhausted by the long duration of the war, the republic began to reap a rich harvest. Its field was sown with the savings of a rewarding seed which, though late, bore fruit a hundredfold. But the tree from which Philip gathered fruit was a dead trunk that never again put forth verdance.

It was Philip's ill fortune that all the treasure that he lavished on the oppression of the Provinces only served to enrich them. The continuous flow of Spanish gold had spread riches and luxury throughout Europe. But the ever-increasing needs of Europe were supplied mainly by the Netherlanders who controlled the commerce of the known world and determined the price of all merchandise. Even during the war Philip could not prevent his own subjects from trading with the republic. He could not even desire to do so. He himself furnished the rebels with the means of defraying the cost of their defense. The very war that was to ruin them increased the sale of their goods. The enormous sums expended on his fleets and armies flowed for the most part into the exchequer of the republic which was more or less connected with the trading centers of Flanders and Brabant. Every attack launched by Philip against the rebels worked to their advantage. All the fabulous sums consumed by a forty-year war poured into the sieves of the Danaids and vanished into a bottomless abyss.

The long sluggish struggle was as detrimental to the king as it was advantageous to the rebels. His army was composed for the most part of the remnants of the victorious troops which had earned their laurels under Charles V. Age and long service entitled them to repose. Many of them, enriched by the war, were impatient to return home in order to end in comfort a life of hardship. As they came to believe that they had discharged the obligations of duty and honor, and as they began to reap the rewards of so many battles, their former zeal, their heroic spirit, their discipline relaxed.

ihre Mannszucht ließen in eben dem Grade nach, als sie ihre Ehre und Pflicht gelöst zu haben glaubten und die Früchte so vieler Feldzüge endlich zu ernten anfingen. Dazu kam, daß Truppen, die gewohnt waren, durch das Ungestüm ihres Angriffs jeden Widerstand zu besiegen, ein Krieg ermüden mußte, der weniger mit Menschen als mit Elementen geführt wurde, der mehr die Geduld übte, als die Ruhmbegierde vergnügte, wobei weniger Gefahr als Beschwerlichkeit und Mangel zu bekämpfen war. Weder ihr persönlicher Mut noch ihre lange kriegerische Erfahrung konnten ihnen in einem Lande zu statten kommen, dessen eigentümliche Beschaffenheit oft auch dem Feigsten der Eingebornen über sie Vorteile gab. Auf einem fremden Boden endlich schadete ihnen *eine* Niederlage mehr, als *viele* Siege über einen Feind, der hier zu Hause war, ihnen nützen konnten. Mit den Rebellen war es gerade der umgekehrte Fall. In einem so langwierigen Kriege, wo keine entscheidende Schlacht geschah, mußte der schwächere Feind zuletzt von dem stärkern lernen, kleine Niederlagen ihn an die Gefahr gewöhnen, kleine Siege seine Zuversicht befeuern. Bei Eröffnung des Bürgerkriegs hatte sich die republikanische Armee vor der spanischen im Felde kaum zeigen dürfen; seine lange Dauer übte und härtete sie. Wie die königlichen Heere des Schlagens überdrüssig wurden, war das Selbstvertrauen der Rebellen mit ihrer bessern Kriegszucht und Erfahrung gestiegen. Endlich, nach einem halben Jahrhundert, gingen Meister und Schüler, unüberwunden, als gleiche Kämpfer aus einander.

Ferner wurde im ganzen Verlaufe dieses Kriegs von seiten der Rebellen mit mehr Zusammenhang und Einheit gehandelt als von seiten des Königs. Ehe jene ihr erstes Oberhaupt verloren, war die Verwaltung der Niederlande durch nicht weniger als fünf verschiedene Hände gegangen. Die Unentschlüssigkeit der Herzogin von Parma teilte sich dem Kabinett zu Madrid mit und ließ es in kurzer Zeit beinahe alle Staatsmaximen durchwandern. Herzog Albas unbeugsame Härte, die Gelindigkeit seines Nachfolgers Requesens, Don Johanns von Österreich Hinterlist und Tücke und der lebhafte cäsarische Geist des Prinzen von Parma gaben die-

Moreover, troops that had been accustomed to overcoming all resistance by the impetuosity of their attacks could not help but weary of a war waged not so much against men as against the elements. Instead of gratifying their love of glory, it called for the exercise of patience. They were required to contend with fatigue, discomfort and want rather than with danger. Neither courage nor military experience availed in a country whose peculiar features often gave the advantage even to the most cowardly. The damage inflicted on them by a single defeat on foreign soil was out of all proportion to what they could gain by many victories over an enemy that was battling on its home territory. For the rebels the situation was just the reverse. In so protracted a war in which there were no decisive battles, the weaker party inevitably learned from the stronger the art of defense. Minor defeats accustomed it to danger; minor victories aroused its confidence.

At the beginning of the war the republican army scarcely dared show itself on the field. The long duration of the struggle gave it the opportunity to become practiced and hardened. As the royal armies grew weary of battle, the rebels became increasingly disciplined and experienced and their confidence rose. At last, after a half century, master and pupil parted unvanquished as equals in battle.

Again, throughout the war there was greater unity and organization among the rebels than among the royalists. Before the former lost their first leader, the administration of the Netherlands passed through as many as five hands. The vacillation of the Duchess of Parma communicated itself to the cabinet in Madrid which within a short period of time tried out almost every kind of policy. The inflexible cruelty of Duke Alba, the mildness of his successor, Requesens, the perfidy and cunning of Don John of Austria, the active and imperious mind of the Prince of Parma: each gave a different direction to

301

diesem Krieg ebenso viel entgegengesetzte Richtungen, während daß der Plan der Rebellion in dem einzigen Kopfe, worin er klar und lebendig wohnte, immer derselbe blieb. Das größere Übel war, daß die Maxime mehrenteils das Moment verfehlte, in welchem sie anzuwenden sein mochte. Im Anfang der Unruhen, wo das Übergewicht augenscheinlich noch auf seiten des Königs war, wo ein rascher Entschluß und männliche Stetigkeit die Rebellion noch in der Wiege erdrücken konnten, ließ man den Zügel der Regierung in den Händen eines Weibes schlaffhin und her schwanken. Nachdem die Empörung zum wirklichen Ausbruch gekommen war, die Kräfte der Faktion und des Königs schon mehr im Gleichgewichte standen und eine kluge Geschmeidigkeit allein dem nahen Bürgerkrieg wehren konnte, fiel die Statthalterschaft einem Manne zu, dem zu diesem Posten gerade diese einzige Tugend fehlte. Einem so wachsamen Aufseher, als Wilhelm der Verschwiegene war, entging keiner der Vorteile, die ihm die fehlerhafte Politik seines Gegners gab, und mit stillem Fleiß rückte er langsam sein großes Unternehmen zum Ziele.

Aber warum erschien Philipp der Zweite nicht selbst in den Niederlanden? Warum wollte er lieber die unnatürlichsten Mittel erschöpfen, um nur das einzige nicht zu versuchen, welches nicht fehlschlagen konnte? Die üppige Gewalt des Adels zu brechen, war kein Ausweg natürlicher als die persönliche Gegenwart des Herrn. Neben der Majestät mußte jede Privatgröße versinken, jedes andre Ansehen erlöschen. Anstatt daß die Wahrheit durch so viele unreine Kanäle langsam und trübe nach dem entlegenen Throne floß, daß die verzögerte Gegenwehr dem Werke des Ohngefährs Zeit ließ, zu einem Werke des Verstandes zu reifen, hätte sein eigner durchdringender Blick Wahrheit von Irrtum geschieden; nicht seine Menschlichkeit, kalte Staatskunst allein hätte dem Lande eine Million Bürger gerettet. Je näher ihrer Quelle, desto nachdrücklicher wären die Edikte gewesen; je dichter an ihrem Ziele, desto unkräftiger und verzagter die Streiche des Aufruhrs gefallen. Es kostet unendlich mehr, das Böse, dessen man sich gegen einen abwesenden Feind wohl getrauen mag, ihm ins Angesicht zuzufügen. Die Rebellion schien

the war, while the plan of rebellion remained the same and was pursued by a single active and clear-thinking mind.

An even greater misfortune was that the right moment to apply the principles was generally missed. At the outset of the troubles, when the advantage was still clearly on the king's side, when prompt decisions and masculine firmness might have crushed the rebellion in the cradle, the reins of government were allowed to swing in the hands of a woman. When the discontentment had turned into open revolt, when the strength of the rebel faction was more evenly balanced with that of the king, when only a shrewd flexibility could have averted the impending civil war, the government devolved on a man who was conspicuously lacking in this very quality. As alert an observer as William the Silent did not fail to take every advantage of the faulty policy of his opponent. With quiet industry he slowly moved his great enterprise towards its goal.

But why did not Philip himself appear in the Netherlands? Why did he prefer to employ the most unnatural methods rather than to try the one remedy that could not fail? Nothing could so effectively curb the overweening power of the nobility as the presence of the master. Before royalty all private greatness was overshadowed, all other prestige paled. The truth was allowed to flow slowly and obscurely through so many impure channels to the distant throne that by delayed measures haphazardly conceived expediencies were given time to mature into deliberate plans, while his own penetrating eyes would have separated truth from error. His cold statesmanship, not his humanity, would have saved the land a million citizens. The nearer to their source, the more weight the edicts would have carried; the closer to their target the less power and decision would have animated the blows of the rebellion. It takes infinitely more courage to inflict harm on an enemy in his presence than in his absence.

anfangs selbst vor ihrem Namen zu zittern und schmückte sich
lange Zeit mit dem künstlichen Vorwand, die Sache des Sou-
veräns gegen die willkürlichen Anmaßungen seines Statt-
halters in Schutz zu nehmen. Philipps Erscheinung in Brüssel
hätte dieses Gaukelspiel auf einmal geendigt. Jetzt mußte
sie ihre Vorspiegelung erfüllen, oder die Larve abwerfen und
sich durch ihre wahre Gewalt verdammen. Und welche Erleichterung für die Niederlande, wenn seine Gegenwart ihnen auch nur diejenigen Übel erspart hätte, die ohne sein
Wissen und gegen seinen Willen auf sie gehäuft wurden!
Welcher Gewinn für ihn selbst, wenn sie auch zu nichts weiter gedient hätte, als über die Anwendung der unermeßlichen
Summen zu wachen, die, zu den Bedürfnissen des Kriegs
widerrechtlich gehoben, in den räuberischen Händen seiner Verwalter verschwanden! Was seine Stellvertreter durch
den unnatürlichen Behelf des Schreckens erzwingen mußten,
hätte die Majestät in allen Gemütern schon vorgefunden.
Was jene zu Gegenständen des Abscheus machte, hätte ihm
höchstens Furcht erworben; denn der Mißbrauch angebor-
ner Gewalt drückt weniger schmerzhaft als der Mißbrauch
empfangener. Seine Gegenwart hätte Tausende gerettet,
wenn er auch nichts als ein haushälterischer Despot war;
wenn er auch nicht einmal *der* war, so würde das Schrecken
seiner Person ihm eine Landschaft erhalten haben, die durch
den Haß und die Geringschätzung seiner Maschinen verloren ging.
Gleichwie die Bedrückung des niederländischen Volks eine
Angelegenheit aller Menschen wurde, die ihre Rechte fühl-
ten, ebenso, möchte man denken, hätte der Ungehorsam
und Abfall dieses Volks eine Aufforderung an alle Fürsten
sein sollen, in der Gerechtsame ihres Nachbars ihre eigne
zu schützen. Aber die Eifersucht über Spanien gewann es
diesmal über diese politische Sympathie, und die ersten
Mächte Europens traten, lauter oder stiller, auf die Seite
der Freiheit. Kaiser Maximilian der Zweite, obgleich dem
spanischen Hause durch Bande der Verwandtschaft ver-
pflichtet, gab ihm gerechten Anlaß zu der Beschuldigung,
die Partei der Rebellen insgeheim begünstigt zu haben. Durch
das Anerbieten seiner Vermittlung gestand er ihren Beschwer-

At first the rebellion seemed to tremble at its own name and employed the ingenious pretext that it was defending the cause of the sovereign against the arbitrary pretensions of his own viceroy. Philip's appearance in Brussels would have at once put an end to this tricky game. The rebels would then have been compelled either to make good their pretensions or to cast aside the mask and condemn themselves by showing their true colors.

And what a relief for the Netherlands if the king's presence had spared them only those evils which were inflicted upon them without his knowledge and contrary to his desire. What a gain for the king himself if his presence had enabled him no more than to watch over the expenditure of the vast sums illegally raised on the plea of meeting the exigencies of war, sums which vanished into the thieving hands of his administrators. What the latter were compelled to extort by means of terror the nation would have been disposed to grant to the sovereign majesty. Where his ministers aroused loathing, the monarch would at most have inspired fear. The abuse of hereditary power is less oppressive than the abuse of delegated authority. His presence would have saved thousands if he had been nothing more than an economical despot. Even had he been less, the awe inspired by his person would have preserved for him a territory which was lost through hatred and contempt for his instruments.

Just as the oppression of the people of the Netherlands aroused the sympathy of all who valued their own rights, it might reasonably have been expected that their disobedience and defection would serve as a signal to all princes to protect their own prerogatives by coming to the aid of their neighbor. But jealousy of Spain got the better of political sympathy and the first powers of Europe arrayed themselves more or less openly on the side of freedom.

Although bound to the house of Spain by ties of blood, King Maximilian II entirely justified the Spanish charge that he secretly favored the rebels. By his offer of mediation he implicitly acknowledged the partial justice of

den stillschweigend einen Grad von Gerechtigkeit zu, welches sie aufmuntern mußte, desto standhafter darauf zu beharren. Unter einem Kaiser, der dem spanischen Hof aufrichtig ergeben gewesen wäre, hätte Wilhelm von Oranien schwerlich so viele Truppen und Gelder aus Deutschland gezogen. Frankreich, ohne den Frieden offenbar und förmlich zu brechen, stellte einen Prinzen vom Geblüt an die Spitze der niederländischen Rebellen; die Operationen der letztern wurden größtenteils mit französischem Gelde und Truppen vollführt. Elisabeth von England übte nur eine gerechte Rache und Wiedervergeltung aus, da sie die Aufrührer gegen ihren rechtmäßigen Oberherrn in Schutz nahm, und wenn gleich ihr sparsamer Beistand höchstens nur hinreichte, den gänzlichen Ruin der Republik abzuwehren, so war dieses in einem Zeitpunkt schon unendlich viel, wo ihren erschöpften Mut Hoffnung allein noch hinhalten konnte. Mit diesen beiden Mächten stand Philipp damals noch im Bündnis des Friedens, und beide wurden zu Verrätern an ihm. Zwischen dem Starken und Schwachen ist Redlichkeit oft keine Tugend; dem, der gefürchtet wird, kommen selten die feinern Bande zu gut, welche Gleiches mit Gleichem zusammenhalten. Philipp selbst hatte die Wahrheit aus dem politischen Umgange verwiesen, er selbst die Sittlichkeit zwischen Königen aufgelöst und die Hinterlist zur Gottheit des Kabinetts gemacht. Ohne seiner Überlegenheit jemals froh zu werden, mußte er sein ganzes Leben hindurch mit der Eifersucht ringen, die sie ihm bei andern erweckte. Europa ließ ihn für den Mißbrauch einer Gewalt büßen, von der er in der Tat nie den ganzen Gebrauch gehabt hatte.

Bringt man gegen die Ungleichheit beider Kämpfer, die auf den ersten Anblick so sehr in Erstaunen setzt, alle Zufälle in Berechnung, welche jenen anfeindeten und diesen begünstigten, so verschwindet das Übernatürliche dieser Begebenheit, aber das Außerordentliche bleibt—und man hat einen richtigen Maßstab gefunden, das eigne Verdienst dieser Republikaner um ihre Freiheit angeben zu können. Doch denke man nicht, daß dem Unternehmen selbst eine so genaue Berechnung der Kräfte vorangegangen sei, oder daß sie beim Eintritt in dieses ungewisse Meer schon das Ufer

their complaints, thereby encouraging them to stand their ground more resolutely. Under an emperor sincerely devoted to the interests of the Spanish house, William of Orange could scarcely have drawn so many troops and so much money from Germany. Without openly and formally breaking the peace, France placed a prince of the blood at the head of the Netherland rebels. Their operations were conducted largely with French gold and French troops. Elizabeth of England was only taking a just revenge and retribution when she gave protection to the rebels against their legitimate sovereign. Although her meager aid served only to ward off utter ruin, this was of infinite value at a moment when nothing but hope could uphold their flagging courage.

At the time Philip was bound by peace treaties to both of these powers, yet both betrayed him. Between the weak and the strong honesty often ceases to be a virtue. The more fastidious relations that prevail between equals can seldom be enjoyed by one who is feared. Philip himself had banished truth from political dealings. He himself had done away with morality between kings, and had made underhandedness the deity of cabinets. He never enjoyed the advantages of his great position, but had to contend all his life with the jealousy it aroused in others. Europe made him atone for the abuse of a power which in fact he had never fully possessed.

At first glance, the disparity between the combatants seems utterly astounding. If, however, we weigh all the accidents of fortune which were adverse to Spain and favorable to the Netherlands, we are no longer tempted to attribute the outcome of the struggle to the intervention of a supernatural agent, but the episode remains extraordinary. We can then gauge more fairly the achievement of the republicans in gaining their liberty.

It must not be supposed, however, that a precise calculation of the opposing forces was made in advance, nor that before they embarked on this unknown sea the

gewußt haben, an welchem sie nachher landeten. So reif, als es zuletzt da stand in seiner Vollendung, erschien das Werk nicht in der Idee seiner Urheber, so wenig als vor Luthers Geiste die ewige Glaubens-Trennung, da er gegen den Ablaßkram aufstand. Welcher Unterschied zwischen dem bescheidenen Aufzug jener Bettler in Brüssel, die um eine menschlichere Behandlung als um eine Gnade flehen, und der furchtbaren Majestät eines Freistaats, der mit Königen als seinesgleichen unterhandelt und in weniger als einem Jahrhundert den Thron seiner vormaligen Tyrannen verschenkt! Des Fatums unsichtbare Hand führte den abgedrückten Pfeil in einem höhern Bogen und nach einer ganz andern Richtung fort, als ihm von der Sehne gegeben war. Im Schoße des glücklichen Brabants wird die Freiheit geboren, die, noch ein neugebornes Kind ihrer Mutter entrissen, das verachtete Holland beglücken soll. Aber das Unternehmen selbst darf uns darum nicht kleiner erscheinen, weil es anders ausschlug, als es gedacht worden war. Der Mensch verarbeitet, glättet und bildet den rohen Stein, den die Zeiten herbeitragen; ihm gehört der Augenblick und der Punkt, aber die Weltgeschichte rollt der Zufall. Wenn die Leidenschaften, welche sich bei dieser Begebenheit geschäftig erzeigten, des Werks nur nicht unwürdig waren, dem sie unbewußt dienten—wenn die Kräfte, die sie ausführen halfen, und die einzelnen Handlungen, aus deren Verkettung sie wunderbar erwuchs, nur an sich edle Kräfte, schöne und große Handlungen waren, so ist die Begebenheit groß, interessant und fruchtbar für uns, und es steht uns frei, über die kühne Geburt des Zufalls zu erstaunen, oder einem höhern Verstand unsre Bewunderung zuzutragen.

Die Geschichte der Welt ist sich selbst gleich wie die Gesetze der Natur und einfach wie die Seele des Menschen. Dieselben Bedingungen bringen dieselben Erscheinungen zurück. Auf eben diesem Boden, wo jetzt die Niederländer ihrem spanischen Tyrannen die Spitze bieten, haben vor funfzehnhundert Jahren ihre Stammväter, die Batavier und Belgen, mit ihrem römischen gerungen. Ebenso wie jene einem hochmütigen Beherrscher unwillig untertan, ebenso von habsüchtigen Satrapen mißhandelt, werfen sie mit ähn-

rebels knew on what shore they would ultimately land. At the outset of the undertaking the originator did not have a clear vision of the final result, any more than Luther foresaw the eternal separation of creeds when he began to oppose the sale of indulgences.

What a contrast between that modest procession of suppliants in Brussels, pleading for more humane treatment as a gracious favor and the awesome majesty of a free state which treated with kings as equals and in less than a century disposed of the throne of its former tyrannical overlord. The unseen hand of fate guided the arrow on a higher flight and in quite a different direction from that given it by the bowstring. That liberty which had been snatched from its mother in earliest infancy and which was one day to gladden despised Holland, came to birth in happy Brabant.

But the enterprise is not to be disparaged because the outcome was different from the original plan. Man carves, shapes and polishes the rough stone that is given him by his age. The moment and the place may be his, but chance turns the wheels of history. If the passions involved in this event were not unworthy of the great work they unconsciously served; if the forces which helped to bring it about and the single actions which formed a part of this remarkable chain of circumstances were noble forces, beautiful and great actions, then the entire episode is inspiring, interesting and fruitful for us. We can look upon it with astonishment as the bold product of chance or we can admire it as the work of a higher intelligence.

This history of the world is as consistent as the laws of nature and as simple as the soul of man. Like conditions produce like phenomena. On the same soil where the Netherlanders were now defying their Spanish tyrant, their forefathers, the Batavi and Belgae, fifteen centuries before had battled with their Roman oppressor. These too, like their descendants, were the unwilling subjects of an arrogant ruler, abused by greedy satraps. They too

lichem Trotz ihre Ketten ab und versuchen das Glück in ebenso ungleichem Kampfe. Derselbe Erobererstolz, derselbe Schwung der Nation in dem Spanier des sechzehnten Jahrhunderts und in dem Römer des ersten, dieselbe Tapferkeit und Mannszucht in beider Heeren, dasselbe Schrekken vor ihrem Schlachtenzug. Dort wie hier sehen wir List gegen Übermacht streiten und Standhaftigkeit, unterstützt durch Eintracht, eine ungeheure Macht ermüden, die sich durch Teilung entkräftet hat. Dort wie hier waffnet Privathaß die Nation; ein einziger Mensch, für seine Zeit geboren, deckt ihr das gefährliche Geheimnis ihrer Kräfte auf und bringt ihren stummen Gram zu einer blutigen Erklärung. "Gestehet, Batavier!" redet Claudius Civilis seine Mitbürger in dem heiligen Haine an, "wird uns von diesen Römern noch wie sonst als Bundsgenossen und Freunden oder nicht vielmehr als dienstbaren Knechten begegnet? Ihren Beamten und Statthaltern sind wir ausgeliefert, die, wenn unser Raub, unser Blut sie gesättigt hat, von andern abgelöst werden, welche dieselbe Gewalttätigkeit nur unter andern Namen erneuern. Geschieht es ja endlich einmal, daß uns Rom einen Oberaufseher sendet, so drückt er uns mit einem prahlerischen teuern Gefolge und noch unerträglicherem Stolz. Die Werbungen sind wieder nahe, welche Kinder von Eltern, Brüder von Brüdern auf ewig reißen und eure kraftvolle Jugend der römischen Unzucht überliefern. Jetzt, Batavier, ist der Augenblick unser. Nie lag Rom darnieder wie jetzt. Lasset euch diese *Namen* von Legionen nicht in Schrekken jagen; ihre Läger enthalten nichts als alte Männer und Beute. Wir haben Fußvolk und Reiterei. Germanien ist unser, und Gallien lüstern, sein Joch abzuwerfen. Mag ihnen Syrien dienen und Asien und der Aufgang, der Könige braucht! Es sind noch unter uns, die geboren wurden, ehe man den Römern Schatzung erlegte. Die Götter halten es mit dem Tapfersten." Feierliche Sakramente weihen diese Verschwörung, wie den Geusenbund; wie dieser hüllt sie sich hinterlistig in den Schleier der Unterwürfigkeit, in die Majestät eines großen Namens. Die Kohorten des Civilis schwören am Rheine dem Vespasian in Syrien, wie der Kompromiß Philipp dem Zweiten. Derselbe Kampfplatz erzeugt

cast off their chains with similar spirit and tried their fortunes in unequal combat.

The same pride of conquest, the same national spirit animated the Spaniard of the sixteenth century and the Roman of the first. The same valor and discipline pertained in both armies, their battle array inspired a similar terror. In both cases we see a contest between stratagem and might, where perseverance, reinforced by unanimity, finally wore out a tremendous power weakened by division.

Then as now the armor of the nation was private hatred. A single man, born for his time, revealed to the nation the dangerous secret of its strength and prevailed upon it to transform its silent grief into bloody action. "Admit, Batavians," cries Claudius Civilis to his countrymen in the sacred grove, "that we are no longer treated by these Romans as allies, but as slaves. We are at the mercy of their prefects and centurions who, when they are satiated with our treasure and with our blood, make way for others who under different names in turn commit the same outrages. When at last Rome deigns to send us a legate, he oppresses us with an ostentatious and costly retinue and an even more intolerable pride. We shall soon be faced again with the military drafts that snatch children from their parents, brothers from brothers, and our strong young men are exposed to Roman licentiousness. Batavians, our time has come. Never did Rome lie so prostrate as now. Do not let the *names* of legions terrify you. They have nothing in their camps but old men and plunder. We have foot soldiers and cavalry. Germany is ours. Gaul is eager to throw off its yoke. Let Syria serve them and Asia and the Orient which needs kings. There are many still alive among us who were born before tribute was paid to the Romans. The gods will uphold the brave." This conspiracy, like the League of the Gueux, was consecrated with solemn rites. It too enveloped itself in a veil of submissiveness, in the majesty of a great name. The cohorts of Civilis on the Rhine swore allegiance to Vespasian in Syria as the League swore allegiance to Philip of Spain. The same battleground produced the

denselben Plan der Verteidigung, dieselbe Zuflucht der Verzweiflung. Beide vertrauen ihr wankendes Glück einem befreundeten Elemente; in ähnlichem Bedrängnis rettet Civilis seine Insel—wie funfzehn Jahrhunderte nach ihm Wilhelm von Oranien die Stadt Leiden—durch eine künstliche Wasserflut. Die batavische Tapferkeit deckt die Ohnmacht der Weltbeherrscher auf, wie der schöne Mut ihrer Enkel den Verfall der spanischen Macht dem ganzen Europa zur Schau stellt. Dieselbe Fruchtbarkeit des Geistes in den Heerführern beider Zeiten läßt den Krieg ebenso hartnäckig dauern und beinahe ebenso zweifelhaft enden; aber einen Unterschied bemerken wir doch: die Römer und Batavier kriegen menschlich, denn sie kriegen nicht für die Religion.[1]

[1] Tacitus, Hist. lib. IV. V.

same plan of defense, the same refuge for despair. The rebels of both ages entrusted their precarious fortunes to a friendly element. In a similar plight, Civilis saved his island—just as, fifteen centuries after him, William of Orange was to save the town of Leyden—by an artificial flood. Batavian valor exposed the impotence of the ruler of the world, just as the fine courage of Batavian descendants revealed to all of Europe the decay of Spanish power. In both cases the war was obstinately prolonged by the resourcefulness of the general, in both the final outcome was nearly as ambiguous. There is one notable difference, however. The Romans and Batavians fought humanely, for they were not fighting for religion.

DON CARLOS
INFANT VON SPANIEN

DRITTER AKT

10. AUFTRITT

Der König und Marquis von Posa.

(Dieser geht dem König, sobald er ihn gewahr wird, entgegen und läßt sich vor ihm auf ein Knie nieder, steht auf und bleibt ohne Zeichen der Verwirrung vor ihm stehen.)

KÖNIG *(betrachtet ihn mit einem Blick der Verwunderung).*
Mich schon gesprochen also?
MARQUIS. Nein.
KÖNIG. Ihr machtet
Um meine Krone Euch verdient. Warum
Entziehet Ihr Euch meinem Dank? In meinem
Gedächtnis drängen sich der Menschen viel.
Allwissend ist nur einer. Euch kams zu,
Das Auge Eures Königes zu suchen.
Weswegen tatet Ihr das nicht?
MARQUIS. Es sind
Zween Tage, Sire, daß ich ins Königreich
Zurückgekommen.
KÖNIG. Ich bin nicht gesonnen,
In meiner Diener Schuld zu stehn—erbittet
Euch eine Gnade!
MARQUIS. Ich genieße die Gesetze.
KÖNIG. Dies Recht hat auch der Mörder.
MARQUIS. Wie viel mehr
Der gute Bürger!—Sire, ich bin zufrieden.

314

DON CARLOS
INFANTE OF SPAIN

ACT III

SCENE 10

The King and the Marquis of Posa.

The latter, as soon as he is aware of him, walks toward the King, genuflects before him, rises, and remains standing in front of him without any sign of perturbation.)

KING: *(observes him with a look of amazement.)*
　You have met me before, then?
MARQUIS:　　　　　　　　　No.
KING:　　　　　　　　　　You made
　My Crown indebted to you. Why have you
　Fought shy of seeking thanks from me? Within
　My memory are crowded many people.
　But One alone knows everything. It was
　Your place to seek out the eye of your King.
　Why did you not do so?
MARQUIS:　　　　　　　It was a couple
　Of days ago that I returned, Sire, to
　Your kingdom.
KING:　　　　　I am not inclined to stand
　Indebted to the persons in my service.
　Entreat some favor from me.
MARQUIS:　　　　　　　　　I enjoy the laws.
KING:　The murderer also has that right.
MARQUIS:　　　　　　　　　　　How much
　More the good citizen!—I am content, Sire.

KÖNIG (*vor sich*).
Viel Selbstgefühl und kühner Mut, bei Gott!
Doch das war zu erwarten.—Stolz will ich
Den Spanier. Ich mag es gerne leiden,
Wenn auch der Becher überschäumt.—Ihr tratet
Aus meinen Diensten, hör ich?
MARQUIS. Einem Bessern
Den Platz zu räumen, zog ich mich zurücke.
KÖNIG. Das tut mir leid. Wenn solche Köpfe feiern,
Wie viel Verlust für meinen Staat!—Vielleicht
Befürchtet Ihr, die Sphäre zu verfehlen,
Die Eures Geistes würdig ist.
MARQUIS. O nein!
Ich bin gewiß, daß der erfahrne Kenner,
In Menschenseelen, seinem Stoff, geübt,
Beim ersten Blicke wird gelesen haben,
Was ich ihm taugen kann, was nicht. Ich fühle
Mit demutsvoller Dankbarkeit die Gnade,
Die Eure Königliche Majestät
Durch diese stolze Meinung auf mich häufen;
Doch—(*er hält inne.*)
KÖNIG. Ihr bedenket Euch?
MARQUIS. Ich bin—ich muß
Gestehen, Sire—sogleich nicht vorbereitet,
Was ich als Bürger dieser Welt gedacht,
In Worte Ihres Untertans zu kleiden.—
Denn damals, Sire, als ich auf immer mit
Der Krone aufgehoben, glaubt ich mich
Auch der Notwendigkeit entbunden, ihr
Von diesem Schritte Gründe anzugeben.
KÖNIG. So schwach sind diese Gründe? Fürchtet Ihr
Dabei zu wagen?
MARQUIS. Wenn ich Zeit gewinne,
Sie zu erschöpfen, Sire—mein Leben höchstens.
Die Wahrheit aber setz ich aus, wenn Sie
Mir diese Gunst verweigern. Zwischen Ihrer
Ungnade und Geringschätzung ist mir

KING: *(to himself)*
By God! Much self-reliance and bold spirit.
That was to be expected, though.—I want
A Spaniard to be proud. I even like
It when the cup runs over.—I hear that
You have resigned my service?
MARQUIS: I withdrew
To make room for a better man.
KING: That grieves me.
If heads the like of this make holiday,
How great the loss is for my state.—Perhaps
You are afraid that you will miss the sphere
Which would be worthy of your mind.
MARQUIS: Oh, no!
I feel quite certain the experienced knower
Of human souls—his matter—will have read
With practiced skill and at first glance what worth
I can or cannot be to him. I feel
With humble gratitude the favor which
Your Royal Majesty is heaping on me
By the expression of this proud opinion.
However—   *(He checks himself.)*
KING: You deliberate?
MARQUIS: I am—
I must confess, Sire, not prepared just now
To clothe in words that fit one of your subjects
The things that I thought as world-citizen.—
For at the time, Sire, when I had forever
Cut my connections with the Crown, I felt
Myself released from all necessity
Of giving reasons to it for that step.
KING: Your reasons are that weak? Are you afraid
To venture them?
MARQUIS: If I took time, Sire, to
Exhaust the list—my lifetime would be needed.
But I will jeopardize the truth if you
Refuse that favor. For the choice is left me
Of either your contempt or your displeasure—

Die Wahl gelassen—muß ich mich entscheiden,
So will ich ein Verbrecher lieber als
Ein Tor von Ihren Augen gehen.
KÖNIG (*mit erwartender Miene*). Nun?
MARQUIS.—Ich kann nicht Fürstendiener sein.
(*Der König sieht ihn mit Erstaunen an.*) Ich will
Den Käufer nicht betrügen, Sire.—Wenn Sie
Mich anzustellen würdigen, so wollen
Sie nur die vorgewogne Tat. Sie wollen
Nur meinen Arm und meinen Mut im Felde,
Nur meinen Kopf im Rat. Nicht meine Taten,
Der Beifall, den sie finden an dem Thron,
Soll meiner Taten Endzweck sein. Mir aber,
Mir hat die Tugend eignen Wert. Das Glück,
Das der Monarch mit meinen Händen pflanzte,
Erschüf ich selbst, und Freude wäre mir
Und eigne Wahl, was mir nur Pflicht sein sollte
Und ist das Ihre Meinung? Können Sie
In Ihrer Schöpfung fremde Schöpfer dulden?
Ich aber soll zum Meißel mich erniedern,
Wo ich der Künstler könnte sein?—Ich liebe
Die Menschheit, und in Monarchien darf
Ich niemand lieben als mich selbst.
KÖNIG. Dies Feuer
Ist lobenswert. Ihr möchtet Gutes stiften.
Wie Ihr es stiftet, kann dem Patrioten,
Dem Weisen gleich viel heißen. Suchet Euch
Den Posten aus in meinen Königreichen,
Der Euch berechtigt, diesem edeln Triebe
Genug zu tun.
MARQUIS. Ich finde keinen.
KÖNIG. Wie?
MARQUIS. Was Eure Majestät durch meine Hand
Verbreiten—ist das Menschenglück?—Ist das
Dasselbe Glück, das meine reine Liebe
Den Menschen gönnt?—Vor diesem Glücke würde
Die Majestät erzittern.—Nein! Ein neues
Erschuf der Krone Politik—ein Glück,

If this decision must be made by me,
Then I prefer to go out of your sight
A criminal but not a fool.

KING: (*with expectant look*) Well, then?

MARQUIS: —I cannot be the server of a Prince.
                    (*The King looks at him in astonishment.*)
I will not cheat the buyer, Sire.—If you
Do me the honor of appointing me,
Then you want only the deed preassigned.
You want my arm alone and valor in
The field, my mind in council. Not my deeds,
But their approval found before the throne,
Shall be the goal of action. But for me
Right conduct has a value of its own.
The happiness the Monarch would plant by
My hands, if I myself created it,
Then duty would be joy and my own choice.
But is that your opinion too? Can you
Bear strange creators in your own creation?
Must I descend to be a chisel merely
When I might be the sculptor?—My love is
To all mankind; in monarchies I may
Love no one but myself.

KING: This ardor is
Praiseworthy. You wish to establish Good.
How you establish it is no great matter
To patriots or men of wisdom. Choose
Yourself a post within my range of kingdoms
Which will empower you to give scope to
This noble impulse.

MARQUIS: I have found none.

KING: What?

MARQUIS: That which Your Majesty would spread abroad
By my hand—Is that human happiness?—
Is it the kind of happiness that my
Pure love grants human beings?—Majesty
Would tremble at that happiness.—Oh no!
Crown policy created a new kind—

319

Das sie noch reich genug ist auszuteilen,
Und in dem Menschenherzen neue Triebe,
Die sich von diesem Glücke stillen lassen.
In ihren Münzen läßt sie Wahrheit schlagen,
Die Wahrheit, die sie dulden kann. Verworfen
Sind alle Stempel, die nicht diesem gleichen.
Doch was der Krone frommen kann—ist das
Auch mir genug? Darf meine Bruderliebe
Sich zur Verkürzung meines Bruders borgen?
Weiß ich ihn glücklich—eh er denken darf?
Mich wählen Sie nicht, Sire, Glückseligkeit,
Die Sie uns prägen, auszustreun. Ich muß
Mich weigern, diese Stempel auszugeben.—
Ich kann nicht Fürstendiener sein.
KÖNIG (*etwas rasch*). Ihr seid
Ein Protestant.
MARQUIS (*nach einigem Bedenken*).
Ihr Glaube, Sire, ist auch
Der meinige.
(*Nach einer Pause.*) Ich werde mißverstanden.
Das war es, was ich fürchtete. Sie sehen
Von den Geheimnissen der Majestät
Durch meine Hand den Schleier weggezogen.
Wer sichert Sie, daß mir noch heilig heiße,
Was mich zu schrecken aufgehört? Ich bin
Gefährlich, weil ich über mich gedacht.—
Ich bin es nicht, mein König. Meine Wünsche
Verwesen hier.
(*Die Hand auf die Brust gelegt.*)
Die lächerliche Wut
Der Neuerung, die nur der Ketten Last,
Die sie nicht ganz zerbrechen kann, vergrößert,
Wird mein Blut nie erhitzen. Das Jahrhundert
Ist meinem Ideal nicht reif. Ich lebe
Ein Bürger derer, welche kommen werden.
Kann ein Gemälde Ihre Ruhe trüben?—
Ihr Atem löscht es aus.
KÖNIG. Bin ich der erste,
Der Euch von dieser Seite kennt?

320

That *it* is rich enough to spread abroad,
And in the human heart new impulses
That can be gratified by that new kind.
Upon its coins it has Truth struck, *that* truth
Which it can tolerate. All other stamps
Are thrown away that are not like that *one*.
But what is to the Crown's advantage—will
It be enough for me? Shall my love for
My brother be lent to encroachment on
My brother? Do I know that he is happy
Before he is allowed to think? Do not
Choose me, Sire, to spread happiness that you
Have stamped. I must refuse to pass those stamps.—
I cannot be the server of a Prince.

KING: (*rather suddenly*)
You are a Protestant.

MARQUIS: (*after some reflection*) Your faith, Sire, is
Mine also.   (*after a pause*)
            I have been misunderstood.
That was just what I feared. You see the veil
Withdrawn by my hand from the mysteries
Of majesty. Who will give you assurance
That what has ceased to terrify me will
Still be accounted holy by me? I
Am dangerous because I have done thinking
About myself.—But I am not, my King.
My wishes molder here.
            (*his hand upon his heart*)
            The foolish craze
For revolution, which but makes more heavy
The weight of chains it cannot wholly break,
Will never fire *my* blood. The century
Is not yet ripe for my ideal. I
Live as a citizen of those to come.
Can a mere picture trouble your repose?—
Your breath effaces it.

KING: Am I the first
To know this side of you?

MARQUIS. Von dieser—
Ja!
KÖNIG (*steht auf, macht einige Schritte und bleibt dem Mar-
quis gegenüber stehen. Vor sich*).
Neu zum wenigsten ist dieser Ton!
Die Schmeichelei erschöpft sich. Nachzuahmen
Erniedrigt einen Mann von Kopf.—Auch einmal
Die Probe von dem Gegenteil. Warum nicht?
Das Überraschende macht Glück.—Wenn Ihr
Es so verstehet, gut, so will ich mich
Auf eine neue Kronbedienung richten—
Den starken Geist—
MARQUIS. Ich höre, Sire, wie klein,
Wie niedrig Sie von Menschenwürde denken,
Selbst in des freien Mannes Sprache nur
Den Kunstgriff eines Schmeichlers sehen, und
Mir deucht, ich weiß, wer Sie dazu berechtigt.
Die Menschen zwangen Sie dazu; die haben
Freiwillig ihres Adels sich begeben,
Freiwillig sich auf diese niedre Stufe
Herabgestellt. Erschrocken fliehen sie
Vor dem Gespenste ihrer innern Größe,
Gefallen sich in ihrer Armut, schmücken
Mit feiger Weisheit ihre Ketten aus,
Und Tugend nennt man, sie mit Anstand tragen.
So überkamen Sie die Welt. So ward
Sie Ihrem großen Vater überliefert.
Wie könnten Sie in dieser traurigen
Verstümmlung—Menschen ehren?
KÖNIG. Etwas Wahres
Find ich in diesen Worten.
MARQUIS. Aber schade!
Da Sie den Menschen aus des Schöpfers Hand
In Ihrer Hände Werk verwandelten
Und dieser neugegossnen Kreatur
Zum Gott sich gaben—da versahen Sies
In etwas nur: Sie blieben selbst noch Mensch—
Mensch aus des Schöpfers Hand. Sie fuhren fort,
Als Sterblicher zu leiden, zu begehren;

MARQUIS: This side of—Yes!
KING: (*rises, walks a few paces, and stops opposite
the Marquis.   To himself*)
    At least this tone is novel! Flattery
    Exhausts itself. To imitate the others
    Degrades a man of talent.—Shall the test
    Be made once of the opposite? Why not?
    Surprises make for pleasure.—Good, then. If
    You understand the thing so well, I shall
    Arrange for a new Crown administration—
    For your strong mind—
MARQUIS: I notice, Sire, how small,
    How low you rate the dignity of man,
    And even in the free man's speech see only
    The cunning of the flatterer, and I
    Believe I know who warrants your conception.
    Human beings forced you to it; *they*
    Of their free will sold their nobility,
    Of their free will reduced themselves to this
    Base level. Terrified they flee before
    The ghost of their own inner greatness, take
    A pleasure in their poverty, adorn
    Their chains with wisdom born of cowardice,
    And call it virtue when they wear them with
    Decorum. Thus you overcame the world.
    So it was given you by your great father.
    In this pathetic mutilated form
    How could you—honor human beings?
KING: In
    Your words I find some truth.
MARQUIS: Alas, however!
    When from the hand of the Creator you
    Transformed these men into your handiwork
    And to this newly molded creature set
    Yourself up as a god—you overlooked
    One item: you yourself remained a man—
    A man from the Creator's hand. *You* went
    On suffering as a mortal, and desiring;

Sie brauchen Mitgefühl—und einem Gott
Kann man nur opfern—zittern—zu ihm beten!
Bereuenswerter Tausch! Unselige
Verdrehung der Natur!—Da Sie den Menschen
Zu Ihrem Saitenspiel herunterstürzten,
Wer teilt mit Ihnen Harmonie?
KÖNIG. (Bei Gott,
Er greift in meine Seele!)
MARQUIS. Aber Ihnen
Bedeutet dieses Opfer nichts. Dafür
Sind Sie auch einzig—Ihre eigne Gattung—
Um diesen Preis sind Sie ein Gott.—Und schrecklich,
Wenn das nicht wäre—wenn für diesen Preis,
Für das zertretne Glück von Millionen,
Sie nichts gewonnen hätten! wenn die Freiheit,
Die Sie vernichteten, das einzge wäre,
Das Ihre Wünsche reifen kann?—Ich bitte,
Mich zu entlassen, Sire. Mein Gegenstand
Reißt mich dahin. Mein Herz ist voll—der Reiz
Zu mächtig, vor dem Einzigen zu stehen,
Dem ich es öffnen möchte.
(*Der Graf von Lerma tritt herein und spricht einige Worte leise
mit dem König. Dieser gibt ihm einen Wink, sich zu entfernen,
und bleibt in seiner vorigen Stellung sitzen.*)
KÖNIG (*zum Marquis, nachdem Lerma weggegangen*).
Redet aus!
MARQUIS (*nach einigem Stillschweigen*).
Ich fühle, Sire—den ganzen Wert—
KÖNIG. Vollendet!
Ihr hattet mir noch mehr zu sagen.
MARQUIS. Sire!
Jüngst kam ich an von Flandern und Brabant.—
So viele reiche, blühende Provinzen!
Ein kräftiges, ein großes Volk—und auch
Ein gutes Volk—und Vater dieses Volkes,
Das, dacht ich, das muß göttlich sein!—Da stieß
Ich auf verbrannte menschliche Gebeine—
(*Hier schweigt er still, seine Augen ruhen auf dem König, der
es versucht, diesen Blick zu erwidern, aber betroffen und ver-
wirrt zur Erde sieht.*)
324

Now *you* need sympathy—and with a god
Men can only tremble—sacrifice—
And pray! Regrettable exchange! Unhappy
Distortion of the way of Nature!—Since
You lowered man to be your instrument
Who will share harmony with you?

KING: (By God,
He strikes into my soul!)

MARQUIS: This sacrifice,
However, has no meaning for you. For
You are unique—a class unto yourself—
And at this price you are a god.—How dreadful
If it were *not* so—if at this price, at
Cost of the trampled happiness of millions,
They had gained nothing! if the freedom which
You have annihilated were the only
Thing that could bring your wishes to fruition?—
I beg you to dismiss me, Sire. My subject
Sweeps me away. My heart is full—the charm
Too great of standing with the only man
To whom I would like to reveal it.

(*The Count of Lerma enters and speaks a few words softly
to the King. The latter signs him to withdraw, and remains sitting in his former position.*)

KING: (*to the Marquis after Lerma has gone out*)   Go
On speaking.

MARQUIS: (*after some silence*)
                        Sire, I feel—the entire merit—

KING: Conclude! You had still more to say to me.

MARQUIS: Sire, I have just come from Brabant and Flanders—
So many flourishing, rich provinces!
A great and sturdy people—and a good
People also—Father of that people!
To be that, I thought, must be god-like!—Then
I came upon charred bones of human beings—

(*Here he falls silent. His eyes rest upon the King, who tries
to meet this glance but looks at the ground startled and
confused.*)

325

Sie haben recht. Sie müssen. Daß Sie können,
Was Sie zu müssen eingesehn, hat mich
Mit schauernder Bewunderung durchdrungen.
O schade, daß, in seinem Blut gewälzt,
Das Opfer wenig dazu taugt, dem Geist
Des Opferers ein Loblied anzustimmen!
Daß Menschen nur—nicht Wesen höhrer Art—
Die Weltgeschichte schreiben!—Sanftere
Jahrhunderte verdrängen Philipps Zeiten;
Die bringen mildre Weisheit; Bürgerglück
Wird dann versöhnt mit Fürstengröße wandeln,
Der karge Staat mit seinen Kindern geizen,
Und die Notwendigkeit wird menschlich sein.
KÖNIG. Wann, denkt Ihr, würden diese menschlichen
Jahrhunderte erscheinen, hätt ich vor
Dem Fluch des jetzigen gezittert? Sehet
In meinem Spanien Euch um. Hier blüht
Des Bürgers Glück in nie bewölktem Frieden;
Und diese Ruhe gönn ich den Flamändern.
MARQUIS (*schnell*).
Die Ruhe eines Kirchhofs! Und Sie hoffen
Zu endigen, was Sie begannen? hoffen,
Der Christenheit gezeitigte Verwandlung,
Den allgemeinen Frühling aufzuhalten,
Der die Gestalt der Welt verjüngt? Sie wollen
Allein in ganz Europa—sich dem Rade
Des Weltverhängnisses, das unaufhaltsam
In vollem Laufe rollt, entgegenwerfen?
Mit Menschenarm in seine Speichen fallen?
Sie werden nicht! Schon flohen Tausende
Aus Ihren Ländern froh und arm. Der Bürger,
Den Sie verloren für den Glauben, war
Ihr edelster. Mit offnen Mutterarmen
Empfängt die Fliehenden Elisabeth,
Und furchtbar blüht durch Künste unsres Landes
Brittannien. Verlassen von dem Fleiß
Der neuen Christen, liegt Grenada öde,
Und jauchzend sieht Europa seinen Feind

But you are right. *You* had to. That you *can*
Do what you realized you had to, filled
Me with a horrified astonishment.
A pity that the victim drowned in his
Own blood cannot intone a hymn of praise to
The spirit of the executioner!
Or that mere human beings—and not creatures
Of higher kind—write history!—But gentler
Ages will supplant the times of Philip;
They will bring milder wisdom; welfare of
The citizen will walk with Princes' greatness
In harmony, the thrifty state will cherish
Its children, and Necessity be human.

KING: When do you think these human centuries
Would come about, had I not trembled at
The curse that plagues the present one? Look
About you in this Spain of mine. The welfare
Of citizens blooms here in cloudless peace;
And *this peace* I grant to the Flemish people.

MARQUIS: (*quickly*)
The peace of cemeteries! And you hope
To finish what you have begun? You hope
To halt the transformation of matured
Christendom, the universal springtime
That makes the world's form young again?—You want—
Alone in all of Europe—to oppose
The wheel of universal destiny
Now rolling beyond check in full career,
And thrust your human arm between its spokes?
You will not! Thousands have already fled
From your lands poor but happy. And the subjects
That you have lost for the Faith's sake were your
Most noble ones. With mother's arms wide opened
Elizabeth receives the fugitives,
And with the skills of our lands Britain blooms
Luxuriantly. Granada lies a waste
For want of industry of "the new Christians",
And Europe gloats to see its enemy

327

An selbstgeschlagnen Wunden sich verbluten.
(*Der König ist bewegt; der Marquis bemerkt es und tritt einige
Schritte näher.*)
Sie wollen pflanzen für die Ewigkeit
Und säen Tod? Ein so erzwungnes Werk
Wird seines Schöpfers Geist nicht überdauern.
Dem Undank haben Sie gebaut—umsonst
Den harten Kampf mit der Natur gerungen,
Umsonst ein großes, königliches Leben
Zerstörenden Entwürfen hingeopfert.
Der Mensch ist mehr, als Sie von ihm gehalten.
Des langen Schlummers Bande wird er brechen
Und wiederfordern sein geheiligt Recht.
Zu einem Nero und Busiris wirft
Er Ihren Namen, und—das schmerzt mich; denn
Sie waren gut.
KÖNIG. Wer hat Euch dessen so
Gewiß gemacht?
MARQUIS (*mit Feuer*). Ja, beim Allmächtigen
Ja—ja—ich wiederhol es. Geben Sie,
Was Sie uns nahmen, wieder! Lassen Sie,
Großmütig wie der Starke, Menschenglück
Aus Ihrem Füllhorn strömen—Geister reifen
In Ihrem Weltgebäude! Geben Sie,
Was Sie uns nahmen, wieder! Werden Sie
Von Millionen Königen ein König.

(*Er nähert sich ihm kühn und indem er feste und feurige Blicke
auf ihn richtet.*)
O könnte die Beredsamkeit von allen
Den Tausenden, die dieser großen Stunde
Teilhaftig sind, auf meinen Lippen schweben,
Den Strahl, den ich in diesen Augen merke,
Zur Flamme zu erheben!—Geben Sie
Die unnatürliche Vergöttrung auf,
Die uns vernichtet. Werden Sie uns Muster
Des Ewigen und Wahren. Niemals—niemals
Besaß ein Sterblicher so viel, so göttlich
Es zu gebrauchen. Alle Könige

Bleeding to death from self-inflicted wounds.

> (*The King is moved; the Marquis perceives
> it and comes several steps closer.*)

You want to plant for all eternity,
And you sow death? No work done thus by force
Will last beyond the will of its creator.
You have built for ingratitude—for naught
You have fought your hard fight with Nature, and
For naught expended your great royal life
In sacrifice for projects of destruction.
Man is a greater thing than you have thought him.
And he will burst the bonds of lengthy slumber
And will demand his consecrated rights.
Your name with Nero's and Busiris' he
Will vilify, and—that is painful to me,
For you were good.

KING: Who gave you such assurance
That this is so?

MARQUIS: (*with ardor*)   Yes, by Almighty God!
Yes—Yes—and I repeat it. Give us back
What you have taken from us. Generously,
As a strong man, let human happiness
Stream forth out of your horn of plenty.—Minds
In your world-edifice are ripening.
Give us back what you have taken from us.
Become a King among a million kings.

> (*He approaches him boldly while
> directing firm and fiery glances at him.*)

O, if upon my lips might hover that
Persuasiveness of all the thousands who
Share the concern in this momentous hour,
To fan into a flame the ray that I
Perceive now in your eyes! Abjure all this
Unnatural deification which
Annihilates us, and become our pattern
Of the eternal truth. O never—never
Did mortal man possess so much, to use
In such a god-like fashion. All the kings

Europens huldigen dem spanschen Namen.
Gehn Sie Europens Königen voran.
Ein Federzug von dieser Hand, und neu
Erschaffen wird die Erde. Geben Sie
Gedankenfreiheit!
(*Sich ihm zu Füßen werfend.*)
KÖNIG (*überrascht, das Gesicht weggewandt und dann wie-
der auf den Marquis geheftet*). Sonderbarer Schwärmer!
Doch—stehet auf—ich—
MARQUIS. Sehen Sie sich um
In seiner herrlichen Natur! Auf Freiheit
Ist sie gegründet—und wie reich ist sie
Durch Freiheit! Er, der große Schöpfer, wirft
In einen Tropfen Tau den Wurm und läßt
Noch in den toten Räumen der Verwesung
Die Willkür sich ergetzen—Ihre Schöpfung,
Wie eng und arm! Das Rauschen eines Blattes
Erschreckt den Herrn der Christenheit—Sie müssen
Vor jeder Tugend zittern. Er—der Freiheit
Entzückende Erscheinung nicht zu stören—
Er läßt des Übels grauenvolles Heer
In seinem Weltall lieber toben—ihn,
Den Künstler, wird man nicht gewahr, bescheiden
Verhüllt er sich in ewige Gesetze.
Die sieht der Freigeist, doch nicht ihn. "Wozu
Ein Gott?" sagt er, "die Welt ist sich genug."
Und keines Christen Andacht hat ihn mehr
Als dieses Freigeists Lästerung gepriesen.
KÖNIG. Und wollet Ihr es unternehmen, dies
Erhabne Muster in der Sterblichkeit,
In meinen Staaten nachzubilden?
MARQUIS. Sie,
Sie können es. Wer anders? Weihen Sie
Dem Glück der Völker die Regentenkraft,
Die—ach so lang—des Thrones Größe nur
Gewuchert hatte!—Stellen Sie der Menschheit
Verlornen Adel wieder her! Der Bürger
Sei wiederum, was er zuvor gewesen,

Of Europe venerate the Spanish name.
Walk at the head of all the kings of Europe.
A single pen-stroke will suffice: the world
Will be created new. O give us freedom
Of thought—

>   (*throwing himself at his feet*)

KING: (*taken by surprise, with face averted and then
again fixed on the Marquis*) Fantastic visionary! But—
Stand up—I—

MARQUIS: Cast your eye about you in
The splendor of His Nature! It is founded
On freedom—and how rich it is by virtue
Of freedom! He, the great Creator, casts
The worm into a drop of dew and lets
Free will take its delight amid the very
Death spaces of corruption—Your creation,
How cramped and poor! The rustling of a leaf
Strikes terror in the lord of Christendom—
You must fear every virtue. *He*—lest Freedom's
Delightful presence be disturbed—He sooner
Allows the entire ghastly host of Evil
To rage throughout His universe—Of Him,
The Maker, one is not aware; discreetly
He veils Himself in His eternal laws.
The free-thinker sees *these,* but not *Him.* Why have
A God? says he; the world is self-sufficient.
No Christian's piety has ever praised
Him more than that free-thinker's blasphemy.

KING: And would you undertake to imitate
This pattern of sublimity among
The mortal creatures in my kingdoms?

MARQUIS: You,
You can do so. Who else can? Consecrate
The ruling power to the welfare of
The peoples who—so long—have served but to
Promote the greatness of the throne. Restore
Mankind its lost nobility. And let
The subject be once more what he once was,

Der Krone Zweck!—ihn binde keine Pflicht
Als seiner Brüder gleich ehrwürdge Rechte!
Wenn nun der Mensch, sich selbst zurückgegeben,
Zu seines Werts Gefühl erwacht—der Freiheit
Erhabne, stolze Tugenden gedeihen—
Dann, Sire, wenn Sie zum glücklichsten der Welt
Ihr eignes Königreich gemacht—dann ist
Es Ihre Pflicht, die Welt zu unterwerfen.
KÖNIG (*nach einem großen Stillschweigen*).
Ich ließ Euch bis zu Ende reden.—Anders,
Begreif ich wohl, als sonst in Menschenköpfen
Malt sich in diesem Kopf die Welt—auch will
Ich fremdem Maßstab Euch nicht unterwerfen.
Ich bin der erste, dem Ihr Euer Innerstes
Enthüllt. Ich glaub es, weil ichs weiß. Um dieser
Enthaltung willen, solche Meinungen,
Mit solchem Feuer doch umfaßt, verschwiegen
Zu haben bis auf diesen Tag—um dieser
Bescheidnen Klugheit willen, junger Mann,
Will ich vergessen, daß ich sie erfahren,
Und wie ich sie erfahren. Stehet auf.
Ich will den Jüngling, der sich übereilte,
Als Greis und nicht als König widerlegen.
Ich will es, weil ichs will.—Gift also selbst,
Find ich, kann in gutartigen Naturen
Zu etwas Besserm sich veredeln.—Aber
Flieht meine Inquisition!—Es sollte
Mir leid tun—
MARQUIS. Wirklich? Sollt es das?
KÖNIG (*in seinem Anblick verloren*). Ich habe
Solch einen Menschen nie gesehen.—Nein,
Nein, Marquis! Ihr tut mir zu viel. Ich will
Nicht Nero sein. Ich will es nicht sein—will
Es gegen Euch nicht sein. Nicht alle
Glückseligkeit soll unter mir verdorren.
Ihr selbst, Ihr sollet unter meinen Augen
Fortfahren dürfen, Mensch zu sein.
MARQUIS (*rasch*). Und meine
Mitbürger, Sire?—O! nicht um mich war mirs

The purpose of the Crown,—and let no duty
Bind him but his brothers' equally
Sacred rights. Once man, returned unto
Himself, wakes to awareness of his worth—
And Freedom's proud and lofty virtues thrive—
Then, Sire, when you have made your own realm into
The happiest in the world—then it will be
Your obligation to subject the world.

KING: (*after a great silence*)
I have let you speak to the end—The world,
I understand, is not depicted in
Your mind as in the minds of others—nor
Will I subject you to an alien standard.
I am the first to whom you have revealed your inmost
Thoughts. That much I believe, because I know it.
And for the sake of your forbearance in
Maintaining silence until now on these
Opinions held with such great ardor—for
This prudence and discretion's sake, young man,
I will forget that I have learned of them
And how I learned of them. Arise. I shall
Refute the youth who overstepped the limits,
As one of riper years but not as King.
I shall, because I wish to.—Even poison
Itself, I find, may be transmuted in
High natures into something better.—But
Avoid my Inquisition. It would pain
Me—

MARQUIS: Would it? Really?

KING: (*lost in gazing at him*) Such a human being
I never saw before.—No! No, Marquis!
You have read too much into me. I wish
To be no Nero. That I do not want—
Not in respect to you. Not all
Of happiness shall wither under me.
Beneath my eyes you may yourself continue
To be a human being.

MARQUIS: (*quickly*) Sire, what of
My fellow-citizens? O, I was not

333

Zu tun, nicht meine Sache wollt ich führen.
Und Ihre Untertanen, Sire?
KÖNIG. Und wenn
Ihr so gut wisset, wie die Folgezeit
Mich richten wird, so lerne sie an Euch,
Wie ich mit Menschen es gehalten, als
Ich einen fand.
MARQUIS. O! der gerechteste
Der Könige sei nicht mit einem Male
Der ungerechteste.—In Ihrem Flandern
Sind tausend bessere als ich. Nur Sie—
Darf ich es frei gestehen, großer König?—
Sie sehn jetzt unter diesem sanftern Bilde
Vielleicht zum erstenmal die Freiheit.
KÖNIG (*mit gemildertem Ernst*). Nichts mehr
Von diesem Inhalt, junger Mann.—Ich weiß,
Ihr werdet anders denken, kennet Ihr
Den Menschen erst wie ich.—Doch hätt ich Euch
Nicht gern zum letztenmal gesehn. Wie fang ich
Es an, Euch zu verbinden?
MARQUIS. Lassen Sie
Mich, wie ich bin. Was wär ich Ihnen, Sire,
Wenn Sie auch mich bestächen?
KÖNIG. Diesen Stolz
Ertrag ich nicht. Ihr seid von heute an
In meinen Diensten.—Keine Einwendung!
Ich will es haben.
(*Nach einer Pause.*) Aber wie? Was wollte
Ich denn? War es nicht Wahrheit, was ich wollte?
Und hier find ich noch etwas mehr.—Ihr habt
Auf meinem Thron mich ausgefunden, Marquis.
Nicht auch in meinem Hause?
(*Da sich der Marquis zu bedenken scheint.*)
Ich versteh Euch.
Doch—wär ich auch von allen Vätern der
Unglücklichste, kann ich nicht glücklich sein
Als Gatte?
MARQUIS. Wenn ein hoffnungsvoller Sohn,
Wenn der Besitz der liebenswürdigsten

Concerned with me, I did not wish to plead
My cause. What of your subjects, Sire?—
KING: And if
You know so well how centuries to come
Will judge me, let them learn by you how I
Have acted with a human being when
I found one.
MARQUIS: O let the most just of kings
Be not all of a sudden the most unjust—
In your own Flanders there are thousands better
Than I. And *you* alone—may I assume
The liberty, great King, to speak it frankly?—
Beneath this milder picture *you* are seeing
Freedom now perhaps for the first time.
KING: (*with mitigated seriousness*)
No more, young man, upon this subject.—I
Know you will think quite differently when you
Know human beings as I know them.—Yet
I should not like to have this be the last
Time I see you. What shall I do to win you?
MARQUIS: Let me be as I am. What good would I
Be to you, Sire, were you to bribe me?
KING: This
Pride I cannot endure. You are from this
Day forward in my service—No objections!
I will have it so.
(*after a pause*)   And yet—What was it
I wanted? Was it not truth that I wanted?
I find here something more besides.—You have
Now found me out upon my throne, Marquis;
But in my private life?
                    (*as the Marquis seems to deliberate*)
                          I understand you.
But—Were I not the most unfortunate
Of fathers, can I not be happy as
A husband?
MARQUIS: If a son replete with promise,
If the possession of the loveliest

Gemahlin einem Sterblichen ein Recht
Zu diesem Namen geben, Sire, so sind Sie
Der glücklichste durch beides.
KÖNIG (*mit finstrer Miene*). Nein, ich bins nicht!
Und daß ichs nicht bin, hab ich tiefer nie
Gefühlt als eben jetzt.
(*Mit einem Blicke der Wehmut auf dem Marquis verweilend.*)
MARQUIS. Der Prinz denkt edel
Und gut. Ich hab ihn anders nie gefunden.
KÖNIG. Ich aber hab es.—Was er mir genommen,
Kann keine Krone mir ersetzen—eine
So tugendhafte Königin!
MARQUIS. Wer kann
Es wagen, Sire?
KÖNIG. Die Welt! Die Lästerung!
Ich selbst!—Hier liegen Zeugnisse, die ganz
Unwidersprechlich sie verdammen; andre
Sind noch vorhanden, die das Schrecklichste
Mich fürchten lassen.—Aber, Marquis—schwer,
Schwer fällt es mir, an eines nur zu glauben.
Wer klagt sie an?—Wenn sie—sie fähig sollte
Gewesen sein, so tief sich zu entehren,
O wie viel mehr ist mir zu glauben dann
Erlaubt, daß eine Eboli verleumdet?
Haßt nicht der Priester meinen Sohn und sie?
Und weiß ich nicht, daß Alba Rache brütet?
Mein Weib ist mehr wert als sie alle.
MARQUIS. Sire,
Und etwas lebt noch in des Weibes Seele,
Das über allen Schein erhaben ist
Und über alle Lästerung—es heißt
Weibliche Tugend.
KÖNIG. Ja! Das sag ich auch.
So tief, als man die Königin bezüchtigt,
Herabzusinken, kostet viel. So leicht,
Als man mich überreden möchte, reißen
Der Ehre heilge Bande nicht. Ihr kennt
Den Menschen, Marquis. Solch ein Mann hat mir

Of spouses, gives a mortal man the right
To be so called, Sire, then you are on both
Counts the most fortunate of men.

KING: *(with a dark look)*   No, that
I am not! And I never felt more deeply
Than now that I am not—
(dwelling with a gaze of sadness upon the Marquis)

MARQUIS: The Prince's thoughts
Are good and noble. I have never found
Him otherwise.

KING: But I have.—No crown can
Make up for me what he has taken from me—
A Queen so virtuous!

MARQUIS: Sire, who would dare
Do such a thing?

KING: The world! Its blasphemies!
And I myself!—Here lie the proofs that damn her
Incontrovertibly; and there are others
Available besides, that make me fear
The utmost—But, Marquis, I find it hard,
Hard to believe *one thing.* Who is it that
Accuses her?—If *she*—she ever could
Have brought such deep dishonor on herself,
O how much more may I permit myself
To think an Eboli is slandering?
Does not the Priest hate both my son and her?
And am I not aware that Alba broods
Revenge? My wife is worth more than them all.

MARQUIS: Sire, something else still lives in your wife's soul
That is exalted over all appearance
And over every blasphemy—its name
Is womanly virtue.

KING: Yes! So I say too.
To sink so low as they accuse the Queen
Of sinking, takes a lot. So easily
As they would like to make me think, fine bonds
Of honor do not break. You know mankind,
Marquis. I long have felt the need of such

337

Schon längst gemangelt, Ihr seid gut und fröhlich
Und kennet doch den Menschen auch—drum hab
Ich Euch gewählt—
MARQUIS (*überrascht und erschrocken*). Mich, Sire?
KÖNIG. Ihr standet
Vor Eurem Herrn und habt nichts für Euch selbst
Erbeten—nichts! Das ist mir neu—Ihr werdet
Gerecht sein. Leidenschaft wird Euren Blick
Nicht irren.—Dränget Euch zu meinem Sohn,
Erforscht das Herz der Königin. Ich will
Euch Vollmacht senden, sie geheim zu sprechen.
Und jetzt verlaßt mich! (*Er zieht eine Glocke.*)
MARQUIS. Kann ich es mit *einer*
Erfüllten Hoffnung—dann ist dieser Tag
Der schönste meines Lebens.
KÖNIG (*reicht ihm die Hand zum Kusse*). Er ist kein
Verlorner in dem meinigen.
(*Der Marquis steht auf und geht. Graf Lerma tritt herein.*)
Der Ritter
Wird künftig ungemeldet vorgelassen.

A man as you. You are both good and cheerful
And yet you also know mankind—Therefore
I choose you—
MARQUIS: (*surprised and startled*)
            Me, Sire?
KING: You have stood before
Your lord and have asked nothing for yourself—
Nothing. That is new to me.—You will
Be just. Your glance will not be led astray
By passion—Make your way to my son's favor,
And sound the Queen's heart out. I will send you
Full authorization to speak with them both
In private. Leave me now.
                (*He pulls the bell cord.*)
MARQUIS: Can I do so
With *one* hope realized? If so, this day
Will be the finest of my life.
KING: (*gives him his hand to kiss.*) It is
No lost one in *my* life.
                (*The Marquis rises and leaves.*)
                (*Enter Count Lerma.*)
                The cavalier
Will henceforth be admitted unannounced.

ÜBER DIE ÄSTHETISCHE ERZIEHUNG
DES MENSCHEN IN EINER REIHE VON BRIEFEN

2. BRIEF

ABER sollte ich von der Freiheit, die mir von Ihnen verstattet wird, nicht vielleicht einen bessern Gebrauch machen können, als Ihre Aufmerksamkeit auf dem Schauplatz der schönen Kunst zu beschäftigen? Ist es nicht wenigstens außer der Zeit, sich nach einem Gesetzbuch für die ästhetische Welt umzusehen, da die Angelegenheiten der moralischen ein so viel näheres Interesse darbieten und der philosophische Untersuchungsgeist durch die Zeitumstände so nachdrücklich aufgefordert wird, sich mit dem vollkommensten aller Kunstwerke, mit dem Bau einer wahren politischen Freiheit zu beschäftigen?

Ich möchte nicht gern in einem andern Jahrhundert leben und für ein andres gearbeitet haben. Man ist ebenso gut Zeitbürger, als man Staatsbürger ist; und wenn es unschicklich, ja unerlaubt gefunden wird, sich von den Sitten und Gewohnheiten des Zirkels, in dem man lebt, auszuschließen, warum sollte es weniger Pflicht sein, in der Wahl seines Wirkens dem Bedürfnis und dem Geschmack des Jahrhunderts eine Stimme einzuräumen?

ON THE AESTHETIC EDUCATION OF MAN

Second Letter

But should I not, perhaps, be able to make better use of the liberty you have granted me than by engaging your attention with the field of art? Is it not, to say the least, untimely to be looking for a code of laws for the aesthetic world when the affairs of the moral world offer so much more immediate an interest and the spirit of philosophical inquiry is so vigorously challenged by the circumstances of the time to concern itself with the construction of the most perfect of all works of art, true political freedom?

I should not care to be living in another century nor to have worked for another. We are citizens of an age as well as of a state. And if it is considered improper, or even inadmissible, for a man to dissociate himself from the manners and customs of the circle in which he lives, why should it not also be his duty, in choosing his activity, to give the needs and tastes of his century a voice in the decision?

Diese Stimme scheint aber keineswegs zum Vorteil der Kunst auszufallen; derjenigen wenigstens nicht, auf welche allein meine Untersuchungen gerichtet sein werden. Der Lauf der Begebenheiten hat dem Genius der Zeit eine Richtung gegeben, die ihn je mehr und mehr von der Kunst des Ideals zu entfernen droht. Diese muß die Wirklichkeit verlassen und sich mit anständiger Kühnheit über das Bedürfnis erheben; denn die Kunst ist eine Tochter der Freiheit, und von der Notwendigkeit der Geister, nicht von der Notdurft der Materie will sie ihre Vorschrift empfangen. Jetzt aber herrscht das Bedürfnis und beugt die gesunkene Menschheit unter sein tyrannisches Joch. Der *Nutzen* ist das große Idol der Zeit, dem alle Kräfte fronen und alle Talente huldigen sollen. Auf dieser groben Wage hat das geistige Verdienst der Kunst kein Gewicht, und, aller Aufmunterung beraubt, verschwindet sie von dem lärmenden Markt des Jahrhunderts. Selbst der philosophische Untersuchungsgeist entreißt der Einbildungskraft eine Provinz nach der andern, und die Grenzen der Kunst verengen sich, je mehr die Wissenschaft ihre Schranken erweitert.

Erwartungsvoll sind die Blicke des Philosophen wie des Weltmanns auf den politischen Schauplatz geheftet, wo jetzt, wie man glaubt, das große Schicksal der Menschheit verhandelt wird. Verrät es nicht eine tadelnswerte Gleichgültigkeit gegen das Wohl der Gesellschaft, dieses allgemeine Gespräch nicht zu teilen? So nahe dieser große Rechtshandel, seines Inhalts und seiner Folgen wegen, jeden, der sich Mensch nennt, angeht, so sehr muß er, seiner Verhandlungsart wegen, jeden Selbstdenker insbesondere interessieren. Eine Frage, welche sonst nur durch das blinde Recht des Stärkern beantwortet wurde, ist nun, wie es scheint, vor dem Richterstuhle reiner Vernunft anhängig gemacht, und wer nur immer fähig ist, sich in das Zentrum des Ganzen zu versetzen und sein Individuum zur Gattung zu steigern, darf sich als einen Beisitzer jenes Vernunftgerichts betrachten, so wie er als Mensch und Weltbürger zugleich Partei ist und näher oder entfernter in den Erfolg sich verwickelt sieht. Es ist also nicht bloß seine eigene Sache, die in diesem großen Rechtshandel zur Entscheidung kommt; es soll auch nach

But this voice does not seem to have proved at all advantageous to art, not at least to the art to which I shall confine my examination. The course of events has given a direction to the spirit of the age which threatens to remove it even further from the art of the ideal. This art must abandon reality and rise with becoming boldness above necessity; for art is a daughter of freedom and must receive her instructions from spiritual needs and not from material exigencies. But today necessity is master and forces a degraded humanity to bow beneath its tyrannous yoke. *Utility* is the great idol of the age to which all powers must do service and all talents pay homage. The spiritual merit of art has no weight on these crude scales; deprived of any encouragement, art flees from the noisy marts of our century. Even the spirit of philosophical inquiry wrests one province after another from the imagination. The frontiers of art contract as the domain of science expands.

The eyes of the philosopher as well as those of the man of the world are fixed expectantly on the political arena where at present, so it is believed, the high destiny of mankind is being debated. Does it not show a reprehensible indifference to the welfare of society for a man not to participate in this universal discussion? And while this great case, because of its subject and its consequences closely concerns everyone who calls himself a human being, it must because of the method of procedure be of particular interest to the independent thinker. A question which formerly was answered only by the blind right of the stronger is now, as it seems, brought before the tribunal of pure reason. Anyone who is capable of placing himself in a central position and raising his individuality to the level of the race, may regard himself as an assessor at this court of reason, just as he is at the same time an interested party as human being and as citizen of the world and finds himself implicated to a greater or lesser degree in the issue. Thus it is not merely his own cause that is being decided in this great case;

Gesetzen gesprochen werden, die er als vernünftiger Geist selbst zu diktieren fähig und berechtigt ist.

Wie anziehend müßte es für mich sein, einen solchen Gegenstand mit einem ebenso geistreichen Denker als liberalen Weltbürger in Untersuchung zu nehmen und einem Herzen, das mit schönem Enthusiasmus dem Wohl der Menschheit sich weiht, die Entscheidung heimzustellen! Wie angenehm überraschend, bei einer noch so großen Verschiedenheit des Standorts und bei dem weiten Abstand, den die Verhältnisse in der wirklichen Welt nötig machen, Ihrem vorurteilfreien Geist auf dem Felde der Ideen in dem nämlichen Resultat zu begegnen! Daß ich dieser reizenden Versuchung widerstehe und die Schönheit der Freiheit vorangehen lasse, glaube ich nicht bloß mit meiner Neigung entschuldigen, sondern durch Grundsätze rechtfertigen zu können. Ich hoffe, Sie zu überzeugen, daß diese Materie weit weniger dem Bedürfnis als dem Geschmack des Zeitalters fremd ist, ja daß man, um jenes politische Problem in der Erfahrung zu lösen, durch das ästhetische den Weg nehmen muß, weil es die Schönheit ist, durch welche man zu der Freiheit wandert. Aber dieser Beweis kann nicht geführt werden, ohne daß ich Ihnen die Grundsätze in Erinnerung bringe, durch welche sich die Vernunft überhaupt bei einer politischen Gesetzgebung leitet.

3. BRIEF

DIE Natur fängt mit dem Menschen nicht besser an als mit ihren übrigen Werken: sie handelt für ihn, wo er als freie Intelligenz noch nicht selbst handeln kann. Aber eben das macht ihn zum Menschen, daß er bei dem nicht stille steht, was die bloße Natur aus ihm machte, sondern die Fähigkeit besitzt, die Schritte, welche jene mit ihm antizipierte, durch Vernunft wieder rückwärts zu tun, das Werk der Not in ein Werk seiner freien Wahl umzuschaffen und die physische Notwendigkeit zu einer moralischen zu erheben.

344

the verdict is to be given on the basis of laws which he himself, as a rational spirit, is competent and entitled to dictate.

What an attractive prospect it would be for me to explore such a subject with one who is both a brilliant thinker and a liberal citizen of the world and to press for a verdict from a heart that is dedicated with a fine enthusiasm to the welfare of humanity. What an agreeable surprise, despite the difference in social station and the circumstances of the actual world that inevitably separate us, to meet your unprejudiced mind on the field of ideas as it reaches the same conclusions as my own! The fact that I am resisting this delightful temptation and allowing beauty to take precedence over freedom I believe I cannot merely defend on the grounds of my own inclination, but I can also justify it on principle. I hope to convince you that this subject is far less alien to the need of the age than to its taste, that we must indeed, if we are to solve that political problem in practice, take our path through the aesthetic problem, since it is through beauty that we arrive at freedom. But I cannot supply proof of this until I have reminded you of the principles which generally guide reason in political legislation.

Third Letter

Nature begins with man no better than with the rest of her works. She acts for him where he cannot yet act for himself as a free intelligence. But it is just this that makes him a man, the fact that he does not stop with what Nature made him, but possesses the capacity to retrace with his reason the steps which she anticipated for him, to transform the work of necessity into a work of his free choice and to elevate physical necessity to moral necessity.

Er kommt zu sich aus seinem sinnlichen Schlummer, erkennt sich als Mensch, blickt um sich her und findet sich—in dem Staate. Der Zwang der Bedürfnisse warf ihn hinein, ehe er in seiner Freiheit diesen Stand wählen konnte; die Not richtete denselben nach bloßen Naturgesetzen ein, ehe *er* es nach Vernunftgesetzen konnte. Aber mit diesem Notstaat, der nur aus seiner Naturbestimmung hervorgegangen und auch nur auf diese berechnet war, konnte und kann er als moralische Person nicht zufrieden sein—und schlimm für ihn, wenn er es könnte! Er verläßt also, mit demselben Rechte, womit er Mensch ist, die Herrschaft einer blinden Notwendigkeit, wie er in so vielen andern Stücken durch seine Freiheit von ihr schneidet, wie er, um nur *ein* Beispiel zu geben, den gemeinen Charakter, den das Bedürfnis der Geschlechtsliebe aufdrückte, durch Sittlichkeit auslöscht und durch Schönheit veredelt. So holt er, auf eine künstliche Weise, in seiner Volljährigkeit seine Kindheit nach, bildet sich einen *Naturstand* in der Idee, der ihm zwar durch keine Erfahrung gegeben, aber durch seine Vernunftbestimmung notwendig gesetzt ist, leiht sich in diesem idealischen Stand einen Endzweck, den er in seinem wirklichen Naturstand nicht kannte, und eine Wahl, deren er damals nicht fähig war, und verfährt nun nicht anders, als ob er von vorn anfinge und den Stand der Unabhängigkeit aus heller Einsicht und freiem Entschluß mit dem Stand der Verträge vertauschte. Wie kunstreich und fest auch die blinde Willkür ihr Werk gegründet haben, wie anmaßend sie es auch behaupten und mit welchem Scheine von Ehrwürdigkeit es umgeben mag —er darf es, bei dieser Operation, als völlig ungeschehen betrachten; denn das Werk blinder Kräfte besitzt keine Autorität, vor welcher die Freiheit sich zu beugen brauchte, und alles muß sich dem höchsten Endzwecke fügen, den die Vernunft in seiner Persönlichkeit aufstellt. Auf diese Art entsteht und rechtfertigt sich der Versuch eines mündig gewordenen Volkes, seinen Naturstaat in einen sittlichen umzuformen.

Dieser Naturstaat (wie jeder politische Körper heißen kann, der seine Einrichtung ursprünglich von Kräften, nicht von Gesetzen ableitet) widerspricht nun zwar dem moralischen

He comes to himself out of his sensual slumber, recognizes that he is a man, looks around and finds himself —in the state. The pressure of his needs had thrown him there before he was free to chose his station. Need established it by mere natural laws before he could do so according to the laws of reason. But as a moral being he could not and cannot rest content with this state based on need which had arisen only out of his natural destination and was designed for that alone—and woe to him if he could! By the same right, therefore, that he is a human being, he abandons the rule of blind necessity, as in so many other respects he divorces himself from it by his freedom, as—to take one example—he erases by morality and ennobles through beauty the vulgar character imprinted upon sexual love by exigency. Thus in maturity he artificially recovers his childhood, fashions for himself the idea of a *state of nature* which, while not given him by his own experience, was the necessary goal of his rational destination. In this ideal state he sets himself an ultimate aim which he never knew in his actual state of nature and a choice of which he was not then capable. He now proceeds exactly as though he were starting afresh and substituting with clear insight and free resolve the status of independence for the status of contract. However cleverly and firmly blind and arbitrary force may have laid the foundations of her work, however arrogantly she may maintain it, and though she may surround it with an aura of respectability, he may regard it, during this process, as something that never happened. The work of blind forces possesses no authority before which freedom need bow, and everything must yield to the highest aim that reason sets up in his personality. This is the way in which the attempt of a mature nation to transform its natural state into a moral one originates and is justified.

Now while this natural state (as we may call every political body whose organization is originally based on force rather than on law) is opposed to moral man for whom

Menschen, dem die bloße Gesetzmäßigkeit zum Gesetz dienen soll, aber er ist doch gerade hinreichend für den physischen Menschen, der sich nur darum Gesetze gibt, um sich mit Kräften abzufinden. Nun ist aber der physische Mensch *wirklich*, und der sittliche nur *problematisch*. Hebt also die Vernunft den Naturstaat auf, wie sie notwendig muß, wenn sie den ihrigen an die Stelle setzen will, so wagt sie den physischen und wirklichen Menschen an den problematischen sittlichen, so wagt sie die Existenz der Gesellschaft an ein bloß mögliches (wenn gleich moralisch notwendiges) Ideal von Gesellschaft. Sie nimmt dem Menschen etwas,.das er wirklich besitzt, und ohne welches er nichts besitzt, und weist ihn dafür an etwas an, das er besitzen könnte und sollte; und hätte sie zu viel auf ihn gerechnet, so würde sie ihm für eine Menschheit, die ihm noch mangelt und unbeschadet seiner Existenz mangeln kann, auch selbst die Mittel zur Tierheit entrissen haben, die doch die Bedingung seiner Menschheit ist. Ehe er Zeit gehabt hätte, sich mit seinem Willen an dem Gesetz fest zu halten, hätte sie unter seinen Füßen die Leiter der Natur weggezogen.

Das große Bedenken also ist, daß die physische Gesellschaft in der *Zeit* keinen Augenblick aufhören darf, indem die moralische in der *Idee* sich bildet, daß um der Würde des Menschen willen seine Existenz nicht in Gefahr geraten darf. Wenn der Künstler an einem Uhrwerk zu bessern hat, so läßt er die Räder ablaufen; aber das lebendige Uhrwerk des Staats muß gebessert werden, indem es schlägt, und hier gilt es, das rollende Rad während seines Umschwunges auszutauschen. Man muß also für die Fortdauer der Gesellschaft eine Stütze aufsuchen, die sie von dem Naturstaate, den man auflösen will, unabhängig macht.

Diese Stütze findet sich nicht in dem natürlichen Charakter des Menschen, der, selbstsüchtig und gewalttätig, vielmehr auf Zerstörung als auf Erhaltung der Gesellschaft zielt; sie findet sich ebenso wenig in seinem sittlichen Charakter, der, nach der Voraussetzung, erst gebildet werden soll, und auf den, weil er frei ist und weil er nie erscheint, von dem Gesetzgeber nie gewirkt und nie mit Sicherheit gerechnet werden könnte. Es käme also darauf an, von dem physischen

mere conformity to law must serve as law, it is quite adequate for physical man who imposes laws upon himself only in order to come to terms with force. But physical man is *actual* and moral man merely *problematical.* Therefore when reason abolishes the natural state, as she must inevitably do if she wishes to put her own in its place, she is risking the physical and actual man for the problematical moral man; she is risking the very existence of society for a merely possible (if morally necessary) ideal of society. She takes from man something that he actually possesses, and without which he possesses nothing, and assigns to him in its place something which he could and should possess. If she had overestimated his powers, she would have deprived him of the resources of his animal existence which are the very condition of his humanity, for the sake of a humanity which is still beyond him and can remain so without detriment to his existence. Before he had had time to hold fast to the law with his will, she would have taken the ladder of nature from under his feet.

The great consideration, therefore, is that physical society must not for an instant cease to exist *in time* while moral society is being developed *in idea*, that in the interests of human dignity, its existence must not be endangered. When the mechanic has to repair the works of a clock, he lets the wheels run down. But the living clockwork of the state must be repaired while it is in motion, and here it is a matter of changing the wheels while they are turning. We must therefore look for some support to ensure the continuation of society, to make it independent of the natural state that we wish to abolish.

This support is not to be found in the natural character of man which, being selfish and violent, is far more calculated to destroy society than to preserve it. Nor is it to be found in his moral character which *ex hypothesi* has yet to be formed and upon which, because it is free and is never manifest, the lawgiver can never act and never depend with any certainty. The important thing, therefore, is to dissociate caprice from the physical and

Charakter die Willkür und von dem moralischen die Freiheit abzusondern—es käme darauf an, den erstern mit Gesetzen übereinstimmend, den letztern von Eindrücken abhängig zu machen—es käme darauf an, jenen von der Materie etwas weiter zu entfernen, diesen ihr um etwas näher zu bringen —um einen dritten Charakter zu erzeugen, der, mit jenen beiden verwandt, von der Herrschaft bloßer Kräfte zu der Herrschaft der Gesetze einen Übergang bahnte und, ohne den moralischen Charakter an seiner Entwicklung zu verhindern, vielmehr zu einem sinnlichen Pfand der unsichtbaren Sittlichkeit diente.

7. BRIEF

SOLLTE diese Wirkung vielleicht von dem Staat zu erwarten sein? Das ist nicht möglich, denn der Staat, wie er jetzt beschaffen ist, hat das Übel veranlaßt, und der Staat, wie ihn die Vernunft in der Idee sich aufgibt, anstatt diese bessere Menschheit begründen zu können, müßte selbst erst darauf gegründet werden. Und so hätten mich denn die

freedom from the moral character; to make the first conformable to law, the second dependent on impressions. The physical character must be removed somewhat further from the material and the moral brought somewhat closer to it—so as to create a third character related to both which would pave the way for a transition from the rule of mere force to the rule of law and, without impeding the development of the moral character, would serve as a tangible pledge of an as yet invisible morality.

Seventh Letter

Should we, perhaps, expect this action to come from the state? This is not possible, for the state, as it is now constituted, is responsible for the evil, and the state, as reason conceives it in idea, instead of being able to establish this better humanity, must itself be founded upon it. And so the foregoing inquiries have led me

bisherigen Untersuchungen wieder auf den Punkt zurückgeführt, von dem sie mich eine Zeitlang entfernten. Das
jetzige Zeitalter, weit entfernt, uns diejenige Form der Menschheit aufzuweisen, welche als notwendige Bedingung einer
moralischen Staatsverbesserung erkannt worden ist, zeigt
uns vielmehr das direkte Gegenteil davon. Sind also die von
mir aufgestellten Grundsätze richtig, und bestätigt die Erfahrung mein Gemälde der Gegenwart, so muß man jeden
Versuch einer solchen Staatsveränderung so lange für unzei-
tig und jede darauf gegründete Hoffnung so lange für schi-
märisch erklären, bis die Trennung in dem innern Menschen
wieder aufgehoben und seine Natur vollständig genug entwickelt ist, um selbst die Künstlerin zu sein und der politischen Schöpfung der Vernunft ihre Realität zu verbürgen.
Die Natur zeichnet uns in ihrer physischen Schöpfung den
Weg vor, den man in der moralischen zu wandeln hat. Nicht
eher, als bis der Kampf elementarischer Kräfte in den nie-
drigern Organisationen besänftiget ist, erhebt sie sich zu der
edeln Bildung des physischen Menschen. Ebenso muß der
Elementenstreit in dem ethischen Menschen, der Konflikt
blinder Triebe, fürs erste beruhigt sein, und die grobe Ent-
gegensetzung muß in ihm aufgehört haben, ehe man es wagen
darf, die Mannigfaltigkeit zu begünstigen. Auf der andern
Seite muß die Selbständigkeit seines Charakters gesichert
sein und die Unterwürfigkeit unter fremde despotische Formen einer anständigen Freiheit Platz gemacht haben, ehe
man die Mannigfaltigkeit in ihm der Einheit des Ideals unterwerfen darf. Wo der Naturmensch seine Willkür noch so
gesetzlos mißbraucht, da darf man ihm seine Freiheit kaum
zeigen; wo der künstliche Mensch seine Freiheit noch so
wenig gebraucht, da darf man ihm seine Willkür nicht nehmen. Das Geschenk liberaler Grundsätze wird Verräterei an
dem Ganzen, wenn es sich zu einer noch gärenden Kraft
gesellt und einer schon übermächtigen Natur Verstärkung
zusendet; das Gesetz der Übereinstimmung wird Tyrannei
gegen das Individuum, wenn es sich mit einer schon herrschenden Schwäche und physischen Beschränkung verknüpft
und so den letzten glimmenden Funken von Selbsttätigkeit
und Eigentum auslöscht.

back again to the point from which they drew me for a while. The present age, far from exhibiting the form of humanity that we have recognized to be the necessary condition for the moral reform of the state, shows us rather the precise opposite. If, therefore, the principles I have laid down are correct, and experience bears out my picture of the present age, we must regard any attempt at such a reform of the state as premature and all hope based upon it as chimerical until such time as the division in the inner man has been done away with and his nature has developed completely enough to be itself the artist and to guarantee reality to the political creation of reason.

In her physical creation Nature shows us the path that must be pursued in moral creation. Not until the battle of elemental forces has abated in the lower organizations does she rise to the noble formation of physical man. In the same way the elemental struggle in ethical man, the conflict of blind impulses must first have been quieted, and the crude antagonism within him must have ceased before we may dare to encourage multiplicity. On the other hand, his independence of character must be assured and his subjection to despotic alien forms have given place to a decent freedom before we can subject the multiplicity in him to the unity of the ideal. Where natural man still misuses his caprice so lawlessly, we can scarcely show him his freedom. Where civilized man makes so little use of his freedom, we may not deprive him of his caprice. The gift of liberal principles becomes an act of treachery to the whole when it is associated with a force still in ferment and reinforces an already overpowerful nature. The law of conformity becomes a tyranny against the individual when it is combined with an already dominant weakness and physical limitation and so extinguishes the last glimmering sparks of spontaneity and individuality.

Der Charakter der Zeit muß sich also von seiner tiefen Entwürdigung erst aufrichten, dort der blinden Gewalt der Natur sich entziehen und hier zu ihrer Einfalt, Wahrheit und Fülle zurückkehren—eine Aufgabe für mehr als *ein* Jahrhundert. Unterdessen, gebe ich gerne zu, kann mancher Versuch im einzelnen gelingen; aber am Ganzen wird dadurch nichts gebessert sein, und der Widerspruch des Betragens wird stets gegen die Einheit der Maximen beweisen. Man wird in andern Weltteilen in dem Neger die Menschheit ehren und in Europa sie in dem Denker schänden. Die alten Grundsätze werden bleiben, aber sie werden das Kleid des Jahrhunderts tragen, und zu einer Unterdrückung, welche sonst die Kirche autorisierte, wird die Philosophie ihren Namen leihen. Von der Freiheit erschreckt, die in ihren ersten Versuchen sich immer als Feindin ankündigt, wird man dort einer bequemen Knechtschaft sich in die Arme werfen und hier, von einer pédantischen Kuratel zur Verzweiflung gebracht, in die wilde Ungebundenheit des Naturstands entspringen. Die Usurpation wird sich auf die Schwachheit der menschlichen Natur, die Insurrektion auf die Würde derselben berufen, bis endlich die große Beherrscherin aller menschlichen Dinge, die blinde Stärke, dazwischen tritt und den vorgeblichen Streit der Prinzipien wie einen gemeinen Faustkampf entscheidet.

8. BRIEF

SOLL sich also die Philosophie, mutlos und ohne Hoffnung, aus diesem Gebiete zurückziehen? Während daß sich die Herrschaft der Formen nach jeder andern Richtung erweitert, soll dieses wichtigste aller Güter dem gestaltlosen Zufall preisgegeben sein? Der Konflikt blinder Kräfte soll in der politischen Welt ewig dauern und das gesellige Gesetz nie über die feindselige Selbstsucht siegen?
Nichts weniger! Die Vernunft selbst wird zwar mit dieser rauhen Macht, die ihren Waffen widersteht, unmittelbar den Kampf nicht versuchen und so wenig, als der Sohn des Saturns in der Ilias, selbsthandelnd auf den finstern Schauplatz heruntersteigen. Aber aus der Mitte der Streiter wählt sie sich den würdigsten aus, bekleidet ihn, wie Zeus seinen

The character of the time, therefore, must first recover from its deep degradation; in one place it must extricate itself from the blind power of nature, and in another return to her simplicity, truth and plenitude—a task for more than a single century. Meanwhile, I readily admit, many an attempt may succeed individually; but on the whole, nothing will be improved by them. The contradiction of behavior will always demonstrate against the unity of maxims. In other continents humanity may be respected in the negro, while in Europe it is dishonored in the thinker. The old principles will remain, but they will be clothed in the garb of the century and philosophy will lend its name to an oppression which was formerly authorized by the Church. Terrified of the freedom, which in their first attempts always appears to them as an enemy, men will in one case throw themselves into the arms of a comfortable slavery and in another, driven to despair by a pedantic tutelage, they will escape into the wild libertinism of the natural state. Usurpation will plead the weakness of human nature, insurrection its dignity, until at length the great sovereign of all human affairs, blind force, steps in to decide the sham conflict of principles like a common fist fight.

Eighth Letter

Is philosophy then to retire dejected and despairing from the field? While the mastery of forms is being extended in every other direction, is this most important of all commodities to be left to the mercy of formless chance? Is the conflict of blind forces to continue forever in the political world and is social law never to triumph over hostile self-interest?

By no means! Reason, it is true, will not attempt to struggle directly with this brute power which resists her weapons, and no more than the son of Saturn in the Iliad will she descend in person into the dismal arena to engage in combat. But from the midst of the combatants she will select the worthiest, will equip him, as Zeus did his grandson, with divine weapons and will

Enkel, mit göttlichen Waffen und bewirkt durch seine siegende Kraft die große Entscheidung.

Die Vernunft hat geleistet, was sie leisten kann, wenn sie das Gesetz findet und aufstellt; vollstrecken muß es der mutige Wille und das lebendige Gefühl. Wenn die Wahrheit im Streit mit Kräften den Sieg erhalten soll, so muß sie selbst erst zur *Kraft* werden und zu ihrem Sachführer im Reich der Erscheinungen einen *Trieb* aufstellen; denn Triebe sind die einzigen bewegenden Kräfte in der empfindenden Welt. Hat sie bis jetzt ihre siegende Kraft noch so wenig bewiesen, so liegt dies nicht an dem Verstande, der sie nicht zu entschleiern wußte, sondern an dem Herzen, das sich ihr verschloß, und an dem Triebe, der nicht für sie handelte.

Denn woher diese noch so allgemeine Herrschaft der Vorurteile und diese Verfinsterung der Köpfe bei allem Licht, das Philosophie und Erfahrung aufsteckten? Das Zeitalter ist aufgeklärt, das heißt, die Kenntnisse sind gefunden und öffentlich preisgegeben, welche hinreichen würden, wenigstens unsre praktischen Grundsätze zu berichtigen; der Geist der freien Untersuchung hat die Wahnbegriffe zerstreut, welche lange Zeit den Zugang zu der Wahrheit verwehrten, und den Grund unterwühlt, auf welchem Fanatismus und Betrug ihren Thron erbauten; die Vernunft hat sich von den Täuschungen der Sinne und von einer betrüglichen Sophistik gereinigt, und die Philosophie selbst, welche uns zuerst von ihr abtrünnig machte, ruft uns laut und dringend in den Schoß der Natur zurück—woran liegt es, daß wir noch immer Barbaren sind?

Es muß also, weil es nicht in den Dingen liegt, in den Gemütern der Menschen etwas vorhanden sein, was der Aufnahme der Wahrheit, auch wenn sie noch so hell leuchtete, und der Annahme derselben, auch wenn sie noch so lebendig überzeugte, im Wege steht. Ein alter Weiser hat es empfunden, und es liegt in dem vielbedeutenden Ausdrucke versteckt: *sapere aude.*

Erkühne dich, weise zu sein. Energie des Muts gehört dazu, die Hindernisse zu bekämpfen, welche sowohl die Trägheit der Natur als die Feigheit des Herzens der Belehrung entgegensetzen. Nicht ohne Bedeutung läßt der alte Mythus

bring about the great decision through his victorious strength.

Reason has accomplished all she can in discovering and expounding the law. It is the task of the courageous will and lively feeling to put it into execution. If truth is to gain the victory in the struggle with force, she herself must first become a *force* and appoint some drive as her representative in the realm of phenomena; for drives are the only motive forces in the sensible world. That up to now truth has displayed so little of her victorious strength is due not to the intellect which was incapable of unveiling it, but to the heart which remained closed to it and to the impulse which refused to act in her behalf.

Why then this still universal supremacy of prejudice and intellectual darkness in the face of all the light that has been shed by philosophy and experience? The age is enlightened, that is to say knowledge has been discovered and disseminated which would suffice at least to rectify our practical principles. The spirit of free inquiry has dispelled the erroneous conceptions which for a long time barred the approach to truth and has undermined the foundations on which fanaticism and fraud erected their throne. Reason has been purged of the illusions of the senses and of deceptive sophistry, and philosophy herself, which first caused us to forsake nature, calls us loudly and urgently to return to her bosom—why is it that we are still barbarians?

Since the fault does not lie with things, there must be something in men's temperaments which hinders the reception of truth, however brightly it may shine, and its acceptance, however lively the conviction it may inspire. An ancient sage felt this and it lies concealed in the meaningful maxim: *sapere aude.*

Dare to be wise! Energy of spirit is needed to overcome the obstacles which both indolence of nature and cowardice of heart set in the path of our instruction. It is not without significance that the old myth makes the

die Göttin der Weisheit in voller Rüstung aus Jupiters Haupte steigen; denn schon ihre erste Verrichtung ist kriegerisch. Schon in der Geburt hat sie einen harten Kampf mit den Sinnen zu bestehen, die aus ihrer süßen Ruhe nicht gerissen sein wollen. Der zahlreichere Teil der Menschen wird durch den Kampf mit der Not viel zu sehr ermüdet und abgespannt, als daß er sich zu einem neuen und härtern Kampf mit dem Irrtum aufraffen sollte. Zufrieden, wenn er selbst der sauren Mühe des Denkens entgeht, läßt er andere gern über seine Begriffe die Vormundschaft führen, und geschieht es, daß sich höhere Bedürfnisse in ihm regen, so ergreift er mit durstigem Glauben die Formeln, welche der Staat und das Priestertum für diesen Fall in Bereitschaft halten. Wenn diese unglücklichen Menschen unser Mitleiden verdienen, so trifft unsre gerechte Verachtung die andern, die ein besseres Los von dem Joch der Bedürfnisse frei macht, aber eigene Wahl darunter beugt. Diese ziehen den Dämmerschein dunkler Begriffe, wo man lebhafter fühlt und die Phantasie sich nach eignem Belieben bequeme Gestalten bildet, den Strahlen der Wahrheit vor, die das angenehme Blendwerk ihrer Träume verjagen. Auf eben diese Täuschungen, die das feindselige Licht der Erkenntnis zerstreuen soll, haben sie den ganzen Bau ihres Glücks gegründet, und sie sollten eine Wahrheit so teuer kaufen, die damit anfängt, ihnen alles zu nehmen, was Wert für sie besitzt? Sie müßten schon weise sein, um die Weisheit zu lieben: eine Wahrheit, die derjenige schon fühlte, der der Philosophie ihren Namen gab.
Nicht genug also, daß alle Aufklärung des Verstandes nur insoferne Achtung verdient, als sie auf den Charakter zurückfließt; sie geht auch gewissermaßen von dem Charakter aus, weil der Weg zu dem Kopf durch das Herz muß geöffnet werden. Ausbildung des Empfindungsvermögens ist also das dringendere Bedürfnis der Zeit, nicht bloß weil sie ein Mittel wird, die verbesserte Einsicht für das Leben wirksam zu machen, sondern selbst darum, weil sie zu Verbesserung der Einsicht erweckt.

goddess of wisdom emerge fully armed from the head of Jupiter; for even her first function is warlike. Even at birth she has to wage a hard battle with the senses which do not want to be dragged from their sweet repose. The greater part of humanity is too weary and exhausted from the struggle with want to brace itself for a fresh and sterner struggle with error. Content if they themselves escape the hard labor of thought, most men gladly leave to others the guardianship of their ideas, and if higher needs happen to stir in them, they embrace with eager faith the formulas which state and priesthood hold in readiness for such an occasion. If these unhappy people deserve our sympathy, we may hold in justified contempt those others whom a better lot has freed from the yoke of necessity, but who, by their own choice, continue to bow beneath it. These men prefer the twilight of obscure conceptions where feeling is livelier and fancy fashions comfortable images to suit its own pleasure, to the beams of truth which dispel the fond delusion of their dreams. On these same delusions, which should be dispelled by the hostile light of knowledge, they have based the entire structure of their happiness, and are they to purchase so dearly a truth which begins by depriving them of everything they value? They must already be wise in order to love wisdom: a truth which was felt by the man who gave philosophy its name.

Not only, then, does all intellectual enlightenment deserve our respect only insofar as it reacts upon character; it also proceeds so-to-speak from the character because the path to the head must be opened by the heart. The training of sensibility is therefore the more pressing need of our age, not merely because it will be a means of making the improved understanding effective in living, but for the very reason that it will awaken this improvement.

9. BRIEF

ABER ist hier nicht vielleicht ein Zirkel? Die theoretische Kultur soll die praktische herbeiführen, und die praktische doch die Bedingung der theoretischen sein? Alle Verbesserung im Politischen soll von Veredlung des Charakters ausgehen—aber wie kann sich unter den Einflüssen einer barbarischen Staatsverfassung der Charakter veredeln? Man müßte also zu diesem Zwecke ein Werkzeug aufsuchen, welches der Staat nicht hergibt, und Quellen dazu eröffnen, die sich bei aller politischen Verderbnis rein und lauter erhalten.

Jetzt bin ich an dem Punkt angelangt, zu welchem alle meine bisherigen Betrachtungen hingestrebt haben. Dieses Werkzeug ist die schöne Kunst, diese Quellen öffnen sich in ihren unsterblichen Mustern.

Von allem, was positiv ist und was menschliche Konventionen einführten, ist die Kunst wie die Wissenschaft losgesprochen, und beide erfreuen sich einer absoluten Immunität von der Willkür der Menschen. Der politische Gesetzgeber kann ihr Gebiet sperren, aber darin herrschen kann er nicht. Er kann den Wahrheitsfreund ächten, aber die Wahrheit besteht; er kann den Künstler erniedrigen, aber die Kunst kann er nicht verfälschen. Zwar ist nichts gewöhnlicher, als daß beide, Wissenschaft und Kunst, dem Geist des Zeitalters huldigen und der hervorbringende Geschmack von dem beurteilenden das Gesetz empfängt. Wo der Charakter straff wird und sich verhärtet, da sehen wir die Wissenschaft streng ihre Grenzen bewachen und die Kunst in den schweren Fesseln der Regel gehn; wo der Charakter erschlafft und sich auflöst, da wird die Wissenschaft zu gefallen und die Kunst zu vergnügen streben. Ganze Jahrhunderte lang zeigen sich die Philosophen wie die Künstler geschäftig, Wahrheit und Schönheit in die Tiefen gemeiner Menschheit hinabzutauchen; jene gehen darin unter, aber mit eigner unzerstörbarer Lebenskraft ringen sich diese siegend empor.

Der Künstler ist zwar der Sohn seiner Zeit, aber schlimm für ihn, wenn er zugleich ihr Zögling oder gar noch ihr Günstling ist. Eine wohltätige Gottheit reiße den Säugling bei Zeiten von seiner Mutter Brust, nähre ihn mit der Milch eines

But is this not perhaps a circle? Is theoretical culture
to bring about practical culture while at the same time
the practical is to be the condition of the theoretical?
All improvement in the political sphere is to proceed
from the ennoblement of character—but how, under the
influence of a barbarous constitution, can character be
ennobled? We would have for this purpose to search for
an instrument not provided by the state with which
to open up wellsprings that will remain pure and clear
despite àll political corruption.

I have now reached the point toward which all my
previous observations have been directed. This instrument is fine art, and these wellsprings are opened up in
its immortal patterns.

Art, like science, is free of everything that is positive
or established by human conventions, and both rejoice
in an absolute immunity from human arbitrariness. The
political legislator can close off their domain, but he
cannot govern it. He can ostracize the friend of truth,
but truth endures. He can humiliate the artist, but art
he cannot debase. Nothing, it is true, is more common
than for both science and art to pay homage to the
spirit of the age and for productive taste to accept the
law of critical taste. Where character becomes rigid and
obdurate, we see science keeping a strict watch over
her frontiers and art moving in the heavy shackles of
rules. Where character is devitalized and loose, science
will strive to please and art to amuse. For entire centuries philosophers and artists have been seen to engage
in plunging truth and beauty into the depths of vulgar
humanity; the philosophers and artists perish there,
but truth and beauty fight their way victoriously back
to the surface with their own indestructible vitality.

The artist is admittedly the child of his time, but woe
to him if he is also its disciple, or even its favorite. May
some beneficent deity snatch the infant in time from
his mother's breast, nourish him with the milk of a bet-

bessern Alters und lasse ihn unter fernem griechischen Himmel zur Mündigkeit reifen. Wenn er dann Mann geworden ist, so kehre er, eine fremde Gestalt, in sein Jahrhundert zurück; aber nicht, um es mit seiner Erscheinung zu erfreuen, sondern furchtbar wie Agamemnons Sohn, um es zu reinigen. Den Stoff zwar wird er von der Gegenwart nehmen, aber die Form von einer edleren Zeit, ja jenseits aller Zeit, von der absoluten unwandelbaren Einheit seines Wesens entlehnen. Hier aus dem reinen Äther seiner dämonischen Natur rinnt die Quelle der Schönheit herab, unangesteckt von der Verderbnis der Geschlechter und Zeiten, welche tief unter ihr in trüben Strudeln sich wälzen. Seinen Stoff kann die Laune entehren, wie sie ihn geadelt hat, aber die keusche Form ist ihrem Wechsel entzogen. Der Römer des ersten Jahrhunderts hatte längst schon die Kniee vor seinen Kaisern gebeugt, als die Bildsäulen noch aufrecht standen; die Tempel blieben dem Auge heilig, als die Götter längst zum Gelächter dienten, und die Schandtaten eines Nero und Commodus beschämte der edle Stil des Gebäudes, das seine Hülle dazu gab. Die Menschheit hat ihre Würde verloren, aber die Kunst hat sie gerettet und aufbewahrt in bedeutenden Steinen; die Wahrheit lebt in der Täuschung fort, und aus dem Nachbilde wird das Urbild wieder hergestellt werden. So wie die edle Kunst die edle Natur überlebte, so schreitet sie derselben auch in der Begeisterung, bildend und erweckend, voran. Ehe noch die Wahrheit ihr siegendes Licht in die Tiefen der Herzen sendet, fängt die Dichtungskraft ihre Strahlen auf, und die Gipfel der Menschheit werden glänzen, wenn noch feuchte Nacht in den Tälern liegt.

Wie verwahrt sich aber der Künstler vor den Verderbnissen seiner Zeit, die ihn von allen Seiten umfangen? Wenn er ihr Urteil verachtet. Er blicke aufwärts nach seiner Würde und dem Gesetz, nicht niederwärts nach dem Glück und nach dem Bedürfnis. Gleich frei von der eiteln Geschäftigkeit, die in den flüchtigen Augenblick gern ihre Spur drücken möchte, und von dem ungeduldigen Schwärmergeist, der auf die dürftige Geburt der Zeit den Maßstab des Unbedingten anwendet, überlasse er dem Verstande, der hier

ter age and permit him to grow to maturity under the distant skies of Greece. Then, when he has become a man, let him return to his century, an alien figure; but not to gladden it by his appearance, but rather, an object of terror like Agamemnon's son, to purge it. His subject matter, it is true, he will take from the present age, but his form he will borrow from a nobler time, indeed from beyond all time, from the absolute, unchangeable unity of his being. From here, the pure aether of his daemonic nature, flows the wellspring of beauty, untainted by the corruption of generations and ages that wallow in the dark eddies far below. A whim can degrade his material as it has dignified it, but the chaste form is removed from the changing moods. The Roman of the first century had long since bent the knee before his emperors when the statues of the gods still stood erect. The temples remained holy in men's eyes long after the gods had become objects of ridicule, and the infamous crimes of a Nero and a Commodus were put to shame by the noble style of the building that housed them. Humanity has lost its dignity, but art has rescued and preserved it in significant stone. Truth lives on in deception, and the original will be reconstructed from the copy. As noble art has outlived noble nature, so too she marches ahead of it, fashioning and awakening by her inspiration. Before ever truth sends her triumphant light into the depths of the heart, the power of poetry catches its rays and the peaks of humanity will gleam when the humid night still lingers in the valleys.

But how does the artist protect himself from the corruptions of his time that hem him in on all sides? By despising its opinion. Let him look upwards to his own dignity and to law, not downwards toward happiness and everyday needs. Free alike from vain activity, which would gladly set its mark on the fleeting moment, and from the impatient spirit of extravagant enthusiasm, which applies the measure of the absolute to the sorry productions of time, let him relinquish the sphere of

einheimisch ist, die Sphäre des Wirklichen; er aber strebe, aus dem Bunde des Möglichen mit dem Notwendigen das Ideal zu erzeugen. Dieses präge er aus in Täuschung und Wahrheit, präge es in die Spiele seiner Einbildungskraft und in den Ernst seiner Taten, präge es aus in allen sinnlichen und geistigen Formen und werfe es schweigend in die unendliche Zeit.

Aber nicht jedem, dem dieses Ideal in der Seele glüht, wurde die schöpferische Ruhe und der große geduldige Sinn verliehen, es in den verschwiegnen Stein einzudrücken oder in das nüchterne Wort auszugießen und den treuen Händen der Zeit zu vertrauen. Viel zu ungestüm, um durch dieses ruhige Mittel zu wandern, stürzt sich der göttliche Bildungstrieb oft unmittelbar auf die Gegenwart und auf das handelnde Leben und unternimmt, den formlosen Stoff der moralischen Welt umzubilden. Dringend spricht das Unglück seiner Gattung zu dem fühlenden Menschen, dringender ihre Entwürdigung, der Enthusiasmus entflammt sich, und das glühende Verlangen strebt in kraftvollen Seelen ungeduldig zur Tat. Aber befragte er sich auch, ob diese Unordnungen in der moralischen Welt seine Vernunft beleidigen oder nicht vielmehr seine Selbstliebe schmerzen? Weiß er es noch nicht, so wird er es an dem Eifer erkennen, womit er auf bestimmte und beschleunigte Wirkungen dringt. Der reine moralische Trieb ist aufs Unbedingte gerichtet, für ihn gibt es keine Zeit, und die Zukunft wird ihm zur Gegenwart, sobald sie sich aus der Gegenwart notwendig entwickeln muß. Vor einer Vernunft ohne Schranken ist die Richtung zugleich die Vollendung, und der Weg ist zurückgelegt, sobald er eingeschlagen ist.

Gib also, werde ich dem jungen Freund der Wahrheit und Schönheit zur Antwort geben, der von mir wissen will, wie er dem edeln Trieb in seiner Brust, bei allem Widerstande des Jahrhunderts, Genüge zu tun habe, gib der Welt, auf die du wirkst, die *Richtung* zum Guten, so wird der ruhige Rhythmus der Zeit die Entwicklung bringen. Diese Richtung hast du ihr gegeben, wenn du, lehrend, ihre Gedanken zum Notwendigen und Ewigen erhebst, wenn du, handelnd oder bildend, das Notwendige und Ewige in einen Gegen-

the actual to the intellect which is at home in it; but let him strive to produce the ideal from the union of the possible with the necessary. Let him imprint it on illusion and truth, imprint it in the play of his imagination and the seriousness of his actions, imprint it on all sensuous and spiritual forms and cast it silently into infinite time.

But not everyone with this ideal glowing in his soul has been vouchsafed the creative peace and the great patience of temperament to stamp it on the silent stone or to pour it into the sober word and entrust it to the faithful hands of time. Much too impetuous to proceed by such quiet means, the divine creative impulse often plunges directly into the present and into practical life, and undertakes to transform the formless substance of the moral world. The unhappiness of the human race speaks urgently to the sensitive man, its degradation still more urgently. Enthusiasm is kindled and burning desire strives impatiently for action in vigorous souls. But has he also asked himself whether these disorders in the moral world offend his reason or whether they do not rather hurt his self-love? If he does not yet know the answer, he will discover it from the eagerness with which he presses for definite and rapid results. The pure moral impulse is directed toward the absolute. Time does not exist for it, and the future becomes the present as soon as it must of necessity develop from the present. For an intelligence without limitations the direction is also the completion, and the road has been traveled once it is chosen.

Give then, I shall reply to the young friend of truth and beauty who wants to learn from me how he can satisfy the noble impulse in his breast in the face of all the opposition of his century—give the world you are influencing the direction towards the good, and the quiet rhythm of time will bring about the development. You have given it this direction if by your teaching you elevate its thoughts to the necessary and the eternal,

stand ihrer Triebe verwandelst. Fallen wird das Gebäude des Wahns und der Willkürlichkeit, fallen muß es, es ist schon gefallen, sobald du gewiß bist, daß es sich neigt; aber in dem innern, nicht bloß in dem äußern Menschen muß es sich neigen. In der schamhaften Stille deines Gemüts erziehe die siegende Wahrheit, stelle sie aus dir heraus in der Schönheit, daß nicht bloß der Gedanke ihr huldige, sondern auch der Sinn ihre Erscheinung liebend ergreife. Und damit es dir nicht begegne, von der Wirklichkeit das Muster zu empfangen, das du ihr geben sollst, so wage dich nicht eher in ihre bedenkliche Gesellschaft, bis du eines idealischen Gefolges in deinem Herzen versichert bist. Lebe mit deinem Jahrhundert, aber sei nicht sein Geschöpf; leiste deinen Zeitgenossen, aber was sie bedürfen, nicht was sie loben. Ohne ihre Schuld geteilt zu haben, teile mit edler Resignation ihre Strafen und beuge dich mit Freiheit unter das Joch, das sie gleich schlecht entbehren und tragen. Durch den standhaften Mut, mit dem du ihr Glück verschmähest, wirst du ihnen beweisen, daß nicht deine Feigheit sich ihren Leiden unterwirft. Denke sie dir, wie sie sein sollten, wenn du auf sie zu wirken hast, aber denke sie dir, wie sie sind, wenn du für sie zu handeln versucht wirst. Ihren Beifall suche durch ihre Würde, aber auf ihren Unwert berechne ihr Glück, so wird dein eigener Adel dort den ihrigen aufwecken und ihre Unwürdigkeit hier deinen Zweck nicht vernichten. Der Ernst deiner Grundsätze wird sie von dir scheuchen, aber im Spiele ertragen sie sie noch; ihr Geschmack ist keuscher als ihr Herz, und hier mußt du den scheuen Flüchtling ergreifen. Ihre Maximen wirst du umsonst bestürmen, ihre Taten umsonst verdammen, aber an ihrem Müßiggange kannst du deine bildende Hand versuchen. Verjage die Willkür, die Frivolität, die Rohigkeit aus ihren Vergnügungen, so wirst du sie unvermerkt auch aus ihren Handlungen, endlich aus ihren Gesinnungen verbannen. Wo du sie findest, umgib sie mit edeln, mit großen, mit geistreichen Formen, schließe sie ringsum mit den Symbolen des Vortrefflichen ein, bis der Schein die Wirklichkeit und die Kunst die Natur überwindet.

if by your actions or your creations you transform the necessary and the eternal into the object of its drives. The edifice of folly and arbitrariness will collapse, it must collapse. It has already collapsed as soon as you are certain that it is leaning; but it must lean in the inner and not merely in the outer man. In the modest stillness of your heart you must foster victorious truth, externalize it in beauty, so that thought alone does not pay homage to it, but sense too may lovingly grasp its manifestations. And so that it does not happen that you take from reality the pattern you are to give it, do not venture into its dubious society until you are assured of an ideal following in your heart. Live with your century, but do not be its creature; do for your contemporaries that which they need, not that which they praise. Without sharing their guilt, share their penalties with noble resignation, and bow freely beneath the yoke which they do without and bear with equally bad grace. By the steadfast courage with which you scorn their happiness, you will prove to them that it is not your cowardice that submits to their sufferings. Think of them as they are to be when you have to influence them, but think of them as they are when you are tempted to act in their behalf. Seek their approbation through their dignity, but judge their happiness by their unworthiness; thus, on the one hand, your own nobility will awaken theirs and on the other, their unworthiness will not defeat your purpose. The seriousness of your principles will frighten them away from you, but in play they will continue to tolerate them; their taste is purer than their hearts, and it is here that you must take hold of the timid fugitive. You will attack their maxims in vain, in vain condemn their acts; but you can try your creative hand on their idleness. Drive out arbitrariness, frivolity and coarseness from their pleasures, and you will imperceptibly banish them also from their actions and finally from their thinking. Wherever you find them, surround them with great, noble and ingenious forms. Enclose them all around with the symbols of excellence until reality is overcome by appearance and nature by art.

WALLENSTEIN

PROLOG

Gesprochen bei Wiedereröffnung der Schaubühne in Weimar im Oktober 1798

DER scherzenden, der ernsten Maske Spiel,
Dem ihr so oft ein willig Ohr und Auge
Geliehn, die weiche Seele hingegeben,
Vereinigt uns aufs neu in diesem Saal—
Und sieh! er hat sich neu verjüngt, ihn hat
Die Kunst zum heitern Tempel ausgeschmückt,
Und ein harmonisch hoher Geist spricht uns
Aus dieser edeln Säulenordnung an
Und regt den Sinn zu festlichen Gefühlen.

Und doch ist dies der alte Schauplatz noch,
Die Wiege mancher jugendlichen Kräfte,
Die Laufbahn manches wachsenden Talents.
Wir sind die alten noch, die sich vor euch
Mit warmem Trieb und Eifer ausgebildet.
Ein edler Meister stand auf diesem Platz,
Euch in die heitern Höhen seiner Kunst
Durch seinen Schöpfergenius entzückend.
O! möge dieses Raumes neue Würde
Die Würdigsten in unsre Mitte ziehn,
Und eine Hoffnung, die wir lang gehegt,
Sich uns in glänzender Erfüllung zeigen.
Ein großes Muster weckt Nacheiferung
Und gibt dem Urteil höhere Gesetze.
So stehe dieser Kreis, die neue Bühne
Als Zeugen des vollendeten Talents.
Wo möcht es auch die Kräfte lieber prüfen,

WALLENSTEIN

*Spoken at the reopening of the stage in Weimar in
October, 1798*

The sport of jesting and of earnest masks,
To which you have lent willing ears and eyes
So often, and committed tender hearts,
Unites us once again within this hall.
Behold how it has been rejuvenated.
Art has adorned it as a cheerful temple,
And a harmonious lofty spirit speaks
To us out of this noble order of columns
And stirs our minds to high and solemn feelings.

Yet this is still the well known stage of old,
The cradle of how many youthful spirits,
The highroad of how much evolving talent.
We are ourselves the same who formerly
Acquired our skills with eager warmth before you.
A noble master has stood on this stage
Who charmed you to the heights of his great art
By virtue of his own creative genius.
O, may this room's new-founded dignity
Attract the worthiest into our midst,
And may *one* hope that we have cherished long
Be realized in brilliance of fulfillment.
A splendid model rouses emulation,
Establishes more lofty laws of judgment.
Hence let this building stand, and this new stage,
In testimony of perfected talent.
Where better might it test its powers out,

Den alten Ruhm erfrischen und verjüngen,
Als hier vor einem auserlesnen Kreis,
Der, rührbar jedem Zauberschlag der Kunst,
Mit leisbeweglichem Gefühl den Geist
In seiner flüchtigsten Erscheinung hascht?

Denn schnell und spurlos geht des Mimen Kunst,
Die wunderbare, an dem Sinn vorüber,
Wenn das Gebild des Meißels, der Gesang
Des Dichters nach Jahrtausenden noch leben.
Hier stirbt der Zauber mit dem Künstler ab,
Und wie der Klang verhallet in dem Ohr,
Verrauscht des Augenblicks geschwinde Schöpfung,
Und ihren Ruhm bewahrt kein dauernd Werk.
Schwer ist *die* Kunst, vergänglich ist ihr Preis,
Dem Mimen flicht die Nachwelt keine Kränze;
Drum muß er geizen mit der Gegenwart,
Den Augenblick, der sein ist, ganz erfüllen,
Muß seiner Mitwelt mächtig sich versichern
Und im Gefühl der Würdigsten und Besten
Ein lebend Denkmal sich erbaun— So nimmt er
Sich seines Namens Ewigkeit voraus.
Denn wer den Besten seiner Zeit genug
Getan, der hat gelebt für alle Zeiten.

Die neue Ära, die der Kunst Thaliens
Auf dieser Bühne heut beginnt, macht auch
Den Dichter kühn, die alte Bahn verlassend,
Euch aus des Bürgerlebens engem Kreis
Auf einen höhern Schauplatz zu versetzen,
Nicht unwert des erhabenen Moments
Der Zeit, in dem wir strebend uns bewegen.
Denn nur der große Gegenstand vermag
Den tiefen Grund der Menschheit aufzuregen;
Im engen Kreis verengert sich der Sinn,
Es wächst der Mensch mit seinen größern Zwecken.

Und jetzt an des Jahrhunderts ernstem Ende,
Wo selbst die Wirklichkeit zur Dichtung wird,

Refreshing and regaining former fame,
Than here before this chosen audience,
Which, sensitive to every stroke of Art's
Enchantment, seizes with responsive feeling
Upon the mind's most fleeting apparitions?

For swiftly over our awareness passes
The wondrous art of mimes without a trace,
Whereas the sculptor's statue and the song
Of poets live beyond the centuries.
Here, when the artist ends, his magic ends,
And as the sound recedes upon our ears
The moment's quick creation dies in echoes,
Its fame preserved by no enduring work.
Hard is this art, its praise is transitory;
For mimes, posterity entwines no garlands.
Therefore they must be greedy of the present
And fill the moment which is theirs, completely,
Assure themselves of their contemporaries
And in the feelings of the best and noblest
Build living monuments. In this way they
Anticipate their names' eternity.
For he who does sufficient for the best
Of his own time, has lived for all the ages.

And this new era which today begins
For Thalia's art upon this stage has made
The poet bold as well, to quit old paths
And from the narrow sphere of middle class
Existence lift you to a higher scene
Not unbefitting the exalted moment
Of time in which we strive and have our life.
For only subjects of high consequence
Can stir the deepest depths of human kind;
The mind grows narrow in a narrow sphere
And man grows great with greater purposes.

Now at this century's impressive close,
As actuality itself is turned

Wo wir den Kampf gewaltiger Naturen
Um ein bedeutend Ziel vor Augen sehn
Und um der Menschheit große Gegenstände,
Um Herrschaft und um Freiheit wird gerungen—
Jetzt darf die Kunst auf ihrer Schattenbühne
Auch höhern Flug versuchen, ja sie muß,
Soll nicht des Lebens Bühne sie beschämen.

Zerfallen sehen wir in diesen Tagen
Die alte feste Form, die einst vor hundert
Und funfzig Jahren ein willkommner Friede
Europens Reichen gab, die teure Frucht
Von dreißig jammervollen Kriegesjahren.
Noch einmal laßt des Dichters Phantasie
Die düstre Zeit an euch vorüberführen,
Und blicket froher in die Gegenwart
Und in der Zukunft hoffnungsreiche Ferne.

In jenes Krieges Mitte stellt euch jetzt
Der Dichter. Sechzehn Jahre der Verwüstung,
Des Raubs, des Elends sind dahingeflohn,
In trüben Massen gäret noch die Welt,
Und keine Friedenshoffnung strahlt von fern.
Ein Tummelplatz von Waffen ist das Reich,
Verödet sind die Städte, Magdeburg
Ist Schutt, Gewerb und Kunstfleiß liegen nieder,
Der Bürger gilt nichts mehr, der Krieger alles,
Straflose Frechheit spricht den Sitten Hohn,
Und rohe Horden lagern sich, verwildert
Im langen Krieg, auf dem verheerten Boden.

Auf diesem finstern Zeitgrund malet sich
Ein Unternehmen kühnen Übermuts
Und ein verwegener Charakter ab.
Ihr kennet ihn—den Schöpfer kühner Heere,
Des Lagers Abgott und der Länder Geißel,
Die Stütze und den Schrecken seines Kaisers,
Des Glückes abenteuerlichen Sohn,
Der, von der Zeiten Gunst emporgetragen,

To art, as we see mighty natures locked
In struggle for a goal of lofty import,
As conflict rages for the mighty ends
Of man, for masterdom, for freedom, now
Art is allowed assay of higher flight
Upon its shadow-stage; indeed it must be,
Lest it be put to shame by life's own stage.

Amid these days we see the old fixed form
Disintegrate, which in its time a hundred
And fifty years ago a welcome peace
Imposed on Europe's realms, the precious fruit
Acquired by thirty dismal years of war.
Now once again permit the poet's fancy
To bring before your eyes that sombre age,
While more content you gaze about the present
And toward the hopeful distance of the future.

Into the middle of that war the poet
Now takes you. Sixteen years of devastation,
Of pillage, and of misery have passed.
Dark masses of the world are still in ferment
And from afar there shines no hope of peace.
The Empire is a rumpus-field for weapons,
Deserted are the cities, Magdeburg
In ashes, art and industry are prostrate,
The citizen is naught, the soldier all,
Unpunished insolence makes mock of custom,
And rude hordes, lawless grown in lengthy war,
Make couches on the devastated ground.

Against this lowering background there is painted
An undertaking of audacious pride
And an impetuous, headstrong character.
You know him—the creator of bold armies,
The idol of the camp and scourge of countries,
The prop and yet the terror of his Emperor,
Dame Fortune's fabulous adopted son,
Who, lifted by the favor of the times,

Der Ehre höchste Staffeln rasch erstieg
Und, ungesättigt immer weiter strebend,
Der unbezähmten Ehrsucht Opfer fiel.
Von der Parteien Gunst und Haß verwirrt
Schwankt sein Charakterbild in der Geschichte;
Doch euren Augen soll ihn jetzt die Kunst,
Auch eurem Herzen menschlich näher bringen.
Denn jedes Äußerste führt *sie*, die alles
Begrenzt und bindet, zur Natur zurück,
Sie sieht den Menschen in des Lebens Drang
Und wälzt die größre Hälfte seiner Schuld
Den unglückseligen Gestirnen zu.

Nicht *er* ists, der auf dieser Bühne heut
Erscheinen wird. Doch in den kühnen Scharen,
Die sein Befehl gewaltig lenkt, sein Geist
Beseelt, wird euch sein Schattenbild begegnen,
Bis ihn die scheue Muse selbst vor euch
Zu stellen wagt in lebender Gestalt;
Denn seine Macht ists, die sein Herz verführt,
Sein Lager nur erkläret sein Verbrechen.

Darum verzeiht dem Dichter, wenn er euch
Nicht raschen Schritts mit *einem* Mal ans Ziel
Der Handlung reißt, den großen Gegenstand
In einer Reihe von Gemälden nur
Vor euren Augen abzurollen wagt.
Das heutge Spiel gewinne euer Ohr
Und euer Herz den ungewohnten Tönen;
In jenen Zeitraum führ es euch zurück,
Auf jene fremde kriegerische Bühne,
Die unser Held mit seinen Taten bald
Erfüllen wird.

Und wenn die Muse heut,
Des Tanzes freie Göttin und Gesangs,
Ihr altes deutsches Recht, des Reimes Spiel,
Bescheiden wieder fordert—tadelts nicht!
Ja danket ihrs, daß sie das düstre Bild

374

Climbed rapidly the highest rungs or honor
And, never sated, striving ever further,
Fell victim to intemperate ambition.
Blurred by the favor and the hate of parties,
His image wavers in our history.
But Art shall now bring him more humanly
And closer to your eyes and to your hearts.
For Art, which binds and limits everything,
Brings all extremes back to the sphere of Nature.
It sees this man amid the press of life
And shows the greater half of his wrong-doing
To be the guilt of inauspicious stars.

  It is not he who will appear upon
This stage today. But in the daring hosts
Which his command with power sways, his spirit
Inspires, you will behold his shadow-self
Until the cautious Muse shall venture to
Produce him in his living form before you.
It is his power which misleads his heart:
His camp alone will make his crime quite clear.

  Forgive the poet therefore if he does not
Sweep you with rapid step and all at once
Straight to his story's goal, but only ventures
To set his mighty subject forth before you
In series, one by one, of pictures merely.
May this day's play persuade your ears and win
Your hearts as well to unfamiliar tones;
May it transport you to that former epoch
And to that far-off theatre of war
Which soon will be preempted by our hero
And his exploits

    And if today the Muse,
Unfettered goddess of the dance and song,
Should modestly claim her old German right
Once more to sport with rhyme,—do not reprove her.
But thank her for transposing that grim picture

Der Wahrheit in das heitre Reich der Kunst
Hinüberspielt, die Täuschung, die sie schafft,
Aufrichtig selbst zerstört und ihren Schein
Der Wahrheit nicht betrüglich unterschiebt;
Ernst ist das Leben, heiter ist die Kunst.

Of truth into the cheerful realm of Art,
Herself destroying her illusion in
Good faith, not substituting with deceit
The semblances of Truth for Truth itself:
For life is stern, but art serenely joyous.

DIE KRANICHE DES IBYKUS

ZUM Kampf der Wagen und Gesänge,
Der auf Korinthus' Landesenge
Der Griechen Stämme froh vereint,
Zog Ibykus, der Götterfreund.
Ihm schenkte des Gesanges Gabe,
Der Lieder süßen Mund Apoll;
So wandert er, an leichtem Stabe,
Aus Rhegium, des Gottes voll.

Schon winkt auf hohem Bergesrücken
Akrokorinth des Wandrers Blicken,
Und in Poseidons Fichtenhain
Tritt er mit frommem Schauder ein.
Nichts regt sich um ihn her, nur Schwärme
Von Kranichen begleiten ihn,
Die fernhin nach des Südens Wärme
In graulichtem Geschwader ziehn.

"Seid mir gegrüßt, befreundte Scharen,
Die mir zur See Begleiter waren!
Zum guten Zeichen nehm ich euch,
Mein Los, es ist dem euren gleich:
Von fern her kommen wir gezogen
Und flehen um ein wirtlich Dach.
Sei uns der Gastliche gewogen,
Der von dem Fremdling wehrt die Schmach!"

Und munter fördert er die Schritte
Und sieht sich in des Waldes Mitte—
Da sperren, auf gedrangem Steg,
Zwei Mörder plötzlich seinen Weg.
Zum Kampfe muß er sich bereiten,
Doch bald ermattet sinkt die Hand,
Sie hat der Leier zarte Saiten,
Doch nie des Bogens Kraft gespannt.

Er ruft die Menschen an, die Götter,
Sein Flehen dringt zu keinem Retter,
Wie weit er auch die Stimme schickt,

THE CRANES OF IBYCUS

To strife of chariots and songs,
That joy-united Grecian throngs
On Corinth's isthmus-land attend,
Went Ibycus, the god's own friend.
To him had fair Apollo granted
Two lips all sweet with song and lay;
On light staff leaning, god-enchanted,
From Rhegium forth he made his way.

Acrocorinth, on mountain risen,
Already greets the wand'rer's vision,
And he begins, with pious dread,
Poseidon's grove of firs to tread.
Naught stirs all round him save a swarm
Of cranes, who share his wand'rer's way,
Who far to regions south and warm
Wing on and on in squadron gray.

"O friendly hosts, all hail to ye
Who shared my sail across the sea!
I deem ye as a fav'ring sign,
Your destiny's akin to mine:
From lands afar we wand'rers stray
And pray for some kind shelt'ring-place.
May Zeus-protector guide our way,
Who guards the stranger from disgrace!"

And carefree he the wood doth enter
And reaches soon the dark grove's center—
There, on a narrow bridge, by force
Two murd'rers sudden bar his course.
For mortal strife he must make ready,
But soon his wearied hand sinks low;
For gentle lyre-strings 'twas steady,
It ne'er had strung the deadly bow.

To men, to gods he pleads entreaty,
His prayer finds no saviour's pity,
However far his voice he sends,

Nichts Lebendes wird hier erblickt.
"So muß ich hier verlassen sterben,
Auf fremdem Boden, unbeweint,
Durch böser Buben Hand verderben,
Wo auch kein Rächer mir erscheint!"

Und schwer getroffen sinkt er nieder,
Da rauscht der Kraniche Gefieder,
Er hört, schon kann er nicht mehr sehn,
Die nahen Stimmen furchtbar krähn.
"Von euch, ihr Kraniche dort oben,
Wenn keine andre Stimme spricht,
Sei meines Mordes Klag erhoben!"
Er ruft es, und sein Auge bricht.

Der nackte Leichnam wird gefunden,
Und bald, obgleich entstellt von Wunden,
Erkennt der Gastfreund in Korinth
Die Züge, die ihm teuer sind.
"Und muß ich so dich wiederfinden,
Und hoffte mit der Fichte Kranz
Des Sängers Schläfe zu umwinden,
Bestrahlt von seines Ruhmes Glanz!"

Und jammernd hörens alle Gäste,
Versammelt bei Poseidons Feste,
Ganz Griechenland ergreift der Schmerz,
Verloren hat ihn jedes Herz;
Und stürmend drängt sich zum Prytanen
Das Volk, es fordert seine Wut,
Zu rächen des Erschlagnen Manen,
Zu sühnen mit des Mörders Blut.

Doch wo die Spur, die aus der Menge,
Der Völker flutendem Gedränge,
Gelocket von der Spiele Pracht,
Den schwarzen Täter kenntlich macht?
Sinds Räuber, die ihn feig erschlagen?
Tats neidisch ein verborgner Feind?
Nur Helios vermags zu sagen,
Der alles Irdische bescheint.

Naught living to his cry attends.
"Then must I perish here forsaken,
On foreign soil, unmourned and still,
My life by churlish fellows taken,
No one my vengeance to fulfill!"

And stricken deep he sinks, eyes blurring,
When, lo! the wings of cranes come whirring,
He hears—though he no more can see—
Their slender throats screech fearfully.
"By you, o cranes, there over me,
If no one else the utt'rance make,
Be borne to man my murder plea!"
He speaks it, and his dim eyes break.

Ere long the naked corpse is found,
And though defaced by many a wound,
His host in Corinth swift can tell
Those features that he loved so well:
"And is it thus that I must find thee,
And I had hoped with poet-crown,
With gentle spruce-wreath to entwine thee,
Illumined by thy bright renown!"

And one great sigh of sad lamenting
Shakes all Poseidon's feast attending.
All Greece is torn by sorrow's smart,
His loss burns deep in every heart;
The people throng in raging seas
Before their judge, his wrath to urge,
The slain man's manes to appease,
With murd'rer's blood his death to purge.

But where's the trace that from the surging
Of undulating peoples merging,
Allured by sportive glories bright,
Shall bring the murd'rer back to light?
Did robbers craven make the kill?
Was't envy of some secret foe?
That Helios alone can tell,
Whose rays illume all things below.

Er geht vielleicht mit frechem Schritte
Jetzt eben durch der Griechen Mitte,
Und während ihn die Rache sucht,
Genießt er seines Frevels Frucht;
Auf ihres eignen Tempels Schwelle
Trotzt er vielleicht den Göttern, mengt
Sich dreist in jene Menschenwelle,
Die dort sich zum Theater drängt.

Denn Bank an Bank gedränget sitzen,
Es brechen fast der Bühne Stützen,
Herbeigeströmt von fern und nah,
Der Griechen Völker wartend da;
Dumpfbrausend wie des Meeres Wogen,
Von Menschen wimmelnd, wächst der Bau
In weiter stets geschweiftem Bogen
Hinauf bis in des Himmels Blau.

Wer zählt die Völker, nennt die Namen,
Die gastlich hier zusammenkamen?
Von Cekrops' Stadt, von Aulis' Strand,
Von Phocis, vom Spartanerland,
Von Asiens entlegner Küste,
Von allen Inseln kamen sie
Und horchen von dem Schaugerüste
Des Chores grauser Melodie,

Der streng und ernst, nach alter Sitte,
Mit langsam abgemeßnem Schritte
Hervortritt aus dem Hintergrund,
Umwandelnd des Theaters Rund.
So schreiten keine irdschen Weiber,
Die zeugete kein sterblich Haus!
Es steigt das Riesenmaß der Leiber
Hoch über menschliches hinaus.

Ein schwarzer Mantel schlägt die Lenden,
Sie schwingen in entfleischten Händen
Der Fackel düsterrote Glut,
In ihren Wangen fließt kein Blut;
Und wo die Haare lieblich flattern,

E'en now, perchance, with saunter shameless
He walks the Grecian crowd, still blameless—
Whilst vengeance follows in pursuit,
He gloats o'er his transgression's fruit;
The very gods perchance he braves
Upon the threshold of their fane—
Joins boldly in the human waves
That surge yon theater to gain.

For gathered there from far and near,
Close-packed on benches, tier on tier,
The tribes of Greece sit waiting all—
The burdened stage bids fair to fall;
Deep rumbling, full—as sea-surf roars,
The teeming arch, a human sea,
In ever-widening span upsoars
Into the sky's blue canopy.

Who knows the nation, who the name
Of all who here together came?
From Theseus' town, from Aulis' strand,
From Phocis, from the Spartan's land,
Yea, e'en from Asia's coast far distant,
From every island they did throng,
And now, by yonder show-stage, listened
To Grecian chorus' gruesome song.

Severe and stern in custom treasured,
With stolid steps sedate and measured
It marches forth from background dark,
And circles round the theater's arc.
That stride is not of women mortal,
No earthly race gave birth to them!
Their giant forms tower up transportal
High o'er the puny sons of men.

About their thighs black cloaks hang clinging,
Their fleshless hands are steadfast swinging
Dull torches of half-hidden glow,
While in their cheeks no blood dares flow;
And there where lovely locks loose flutter

Um Menschenstirnen freundlich wehn,
Da sieht man Schlangen hier und Nattern
Die giftgeschwollnen Bäuche blähn.

Und schauerlich gedreht im Kreise
Beginnen sie des Hymnus Weise,
Der durch das Herz zerreißend dringt,
Die Bande um den Frevler schlingt.
Besinnungraubend, herzbetörend
Schallt der Erinnyen Gesang,
Er schallt, des Hörers Mark verzehrend,
Und duldet nicht der Leier Klang:

"Wohl dem, der frei von Schuld und Fehle
Bewahrt die kindlich reine Seele!
Ihm dürfen wir nicht rächend nahn,
Er wandelt frei des Lebens Bahn.
Doch wehe, wehe, wer verstohlen
Des Mordes schwere Tat vollbracht!
Wir heften uns an seine Sohlen,
Das furchtbare Geschlecht der Nacht.

"Und glaubt er fliehend zu entspringen,
Geflügelt sind wir da, die Schlingen
Ihm werfend um den flüchtgen Fuß,
Daß er zu Boden fallen muß.
So jagen wir ihn, ohn Ermatten,
Versöhnen kann uns keine Reu,
Ihn fort und fort bis zu den Schatten,
Und geben ihn auch dort nicht frei."

So singend tanzen sie den Reigen,
Und Stille wie des Todes Schweigen
Liegt überm ganzen Hause schwer,
Als ob die Gottheit nahe wär.
Und feierlich, nach alter Sitte,
Umwandelnd des Theaters Rund,
Mit langsam abgemeßnem Schritte
Verschwinden sie im Hintergrund.

Und zwischen Trug und Wahrheit schwebet
Noch zweifelnd jede Brust und bebet,

Right friendly round a mortal brow,
Here one sees snakes and vipers clutter,
Their bodies poison-swelled enow.

And in a fearful circle rounded,
The dread and awesome song is sounded,
That rending fills each heart with fear,
And locks the sinner in its sphere.
To dim the senses, hearts to harrow,
Echoes the furies' fateful chant,
Resounds, devours the listener's marrow,
Permits no lyres' accompaniment:

"Yea, happy he, who's free of error!
On him we dare not wreak our terror.
Who keeps his soul childlike and pure,
Traverses life wrath-free and sure.
But woe to him, who dark and hidden
Hath done the deed of murder base!
We fasten on his steps unbidden,
Dark night's avenging, awful race.

And if he thinks to 'scape by fleeing,
On wings we come, our nets all-seeing
About his fleeting feet we cast,
So that he needs must fall at last.
Thus do we hunt him, tiring never,
Repentance vain we never heed,
Straight on, e'en to the shades' own river,
And even there he is not freed."

Thus on they dance and chant in chillness,
And silence, like unto death's stillness,
Lies heavy over house and sky
As if the deity were nigh.
And solemnly, in custom treasured,
Encircling all the theater's arc,
With stolid step sedate and measured
They vanish in the background dark.

And twixt deceit and truth still wavers
Each human doubting breast, and quavers,

Und huldiget der furchtbarn Macht,
Die richtend im Verborgnen wacht,
Die unerforschlich, unergründet
Des Schicksals dunkeln Knäuel flicht,
Dem tiefen Herzen sich verkündet,
Doch fliehet vor dem Sonnenlicht.

Da hört man auf den höchsten Stufen
Auf einmal eine Stimme rufen:
"Sieh da! Sieh da, Timotheus,
Die Kraniche des Ibykus!"—
Und finster plötzlich wird der Himmel,
Und über dem Theater hin
Sieht man, in schwärzlichtem Gewimmel,
Ein Kranichheer vorüberziehn.

"Des Ibykus!"—Der teure Name
Rührt jede Brust mit neuem Grame,
Und wie im Meere Well auf Well,
So läufts von Mund zu Munde schnell:
"Des Ibykus, den wir beweinen,
Den eine Mörderhand erschlug!
Was ists mit dem? Was kann er meinen?
Was ists mit diesem Kranichzug?"

Und lauter immer wird die Frage,
Und ahnend fliegts mit Blitzesschlage
Durch alle Herzen: "Gebet Acht,
Das ist der Eumeniden Macht!
Der fromme Dichter wird gerochen,
Der Mörder bietet selbst sich dar!
Ergreift ihn, der das Wort gesprochen,
Und ihn, an dens gerichtet war!"

Doch dem war kaum das Wort entfahren,
Möcht ers im Busen gern bewahren;
Umsonst! der schreckenbleiche Mund
Macht schnell die Schuldbewußten kund.
Man reißt und schleppt sie vor den Richter,
Die Szene wird zum Tribunal,
Und es gestehn die Bösewichter,
Getroffen von der Rache Strahl.

And homage pays to that dread might
That judging watches, hid from sight,
That, fathomless and unexposed,
Entwines the obscure skein of fate;
In bosom depths it is disclosed,
Howe'er it flees from sunlight's hate.

Then sudden from the tier most high
A voice is heard by all to cry:
"See there, see there, Timotheus!
The cranes, the cranes of Ibycus!"
And swift a darkness dims the heaven,
And o'er the theater and away
One sees in teeming swarm of ebon
A troop of cranes wing on its way.

"Of Ibycus!"—That name so treasured
Moves every breast with grief fresh-measured—
As waves on waves in oceans rise,
From mouth to mouth it swiftly flies:
"Of Ibycus, whom we are mourning,
Who fell for fiendish murd'rers' gains?
What is't with him? What means his warning?
And what imports this swarm of cranes?"

And louder ever grow the cries,
With lightning-speed foreboding flies
Through every heart: "'Tis clear as light,
This is th' avenging furies' might!
The poet's manes are appeased,
The murd'rer seeks his own arrest!
Let him who spoke the word be seized,
And him, to whom it was addressed."

That word he had no sooner uttered,
Than he had fain his bosom fettered,—
In vain! Mouths pale with terror's hue
Full swift reveal the guilty two.
Before the judge they're dragged in passion,
A jury gathers at his call,
And both the culprits make confession,
As 'neath the vengeance-stroke they fall.

DAS LIED VON DER GLOCKE

Vivos voco. Mortuos plango. Fulgura frango

FEST gemauert in der Erden
Steht die Form, aus Lehm gebrannt.
Heute muß die Glocke werden!
Frisch, Gesellen, seid zur Hand!
Von der Stirne heiß
Rinnen muß der Schweiß,
Soll das Werk den Meister loben;
Doch der Segen kommt von oben.

Zum Werke, das wir ernst bereiten,
Geziemt sich wohl ein ernstes Wort;
Wenn gute Reden sie begleiten,
Dann fließt die Arbeit munter fort.
So laßt uns jetzt mit Fleiß betrachten,
Was durch die schwache Kraft entspringt:
Den schlechten Mann muß man verachten,
Der nie bedacht, was er vollbringt.
Das ists ja, was den Menschen zieret,
Und dazu ward ihm der Verstand,
Daß er im innern Herzen spüret,
Was er erschafft mit seiner Hand.

Nehmet Holz vom Fichtenstamme,
Doch recht trocken laßt es sein,
Daß die eingepreßte Flamme
Schlage zu dem Schwalch hinein!
Kocht des Kupfers Brei,
Schnell das Zinn herbei!
Daß die zähe Glockenspeise
Fließe nach der rechten Weise!

Was in des Dammes tiefer Grube
Die Hand mit Feuers Hilfe baut,

SONG OF THE BELL

Vivos voco. Mortuos plango. Fulgura frango.

Fastened deep in firmest earth,
  Stands the mold of well burnt clay.
Now we'll give the bell its birth;
  Quick, my friends, no more delay!
    From the heated brow
    Sweat must freely flow,
If to your master praise be given:
But the blessing comes from Heaven.

To the work we now prepare
  A serious thought is surely due;
And cheerfully the toil we'll share,
  If cheerful words be mingled too.
Then let us still with care observe
  What from our strength, yet weakness, springs;
For he respect can ne'er deserve
  Who hands alone to labor brings.
'Tis only this which honors man;
  His mind with heavenly fire was warmed,
That he with deepest thought might scan
  The work which his own hand has formed.

With splinters of the driest pine
  Now feed the fire below;
Then the rising flame shall shine,
  And the melting ore shall flow.
    Boils the brass within,
    Quickly add the tin;
That the thick metallic mass
Rightly to the mold may pass.

What with the aid of fire's dread power
  We in the dark, deep pit now hide,

Hoch auf des Turmes Glockenstube,
Da wird es von uns zeugen laut.
Noch dauern wirds in späten Tagen
Und rühren vieler Menschen Ohr
Und wird mit dem Betrübten klagen
Und stimmen zu der Andacht Chor.
Was unten tief dem Erdensohne
Das wechselnde Verhängnis bringt,
Das schlägt an die metallne Krone,
Die es erbaulich weiter klingt.

Weiße Blasen seh ich springen,
Wohl! die Massen sind im Fluß.
Laßts mit Aschensalz durchdringen,
Das befördert schnell den Guß.
Auch von Schaume rein
Muß die Mischung sein,
Daß vom reinlichen Metalle
Rein und voll die Stimme schalle.

Denn mit der Freude Feierklange
Begrüßt sie das geliebte Kind
Auf seines Lebens erstem Gange,
Den es in Schlafes Arm beginnt;
Ihm ruhen noch im Zeitenschoße
Die schwarzen und die heitern Lose,
Der Mutterliebe zarte Sorgen
Bewachen seinen goldnen Morgen.—
Die Jahre fliehen pfeilgeschwind.
Vom Mädchen reißt sich stolz der Knabe,
Er stürmt ins Leben wild hinaus,
Durchmißt die Welt am Wanderstabe.
Fremd kehrt er heim ins Vaterhaus,
Und herrlich, in der Jugend Prangen,
Wie ein Gebild aus Himmels Höhn,
Mit züchtigen, verschämten Wangen
Sieht er die Jungfrau vor sich stehn.
Da faßt ein namenloses Sehnen
Des Jünglings Herz, er irrt allein,
Aus seinen Augen brechen Tränen,
Er flieht der Brüder wilden Reihn.

Shall, on some lofty, sacred tower,
  Tell of our skill and form our pride.
And it shall last to days remote,
  Shall thrill the ear of many a race;
Shall sound with sorrow's mournful note,
  And call to pure devotion's grace.
Whatever to the sons of earth
  Their changing destiny brings down,
To the deep, solemn clang gives birth,
  That rings from out this metal crown.

See, the boiling surface, whitening,
  Shows the whole is mixing well;
Add the salts, the metal brightening,
  Ere flows out the liquid bell.
    Clear from foam or scum
    Must the mixture come,
That with a rich metallic note
The sound aloft in air may float.

Now with joy and festive mirth
  Salute that loved and lovely child,
Whose earliest moments on the earth
  Are passed in sleep's dominion mild.
While on Time's lap he rests his head,
The fatal sisters spin their thread;
  A mother's love, with softest rays,
  Gilds o'er the morning of his days.—
But years with arrowy haste are fled.
His nursery bonds he proudly spurns;
  He rushes to the world without;
After long wandering, home he turns,
  Arrives a stranger and in doubt.
There, lovely in her beauty's youth,
  A form of heavenly mold he meets,
Of modest air and simple truth;
  The blushing maid he bashful greets.
A nameless feeling seizes strong
  On his young heart. He walks alone;
To his moist eyes emotions throng;
  His joy in ruder sports has flown.

391

Errötend folgt er ihren Spuren
Und ist von ihrem Gruß beglückt,
Das Schönste sucht er auf den Fluren,
Womit er seine Liebe schmückt.
O zarte Sehnsucht, süßes Hoffen,
Der ersten Liebe goldne Zeit!
Das Auge sieht den Himmel offen,
Es schwelgt das Herz in Seligkeit—
O daß sie ewig grünen bliebe,
Die schöne Zeit der jungen Liebe!

Wie sich schon die Pfeifen bräunen!
Dieses Stäbchen tauch ich ein:
Sehn wirs überglast erscheinen,
Wirds zum Gusse zeitig sein.
Jetzt, Gesellen, frisch!
Prüft mir das Gemisch,
Ob das Spröde mit dem Weichen
Sich vereint zum guten Zeichen.

Denn wo das Strenge mit dem Zarten,
Wo Starkes sich und Mildes paarten,
Da gibt es einen guten Klang.
Drum prüfe, wer sich ewig bindet,
Ob sich das Herz zum Herzen findet!
Der Wahn ist kurz, die Reu ist lang.—
Lieblich in der Bräute Locken
Spielt der jungfräuliche Kranz,
Wenn die hellen Kirchenglocken
Laden zu des Festes Glanz.

Ach! des Lebens schönste Feier
Endigt auch den Lebensmai,
Mit dem Gürtel, mit dem Schleier
Reißt der schöne Wahn entzwei.
Die Leidenschaft flieht,
Die Liebe muß bleiben;
Die Blume verblüht,
Die Frucht muß treiben.
Der Mann muß hinaus
Ins feindliche Leben,
Muß wirken und streben

He follows, blushing, where she goes;
　And should her smile but welcome him,
The fairest flower, the dewy rose,
　To deck her beauty seems too dim.
O tenderest passion! Sweetest hope!
　The golden hours of earliest love!
Heaven's self to him appears to ope;
　He feels a bliss this earth above.
O, that it could eternal last!
That youthful love were never past!

See how brown the liquid turns!
　Now this rod I thrust within;
If it's glazed before it burns,
Then the casting may begin.
　　Quick, my lads, and steady,
　　　If the mixture's ready!
When the strong and weaker blend,
Then we hope a happy end:

Whenever strength with softness joins,
When with the rough the mild combines,
　Then all is union sweet and strong.
Consider, ye who join your hands,
If hearts are twined in mutual bands;
　For passion's brief, repentance long.
How lovely in the maiden's hair
The bridal garland plays!
And merry bells invite us there,
Where mingle festive lays.
Alas! that all life's brightest hours
　Are ended with its earliest May!
That from those sacred nuptial bowers
　The dear deceit should pass away!
　　　Though passion may fly,
　　　　Yet love will endure;
　　　The flower must die,
　　　　The fruit to insure.
　　　The man must without,
　　　　Into struggling life;
　　　　With toiling and strife,
　　　　He must plan and contrive;

Und pflanzen und schaffen,
Erlisten, erraffen,
Muß wetten und wagen,
Das Glück zu erjagen.
Da strömet herbei die unendliche Gabe,
Es füllt sich der Speicher mit köstlicher Habe,
Die Räume wachsen, es dehnt sich das Haus.
Und drinnen waltet
Die züchtige Hausfrau,
Die Mutter der Kinder,
Und herrschet weise
Im häuslichen Kreise,
Und lehret die Mädchen
Und wehret den Knaben,
Und reget ohn Ende
Die fleißigen Hände,
Und mehrt den Gewinn
Mit ordnendem Sinn,
Und füllet mit Schätzen die duftenden Laden,
Und dreht um die schnurrende Spindel den Faden,
Und sammelt im reinlich geglätteten Schrein
Die schimmernde Wolle, den schneeigten Lein,
Und füget zum Guten den Glanz und den Schimmer,
Und ruhet nimmer.

Und der Vater mit frohem Blick
Von des Hauses weitschauendem Giebel
Überzählet sein blühend Glück,
Siehet der Pfosten ragende Bäume
Und der Scheunen gefüllte Räume
Und die Speicher, vom Segen gebogen,
Und des Kornes bewegte Wogen,
Rühmt sich mit stolzem Mund:
Fest, wie der Erde Grund,
Gegen des Unglücks Macht
Steht mir des Hauses Pracht!—
Doch mit des Geschickes Mächten
Ist kein ewger Bund zu flechten,
Und das Unglück schreitet schnell.

Must be prudent to thrive;
With boldness must dare,
Good fortune to share.
'Tis by means such as these, that abundance is poured
In a full, endless stream, to increase all his hoard,
While his house to a palace spreads out.

Within doors governs
The modest, careful wife,
The children's kind mother;
And wise is the rule
Of her household school.
She teaches the girls,
And she warns the boys;
She directs all the bands
Of diligent hands,
And increases their gain
By her orderly reign.
And she fills with her treasures her sweet-scented chests;
From the toil of her spinning-wheel scarcely she rests;
And she gathers in order, so cleanly and bright,
The softest of wool, and the linen snow-white:
The useful and pleasant she mingles ever,
And is slothful never.

The father, cheerful, from the door,
His wide-extended homestead eyes;
Tells all his smiling fortunes o'er;
The future columns in his trees,
His barn's well furnished stock he sees,
His granaries e'en now o'erflowing,
While yet the waving corn is growing.
He boasts with swelling pride,
"Firm as the mountain's side
Against the shock of fate
Is now my happy state."
Who can discern futurity?
Who can insure prosperity?
Quick misfortune's arrow flies.

Wohl! nun kann der Guß beginnen,
Schön gezacket ist der Bruch.
Doch, bevor wirs lassen rinnen,
Betet einen frommen Spruch.
Stoßt den Zapfen aus!
Gott bewahr das Haus!
Rauchend in des Henkels Bogen
Schießts mit feuerbraunen Wogen.

Wohltätig ist des Feuers Macht,
Wenn sie der Mensch bezähmt, bewacht,
Und was er bildet, was er schafft,
Das dankt er dieser Himmelskraft;
Doch furchtbar wird die Himmelskraft,
Wenn sie der Fessel sich entrafft,
Einhertritt auf der eignen Spur
Die freie Tochter der Natur.
Wehe, wenn sie losgelassen,
Wachsend ohne Widerstand
Durch die volkbelebten Gassen
Wälzt den ungeheuren Brand!
Denn die Elemente hassen
Das Gebild der Menschenhand.
Aus der Wolke
Quillt der Segen,
Strömt der Regen;
Aus der Wolke, ohne Wahl,
Zuckt der Strahl!
Hört ihrs wimmern hoch vom Turm!
Das ist Sturm!
Rot wie Blut
Ist der Himmel,
Das ist nicht des Tages Glut!
Welch Getümmel
Straßen auf!
Dampf wallt auf!
Flackernd steigt die Feuersäule,
Durch der Straße lange Zeile
Wächst es fort mit Windeseile,

Now we may begin to cast;
   All is right and well prepared:
Yet, ere the anxious moment's past,
   A pious hope by all be shared.
      Strike the stopper clear!
      God preserve us here!
Sparkling, to the rounded mold
It rushes hot, like liquid gold.

How useful is the power of flame,
If human skill control and tame!
And much of all that man can boast,
Without this child of Heaven, were lost.
But frightful is her changing mien,
When, bursting from her bonds, she's seen
To quit the safe and quiet hearth,
And wander lawless o'er the earth.
Woe to those whom then she meets!
   Against her fury who can stand?
Along the thickly peopled streets
   She madly hurls her fearful brand.
Then the elements, with joy,
Man's best handiwork destroy.
      From the clouds
      Falls amain
      The blessed rain:
      From the clouds alike
      Lightnings strike.
Ringing loud the fearful knell
      Sounds the bell.
    Dark blood-red
      Are all the skies;
But no dawning light is spread.
      What wild cries
      From the streets arise!
      Smoke dims the eyes.
Flickering mounts the fiery glow
Along the street's extended row,
Fast as fiercest winds can blow.

Kochend wie aus Ofens Rachen
Glühn die Lüfte, Balken krachen,
Pfosten stürzen, Fenster klirren,
Kinder jammern, Mütter irren,
Tiere wimmern
Unter Trümmern,
Alles rennet, rettet, flüchtet,
Taghell ist die Nacht gelichtet.
Durch der Hände lange Kette
Um die Wette
Fliegt der Eimer, hoch im Bogen
Spritzen Quellen, Wasserwogen.
Heulend kommt der Sturm geflogen,
Der die Flamme brausend sucht.
Prasselnd in die dürre Frucht
Fällt sie, in des Speichers Räume,
In der Sparren dürre Bäume,
Und als wollte sie im Wehen
Mit sich fort der Erde Wucht
Reißen in gewaltger Flucht,
Wächst sie in des Himmels Höhen
Riesengroß!
Hoffnungslos
Weicht der Mensch der Götterstärke,
Müßig sieht er seine Werke
Und bewundernd untergehen.

Leergebrannt
Ist die Stätte,
Wilder Stürme rauhes Bette;
In den öden Fensterhöhlen
Wohnt das Grauen,
Und des Himmels Wolken schauen
Hoch hinein.

Einen Blick
Nach dem Grabe
Seiner Habe
Sendet noch der Mensch zurück—
Greift fröhlich dann zum Wanderstabe.

Bright, as with a furnace flare,
And scorching, is the heated air;
Beams are falling, children crying,
Windows breaking, mothers flying,
Creatures moaning, crushed and dying,—
All is uproar, hurry, flight,
And light as day the dreadful night.
Along the eager living lane,
      Though all in vain,
Speeds the bucket. The engine's power
Sends the artificial shower.
But see, the heavens still threatening lower!
The winds rush roaring to the flame.
Cinders on the store-house frame,
And its drier stores, fall thick;
While kindling, blazing, mounting quick,
As though it would, at one fell sweep,
    All that on the earth is found
    Scatter wide in ruin round,
Swells the flame to heaven's blue deep,
        With giant size.
        Hope now dies.
    Man must yield to Heaven's decrees.
    Submissive, yet appalled, he sees
His fairest works in ashes sleep.

        All burnt over
        Is the place,
The storm's wild home. How changed its face!
    In the empty, ruined wall
        Dwells dark horror;
    While heaven's clouds in shadow fall
        Deep within.

        One look,
      In memory sad,
      Of all he had,
    The unhappy sufferer took,—
Then found his heart might yet be glad.

Was Feuers Wut ihm auch geraubt,
Ein süßer Trost ist ihm geblieben:
Er zählt die Häupter seiner Lieben,
Und sieh! ihm fehlt kein teures Haupt.

In die Erd ists aufgenommen,
Glücklich ist die Form gefüllt;
Wirds auch schön zu Tage kommen,
Daß es Fleiß und Kunst vergilt?
Wenn der Guß mißlang?
Wenn die Form zersprang?
Ach! vielleicht, indem wir hoffen,
Hat uns Unheil schon getroffen.

Dem dunkeln Schoß der heilgen Erde
Vertrauen wir der Hände Tat,
Vertraut der Sämann seine Saat
Und hofft, daß sie entkeimen werde
Zum Segen, nach des Himmels Rat.
Noch köstlicheren Samen bergen
Wir trauernd in der Erde Schoß
Und hoffen, daß er aus den Särgen
Erblühen soll zu schönerm Los.

Von dem Dome,
Schwer und bang,
Tönt die Glocke
Grabgesang.
Ernst begleiten ihre Trauerschläge
Einen Wandrer auf dem letzten Wege.

Ach! die Gattin ists, die teure,
Ach! es ist die treue Mutter,
Die der schwarze Fürst der Schatten
Wegführt aus dem Arm des Gatten,
Aus der zarten Kinder Schar,
Die sie blühend ihm gebar,
Die sie an der treuen Brust
Wachsen sah mit Mutterlust—
Ach! des Hauses zarte Bande
Sind gelöst auf immerdar,

However hard his lot to bear,
His choicest treasures still remain:
He calls for each with anxious pain,
    And every loved one's with him there.

To the earth it's now committed.
    With success the mold is filled.
To skill and care alone's permitted
    A perfect work with toil to build.
        Is the casting right?
        Is the mold yet tight?
Ah! while now with hope we wait,
Mischance, perhaps, attends its fate.

To the dark lap of mother earth
    We now confide what we have made;
    As in earth too the seed is laid,
In hope the seasons will give birth
    To fruits that soon may be displayed.
And yet more precious seed we sow
    With sorrow in the world's wide field;
And hope, though in the grave laid low,
    A flower of heavenly hue 't will yield.

        Slow and heavy
        Hear it swell!
        'Tis the solemn
        Passing bell!
Sad we follow, with these sounds of woe,
Those who on this last, long journey go.

    Alas! the wife,—it is the dear one,—
    Ah, it is the faithful mother,
    Whom the shadowy king of fear
    Tears from all that life holds dear;—
    From the husband,—from the young,
    The tender blossoms, that have sprung
    From their mutual, faithful love,
    'Twas hers to nourish, guide, improve.
    Ah! the chain which bound them all
        Is for ever broken now;

Denn sie wohnt im Schattenlande,
Die des Hauses Mutter war,
Denn es fehlt ihr treues Walten.
Ihre Sorge wacht nicht mehr,
An verwaister Stätte schalten
Wird die Fremde, liebeleer.

Bis die Glocke sich verkühlet,
Laßt die strenge Arbeit ruhn;
Wie im Laub der Vogel spielet,
Mag sich jeder gütlich tun.
Winkt der Sterne Licht,
Ledig aller Pflicht
Hört der Pursch die Vesper schlagen,
Meister muß sich immer plagen.

Munter fördert seine Schritte
Fern im wilden Forst der Wandrer
Nach der lieben Heimathütte.
Blöckend ziehen heim die Schafe,
Und der Rinder
Breitgestirnte, glatte Scharen
Kommen brüllend,
Die gewohnten Ställe füllend.
Schwer herein
Schwankt der Wagen,
Kornbeladen;
Bunt von Farben
Auf den Garben
Liegt der Kranz,
Und das junge Volk der Schnitter
Fliegt zum Tanz.
Markt und Straße werden stiller,
Um des Lichts gesellge Flamme
Sammeln sich die Hausbewohner,
Und das Stadttor schließt sich knarrend
Schwarz bedecket
Sich die Erde,
Doch den sichern Bürger schrecket
Nicht die Nacht.

She cannot hear their tender call,
  Nor see them in affliction bow.
Her true affection guards no more;
  Her watchful care wakes not again:
O'er all the once loved orphan's store
  The indifferent stranger now must reign.

Till the bell is safely cold,
  May our heavy labor rest;
Free as the bird, by none controlled,
  Each may do what pleases best.
    With approaching night,
    Twinkling stars are bright.
Vespers call the boys to play;
The master's toils end not with day.

Cheerful in the forest gloom,
  The wandered turns his weary steps
To his loved, though lowly home.
  Bleating flocks draw near the fold;
    And the herds,
Wide-horned, and smooth, slow-pacing come
    Lowing from the hill,
    The accustomed stall to fill.
      Heavy rolls
      Along the wagon,
      Richly loaded.
      On the sheaves,
      With gayest leaves
      They form the wreath;
And the youthful reapers dance
      Upon the heath.
Street and market all are quiet,
And round each domestic light
Gathers now a circle fond,
While shuts the creaking city-gate.
      Darkness hovers
      O'er the earth.
Safety still each sleeper covers
      As with light,

Die den Bösen gräßlich wecket,
Denn das Auge des Gesetzes wacht.
Heilge Ordnung, segenreiche
Himmelstochter, die das Gleiche
Frei und leicht und freudig bindet,
Die der Städte Bau gegründet,
Die herein von den Gefilden
Rief den ungesellgen Wilden,
Eintrat in der Menschen Hütten,
Sie gewöhnt zu sanften Sitten
Und das teuerste der Bande
Wob, den Trieb zum Vaterlande!

Tausend fleißge Hände regen,
Helfen sich in munterm Bund,
Und in feurigem Bewegen
Werden alle Kräfte kund.
Meister rührt sich und Geselle
In der Freiheit heilgem Schutz,
Jeder freut sich seiner Stelle,
Bietet dem Verächter Trutz.
Arbeit ist des Bürgers Zierde,
Segen ist der Mühe Preis;
Ehrt den König seine Würde,
Ehret uns der Hände Fleiß.

Holder Friede,
Süße Eintracht,
Weilet, weilet
Freundlich über dieser Stadt!
Möge nie der Tag erscheinen,
Wo des rauhen Krieges Horden
Dieses stille Tal durchtoben,
Wo der Himmel,
Den des Abends sanfte Röte
Lieblich malt,
Von der Dörfer, von der Städte
Wildem Brande schrecklich strahlt!

Nun zerbrecht mir das Gebäude,
Seine Absicht hats erfüllt,

That the deeds of crime discovers;
   For wakes the law's protecting might.

Holy Order! rich with all
The gifts of Heaven, that best we call,—
Freedom, peace, and equal laws,—
Of common good the happy cause!
She the savage man has taught
What the arts of life have wrought;
Changed the rude hut to comfort, splendor,
And filled fierce hearts with feelings tender
And yet a dearer bond she wove,—
Our home, our country, taught to love.

A thousand active hands, combined
   For mutual aid, with zealous heart,
In well apportioned labor find
   Their power increasing with their art.
Master and workmen all agree,
   Under sweet Freedom's holy care,
And each, content in his degree,
   Warns every scorner to beware.
Labor is the poor man's pride,—
   Success by toil alone is won.
Kings glory in possessions wide—
   We glory in our work well done.

      Gentle peace!
      Sweet union!
      Linger, linger,
Kindly over this our home!
   Never may the day appear,
   When the hordes of cruel war
Through this quiet vale shall rush;
      When the sky,
With the evening's softened air,
      Blushing red,
Shall reflect the frightful glare
   Of burning towns in ruin dread.

Now break up the useless mold:
   Its only purpose is fulfilled.

Daß sich Herz und Auge weide
An dem wohlgelungnen Bild.
Schwingt den Hammer, schwingt,
Bis der Mantel springt!
Wenn die Glock soll auferstehen,
Muß die Form in Stücken gehen.

Der Meister kann die Form zerbrechen
Mit weiser Hand, zur rechten Zeit,
Doch wehe, wenn in Flammenbächen
Das glühnde Erz sich selbst befreit!
Blindwütend, mit des Donners Krachen,
Zersprengt es das geborstne Haus,
Und wie aus offnem Höllenrachen
Speit es Verderben zündend aus.
Wo rohe Kräfte sinnlos walten,
Da kann sich kein Gebild gestalten;
Wenn sich die Völker selbst befrein,
Da kann die Wohlfahrt nicht gedeihn.

Weh, wenn sich in dem Schoß der Städte
Der Feuerzunder still gehäuft,
Das Volk, zerreißend seine Kette,
Zur Eigenhilfe schrecklich greift!
Da zerret an der Glocke Strängen
Der Aufruhr, daß sie heulend schallt
Und, nur geweiht zu Friedensklängen,
Die Losung anstimmt zur Gewalt.

Freiheit und Gleichheit! hört man schallen,
Der ruhge Bürger greift zur Wehr,
Die Straßen füllen sich, die Hallen,
Und Würgerbanden ziehn umher;
Da werden Weiber zu Hyänen
Und treiben mit Entsetzen Scherz,
Noch zuckend, mit des Panthers Zähnen,
Zerreißen sie des Feindes Herz.
Nichts Heiliges ist mehr, es lösen
Sich alle Bande frommer Scheu,
Der Gute räumt den Platz dem Bösen,
Und alle Laster walten frei.

May our eyes, well pleased, behold
  A work to prove us not unskilled.
    Wield the hammer, wield,
    Till the frame shall yield!
That the bell to light may rise,
The form in thousand fragments flies.

The master may destroy the mold
  With careful hand, and judgment wise.
But, woe!— in streams of fire, if rolled,
  The glowing metal seek the skies!
Loud bursting with the clash of thunder,
  It throws aloft the broken ground;
Like a volcano rends asunder,
  And spreads in burning ruin round.
When reckless power by force prevails,
  The reign of peace and art is o'er;
And when a mob e'en wrong assails,
  The public welfare is no more.

Alas! when in the peaceful state
  Conspiracies are darkly forming;
The oppressed no longer patient wait;
  With fury every breast is storming.
Then whirls the bell with frequent clang;
  And Uproar, with her howling voice,
Has changed the note, that peaceful rang,
  To wild confusion's dreadful noise.

Freedom and equal rights they call,—
  And peace gives way to sudden war;
The street is crowded, and the hall,—
  And crime is unrestrained by law:
E'en woman, to a fury turning,
  But mocks at every dreadful deed;
Against the hated madly burning,
  With horrid joy she sees them bleed.
Now naught is sacred;—broken lies
  Each holy law of honest worth;
The bad man rules, the good man flies,
  And every vice walks boldly forth.

Gefährlich ists, den Leu zu wecken,
Verderblich ist des Tigers Zahn,
Jedoch der schrecklichste der Schrecken,
Das ist der Mensch in seinem Wahn.
Weh denen, die dem Ewigblinden
Des Lichtes Himmelsfackel leihn!
Sie strahlt ihm nicht, sie kann nur zünden
Und äschert Städt und Länder ein.

Freude hat mir Gott gegeben!
Sehet! wie ein goldner Stern
Aus der Hülse, blank und eben,
Schält sich der metallne Kern.
Von dem Helm zum Kranz
Spielts wie Sonnenglanz,
Auch des Wappens nette Schilder
Loben den erfahrnen Bilder.

Herein! herein!
Gesellen alle, schließt den Reihen,
Daß wir die Glocke taufend weihen!
Concordia soll ihr Name sein.
Zur Eintracht, zu herzinnigem Vereine
Versammle sie die liebende Gemeine.

Und dies sei fortan ihr Beruf,
Wozu der Meister sie erschuf:
Hoch überm niedern Erdenleben
Soll sie in blauem Himmelszelt
Die Nachbarin des Donners schweben
Und grenzen an die Sternenwelt,
Soll eine Stimme sein von oben,
Wie der Gestirne helle Schar,
Die ihren Schöpfer wandelnd loben
Und führen das bekränzte Jahr.
Nur ewigen und ernsten Dingen
Sei ihr metallner Mund geweiht,
Und stündlich mit den schnellen Schwingen
Berühr im Fluge sie die Zeit;
Dem Schicksal leihe sie die Zunge,
Selbst herzlos, ohne Mitgefühl,

There's danger in the lion's wrath,
   Destruction in the tiger's jaw;
But worse than death to cross the path
   Of man, when passion is his law.
Woe, woe to those who strive to light
   The torch of truth by passion's fire!
It guides not;—it but glares through night
   To kindle freedom's funeral pyre.

God has given us joy tonight!
   See how, like the golden grain
From the husk, all smooth and bright,
   The shining metal now is ta'en!
     From top to well formed rim,
     Not a spot is dim;
E'en the motto, neatly raised,
Shows a skill may well be praised.

     Around, around
Companions all, take your ground,
And name the bell with joy profound!
CONCORDIA is the word we've found
Most meet to express the harmonious sound,
That calls to those in friendship bound.

Be this henceforth the destined end
To which the finished work we send
High over every meaner thing,
  In the blue canopy of heaven,
Near to the thunder let it swing,
  A neighbor to the stars be given.
Let its clear voice above proclaim,
  With brightest troops of distant suns,
The praise of our Creator's name,
  While round each circling season runs.
To solemn thoughts of heart-felt power
  Let its deep note full oft invite,
And tell, with every passing hour,
  Of hastening time's unceasing flight.
Still let it mark the course of fate;
  Its cold, unsympathizing voice

Begleite sie mit ihrem Schwunge
Des Lebens wechselvolles Spiel.
Und wie der Klang im Ohr vergehet,
Der mächtig tönend ihr entschallt,
So lehre sie, daß nichts bestehet,
Daß alles Irdische verhallt.
Jetzo mit der Kraft des Stranges
Wiegt die Glock mir aus der Gruft,
Daß sie in das Reich des Klanges
Steige, in die Himmelsluft.
Ziehet, ziehet, hebt!
Sie bewegt sich, schwebt.
Freude dieser Stadt bedeute,
Friede sei ihr erst Geläute.

Attend on every changing state
  Of human passions, griefs, and joys.
And as the mighty sound it gives
  Dies gently on the listening ear,
We feel how quickly all that lives
  Must change, and fade, and disappear.

Now, lads, join your strength around!
  Lift the bell to upper air!
And in the kingdom wide of sound
  Once placed, we'll leave it there.
    All together! heave!
    Its birth-place see it leave!—
Joy to all within its bound!
Peace its first, its latest sound!

  Translated by Henry Wadsworth Longfellow

MARIA STUART

DRITTER AUFZUG

4. AUFTRITT
Die Vorigen. Elisabeth. Graf Leicester. Gefolge.

ELISABETH (*zu Leicester*). Wie heißt der Landsitz?
LEICESTER.   Fotheringhayschloß.
ELISABETH (*zu Shrewsbury*).
Schickt unser Jagdgefolg voraus nach London,
Das Volk drängt allzuheftig in den Straßen,
Wir suchen Schutz in diesem stillen Park.
(*Talbot entfernt das Gefolge. Sie fixiert mit den Augen die
Maria, indem sie zu Paulet weiter spricht.*)
Mein gutes Volk liebt mich zu sehr. Unmäßig,
Abgöttisch sind die Zeichen seiner Freude,
So ehrt man einen Gott, nicht einen Menschen.
MARIA (*welche diese Zeit über halb ohnmächtig auf die
Amme gelehnt war, erhebt sich jetzt, und ihr Auge begegnet dem
gespannten Blick der Elisabeth. Sie schaudert zusammen und
wirft sich wieder an der Amme Brust*).
O Gott, aus diesen Zügen spricht kein Herz!
ELISABETH. Wer ist die Lady?
(*Ein allgemeines Schweigen.*)
LEICESTER.—Du bist zu Fotheringhay, Königin.
ELISABETH (*stellt sich überrascht und erstaunt, einen fin-
stern Blick auf Leicestern richtend*).
Wer hat mir das getan? Lord Leicester!

MARY STUART

ACT III

SCENE 4

Enter Elizabeth, the Earl of Leicester, and retinue.

ELIZABETH: *(to Leicester)*   What castle is this?
LEICESTER: Castle Fotheringhay.
ELIZABETH: *(to Shrewsbury)*
  Send our hunting party on ahead
  To London. People throng the roads too much.
  We shall seek shelter in this quiet park.
(Talbot dismisses the retinue. She fixes her eyes on Mary
  while she goes on talking with Leicester.)
  My people love me far too much. Their joy
  Is quite immoderate, idolatrous.
  God may be honored so, but not mere mortals.
MARY: *(who all this time has been leaning on the nurse's bos-*
    om, rises now, and her eye encounters the intent gaze of
    Elizabeth. She shudders and throws herself back on the
    nurse's bosom.)
  O God, no heart speaks from that countenance!
ELIZABETH: Who is the Lady?
                (General silence.)
LEICESTER: —You are at Castle Fotheringhay, my Queen.
ELIZABETH: *(pretends to be surprised and astonished*
    and fixes a dark look on Leicester.)
  Who has done this to me? Lord Lester!

LEICESTER. Es ist geschehen, Königin—Und nun
Der Himmel deinen Schritt hieher gelenkt,
So laß die Großmut und das Mitleid siegen.
SHREWSBURY. Laß dich erbitten, königliche Frau,
Dein Aug auf die Unglückliche zu richten,
Die hier vergeht vor deinem Anblick.
(*Maria rafft sich zusammen und will auf die Elisabeth zugehen,
steht aber auf halbem Weg schaudernd still, ihre Gebärden
drücken den heftigsten Kampf aus.*)
ELISABETH.   Wie, Mylords?
Wer war es denn, der eine Tiefgebeugte
Mir angekündigt? Eine Stolze find ich,
Vom Unglück keineswegs geschmeidigt.
MARIA.   Seis!
Ich will mich auch noch diesem unterwerfen.
Fahr hin, ohnmächtger Stolz der edeln Seele!
Ich will vergessen, wer ich bin, und was
Ich litt; ich willl vor ihr mich niederwerfen,
Die mich in diese Schmach herunterstieß.
(*Sie wendet sich gegen die Königin.*)
Der Himmel hat für Euch entschieden, Schwester!
Gekrönt vom Sieg ist Euer glücklich Haupt,
Die *Gottheit* bet ich an, die Euch erhöhte!
(*Sie fällt vor ihr nieder.*)
Doch seid auch *Ihr* nun edelmütig, Schwester!
Laßt mich nicht schmachvoll liegen, Eure Hand
Streckt aus, reicht mir die königliche Rechte,
Mich zu erheben von dem tiefen Fall.
ELISABETH (*zurücktretend*).
Ihr seid an Eurem Platz, Lady Maria!
Und dankend preis ich meines Gottes Gnade,
Der nicht gewollt, daß ich zu Euren Füßen
So liegen sollte, wie Ihr jetzt zu meinen.
MARIA (*mit steigendem Affekt*).
Denkt an den Wechsel alles Menschlichen!
Es leben Götter, die den Hochmut rächen!
Verehret, fürchtet sie, die schrecklichen,

LEICESTER: Well, it has happened, Queen— And so, now that
    Your footsteps have been guided here by Heaven,
    Let generosity and mercy triumph.
SHREWSBURY: Allow us to entreat you, royal Lady,
    To cast your eye on this unfortunate
    Here overwhelmed before your gaze.
(*Mary collects herself and starts to walk toward Elizabeth,
    then stops half way with a shudder; her gestures express
    the most vehement struggle.*)
ELIZABETH: What's this, my Lords?
    Who was it then that told me of a woman
    In deep humility? I find a proud one
    No wise subdued by adverse fortune.
MARY: Be
    It so! I shall submit even to this.
    Hence, impotent pride of the noble soul!
    I shall forget now who I am and what
    I have endured; I shall bow down before her
    Who thrust me down to this ignominy.
                    (*She turns toward the Queen.*)
    Heaven has decided for you, Sister!
    Crowned with triumph is your happy brow,
    And I adore the deity that raised
    You up.   (*She kneels before her.*)
    Be generous in turn, my Sister!
    Let me not lie here in ignominy.
    Stretch forth your hand, your royal right hand give
    Me now, to raise me up from my deep fall!
ELIZABETH: (*stepping back*)
    Lady Mary, you are in your place!
    And thankfully I praise the favor of
    My God, who did not will that I should lie
    At your feet as you now lie here at mine.
MARY: (*with rising emotion*)
    Think of the change that comes to all things human!
    Gods do exist who punish arrogance!
    Revere them, dread them, they are terrible, —

                                        415

Die mich zu Euren Füßen niederstürzen—
Um dieser fremden Zeugen willen, ehrt
In mir Euch selbst, entweihet, schändet nicht
Das Blut der Tudor, das in meinen Adern
Wie in den Euren fließt—O Gott im Himmel!
Steht nicht da, schroff und unzugänglich, wie
Die Felsenklippe, die der Strandende
Vergeblich ringend zu erfassen strebt.
Mein Alles hängt, mein Leben, mein Geschick
An meiner Worte, meiner Tränen Kraft:
Löst *mir* das Herz, daß ich das Eure rühre!
Wenn Ihr mich anschaut mit dem Eisesblick,
Schließt sich das Herz mir schaudernd zu, der Strom
Der Tränen stockt, und kaltes Grausen fesselt
Die Flehensworte mir im Busen an.
ELISABETH (*kalt und streng*).
Was habt Ihr mir zu sagen, Lady Stuart?
Ihr habt mich sprechen wollen. Ich vergesse
Die Königin, die schwer beleidigte,
Die fromme Pflicht der Schwester zu erfüllen,
Und meines Anblicks Trost gewähr ich Euch.
Dem Trieb der Großmut folg ich, setze mich
Gerechtem Tadel aus, daß ich so weit
Heruntersteige—denn Ihr wißt,
Daß Ihr mich habt ermorden lassen wollen.
MARIA. Womit soll ich den Anfang machen, wie
Die Worte klüglich stellen, daß sie Euch
Das Herz ergreifen, aber nicht verletzen!
O Gott, gib meiner Rede Kraft und nimm
Ihr jeden Stachel, der verwunden könnte!
Kann ich doch für mich selbst nicht sprechen, ohne Euch
Schwer zu verklagen, und das will ich nicht.
—Ihr habt an mir gehandelt, wie nicht recht ist,
Denn ich bin eine Königin wie Ihr,
Und Ihr habt als Gefangne mich gehalten;
Ich kam zu Euch als eine Bittende,
Und Ihr, des Gastrechts heilige Gesetze,

And they have cast me down before your feet—
For the sake of these stranger witnesses,
Respect yourself in me! Do not dishonor
Or put to shame the Tudor blood that flows
In my veins as in yours— O God in Heaven!
Do not stand there so inaccessible
And rugged, like a cliff that drowning men
Vainly strive and struggle to attain.
My life, my destiny, my all, now hangs
Upon the power of my words and tears.
Release my heart so that I may touch yours!
When you look at me with that icy glance,
My heart shrinks shuddering and closes shut,
The stream of tears is stopped, and frigid horror
Chokes my words of entreaty in my bosom.

ELIZABETH: (coldly and severely)
What do you have to tell me, Lady Stuart?
You wished to speak to me. I disregard
My Queenship, my profoundly outraged Queenship,
So I may do my duty as a sister.
I grant the solace of beholding me.
My generous impulse leads me on, and I
Expose myself to righteous censure by
Such low descending— for, as you
Well know, you did attempt to have me murdered.

MARY: Where shall I start, how shall I prudently
Contrive my words so that they may have their
Effect upon your heart, yet not offend it!
O God, lend power to my speech and take
From it all thorns that could cause any wounds!
I cannot any way plead for myself without
Accusing you, and that I do not want.
—You have dealt with me in a way that is
Not proper, for I am, like you, a Queen,
And you have held me as a prisoner.
I came to you a suppliant, and you,
Scorning in me the sacred rights of nations
And sacred laws of hospitality,

Der Völker heilig Recht in mir verhöhnend,
Schloßt mich in Kerkermauern ein, die Freunde,
Die Diener werden grausam mir entrissen,
Unwürdgem Mangel werd ich preisgegeben,
Man stellt mich vor ein schimpfliches Gericht—
Nichts mehr davon! Ein ewiges Vergessen
Bedecke, was ich Grausames erlitt.
—Seht! Ich will alles eine Schickung nennen:
Ihr seid nicht schuldig, *ich* bin auch nicht schuldig,
Ein böser Geist stieg aus dem Abgrund auf,
Den Haß in unsern Herzen zu entzünden,
Der unsre zarte Jugend schon entzweit.
Er wuchs mit uns, und böse Menschen fachten
Der unglückselgen Flamme Atem zu.
Wahnsinnge Eiferer bewaffneten
Mit Schwert und Dolch die unberufne Hand—
Das ist das Fluchgeschick der Könige,
Daß sie, entzweit, die Welt in Haß zerreißen
Und jeder Zwietracht Furien entfesseln.
—Jetzt ist kein fremder Mund mehr zwischen uns,
(*nähert sich ihr zutraulich und mit schmeichelndem Ton*)
Wir stehn einander selbst nun gegenüber.
Jetzt, Schwester, redet! Nennt mir meine Schuld,
Ich will Euch völliges Genügen leisten.
Ach, daß Ihr damals mir Gehör geschenkt,
Als ich so dringend Euer Auge suchte!
Es wäre nie so weit gekommen, nicht
An diesem traurgen Ort geschähe jetzt
Die unglückselig traurige Begegnung.
ELISABETH. Mein guter Stern bewahrte mich davor,
Die Natter an den Busen mir zu legen.
—Nicht die Geschicke, Euer schwarzes Herz
Klagt an, die wilde Ehrsucht Eures Hauses.
Nichts Feindliches war zwischen uns geschehn,
Da kündigte mir Euer Ohm, der stolze,
Herrschwütge Priester, der die freche Hand
Nach allen Kronen streckt, die Fehde an,
Betörte Euch, mein Wappen anzunehmen,

Had me shut up in prison walls; my friends
And servants were most cruelly removed;
I was myself left in unseemly hardship;
I was called up to an outrageous court—
No more of that! Oblivion shall forever
Enshroud the cruel things I have endured.
—See! I shall term those things of fate's contriving,
You are not guilty, nor am *I* to blame.
An evil spirit rose from the abyss
To kindle hot the hatred in our hearts
That had already split our tender childhood.
It grew with us, and wicked people fanned
The wretched flame and blew their breath upon it;
Insane fanatics armed with sword and dagger
Officious hands that never had been summoned—
For this is the accursed fate of rulers,
That once they are at odds, they rend the world
And set at large the Furies of all discord.
—There is no alien mouth to come between
Us now,
(*approaching her trustingly and with caressing tone*)
            we stand here in each other's presence.
Now, Sister, speak! Name my offense to me
And I will render total satisfaction.
If only you had given me a hearing
When I so urgently besought your eye!
Things never would have gone so far, nor would
There now be taking place in this sad spot
This sorry and unfortunate encounter!
ELIZABETH: My lucky star protected me from putting
The adder in my bosom.— You should not
Accuse the fates, but rather your black heart,
The wild ambition of your family.
Between us nothing hostile had occurred.
And then your uncle, that ambition-crazed
Proud priest that stretches out his impious hand
To seize all crowns, threw down·his challenge to me,
Befooled you till you took my coat-of-arms,

Euch meine Königstitel zuzueignen,
Auf Tod und Leben in den Kampf mit mir
Zu gehn—Wen rief er gegen mich nicht auf?
Der Priester Zungen und der Völker Schwert,
Des frommen Wahnsinns fürchterliche Waffen;
Hier selbst, im Friedenssitze meines Reichs,
Blies er mir der Empörung Flammen an—
Doch Gott ist mit mir, und der stolze Priester
Behält das Feld nicht—Meinem Haupte war
Der Streich gedrohet, und das Eure fällt!
MARIA. Ich steh in Gottes Hand. Ihr werdet Euch
So blutig Eurer Macht nicht überheben—
ELISABETH. Wer soll mich hindern? Euer Oheim gab
Das Beispiel allen Königen der Welt,
Wie man mit seinen Feinden Frieden macht:
Die Sankt Barthelemi sei meine Schule!
Was ist mir Blutsverwandtschaft, Völkerrecht?
Die Kirche trennet aller Pflichten Band,
Den Treubruch heiligt sie, den Königsmord,
Ich übe nur, was Eure Priester lehren.
Sagt! Welches Pfand gewährte mir für Euch,
Wenn ich großmütig Eure Bande löste?
Mit welchem Schloß verwahr ich Eure Treue,
Das nicht Sankt Peters Schlüssel öffnen kann?
Gewalt nur ist die einzge Sicherheit,
Kein Bündnis ist mit dem Gezücht der Schlangen.
MARIA. O, das ist Euer traurig finstrer Argwohn!
Ihr habt mich stets als eine Feindin nur
Und Fremdlingin betrachtet. Hättet Ihr
Zu Eurer Erbin mich erklärt, wie mir
Gebührt, so hätten Dankbarkeit und Liebe
Euch eine treue Freundin und Verwandte
In mir erhalten.
ELISABETH. Draußen, Lady Stuart,
Ist Eure Freundschaft, Euer Haus das Papsttum,
Der Mönch ist Euer Bruder—Euch! zur Erbin
Erklären! Der verräterische Fallstrick!
Daß Ihr bei meinem Leben noch mein Volk
Verführtet, eine listige Armida,

Till you assumed my royal title, till
You entered with me into battle to
The death— Whom did he not enlist against me?
The tongues of priests, the swords of nations, and
The frightful weapons of religious frenzy;
Here in the peaceful seat of my own kingdom
He blew the flames of revolution up—
But God is with me, and that haughty priest
Has not maintained the field— The blow was aimed
At my head, but it is your head that falls!

MARY: I stand here in the hands of God. You will not
Presume so brutally upon your power—

ELIZABETH: Who is to hinder me? Your uncle set
The model for all monarchs of this world
Of *how* to make peace with one's enemies.
The Saint Bartholomew shall be my school!
What is blood-kinship, or the law of nations,
To me? The Church absolves all bonds of duty
And blesses breach of faith and regicide;
I practice only what your own priests teach.
What pledge would guarantee you for me if
I were so generous to set you free?
What lock would I put on your loyalty
Without Saint Peter's key unlocking it?
The only safety lies with force, for with
The breed of serpents can be no alliance.

MARY: That is your sorry, sinister suspicion!
You always looked upon me only as
An enemy and stranger. If you had
Proclaimed me as your heir, as was my due,
Then gratitude and love would have retained
A loyal friend and relative in me.

ELIZABETH: Out yonder, Lady Stuart is your circle
Of friends, your home is with the Papacy,
Your brother is the monk— Proclaim you as
My heir! A treacherous, deceiving snare!
So that you might seduce my people in
My lifetime, so that like a sly Armida

421

Die edle Jugend meines Königreichs
In Eurem Buhlernetze schlau verstricktet—
Daß alles sich der neu aufgehnden Sonne
Zuwendete, und ich—
MARIA.   Regiert in Frieden!
Jedwedem Anspruch auf dies Reich entsag ich.
Ach, meines Geistes Schwingen sind gelähmt,
Nicht Größe lockt mich mehr—Ihr habts erreicht,
Ich bin nur noch der Schatten der Maria.
Gebrochen ist in langer Kerkerschmach
Der edle Mut—Ihr habt das Äußerste an mir
Getan, habt mich zerstört in meiner Blüte!
—Jetzt macht ein Ende, Schwester. Sprecht es aus,
Das Wort, um dessentwillen Ihr gekommen,
Denn nimmer will ich glauben, daß Ihr kamt,
Um Euer Opfer grausam zu verhöhnen.
Sprecht dieses Wort aus. Sagt mir: "Ihr seid frei,
Maria! Meine Macht habt Ihr gefühlt,
Jetzt lernet meinen Edelmut verehren."
Sagts, und ich will mein Leben, meine Freiheit
Als ein Geschenk aus Eurer Hand empfangen.
—Ein Wort macht alles ungeschehn. Ich warte
Darauf. O laßt michs nicht zu lang erharren!
Weh Euch, wenn Ihr mit diesem Wort nicht endet!
Denn wenn Ihr jetzt nicht segenbringend, herrlich,
Wie eine Gottheit von mir scheidet—Schwester!
Nicht um dies ganze reiche Eiland, nicht
Um alle Länder, die das Meer umfaßt,
Möcht ich vor Euch so stehn, wie Ihr vor mir!
ELISABETH. Bekennt Ihr endlich Euch für überwunden?
Ists aus mit Euren Ränken? Ist kein Mörder
Mehr unterweges? Will kein Abenteurer
Für Euch die traurge Ritterschaft mehr wagen?
—Ja, es ist aus, Lady Maria. Ihr verführt
Mir keinen mehr. Die Welt hat andre Sorgen.
Es lüstet keinen, Euer—vierter Mann
Zu werden, denn Ihr tötet Eure Freier,
Wie Eure Männer!

You might entice the young men of my kingdom
By cunning to your nets for paramours—
So everyone could turn to the newly rising
Sun, while I meanwhile should—

MARY: Rule in peace!
All claims upon this kingdom I renounce.
Alas, my spirit's pinions have been lamed,
I am no longer lured by greatness.— You
Have gained your end. I now am but the shadow
Of Mary. Prison's shame has broken my
Proud spirit.—You have done your uttermost
To me, you have destroyed me in my bloom!
—Now, Sister, make an end! Pronounce those words
Which you have come here to pronounce. For never
Will I believe that you have come here to
Make cruel mockery of me as victim.
Pronounce those words! Say to me: "Mary, you
Are free! My power you have felt, but now
You shall revere my generosity."
Say that, and from your hand I shall accept
My life, my freedom, as a gift.— One word,
And all will be as if it never happened.
I wait. O let me not await too long!
And woe to you if you do not close with
Those words! For if you do not leave me now
With blessing, grandly, like a goddess,—Sister!
Not for this whole rich island, not for all
The countries that the sea surrounds, would I
Stand here before you as you stand with me!

ELIZABETH: Do you admit at last that you are beaten?
Are your plots done? No other murderer
Is on his way? Will no adventurer
Attempt his sorry chivalry for you?
—Yes, Lady Mary, all is over. You
Will tempt no more. The world has other cares.
No one is anxious to be your—fourth husband,
Because you kill your suitors as you kill
Your husbands!

MARIA (*auffahrend*). Schwester! Schwester!
O Gott! Gott! Gib mir Mäßigung!
ELISABETH (*sieht sie lange mit einem Blick stolzer Verach-*
tung an).
Das also sind die Reizungen, Lord Leicester,
Die ungestraft kein Mann erblickt, daneben
Kein andres Weib sich wagen darf zu stellen!
Fürwahr! *Der* Ruhm war wohlfeil zu erlangen:
Es kostet nichts, die *allgemeine* Schönheit
Zu sein, als die *gemeine* sein für *alle*!
MARIA. Das ist zu viel!
ELISABETH (*höhnisch lachend*). Jetzt zeigt Ihr Euer wahres
Gesicht, bis jetzt wars nur die Larve.
MARIA (*von Zorn glühend, doch mit einer edeln Würde*).
Ich habe menschlich, jugendlich gefehlt,
Die Macht verführte mich, ich hab es nicht
Verheimlicht und verborgen, falschen Schein
Hab ich verschmäht mit königlichem Freimut.
Das Ärgste weiß die Welt von mir, und ich
Kann sagen, ich bin besser als mein Ruf.
Weh Euch, wenn sie von Euren Taten einst
Den Ehrenmantel zieht, womit Ihr gleißend
Die wilde Glut verstohlner Lüste deckt.
Nicht Ehrbarkeit habt Ihr von Eurer Mutter
Geerbt: man weiß, um welcher Tugend willen
Anna von Boleyn das Schafott bestiegen.
SHREWSBURY (*tritt zwischen beide Königinnen*).
O Gott des Himmels! Muß es dahin kommen!
Ist das die Mäßigung, die Unterwerfung,
Lady Maria?
MARIA.   Mäßigung! Ich habe
Ertragen, was ein Mensch ertragen kann.
Fahr hin, lammherzige Gelassenheit,
Zum Himmel fliehe, leidende Geduld,
Spreng endlich deine Bande, tritt hervor
Aus deiner Höhle, langverhaltner Groll—
Und *du*, der dem gereizten Basilisk

MARY: (*flaring up*)   Sister! Sister!
 O God! God! Give me self-control!
ELIZABETH: (*looks up at her with a long look of proud
                        contempt*)
 So these, my Lord of Lester, are the charms
 Which no man with impunity has seen,
 With which no other woman dares to vie!
 Indeed! *This* fame was cheap to come by: it
 Costs nothing to become the world-wide beauty
 But to have all the world hold one in common!
MARY: That is too much!
ELIZABETH: '(*with a sneering laugh*)
                        You show your true face now.
 Till now we only saw the mask.
MARY: (*with burning anger, though with noble dignity*)
 I erred, but in a human, youthful way.
 I was seduced by power. I did not
 Conceal or make a secret of it. With
 A royal candor I disdained false seeming.
 The world has known the worst of me, and I
 Can say that I am better than my name.
 But woe to you if from your deeds they once
 Rip off the cloak of honor which you use
 To hide the wild heat of your secret lusts.
 It was not chastity your mother left you;
 We all know what the virtue was for which
 Anne Boleyn climbed the scaffold to the block.
SHREWSBURY: (*stepping between the two Queens*)
 O God in Heaven! Must it come to this!
 Is this your self-control and your submission,
 Lady Mary?
MARY: Self-control! I have
 Endured all that a mortal can endure.
 Hence and be gone, lamb-hearted resignation!
 Fly up to Heaven, patient tolerance!
 Burst from your bonds at last, and from your cavern
 Come forth, you long-suppressed resentment now!
 And you who gave the angered basilisk

Den Mordblick gab, leg auf die Zunge mir
Den giftgen Pfeil—
SHREWSBURY. O sie ist außer sich!
Verzeih der Rasenden, der schwer Gereizten!
(*Elisabeth, für Zorn sprachlos, schießt wütende Blicke auf Marien.*)
LEICESTER (*in der heftigsten Unruhe, sucht die Elisabeth hinwegzuführen*).   Höre
Die Wütende nicht an! Hinweg, hinweg
Von diesem unglückselgen Ort!
MARIA. Der Thron von England ist durch einen Bastard
Entweiht, der Briten edelherzig Volk
Durch eine listge Gauklerin betrogen.
—Regierte Recht, so läget *Ihr* vor mir
Im Staube jetzt, denn *ich* bin Euer König.
(*Elisabeth geht schnell ab, die Lords folgen ihr in der höchsten Bestürzung.*)

His murderous glance, lay now upon my tongue
The poisoned dart—

SHREWSBURY: She is beside herself!
Forgive this mad and deeply injured woman!

(*Elizabeth, speechless with anger, is darting furious looks at Mary.*)

LEICESTER: (*in the most vehement agitation, tries to lead Elizabeth away.*)

                              Do

Not listen to this frenzied woman! Come
Away from this unhappy place.

MARY: A bastard has profaned the throne of England,
The noble-hearted British people has
Been cheated by a crafty, cheap impostor.
—If right prevailed, you would be lying in
The dust before me, for *I* am your King.

(*Elizabeth swiftly leaves. The Lords follow her in the greatest dismay.*)

WILHELM TELL

DRITTER AUFZUG

3. SZENE

FRIESSHARDT (*schreit*). Aufruhr und Empörung!
(*Man hört Jagdhörner.*)
WEIBER. Da kommt der Landvogt!
FRIESSHARDT (*erhebt die Stimme*). Meuterei! Empörung!
STAUFFACHER. Schrei, bis du berstest, Schurke!
RÖSSELM. und MELCHTHAL. Willst du schweigen?
FRIESSHARDT (*ruft noch lauter*).
Zu Hülf, zu Hülf den Dienern des Gesetzes!
WALTHER FÜRST.
Da ist der Vogt! Weh uns, was wird das werden?

Geßler zu Pferd, den Falken auf der Faust, Rudolf der Har-
ras, Bertha und Rudenz, ein großes Gefolge von bewaffneten
Knechten, welche einen Kreis von Piken um die ganze Szene
schließen.

RUDOLF DER HARRAS. Platz, Platz dem Landvogt!
GESSLER. Treibt sie auseinander!
Was läuft das Volk zusammen? Wer ruft Hilfe?
(*Allgemeine Stille.*) Wer wars? Ich will es wissen.
(*Zu Frießhardt.*) Du tritt vor!
Wer bist du, und was hältst du diesen Mann?
(*Er gibt den Falken einem Diener.*)

WILLIAM TELL

ACT III

SCENE 3

HARDHEART: *(shouting)*   Rebellion and revolt!

THE WOMEN: Here comes the Bailiff!

HARDHEART: *(raises his voice)*   Mutiny! Revolt!

STAUFFACHER: Shout so you burst, you rascal!

RÖSSELMANN AND MELCHTAL: Shut your mouth!

HARDHEART: *(shouts louder still)*

    Help! Help! Help for the servants of the law!

WALTER FÜRST: Here is the Bailiff! What will happen to us!

>   *(Enter Gessler on horseback with his falcon on his wrist, Rudolf the Equerry, Berta and Rudenz, and a large retinue of armed servants who form a ring of pikes around the entire stage.)*

RUDOLF THE EQUERRY: Make way there for the Bailiff!

GESSLER: Scatter them!

    Why all this crowd of people? Who cried help?

>   *(General silence.)*

    Who was it? I want to know.

>   *(to Hardheart)*
>   You there, step forward!

    Who are you, and why have you seized this man?

>   *(He hands the falcon to a servant.)*

FRIESSHARDT.
Gestrenger Herr, ich bin dein Waffenknecht
Und wohlbestellter Wächter bei dem Hut.
Diesen Mann ergriff ich über frischer Tat,
Wie er dem Hut den Ehrengruß versagte.
Verhaften wollt ich ihn, wie du befahlst,
Und mit Gewalt will ihn das Volk entreißen.
GESSLER (*nach einer Pause*).
Verachtest du so deinen Kaiser, Tell,
Und mich, der hier an seiner Statt gebietet,
Daß du die Ehr versagst dem Hut, den ich
Zur Prüfung des Gehorsams aufgehangen?
Dein böses Trachten hast du mir verraten.
TELL. Verzeiht mir, lieber Herr! Aus Unbedacht,
Nicht aus Verachtung Eurer ists geschehn.
Wär ich besonnen, hieß ich nicht der Tell.
Ich bitt um Gnad, es soll nicht mehr begegnen.
GESSLER (*nach einigem Stillschweigen*).
Du bist ein Meister auf der Armbrust, Tell,
Man sagt, du nehmst es auf mit jedem Schützen?
WALTHER TELL.
Und das muß wahr sein, Herr—'nen Apfel schießt
Der Vater dir vom Baum auf hundert Schritte.
GESSLER. Ist das dein Knabe, Tell?
TELL. Ja, lieber Herr.
GESSLER. Hast du der Kinder mehr?
TELL. Zwei Knaben, Herr.
GESSLER. Und welcher ists, den du am meisten liebst?
TELL. Herr, beide sind sie mir gleich liebe Kinder.
GESSLER. Nun, Tell! Weil du den Apfel triffst vom Baume
Auf hundert Schritte, so wirst du deine Kunst
Vor mir bewähren müssen. Nimm die Armbrust—
Du hast sie gleich zur Hand—und mach dich fertig,
Einen Apfel von des Knaben Kopf zu schießen.
Doch will ich raten, ziele gut, daß du
Den Apfel treffest auf den ersten Schuß;
Denn fehlst du ihn, so ist dein Kopf verloren.
(*Alle geben Zeichen des Schreckens.*)
TELL. Herr—welches Ungeheure sinnet Ihr
Mir an?—Ich soll vom Haupte meines Kindes—
430

HARDHEART: Most gracious Lord, I am your man-at-arms
And your appointed guard here by the hat.
I caught this man right in the act of failing
To do obeisance before the hat.
I started to arrest him as you ordered,
And these folks want to stop me now by force.

GESSLER: *(after a pause)*
Do you disdain your Emperor so greatly,
Then, Tell, and me, who rules here in his stead,
That you refuse the honors to the hat
Which I hung up to test obedience?
You have betrayed your evil purposes.

TELL: Forgive me, Sir. It was from thoughtlessness
I did so, not from disrespect for you.
My name would not be Tell if I were cautious.
I beg your pardon. It won't occur again.

GESSLER: *(after a silence)*
You are a master at the crossbow, Tell.
They say you will compete with any archer?

WALTER TELL: And that's the truth, Sir. He can shoot an apple
Out of a tree a hundred paces off.

GESSLER: Is that your boy there, Tell?

TELL: Yes, gracious Lord.

GESSLER: Do you have other children?

TELL: Two boys, Sir.

GESSLER: And which one is it that you love the most?

TELL: Sir, I love both my children equally.

GESSLER: Well, Tell, since you can shoot an apple from
The tree a hundred paces off, you shall
Put your skill to the test.—So take your crossbow—
You have it right there with you—and prepare
To shoot an apple off from your boy's head.
But I advise you to aim well so that
You hit the apple with a single shot,
For if you miss it your own head is lost.

(Everyone shows signs of horror.)

TELL: Sir—what atrocious thing are you requiring
Of me?—An apple from my own child's head—

431

Nein, nein doch, lieber Herr, das kömmt Euch nicht
Zu Sinn—verhüts der gnädge Gott!—das könnt Ihr
Im Ernst von einem Vater nicht begehren!
GESSLER. Du wirst den Apfel schießen von dem Kopf
Des Knaben. Ich begehrs und wills.
TELL. Ich soll
Mit meiner Armbrust auf das liebe Haupt
Des eignen Kindes zielen? Eher sterb ich!
GESSLER. Du schießest oder stirbst *mit* deinem Knaben.
TELL. Ich soll der Mörder werden meines Kinds?
Herr, Ihr habt keine Kinder, wisset nicht,
Was sich bewegt in eines Vaters Herzen.
GESSLER. Ei, Tell, du bist ja plötzlich so besonnen!
Man sagte mir, daß du ein Träumer seist
Und dich entfernst von andrer Menschen Weise.
Du liebst das Seltsame—drum hab ich jetzt
Ein eigen Wagstück für dich ausgesucht.
Ein andrer wohl bedächte sich—du drückst
Die Augen zu und greifst es herzhaft an.
BERTHA. Scherzt nicht, o Herr! mit diesen armen Leuten!
Ihr seht sie bleich und zitternd stehn. So wenig
Sind sie Kurzweils gewohnt aus Eurem Munde.
GESSLER. Wer sagt Euch, daß ich scherze?
(*Greift nach einem Baumzweige, der über ihn herhängt.*)
Hier ist der Apfel.
Man mache Raum—er nehme seine Weite,
Wies Brauch ist—achtzig Schritte geb ich ihm—
Nicht weniger, noch mehr. Er rühmte sich,
Auf ihrer hundert seinen Mann zu treffen.
Jetzt, Schütze, triff und fehle nicht das Ziel!
RUDOLF DER HARRAS.
Gott, das wird ernsthaft.—Falle nieder, Knabe,
Es gilt, und fleh den Landvogt um dein Leben!
WALTHER FÜRST (*beiseite zu Melchthal, der kaum seine Ungeduld bezwingt*).
Haltet an Euch, ich fleh Euch drum, bleibt ruhig!
BERTHA (*zum Landvogt*).
Laßt es genug sein, Herr! Unmenschlich ists,

Oh no, no, gracious Lord, that can't be what
You mean—Merciful God forbid!—You cannot
Ask that of any father seriously.

GESSLER: Yes, you will shoot the apple off from that
Boy's head. That is my order and my will.

TELL: I am supposed to aim my crossbow at
My own child's much-loved head? I'd rather die!

GESSLER: You will die *with* the boy unless you shoot.

TELL: I am to be my own child's murderer!
You have no children, Sir, you do not know
What things go on inside a father's heart.

GESSLER: Why, Tell, you are so cautious suddenly!
They told me that you were a dreamer and
Aloof from other people's ways of action.
You love odd things—That's why I have selected
Such a unique objective for your daring.
Another man might well be cautious—*you*
Will shut your eyes and do it like a man.

BERTA: Sir, do not push this jest with these poor people.
You see them standing here all pale and trembling—
They are so little used to jests from you.

GESSLER: Who told you I was jesting?

(*He reaches for a branch of the tree   that hangs above him.*)
                                        Here is the apple.
Make room there—let him take his distance as
The custom is—I give him eighty paces,
No less, no more. He boasted that he could
Hit his man from a hundred paces off.
Now, Archer, hit your mark and do not miss.

RUDOLF THE EQUERRY:
My God, he means it. Get down on your knees
There, Boy, and beg the Bailiff for your life.

WALTER FÜRST: (*aside to Melchtal, who can hardly control
                              his impatience*)
Control yourself, I beg you. Keep your head.

BERTA: (*to the Bailiff*)
Sir, call a halt to this! It is inhuman

Mit eines Vaters Angst also zu spielen.
Wenn dieser arme Mann auch Leib und Leben
Verwirkt durch seine leichte Schuld, bei Gott!
Er hätte jetzt zehnfachen Tod empfunden.
Entlaßt ihn ungekränkt in seine Hütte,
Er hat Euch kennen lernen; dieser Stunde
Wird er und seine Kindeskinder denken.
GESSLER. Öffnet die Gasse!—Frisch! Was zauderst du?
Dein Leben ist verwirkt, ich kann dich töten,
Und sieh, ich lege gnädig dein Geschick
In deine eigne kunstgeübte Hand.
Der kann nicht klagen über harten Spruch,
Den man zum Meister seines Schicksals macht.
Du rühmst dich deines sichern Blicks! Wohlan!
Hier gilt es, Schütze, deine Kunst zu zeigen;
Das Ziel ist würdig, und der Preis ist groß!
Das Schwarze treffen in der Scheibe, das
Kann auch ein andrer; der ist mir der Meister,
Der seiner Kunst gewiß ist überall,
Dems Herz nicht in die Hand tritt noch ins Auge.
WALTHER FÜRST (*wirft sich vor ihm nieder*).
Herr Landvogt, wir erkennen Eure Hoheit,
Doch lasset Gnad vor Recht ergehen, nehmt
Die Hälfte meiner Habe, nehmt sie ganz,
Nur dieses Gräßliche erlasset einem Vater!
WALTHER TELL.
Großvater, knie nicht vor dem falschen Mann!
Sagt, wo ich hinstehn soll. Ich fürcht mich nicht,
Der Vater trifft den Vogel ja im Flug,
Er wird nicht fehlen auf das Herz des Kindes.
STAUFFACHER.
Herr Landvogt, rührt Euch nicht des Kindes Unschuld?
RÖSSELM. O denkt, daß ein Gott im Himmel ist,
Dem Ihr müßt Rede stehn für Eure Taten.
GESSLER (*zeigt auf den Knaben*).
Man bind ihn an die Linde dort!
WALTHER TELL. Mich binden?
Nein, ich will nicht gebunden sein. Ich will
Still halten wie ein Lamm und auch nicht atmen.

434

To play this way with any father's anguish.
If this poor man should have deserved to die
Because of his slight guilt, by God in heaven,
He has already perished ten times over.
Release him to his hut unharmed. He has
Learned who you are by now. This hour will be
Remembered by him and his children's children.

GESSLER: Open a lane there—Quick, what are you waiting
There for? Your life is forfeit, I can kill you.
You see how in my mercy I have placed
Your fate into your own well-practiced hand.
A man cannot complain of a harsh sentence
When he is made the master of his fate.
You boast of your keen eye. All right! Here is
Your chance now, *Archer*, to display your skill.
The aim is worthy and the prize is large.
A bull's-eye hit is something any man
Can manage; I call Master only one
Who is sure of his skill in any place,
Whose heart is neither in his hand nor eye.

WALTER FÜRST: (*throws himself down before him*)
Lord Bailiff, we acknowledge your high power.
But now let mercy pass for justice! Take
The half of my possessions, take them all,
But spare a father from this ghastly thing!

WALTER TELL: Grandfather, do not kneel to that false man!
Just tell me where to stand. I'm not afraid.
Why, Father hits a bird in flight, so he
Won't miss when he aims at his own child's heart.

STAUFFACHER: Lord Bailiff, does this innocence not move you?

RÖSSELMANN: Remember that there is a God in heaven
Whom you must answer to for all your doings.

GESSLER: (*points to the boy*)
Tie him to that linden tree.

WALTER TELL: Tie me!
No, I will not be tied. I will hold still
Just like a lamb and I won't even breathe.

Wenn ihr mich bindet, nein, so kann ichs nicht,
So werd ich toben gegen meine Bande.
RUDOLF DER HARRAS.
Die Augen nur laß dir verbinden, Knabe!
WALTHER TELL.
Warum die Augen? Denket Ihr, ich fürchte
Den Pfeil von Vaters Hand? Ich will ihn fest
Erwarten und nicht zucken mit den Wimpern.
—Frisch, Vater, zeigs, daß du ein Schütze bist!
Er glaubt dirs nicht, er denkt uns zu verderben—
Dem Wütrich zum Verdrusse schieß und triff!
(*Er geht an die Linde, man legt ihm den Apfel auf.*)
MELCHTHAL (*zu den Landleuten*).
Was? Soll der Frevel sich vor unsern Augen
Vollenden? Wozu haben wir geschworen?
STAUFFACHER. Es ist umsonst. Wir haben keine Waffen;
Ihr seht den Wald von Lanzen um uns her.
MELCHTHAL. O hätten wirs mit frischer Tat vollendet!
Verzeihs Gott denen, die zum Aufschub rieten!
GESSLER (*zum Tell*).
Ans Werk! Man führt die Waffen nicht vergebens.
Gefährlich ists, ein Mordgewehr zu tragen,
Und auf den Schützen springt der Pfeil zurück.
Dies stolze Recht, das sich der Bauer nimmt,
Beleidiget den höchsten Herrn des Landes.
Gewaffnet sei niemand, als wer gebietet.
Freuts euch, den Pfeil zu führen und den Bogen,
Wohl, so will ich das Ziel euch dazu geben.
TELL (*spannt die Armbrust und legt den Pfeil auf*).
Öffnet die Gasse! Platz!
STAUFFACHER.
Was, Tell? Ihr wolltet?—Nimmermehr! Ihr zittert,
Die Hand erbebt Euch, Eure Kniee wanken—
TELL (*läßt die Armbrust sinken*).
Mir schwimmt es vor den Augen!
WEIBER. Gott im Himmel!
TELL (*zum Landvogt*).
Erlasset mir den Schuß! Hier ist mein Herz!

But if you tie me, no, then I can't do it,
Then I will surely fight against my bonds.
RUDOLF THE EQUERRY:
Just let them put a blindfold on your eyes, Boy.
WALTER TELL: Why on my eyes? Do you think I'm afraid of
The arrow from my father's hand? I'll face
It firmly and won't even blink my eyes.
Come, Father, show them that you are an archer!
He can't believe it, he thinks he'll destroy us.
To spite the tyrant shoot and hit the mark!
              (*He goes over to the linden tree where the
                   apple is placed on his head.*)
MELCHTAL: (*to the countrymen*)
What? Is this outrage to be carried through
Before our eyes? What did we take the oath for?
STAUFFACHER: It is no use. We have no weapons with us.
You see the forest of their pikes around us.
MELCHTAL: O if we only had gone straight to action!
May God forgive those who advised postponement!
GESSLER: (*to Tell*)
To work now! Weapons are not borne for nothing.
It's dangerous to carry murder-weapons,
The arrow may rebound upon the archer.
This proud right which the peasants have assumed
Offends the sovereign ruler of this country.
None but those in command should carry arms.
If you like wielding arrows and the bow,
Well, I will designate a target for you.
TELL: (*stretches the crossbow and inserts the arrow*)
Open a lane! Make room!
STAUFFACHER:
What, Tell? You mean to—Never! You're unsteady,
Your hand is shaking and your knees are trembling—
TELL: (*lets the crossbow sink down*)
My eyes are dazzling!
WOMEN: O Lord God in heaven!
TELL: (*to the Bailiff*)
Excuse me from this shot. Here is my heart!

(Er reißt die Brust auf.)
Ruft Eure Reisigen und stoßt mich nieder!
GESSLER. Ich will dein Leben nicht, ich will den Schuß.
—Du kannst ja alles, Tell, an nichts verzagst du;
Das Steuerruder führst du wie den Bogen;
Dich schreckt kein Sturm, wenn es zu retten gilt.
Jetzt, Retter, hilf dir selbst—du rettest alle!

*(Tell steht in fürchterlichem Kampf, mit den Händen zuckend
und die rollenden Augen bald auf den Landvogt, bald zum
Himmel gerichtet. Plötzlich greift er in seinen Köcher, nimmt
einen zweiten Pfeil heraus und steckt ihn in seinen Goller. Der
Landvogt bemerkt alle diese Bewegungen.)*

WALTHER TELL *(unter der Linde)*.
Vater, schieß zu! Ich fürcht mich nicht!
TELL. Es muß! *(Er rafft sich zusammen und legt an.)*
RUDENZ *(der die ganze Zeit über in der heftigsten Spannung
gestanden und mit Gewalt an sich gehalten, tritt hervor)*.
Herr Landvogt, weiter werdet Ihrs nicht treiben,
Ihr werdet nicht! Es war nur eine Prüfung—
Den Zweck habt Ihr erreicht. Zu weit getrieben,
Verfehlt die Strenge ihres weisen Zwecks,
Und allzu straff gespannt zerspringt der Bogen.
GESSLER. Ihr schweigt, bis man Euch aufruft.
RUDENZ. Ich will reden!
Ich darfs! Des Königs Ehre ist mir heilig;
Doch solches Regiment muß Haß erwerben.
Das ist des Königs Wille nicht—ich darfs
Behaupten—solche Grausamkeit verdient
Mein Volk nicht; dazu habt Ihr keine Vollmacht.
GESSLER. Ha, Ihr erkühnt Euch?
RUDENZ. Ich hab still geschwiegen
Zu allen schweren Taten, die ich sah;
Mein sehend Auge hab ich zugeschlossen,
Mein überschwellend und empörtes Herz
Hab ich hinabgedrückt in meinen Busen.

(He tears open his shirt.)
Call to your mounted men and mow me down!
GESSLER: I do not want your life. I want this shot.
There's nothing you can't do, Tell, nothing daunts you;
You steer a boat as well as bend the bow,
No storm dismays you when there's need of rescue.
Now, Savior, help yourself—you have saved others!
> *(Tell stands in ghastly struggle, his hands*
> *twitching and his rolling eyes directed now*
> *on the Bailiff, now toward heaven. Suddenly*
> *he reaches into his quiver, takes out a sec-*
> *ond arrow, and sticks it into his doublet.*
> *The Bailiff notes all these actions.)*
WALTER TELL: *(under the linden tree)*
Shoot, Father! I'm not afraid.
TELL: It must be done!
RUDENZ: *(who all this time has stood in the greatest*
suspense and kept control of himself by sheer force,
now comes forward.)
Lord Bailiff, you're not going to press this further,
You surely will not—It was just a test—
You have achieved your end—Severity
When pressed too far will miss its own wise goal,
And over-tightly stretched, a bow will snap.
GESSLER: You will be silent till you're called.
RUDENZ: I *shall* speak,
I have a right to! I hold the King's honor
Sacred, but such rule as this breeds hatred.
This is not the King's will—that I maintain—
Such cruelty as this my people do not
Deserve. You do not have authority
For this.
GESSLER: Ha! You turn bold!
RUDENZ: I have kept silent
At all these grievous actions I have seen,
I shut my eyes when they saw all too clearly,
My overflowing and indignant heart
I forcibly repressed within my bosom.

Doch länger schweigen wär Verrat zugleich
An meinem Vaterland und an dem Kaiser.
BERTHA (*wirft sich zwischen ihn und den Landvogt*).
O Gott, Ihr reizt den Wütenden noch mehr.
RUDENZ. Mein Volk verließ ich, meinen Blutsverwandten
Entsagt ich, alle Bande der Natur
Zerriß ich, um an Euch mich anzuschließen.
Das Beste aller glaubt ich zu befördern,
Da ich des Kaisers Macht befestigte.
Die Binde fällt von meinen Augen—schaudernd
Seh ich an einen Abgrund mich geführt.
Mein freies Urteil habt Ihr irr geleitet,
Mein redlich Herz verführt—ich war daran,
Mein Volk in bester Meinung zu verderben.
GESSLER. Verwegner, diese Sprache deinem Herrn?
RUDENZ. Der Kaiser ist mein Herr, nicht Ihr. Frei bin ich
Wie Ihr geboren, und ich messe mich
Mit Euch in jeder ritterlichen Tugend.
Und stündet Ihr nicht hier in Kaisers Namen,
Den ich verehre, selbst wo man ihn schändet,
Den Handschuh wärf ich vor Euch hin, Ihr solltet
Nach ritterlichem Brauch mir Antwort geben.
—Ja, winkt nur Euren Reisigen! Ich stehe
Nicht wehrlos da wie die—
(*auf das Volk zeigend*) Ich hab ein Schwert,
Und wer mir naht—
STAUFFACHER (*ruft*). Der Apfel ist gefallen!

(*Indem sich alle nach dieser Seite gewendet und Bertha zwischen Rudenz und den Landvogt sich geworfen, hat Tell den Pfeil abgedrückt.*)

RÖSSELMANN. Der Knabe lebt!
VIELE STIMMEN. Der Apfel ist getroffen!

(*Walther Fürst schwankt und droht zu sinken, Bertha hält ihn.*)

GESSLER (*erstaunt*). Er hat geschossen? Wie? Der Rasende!

But any further silence would be treason
Both to my fatherland and to the Emperor.
BERTA: (*throws herself between him and Gessler.*)
You will provoke this raging madman further.
RUDENZ: My people I abandoned, I forsook
The kindred of my blood, I tore asunder
All bonds of Nature to join you. I thought
That I was furthering the good of all
By strengthening the Emperor's power—but
The blind has fallen from my eyes. With horror
I see I have been led up to the brink
Of an abyss.—You have misled my judgment,
Deceived my upright heart—With all the best
Intentions I was ready to destroy
My people.
GESSLER: Rash man, such talk to your Lord!
RUDENZ: The Emperor is my Lord, not you—I was
Born free as you, and I will pit myself
Against you any day in knightly virtue.
And if you did not stand here for the Emperor,
Whom I revere, though you disgrace him now,
I would throw down my glove before you and
You would by knightly custom answer to me.
Yes, call your mounted men. I do not stand
Defenseless here like *them*—
(*pointing toward the people*)
I have a sword,
If they come near me—
STAUFFACHER: (*shouts*) He has hit the apple!
(*While everyone has been looking this way and while
Berta has thrown herself between Rudenz and the
Bailiff, Tell has shot his arrow.*)
RÖSSELMANN: The boy's alive!
MANY VOICES: And he has hit the apple!
(*Walter Fürst staggers and is about to fall.
Berta supports him.*)
GESSLER: (*amazed*)
He shot that arrow? What? The man is crazy!

441

BERTHA. Der Knabe lebt! Kommt zu Euch, guter Vater!
WALTHER TELL (*kommt mit dem Apfel gesprungen*).
Vater, hier ist der Apfel! Wußt ichs ja,
Du würdest deinen Knaben nicht verletzen!
TELL (*stand mit vorgebognem Leib, als wollt er dem Pfeil folgen, die Armbrust entsinkt seiner Hand. Wie er den Knaben kommen sieht, eilt er ihm mit ausgebreiteten Armen entgegen und hebt ihn mit heftiger Inbrunst zu seinem Herzen hinauf; in dieser Stellung sinkt er kraftlos zusammen. Alle stehen gerührt*).
BERTHA. O gütger Himmel!
WALTHER FÜRST (*zu Vater und Sohn*).
Kinder! meine Kinder!
STAUFFACHER. Gott sei gelobt!
LEUTHOLD. Das war ein Schuß! Davon
Wird man noch reden in den spätsten Zeiten.
RUDOLF DER HARRAS.
Erzählen wird man von dem Schützen Tell,
Solang die Berge stehn auf ihrem Grunde.
(*Reicht dem Landvogt den Apfel.*)
GESSLER. Bei Gott! der Apfel mitten durch geschossen!
Es war ein Meisterschuß, ich muß ihn loben.
RÖSSELM. Der Schuß war gut, doch wehe dem, der ihn
Dazu getrieben, daß er Gott versuchte!
STAUFFACHER.
Kommt zu Euch, Tell, steht auf, Ihr habt Euch männlich
Gelöst und frei könnt Ihr nach Hause gehen.
RÖSSELMANN.
Kommt, kommt und bringt der Mutter ihren Sohn!
(*Sie wollen ihn wegführen.*)
GESSLER. Tell, höre!
TELL (*kommt zurück*). Was befehlt Ihr, Herr?
GESSLER. Du stecktest
Noch einen zweiten Pfeil zu dir—ja, ja,
Ich sah es wohl—was meintest du damit?
TELL (*verlegen*).
Herr, das ist also bräuchlich bei den Schützen.
GESSLER. Nein, Tell, die Antwort lass ich dir nicht gelten,
Es wird was anders wohl bedeutet haben.

BERTA: The boy's alive! Compose yourself, good Father!

WALTER TELL: *(comes running with the apple.)*
Father, here is the apple. I knew all
The time that you would not hit your own son.

(Tell has stood with his body bent forward as if he were trying to follow the arrow; the crossbow drops from his hand. As he sees the boy coming he runs to meet him with outstretched arms and with ardent emotion lifts him to his heart. In this posture he collapses unconscious. Everyone stands moved.)

BERTA: O gracious Heaven!

WALTER FÜRST: *(to father and son)* Children! O my children!

STAUFFACHER: Praise be to God!

FOLKLOVE: That was a shot! It will
Be talked about until the end of time!

RUDOLF THE EQUERRY: They'll talk of Tell the Archer as long as
These mountains still remain on their foundations.
(He hands the Bailiff the apple.)

GESSLER: By God, the apple is shot through the center!
It was a master shot, and I must praise it.

RÖSSELMANN: The shot was good. But woe to him that forced
Him to it, making him tempt God thereby.

STAUFFACHER: Come to your senses, Tell, stand up. You have
Redeemed yourself and are free to go home.

RÖSSELMANN: Come on, and bring the son back to his mother!
(They start to lead him away.)

GESSLER: Tell, listen!

TELL: *(comes back.)* What is your command, my Lord?

GESSLER: You hid a second arrow on your person—Yes,
I noticed it—What did you mean by that?

TELL: *(embarrassed)*
That is a sort of custom, Sir, with archers.

GESSLER: No, Tell, I will not let that answer pass.
There must have been some other meaning to it.

Sag mir die Wahrheit frisch und fröhlich, Tell;
Was es auch sei, dein Leben sichr ich dir.
Wozu der zweite Pfeil?
TELL. Wohlan, o Herr,
Weil Ihr mich meines Lebens habt gesichert,
So will ich Euch die Wahrheit gründlich sagen.
(*Er zieht den Pfeil aus dem Goller und sieht den Landvogt
mit einem furchtbaren Blick an.*)
Mit diesem zweiten Pfeil durchschoß ich—Euch,
Wenn ich mein liebes Kind getroffen hätte,
Und Eurer, wahrlich! hätt ich nicht gefehlt.
GESSLER. Wohl, Tell! Des Lebens hab ich dich gesichert;
Ich gab mein Ritterwort, das will ich halten.
Doch weil ich deinen bösen Sinn erkannt,
Will ich dich führen lassen und verwahren,
Wo weder Mond noch Sonne dich bescheint,
Damit ich sicher sei vor deinen Pfeilen.
Ergreift ihn, Knechte! Bindet ihn!
(*Tell wird gebunden.*)
STAUFFACHER. Wie, Herr?
So könntet Ihr an einem Manne handeln,
An dem sich Gottes Hand sichtbar verkündigt?
GESSLER. Laß sehn, ob sie ihn zweimal retten wird!
—Man bring ihn auf mein Schiff! Ich folge nach
Sogleich, ich selbst will ihn nach Küßnacht führen.
RÖSSELM. Das dürft Ihr nicht, das darf der Kaiser nicht,
Das widerstreitet unserm Freiheitsbriefen!
GESSLER. Wo sind sie? Hat der Kaiser sie bestätigt?
Er hat sie nicht bestätigt! Diese Gunst
Muß erst erworben werden durch Gehorsam.
Rebellen seid ihr alle gegen Kaisers
Gericht und nährt verwegene Empörung.
Ich kenn euch alle, ich durchschau euch ganz;
Den nehm ich jetzt heraus aus eurer Mitte,
Doch alle seid ihr teilhaft seiner Schuld.
Wer klug ist, lerne schweigen und gehorchen.

(*Er entfernt sich, Bertha, Rudenz, Harras und Knechte folgen,
Frießhardt und Leuthold bleiben zurück.*)

Now speak the truth quite frankly, Tell. Whatever
It is, I guarantee your life. What was
That second arrow for?

TELL: All right, then, Sir,
Since you have guaranteed my life, I will
Tell you the truth in its entirety.

         (He draws the arrow out of his doublet and
         gazes at the Bailiff with a dreadful glance.)

I would have used this second arrow to—
Shoot *you*, if I had hit my own dear child,
And *you*—there would have been no missing there.

GESSLER: Well, Tell I guaranteed your life for you,
I gave my knightly word, and I will keep it.
But since I have perceived your evil thought,
I'll have you taken and put under guard
Where neither moon nor sun will shine on you
So I may be in safety from your arrows.
Arrest him there, you men, and tie him up!

                  (Tell is bound.)

STAUFFACHER: What, Sir? How can you treat a man this way
In whom God's hand is clearly manifest?

GESSLER: Let's see if it saves him a second time.
Put him aboard my ship. I'll come at once
Myself to pilot him across to Küssnacht.

RÖSSELMANN: You can't do that! The Emperor can't do that!
That goes against the charters of our freedom!

GESSLER: Where are they? Has the Emperor confirmed them?
No, he has not confirmed them; such a favor
Has to be earned first by obedience.
You all are rebels to the Emperor's courts
And fostering an impudent rebellion.
I know the lot of you. I see right through you.
I'm taking this one from your midst right now,
But all of you are sharers in his guilt.
The wise will learn obedience and silence.

     (He withdraws. Berta, Rudenz, the Equerry, and serv-
     ants follow him. Hardheart and Folklove remain
     behind.)

WALTHER FÜRST (*in heftigem Schmerz*).
Es ist vorbei; er hats beschlossen, mich
Mit meinem ganzen Hause zu verderben.
STAUFFACHER (*zum Tell*).
O warum mußtet Ihr den Wütrich reizen!
TELL. Bezwinge sich, wer meinen Schmerz gefühlt!
STAUFFACHER. O nun ist alles, alles hin! Mit Euch
Sind wir gefesselt alle und gebunden!
LANDLEUTE (*umringen den Tell*).
Mit Euch geht unser letzter Trost dahin!
LEUTHOLD (*nähert sich*).
Tell, es erbarmt mich—doch ich muß gehorchen.
TELL. Lebt wohl!
WALTHER TELL (*sich mit heftigem Schmerz an ihn schmie-gend*). O Vater! Vater! lieber Vater!
TELL (*hebt die Arme zum Himmel*).
Dort droben ist dein Vater! den ruf an!
STAUFFACHER.
Tell, sag ich Eurem Weibe nichts von Euch?
TELL (*hebt den Knaben mit Inbrunst an seine Brust*).
Der Knab ist unverletzt; mir wird Gott helfen.
(*Reißt sich schnell los und folgt den Waffenknechten.*)

WALTER FÜRST: It's over now. He has made up his mind
   To ruin me and all my family.
STAUFFACHER: (to Tell)
   Why did you have to rouse the tyrant's fury?
TELL: Let them control themselves who felt my anguish.
STAUFFACHER: Now everything is lost, yes, everything!
   And we are all in chains and fetters with you!
COUNTRYMEN: (gather around Tell)
   With you our last support has given way.
FOLKLOVE: (comes up)
   Tell, I am sorry—but I must obey.
TELL: Farewell.
WALTER TELL: (clinging to him with intense sorrow)
   'O Father! Father! Dearest Father!
TELL: (raises his arms to heaven)
   Up yonder is your Father. Call on Him!
STAUFFACHER: Tell, shall I take your wife some word from you?
TELL: (lifts the boy with fervor to his bosom.)
   The boy is safe. God will look after me.
        (He tears himself away quickly and follows the
                men-at-arms.)

INDEX

Page references in italics denote the selection itself.